D1171037

The Race to the New World

DOUGLAS HUNTER

THE
RACE
TO THE
NEW
WORLD

CHRISTOPHER COLUMBUS,
JOHN CABOT, *and a* LOST HISTORY
of DISCOVERY

Douglas & McIntyre
D&M PUBLISHERS INC.
Vancouver/Toronto

Douglas & McIntyre
An imprint of D&M Publishers Inc.
2323 Quebec Street, Suite 201
Vancouver BC Canada V5T 4S7
www.douglas-mcintyre.com

Cataloguing data available from Library and Archives Canada
ISBN 978-1-55365-857-3 (cloth) · ISBN 978-1-55365-858-0 (ebook)

Jacket design by Peter Cocking and Heather Pringle
Jacket illustration by Gordon Miller
Printed and bound in Canada by Friesens
Text printed on acid-free paper

We gratefully acknowledge the financial support of the Canada Council
for the Arts, the British Columbia Arts Council, the Province of British
Columbia through the Book Publishing Tax Credit, and the Government
of Canada through the Canada Book Fund for our publishing activities.

In memory of Alicia B. Gould, Alwyn Ruddock,
and Louis-André Vigneras, who began the voyage
but were unable to reach the distant shore

CONTENTS

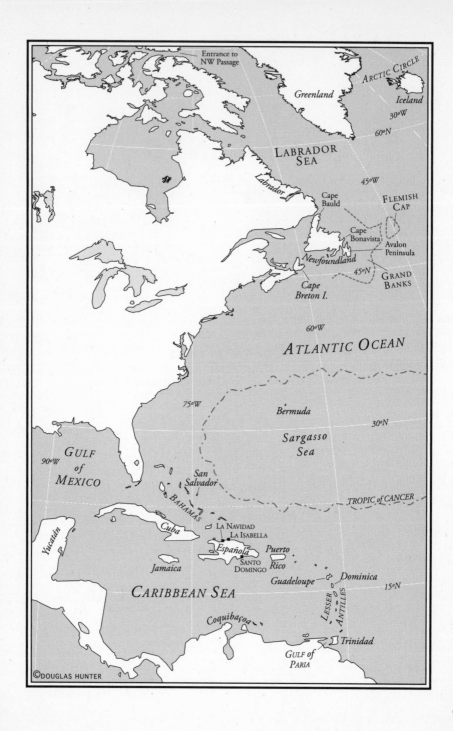

Entrance to
NW Passage

Greenland

ARCTIC CIRCLE

Iceland

30°W

60°N

LABRADOR
SEA

45°W

Labrador

Cape
Bauld

FLEMISH
CAP

Cape
Bonavista

Avalon
Peninsula

Newfoundland

45°N

GRAND
BANKS

*Cape
Breton I.*

60°W

ATLANTIC OCEAN

75°W

Bermuda

30°N

*Sargasso
Sea*

GULF
of
MEXICO

90°W

*San
Salvador*

TROPIC of CANCER

BAHAMAS

Cuba

LA NAVIDAD
LA ISABELLA

Yucatán

Española

*Puerto
Rico*

SANTO
DOMINGO

Jamaica

Guadeloupe

Dominica

15°N

CARIBBEAN SEA

LESSER
ANTILLES

Coquibaçoa

Trinidad

©DOUGLAS HUNTER

*GULF of
PARIA*

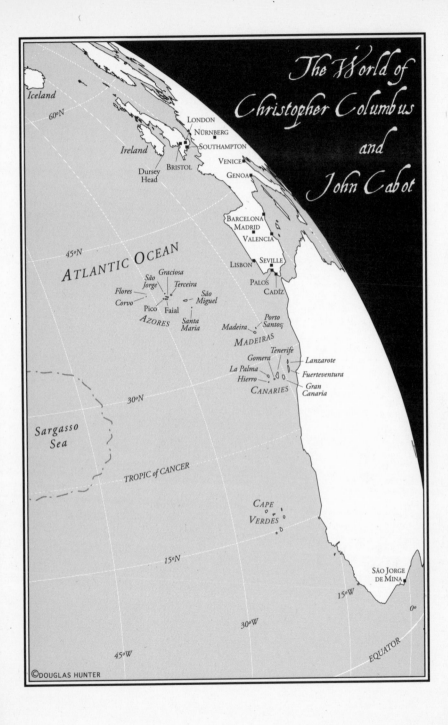

The World of
Christopher Columbus
and
John Cabot

Iceland

60°N

London
Nürnberg
Southampton
Ireland
Dursey
Head   Bristol   Venice
                            Genoa

45°N   ATLANTIC OCEAN
                                          Barcelona
                                          Madrid
                                          Valencia
                            Graciosa   Lisbon   Seville
                  São   Terceira
         Flores Jorge   Palos
         Corvo   São   Cadíz
              Pico   Faial   Miguel
              AZORES   Santa
                            Maria   Porto
                                   Madeira Santo
                                       MADEIRAS
                                           Tenerife
                                    Gomera   Lanzarote
                                  La Palma   Fuerteventura
30°N   Hierro   Gran
                                      CANARIES   Canaria

     Sargasso
       Sea

                    TROPIC of CANCER

                              CAPE
                              VERDES

          15°N
                                              São Jorge
                                              de Mina
                                          15°W   0°

                    30°W

     45°W
                                              EQUATOR

©DOUGLAS HUNTER

INTRODUCTION

ON FEBRUARY 17, 2006, a 418-word obituary for Alwyn Amy Ruddock appeared in *The Guardian*. Written by Edith Emma Mason, a former colleague in the history department at the University of London's Birkbeck College, it briefly recapped the life work of an eighty-nine-year-old woman who had died on December 21, 2005.

Ruddock was a respected economic historian who had made what were widely believed to be breakthrough finds about the voyages of discovery to the New World in the late fifteenth century by the Venetian known to the English-speaking world as John Cabot. Mason noted how Ruddock had produced "a draft of a book about Cabot, but destroyed it because it did not meet her exacting standards. She began work on the book again, but her progress was slowed by failing eyesight and declining health."

This second version of the Cabot book was never completed, stated Mason, who concluded by observing that Ruddock "left strict orders that all research papers were to be destroyed at her death." Ruddock's will had indeed instructed her trustees "to burn shred or otherwise destroy all my letters and photographs both personal and professional microfilms unfinished writings and other research and notes in my possession at the time of my death if this has not already been done prior to my death . . . as soon as possible after my death."

On March 22, 2006, Evan Jones received a copy of the obituary from a colleague. A senior lecturer at the University of Bristol who specializes in Bristol maritime history of the fifteenth to seventeenth centuries, Jones was too young to have known Ruddock, but he knew her reputation and all about the Cabot book that never was. Mobilizing the Bristol historical community, Jones was able to confirm his worst fears: Ruddock's unpublished life's work had long since been fed through a shredder, stuffed into seventy-eight bags, and unceremoniously disposed of. A close friend and neighbor of Ruddock's who was one of the estate's beneficiaries and trustees had been compensated an additional five thousand pounds under the will's terms for doing her posthumous bidding.

The revelation was a stunning coda to a perplexing and tragic career. What little Ruddock had published on Cabot was first-class stuff. Her proof that the letter by "John Day" to Christopher Columbus describing Cabot's first English voyages actually was written by a prominent London merchant named Hugh Say was exemplary of her analytical and archival skills. In waiting for her book, scholars were persuaded for four decades that Ruddock was poised to turn the story of Cabot and the discovery of North America (in her own words) "upside down."

In 1967, Ruddock had teasingly allowed in a letter to the leading exploration scholar David. B. Quinn, with whom she had been associated since her student days in Southampton in the late 1930s: "The documents I've got on Cabot do alter our picture of everything rather radically." She would ultimately claim to have perhaps twenty-three new documents, which was an astounding haul, as it would almost double the number of known documents relating to Cabot's voyages, most of which had been published in 1962.

But the book she had planned, which was well under way by 1966, kept changing its focus, or shifting between an academic and a popular work, or splitting into two books, and never appearing as promised. Following her retirement in 1976, fellow historians knew little more than that she had turned up important evidence, some of it probably in Italy. She approached Exeter Press in October 1992 with a proposal for a book that would be published in 1997, to coincide with celebrations of the five hundredth anniversary of Cabot's discovery of North America. Her working title, *Columbus, Cabot and the English Discovery of America*, not only included Cabot's rival Christopher Columbus but also intriguingly gave first billing to the Genoese mariner sailing in the service of Spain. Exeter contracted her to write the book, but beyond a 1992 synopsis of short chapter outlines (without a single cited source) and a few subsequent notes to an overly patient editorial staff, Ruddock never turned in a page of the manuscript. After her death, no one came forward who knew exactly what she had, precisely where she'd found it, or how deeply it was going to impact the status quo of exploration history. Tantalized by the prospect of a revolution in their understanding of North America's discovery, scholars had waited for her to reveal her breakthroughs.

And waited, for decades. Historians withheld some of their own work, fearing Ruddock's always-imminent revelations would render their efforts pointless and obsolete; some left the study area largely to her, knowing the head start she had and not wanting to invade her turf. Most certainly some young scholars avoided entering her field altogether. Then Ruddock died, and had the trustee of her estate destroy the photographs, rolls of microfilm, and papers that could tell others what she alone knew.

IN SEPTEMBER 2009, I published the book *Half Moon,* on the 1609 Henry Hudson voyage. Intrigued by the crypto-history of New World discovery as a cultural and historiographical phenomenon, I had already turned my attention to new research on earlier voyages and accounts, both real and imagined. I became intrigued by the story of Alwyn Ruddock, her lost research, and the efforts to track down what she had found. As I learned, there actually had been more than two versions of the stillborn Columbus-Cabot book, and Ruddock had left work on several other major initiatives incomplete, ultimately destroying those as well. When *Half Moon* was published, some new evidence on early English voyages to the New World out of Bristol had just been announced by Evan Jones, who had been on the Ruddock case ever since *The Guardian* obituary was forwarded to him in March 2006. These in fact were old finds, by Margaret Condon from the 1970s, that had been lost by going unpublished during Ruddock's idiosyncratic domination of Cabot scholarship. Jones had managed to bring forward these discoveries and reenlist Condon's research aid in pursuing Ruddock's lost Cabot evidence.

The alternately tragic and infuriating story of Alwyn Ruddock and her deliberately destroyed research is a tale unto itself, and one that I told in *Canada's History* in April 2010. (A longer version, with more detail about Ruddock's career and her relationship and correspondence with Quinn, is archived online at my website. See the bibliography.) It is but a prelude to the tale of the remarkable ongoing sleuthing by Evan Jones and his associates in the Cabot Project, as they hunt down the evidence for Ruddock's otherwise-unsubstantiated claims. The quest has led them everywhere from the National Archives at Kew to archives in Italy to a shoe closet in Ruddock's old house in West Sussex, which turned out to hold vital scraps of her papers that survived the destruction of her estate.

The Cabot Project's evidentiary discoveries support a number of contentions Ruddock made in her synopsis and the supportive notes for the book she promised to Exeter Press. Late in the drafting of this book, Francesco Guidi Bruscoli joined the Cabot Project; following a fresh lead Jones had wrested from the contents of Ruddock's shoe closet, he located in Italy the ledgers of the House of Bardi and found an entry that proved Cabot was a client of the London branch of these Florentine merchant bankers. Other assertions by Ruddock, particularly those surrounding the activities and the ultimate fate of the 1498 Cabot flotilla, remain unproven, as I discuss in the afterword.

As fascinating as Ruddock's research and Jones's diligent and inspired investigations were for me, I was never interested in simply writing the book that Ruddock did not, by appropriating the Exeter Press synopsis that survived her. Nor would I tell the story of Evan Jones's dogged and productive effort with his fellow members of the Cabot Project to follow the evidence trail Ruddock had tried to erase. For one thing, that story is far from over; for another, I think Evan should tell it someday. The Ruddock file was the entry point for a more expansive story I wanted to tell about John Cabot and Christopher Columbus, which was not the same story Ruddock evidently had tried and failed to tell. As important as Ruddock's findings are, they figure secondarily in this book. Nevertheless, the story remains very much one about "lost history," as this book's subtitle indicates.

My decision to call this book a "lost history" of discovery may strike some as curious, given the source notes and bibliography that refer to documentary evidence. Certainly the fact that Ruddock ordered all of her research materials and manuscripts destroyed speaks to that idea of "lost," although it must be remembered that Ruddock never destroyed anything original in an archive, only her notes and copies of material. What *was* lost in the process was her years of ferreting, based on superb archival skills and an intimate knowledge of unindexed materials, some of them in private collections. Ultimately it may all prove to be recoverable. But the idea of "lost" extends well beyond the Ruddock materials, as does the challenge of recovery.

For one thing, we know far too little about the Indigenous perspective on the arrival of Europeans like Columbus and Cabot. When reading surviving European materials we must employ a critical eye, particularly in deciding what if anything written about the people of the New World is factually trustworthy. More to the purpose of this particular book, anyone who has tried to write about early exploration by going beyond secondary sources well knows how thin on the ground that surviving evidence actually is, how little of it exists to buttress the often-presumptuous assertions about the past that clutter standard histories.

Even in returning to "primary sources," we are routinely relying on a published transcription of a document or, more specifically, on a translation of that transcription. We are called upon to make leaps of faith that editors of massive nineteenth-century editorial projects like the *Calendars of State Papers* were not making all-too-free translations of source materials. (Having said that, I remain in awe of the industrious scholarship of late nineteenth- and early twentieth-century archival scholars Henry Harrisse, Henry Vignaud, and H. P. Biggar, whose work remains indispensable.) It is beyond the ability of most (if not all) researchers and writers to make a fresh reassessment of every single document involved in such a collection, particularly when compiling just one of them, as in the case of the *CSP* for Venice, represented a lifetime of work for one editor/translator. But in questioning materials at least selectively, lost aspects of discovery history do emerge. As this book well illustrates, standard translations can be faulty; individuals can be incorrectly identified in annotations. Such human errors have been perpetuated through repetition, confidently sanctified by scholarly footnotes. Source materials need to be reassessed from every angle, because they can yield insights obscured by the institutional processes of producing history.

As well, key sources can be lost in the course of historiography. An important example where Cabot is concerned is the July 25, 1498 letter by the Spanish ambassador in London, Roderigo de Puebla, mentioning Cabot's third voyage for Henry VII. Henry Harrisse transcribed it, untranslated, in his work *Jean et Sébastien Cabot*, published in France in 1882. But H. P. Biggar, who followed him with the influential *The Precursors of Jacques Cartier 1497–1534* in 1911, left it out of his compilation of Cabot documents. James Williamson followed Biggar's lead in omitting it from his standard reference work *The Cabot Voyages and Bristol Discovery under Henry VII*, published in 1962. Because there wasn't much in the short Puebla letter that apparently wasn't in the much longer report by another Spanish diplomat in London, Pedro de Ayala, which was written the very same day, Puebla's missive presumably was thought to be expendable from the Cabot syllabus of documents. Yet as this book shows, it is important to know that Puebla and Ayala, who were venal rivals, were writing to their monarchs about Cabot on the very same day in very similar language.

We also have long known that many key sources, such as ship's logs, have disappeared entirely. When preserved at all (as in the case of the four Columbus voyages), they are known not infrequently through secondary sources. We are in fact incredibly reliant on the work of sixteenth- and seventeenth-century historiographers to tell us much of what we know about the early history of discovery, trusting that the facts they offer are reliable and that the now-lost documents they cite ever actually existed—and if they did, that the quotes, paraphrases, and asserted facts are at all reliable.

At this point you may be concluding that writing reliable (never mind definitive) early exploration history is a hopeless and discouraging task. On the contrary, I find it challenging and engaging. The gaps in documentation, the elusive veracity of what does survive, require what I have in the past cautiously categorized as "imagination," by which I do not mean making things up. You need to be able to absorb a diversity of materials to try to overcome the losses, to bridge the gaps in the record, to understand context and incongruity, and then try to picture with as much common sense as can be summoned what seems to have been going on. Ultimately, for me "lost history" is the history that has not yet been told because we have readily accepted what has already been written as the final word, especially where major figures are concerned. History disappears because we collectively bury it. Some aspects of history, such as the American Civil War, are under constant reassessment and challenge. Other aspects, such as exploration history, require more of us to be asking imaginative, informed questions and entertaining perhaps surprising answers.

The connections I have posited in this book among John Cabot, Christopher Columbus, Martin Behaim and the early Portuguese voyagers, including the

Corte-Reals, arise in part from that haunting institutional aspect of the lost history: primary materials we have known about for a long time but have misunderstood through imperfect and poorly annotated translations. In the case of Cabot, one of the most fundamental pieces of evidence for his exploration career in England—a March 1496 letter from Fernando and Isabel in Spain to Puebla, their ambassador in London—actually identifies Cabot in the original Spanish as *lo de las indias*—"the one from the Indies"—yet this essential fact somehow repeatedly eluded translation, including in the standard one by Biggar that is reproduced in Williamson and is still relied on by historians. A 1494 letter written by Martin Behaim to his cousin was translated from German reasonably well, but the key public figures Behaim referred to have been persistently, grossly misidentified. Recognizing whom Behaim was actually writing about helped to change considerably my understanding of his activities.

Behaim himself has been lost to exploration history for any number of reasons, among them a lack of modern curiosity into his 1493 voyage proposal to João II of Portugal, his overstated reputation for self-aggrandizing exaggeration, and a failure to engage the essential question left to us by nineteenth-century historians: what became of this enigmatic, talented, and driven man after he was last heard from in 1494 and before he died in poverty in 1506? The fact that he would prove to be a compelling bridge between the enterprises of Columbus and Cabot and even the Corte-Reals was not foreseen by me even halfway through the research. It took considerable time, and a steady accumulation of evidence, some of it circumstantial, to persuade me that Behaim could be a crucial missing link in the discovery narrative and even an active cohort of Cabot. In the end, Behaim's career, and its twelve lost years, suggested to me what the perplexing Cabot narrative otherwise could not: how a failed Venetian bridge contractor on the run from powerful men in Seville so quickly managed to reinvent himself as a Columbus doppelgänger who could persuade England's Henry VII to reward him with a handsome letters patent for proving a new westward route to Asia's riches.

Although I had hoped to have something new to say about the intersection of the lives and careers of Cabot and Columbus, I did not expect Columbus to be quite so rewarding as a subject of fresh inquiry. I thought the 1992 quincentennial celebrations already would have encouraged a thorough reassessment, but in fact much of the essential documentary legwork occurred only after that seminal year. The massive thirteen-volume *Repertorium Columbianum* project, which endeavored to provide definitive, scholarly, annotated English translations of a disparate body of documents related to Columbus, was issued between 1996 and 2004. Above and beyond finding indispensable the volumes of that work, I realized that a significant amount of scholarship had been produced in Spain, some of it in the past decade, that addressed key areas of Columbus's activities and milieu and none of which had been translated into English. I cannot claim to have absorbed even a fraction of what has been generated in Spanish journals and books on the broad subject of Columbus and the early Spanish presence in the New World. But in order to make use of key works like Antonio Rumeu de Armas's writing on the Canary Islands, Alicia B. Gould's seminal *Nueva Lista Documentada* on the sailors of the 1492 expedition (with its dense, cascading footnotes further illuminating events, individuals, and activities of succeeding New World voyages), and some of the papers and publications addressing Italian mercantile activity in Spain, I had to make sense of them in their original Spanish. On another language front, Jerome Münzer's manuscript journal of his enlightening tour of Spain and Portugal in 1494–95, which was written in Latin, has never appeared in English translation. The fortunate fact that an annotated scholarly French translation appeared in 2006 gave me access to a work that proved to be far more critical to the story than I had originally imagined, as I had sought it out as a source of descriptions of Seville and Valencia during the time of Cabot and Columbus.

There were limits to my multilingual adventurism. I was aware that M. F. Tiepolo had published an important paper on Cabot's problems with Venetian creditors in 1973; I was not aware that despite its importance to Cabot scholarship, no one apparently had ever translated it from the original Italian. The ever-helpful Evan Jones forwarded me a copy; with the aid of a dictionary, I pressed my Romance languages skills to the snapping point, but they were enough to extract the basic information I needed. I would not, however, trust myself with so critical a fresh translation as that of the 1496 Fernando and Isabel letter, and for that I turned to Janet Ritch, an expert in early French and Spanish who teaches at the University of Toronto and York University and whom I knew from my previous work on Champlain. Janet was invaluable in working through a fiendishly opaque bit of late fifteenth-century Spanish; understanding context was so important to her producing a new translation that raises important questions about Cabot's past and the Spanish sovereigns' attitude to his proposed English endeavor. We went back and forth several times by email, puzzling over the phrasing. Although responsibility for the final interpretation rests with me, I could never have arrived at it without her careful guidance. Janet was also indispensible in translating the 1498 Puebla letter that had been hiding in plain sight in Harrisse's 1882 volume. Conrad Heidenreich, professor emeritus at York University and a leading expert on Samuel de Champlain and his cartography, was invaluable in securing a new translation of the above-mentioned Behaim letter, which first involved transcribing it in comprehensible modern German. This new translation allowed me to see how misunderstood its content has long been and what the letter might actually be telling us about Behaim's activities right before he dropped out of sight.

I would be remiss not to mention another aspect of lost history. Ruddock's failure to produce her long-promised book on Cabot (and Columbus) and her decision to have her papers destroyed are but two examples of how the work of

modern historians has been quite literally lost or thwarted. The American Hispan-
ist scholar Alicia Gould, author of the exhaustive *Nueva Lista Documentada,* was
expected to produce a definitive new biography of Columbus but was felled by an
aneurism while entering the Spanish archives at Simancas in 1953, before she could
make good on that considerable promise. Yet another scholar whose promise of
a groundbreaking work went unfulfilled was Louis-André Vigneras. A naturalized
American born in France, Vigneras was a Romance languages scholar who would
eventually teach at George Washington University and deserves to be known as one
of the great scholars of early Portuguese and Spanish voyages to the New World. He
spent years researching a Columbus book that never materialized. He did produce a
manuscript capturing many of his careful insights into early Portuguese and Spanish voyages, but it was lost in the 1960s, evidently after he gave it to a leading British
academic to read. His only book, *The Discovery of South America and the Andalusian
Voyages,* was severely edited down, resulting in a still-important volume that represents but a shadow of the research he had amassed.

I was extremely fortunate at the outset of this project to make the acquaintance
of Jeffrey Reed, an avocational researcher in Washington, D.C., with a doctorate
from the University of London, who has dedicated himself to recovering Vigneras's
lost scholarship. The world of exploration scholarship as it happens is a small one:
Reed met Alwyn Ruddock through David B. Quinn. The papers of Quinn, who
died in 2002, reside in the Library of Congress and contain numerous letters between him and Ruddock that provide clues to what Ruddock had discovered about
Cabot. Reed took it upon himself to search through the mass of correspondence to
produce a transcription of all the relevant exchanges between Quinn and Ruddock,
which he provided to Evan Jones to aid in his search for Ruddock's lost evidence.
Reed's efforts also turned up in Quinn's papers the archival discoveries by Margaret
Condon in the late 1970s that went unknown until Jones pulled them together and
announced them in 2009. Jones posted online extracts from the file of transcribed
correspondence between Quinn and Ruddock so that anyone can access it. (See
Jones, "The Quinn Papers," in the bibliography.) Reed also provided me with a detailed transcription of the Quinn–Reed exchanges, and in addition to forwarding
me copies of every scholarly paper he thought would assist me, he also shared with
me sections of his Vigneras recovery project in draft form.

At Quinn's urging, Reed had hunted down these lost writings of Vigneras, reas-
sembling them from what he described to me as a "box of junk" in the Library of
Congress. At the time of writing, Reed was hoping that the Vigneras manuscript
eventually would be published. He had sent some of the draft material to me in
hope that they would be of use in my own work, above all to help me understand (as
he remarked at one point) that much of what had been published about Columbus
made no sense. Given the unusual nature of this source, I cannot provide citation
notes that have specific page references. And except for two short translations of

phrases in primary materials, I have not quoted from Vigneras's work out of respect for Reed's project. It deserves to be published; in a future edition of this work, I hope to be able to provide citations that point at a specific published Vigneras source. For now, it is important to me that readers understand the insights Vigneras developed that have gone unrecognized.

I hope this makes it clear why this book has been dedicated to the memories of Gould, Ruddock, and Vigneras. I never met any of them, but they all truly began a voyage that never reached the distant shore, and I have benefited from the efforts they made to get there.

In summary, Christopher Columbus and John Cabot generally have been considered coincidental players in the European push-out into the Atlantic. Sailing for different monarchs in different corners of Europe, their westerly quests separated them by thousands of miles. But we must now view them much differently: as men who began working in the service of Spain but who with Cabot's move to England became rivals. Their actions and achievements over a few short years at the end of the fifteenth century locked in the course of the colonization and exploitation of the Americas. In Columbus, Cabot found inspiration that reached the point of bald mimicry. In Cabot, Columbus found an infuriating doppelgänger, whose exploits for England's Henry VII threatened to undermine his particular claims of discovery and his precarious privileges with the Spanish sovereigns. Through Behaim and Münzer, I have striven to draw links between the major players in the westward search, including the Portuguese. And as the reader will see, none of the exploration careers and voyage schemes is fully comprehensible without accounting for the geopolitics of Renaissance Europe.

To understand the career of either Cabot or Columbus, we now must understand the career of the other. The courses they shaped are more deeply intertwined than previously imagined. Together, they allow us to see one of the most monumental events in world history—the European discovery of two continents in the Western Hemisphere where no one had thought to look for even one—with a fresh and comprehensive vision.

IN ADDITION TO REPEATING my thanks for the assistance of Jeffrey Reed, Janet Ritch, and Conrad Heidenreich, I must make special mention of Evan Jones. As the driving force behind the Cabot Project and a senior lecturer at Bristol University, he has proven to be the antithesis of the secretive and cagey Ruddock. He has been exemplary in placing documents and findings in the public domain, and his willingness to share with me essential details of new discoveries before they have been published has been remarkably generous. In return, I have shared with him some of my ideas about Cabot and Columbus prior to publication. I would like to think that the Cabot Project has kept more of its powder dry than I'm aware of; in any event, I look forward to the day when its complete findings are published. We are in the midst of a renaissance of scholarly research on early English voyages to the New World. Dr. Jones and his colleagues deserve to reap accolades for such a tenacious pursuit of a difficult if fascinating (and at times unorthodox) evidence trail. Already they have reinvigorated scholarship on early exploration in the Atlantic realm that otherwise would have been unlikely to attract the energy and curiosity of a new generation of historians.

Preparing this book required the input, advice, and assistance of a number of additional indispensable people. My doctoral supervisor at York University, Carolyn Podruchny, was both supportive and accommodating as I completed this book in the midst of my course work. My agent, Jeff Gerecke, helped me focus my particular narrative interest in Cabot and Columbus, and of course found the project good homes in publishing houses. The manuscript went through a preliminary shakedown with editor Fiona Serpa and a further fine-tooth combing by copyeditor Debra Manette. Finally, Stacy Nation-Knapper undertook a careful proofing of the page galleys and compiled the splendid index. My thanks to all.

And in closing, I thank my wife Deb for her continued support and encouragement, and for creating and defending the space I need to produce such work.

ONE

IN THE LATE fifteenth century, perhaps 100,000 people lived on the cluster of canal-laced islands within the laguna of the northern Adriatic that comprised the city of Venice. Known to its residents as the Signoria, the compact archipelago was the heart of the Venetian republic of the eastern Mediterranean. The Signoria's artisans produced for export fineries of silk, damasks, satins, and crystal; other goods were sourced by merchants from around the Mediterranean, and from distant England came wool and hides. The republic was renowned foremost for its command of trade in precious commodities of the Orient, which arrived from its Levantine ports of Beirut and Alexandria from as far to the east as Borneo: ginger, cinnamon, cloves, nutmeg, saffron, camphor, rhubarb, ambergris, sugar and molasses, and above all pepper. A Venetian merchant, Marco Polo, had explored the Indies of Asia two centuries earlier, but the Orient's wares reached the Levant through middlemen Muslim traders. Lands such as Cathay, which Europeans understood to be the realm of the Great Khan, remained remote—imperfectly described, riotously imagined, the most tangible and most elementary proof of their existence being found in the holds of Venetian ships and the Signoria's aromatic warehouses.

The business details of import and export, of items common and extraordinary, were hashed out in the confines of the Rialto, a small plaza on the island of the same name—"the richest place in the whole world," as diarist Marin Sanudo boasted in 1493. The Rialto, he explained, was "a piazzetta, not very large at all, where everyone goes both morning and afternoon. Here business deals are made with a single word 'yes' or 'no.' There are large numbers of brokers, who are trustworthy; if not, they are reprimanded. . . . Furthermore, throughout the said island of Rialto there are storehouses, both on ground level and above, filled with goods of every value; it would be a marvelous thing if it were possible to see everything at once, in spite of the fact that much is being sold all the time."

The Rialto plaza was animated by gesticulating, darting shadows: Citizens and nobles who did not hold high office went about somberly clothed in long black robes, with hoods of black cloth or velvet, and black caps. Flitting among the merchants in the 1470s and 1480s was a man whose life proved to be an exercise in constant motion through geography, opportunity, and identity, with no certain beginning and an as yet uncertain ending. He wrote his name in a 1484 Venetian testament in a telling blend of dialects: His first name was true to Venice, rendered as Zuan rather than Giovanni, but he preserved the out-of-town family name Chabotto rather than using the Venetian Caboto, then proceeded to identify himself in the Venetian dialect as being *fo de Ser Zilio*—the son of Zilio. Comfortable in the Venetian tongue, the merchant who would be known to the English-speaking world as John Cabot probably was raised there from a fairly young age, but he had not forgotten that his family had originated outside the laguna.

Citizenship standards fluctuated over the course of Venice's history, answering the ebb and flood of war, conquest, and population-robbing plagues. In 1472, it was decreed that nonnoble citizenship (*popular nostro*) could be conferred by a senate vote on anyone who made his residence in the city for fifteen continuous years and paid his taxes to the Signoria during that period. By a vote of 147 to 0 the senate agreed on March 28, 1476, that Ioani Caboto had met this requirement, which meant he had been living there since at least 1461.

Cabot secured full citizenship (*de intus et extra*), making him recognized as a Venetian both within the republic and when abroad. Only about 10 percent of Venetians (above and beyond nobles) secured full citizenship; its main advantage was the avoidance of duties foreigners had to pay on goods brought to the city. Citizenship thus was necessary for Cabot in trading abroad, which we know he did. But we don't know where he was originally from. There was an unfortunate omission by the careless scribe who produced a 1501 document summarizing the conferrals of citizenship since 1472. He omitted the place of origin of the last six names, and Cabot happened to be one of them.

Being born in any territory held by the greater republic would not make one a full-fledged Venetian. A 1313 law had extended full citizenship to everyone born from Grado, more than fifty miles east on the Adriatic coast, to Cavarzere, eleven miles southwest of Chioggia, and so Cabot could not have been from anywhere in the greater laguna region—including from Chioggia, as one tradition would have it. Don Pedro de Ayala, a Spanish ambassador in London in 1498, called Cabot "another Genoese like Colón [Columbus]." By "Genoese" he could have meant someone from the city, the greater territory surrounding it, or the coastal region of northwest Italy known as Liguria. But Cabot may have come from much farther south, from Gaeta in the Kingdom of Naples, as the family name could be found there until 1443, which suggests that they may have moved on to Venice after that.

Ayala may have been misled about Cabot's origins, but in the Spanish ambassador's mind, John Cabot and Christopher Columbus were two of a kind, in both ambitions and origins. In truth, although their careers were deeply entwined in a race to prove a profitable new route to Asia's riches that would defeat the Levantine monopoly of Venetian merchants, they were very different people, with one determined to remake himself as the other.

THE FACT THAT THE Spanish ambassador Pedro de Ayala was confident Christopher Columbus was Genoese is noteworthy, as few historical figures have engendered as much controversy about their origins. He has been declared the son of a Spanish noble, a secret *converso* Jew from Catalonia, a Portuguese spy, and a French pirate, among numerous other guises. Yet the record within his lifetime is rife with references to his Genoese character. In a trust deed dated February 22, 1498, Columbus himself declared *yo nacio en Genoba*—"I was born in Genoa"—which would seem to settle matters unequivocally.

Angelo Trevisan met Columbus in 1501, while Trevisan was secretary to the Venetian ambassador in Spain. Columbus had been brought home from the Caribbean in 1500 in irons, his reputation in ruins. Trevisan befriended and questioned him, and also copied an unpublished account of the voyages by Pietro Martire d'Anghiera, a Milanese poet and humanist scholar. Martire (known in English historiography as "Peter Martyr") held a prominent position in the Spanish court and drew on his own personal experience with Columbus in composing the manuscript that Trevisan copied. Martire's published writings called Columbus a Ligurian as well as a Genoese. An anonymous libretto about Spanish discoveries in the New World, largely based on Trevisan's writing, was published in Venice in 1504, and it opened with an authoritative and rare description of Columbus: "a Genoese, a man of tall and eminent stature, ruddy, of great intelligence and long in face."

Antonio Gallo, a Genoese notary public and chronicler, was quite familiar with Columbus. In 1502, he received for safekeeping from Columbus two copies of his Book of Privileges—the compilation of capitulations, or agreements with the Spanish monarchs, that secured his hereditary rights in the Indies. Gallo was also chancellor of the Banco di San Giorgio (Bank of St. George), which effectively administered the republic, and received Columbus's communication from Seville that same year in which the explorer promised a 10 percent annuity in relief of Genoa's poor. "Although my body is here," Columbus wrote Gallo from Seville, "my heart is still there."

Gallo wrote in 1506 that Christopher and Bartolomé Columbus were "brothers of Ligurian birth and raised in Genoa among plebeian relatives, and who made a living in the textile trade—for their father was a weaver, and the sons were sometimes carders." Columbus indeed was born in Genoa in 1451, the first of five children of Domenico Colombo and Susanna Fontanarossa; Bartolomé was about four years younger. (As was the case with John Cabot, Columbus's name had a wide variety of spellings in contemporary records. In Spain he was most commonly called Cristóbal Colón.) Domenico Colombo was a master weaver, but he also was a tavernkeeper and cheese maker, in addition to dealing in wool and wine. Christopher Columbus made his debut in the notarial record in 1470 at age nineteen, working with his father, and in 1472 was identified as a *lanaiolo*, or wool worker.

Christopher Columbus's life story, particularly his early years, vanished into a fog of innuendo and speculation almost from the moment of his death, with competing recollections shaping a narrative that is incomplete, sometimes contradictory, and not infrequently incoherent. *Le Historie di Cristoforo Colombo* was a biography attributed to his son, Fernando, an illegitimate if beloved offspring, born around 1488 to Columbus's companion, Beatriz Enriquez de Arana. Fernando participated in the fourth Columbus voyage and, after his father's death, briefly visited Santo Domingo in 1509, where his half-brother Diego served as an incompetent governor. The Fernando biography, published in Venice in 1571, has been influential yet problematic, as five different hands likely were involved in its creation.

"Though they received only a limited education in the years of childhood," Antonio Gallo wrote of Christopher and Bartolomé, "they turned to sailing as youths, in the manner of their countrymen." In the abstract of the 1492 voyage journal produced by Bartolomé de Las Casas (the only version that survives), Columbus attests to a lengthy seafaring career. Las Casas paraphrased him: "I have spent twenty-three years at sea and have not left it for any length of time worth mentioning, and I have seen everything from east to west, by which he means that he has been to the north, that is, to England, and I have been to Guinea."

Columbus probably did visit England, almost twenty years before John Cabot appeared there, as well as the Portuguese trading post of São Jorge de Mina on the Guinea coast of West Africa, but his weary boast of incessant seafaring otherwise was assuredly an overstatement: For one thing, his life after arriving in Spain around 1485 seems to have been largely landlocked. Still, after taking to the sea, Christopher established himself as a Genoese merchant's representative, and during his years in the Portuguese realm, he would have spent considerable time on ships in his mercantile duties and could have reached most or all of the constellations of Atlantic islands possessed by Spain and Portugal: the Madeiras, the Cape Verdes, the Canaries, the Azores. Although the eastern Mediterranean was substantially a Venetian trading monopoly, the island of Chios continued to be operated by Genoese merchants under Ottoman rule, and Columbus probably visited it in the 1470s, as he claimed to have done in the 1492 journal.

"The [Genoese] nation is very powerful at sea, its carracks in particular are the best in the world," recounted a Spanish noble, Pero Tafur, who visited Genoa in 1435, "and had it not been for the great dissensions which the people have had amongst themselves, their dominion would have extended throughout the world. The inhabitants are very industrious and without vice, nor are they addicted to sensual pleasures, for which the nature of the country is unfavourable."

It was true that the Genoese were so fractious that they could not govern themselves and were given over to a succession of neighboring powers. During Columbus's time, from 1464 to 1499, Genoa was ruled by the Duchy of Milan. As mariners and merchants, the Genoese had been leaders in expanding Mediterranean trade into the Atlantic realm. The first record of a Genoese galley in England dates to 1281; the Di Negri (di Negro) family was trading to the Thames by 1304, and by 1306 Genoese merchants were being given the choice of London, Sandwich, or Southampton as a destination for goods in shipping contracts. The rediscovery of the Canary Islands (which most likely were known to the Phoenicians and Romans, and were also called the Fortunate Islands) around the year 1300 is credited to a Genoese, Lancelot Malocello.

The activities and influence of Genoese merchants accelerated in the Andalusia region of southern Spain during Columbus's life. They operated in business networks—chiefly consisting of houses or partnerships involving family members and associates—that linked the major trade centers: Seville, Valencia, Cadíz, Cordóba, and Málaga (after the Granada conquest), to name a few, as well as offshore nodes, such as Mallorca. They dominated trade, manufacturing, coastal shipping, and finance in the western Mediterranean while underwriting Spanish conquests from Granada to the Canaries and, eventually, the New World.

The only firm evidence for Columbus's mercantile activities after departing Genoa in the early 1470s comes from the Portuguese Atlantic realm, in the so-called Assereto document, which contains his testimony in a lawsuit at Genoa on August 25, 1479. The suit involved a sugar deal gone sour and two of Genoa's most prominent merchant and banking families, the Centuriones and the di Negros. Columbus testified that he was in Lisbon when he received an order through Paulo di Negro in July 1478 to buy 600 quintales of Madeiran sugar for Luigi Centurione. Di Negro planned to pay for part of the order with proceeds of a wool sale, but when that fell through, Columbus could ship to Centurione only the part of the order that di Negro had paid for with cash.

Exactly whom Columbus was working for at this time isn't clear. But the deal linked him to the di Negro family, and that helps sort out a particularly tangled narrative mess left by the Fernando Columbus biography. It claimed that Columbus the explorer was related to a notorious corsair named Columbus the Younger and had sailed with him for some time. Between Lisbon and Cape St. Vincent, they set upon four Venetian ships of the annual merchant flotilla, known as the Flanders Galleys, that serviced northern Europe: "[T]hey fought fiercely hand to hand with great hatred and courage; and they were so heaped up together that they mounted from one vessel to another killing each other and striking each other without pity with various hand-arms and implements." Columbus's ship was chained to a Venetian galley, and fire erupted. Columbus leapt into the sea, grabbed an oar to stay afloat, and swam two leagues to shore, thus arriving in Portugal. Or so the story went.

There actually was a notorious corsair whose name was Coulomb (or some variant), but he was French and of no relation to Columbus the explorer. However, a Genoese merchant flotilla was attacked by Coulomb off Portugal in 1476, and one of its captains was a di Negro named Giovanni Antonio. Giovanni Antonio, not Paulo of the 1479 sugar lawsuit, may have been the actual di Negro employer of Columbus in these years, and thus Columbus could have sailed with Giovanni Antonio on the fateful 1476 voyage. Paulo di Negro would command a Genoese relief flotilla that December, picking up the survivors in Lisbon and taking them to England—they would have landed at Southampton—on a trading voyage. That would account for Fernando Columbus's further contention that Columbus visited England with a di Negro around 1477.

One way or another, Columbus was established in Portugal by the mid- to late 1470s and spent some of his time in the Madeiras. He may have served as the local factor for Antonio Spinola, a member of one of Genoa's great merchant, banking, and diplomatic families. Working for Spinola would have granted Columbus the means to travel to every corner of the Portuguese Atlantic realm. He also would have been allied with one of the most influential Genoese families in Spain, Portugal, and England—and in most any other European locale where there was money to be made.

A prominent member of the family in Seville, Gaspar de Spinola, would become a key financial partner of Columbus in his Indies voyages. And the English branch of the Spinola empire would figure in John Cabot's career in England, as its members diversified into diplomacy there and wrote historically crucial letters in the seminal years of 1497 and 1498. Through their networks flowed not only goods and cash but information that was worth its weight in gold.

TWO

WHEN DOING BUSINESS at Madeira, Christopher Columbus was some six hundred miles southwest of Lisbon, surrounded by an ocean thought to be scattered with more islands like it awaiting discovery and colonization. Even the known landfalls were far over the visible horizon. Santa María, the nearest of the Azores group, was more than five hundred miles northwest and eight hundred miles west of Lisbon. The Canary Islands were three hundred miles to the south of Madeira, off the West Africa coast, and the Cape Verdes were more than eight hundred miles farther southwest. The existence of these volcanic archipelagos had been promised by legend and hearsay and scholars of antiquity, and had yielded up to persistent daring and curiosity. Cartographers imagined many more of them, still farther west, and mariners had every reason to expect to find them, given past successes.

The Portuguese led the discovery (or rediscovery) of the Atlantic islands in the fifteenth century. The Madeiras were found and their settlement begun between 1419 and 1425; the first islands in the Azores archipelago were reached in 1427. The first Portuguese expedition to the Canaries, which had already been the subject of a French colonization effort, followed in 1440. Settlement of the Azores then began, and the Portuguese pressed southward along the West African coast, their vessels sighting the Cape Verde Islands sometime between 1456 and 1462.

More distant finds were promised. In 1448, a captain of one of Venice's Flanders Galleys, Andrea Bianco, drew a world map while in London that demonstrated considerable knowledge of Portuguese discoveries, including several unlabeled islands that may have been an early recognition of the Cape Verde archipelago. Farther yet to the southwest, Bianco drew an enigmatic "authentic island" (Ixola Otinticha) that some would argue represented a secret Portuguese discovery of northeastern Brazil.

As the ocean yielded its final confirmable landfalls in that great triangle of trade and colonization—nearly one thousand miles west from Lisbon to the farthermost of the Azores, then fifteen hundred miles south to the Cape Verdes, and some eighteen hundred miles east-northeast, through the Canaries and the Madeiras along the West African coast back to Lisbon—the Portuguese combed through legend and anecdote, looking for some actionable evidence or encouragement. In 1452, Portugal's Diogo de Teive sailed 150 leagues (about 450 miles) to the southwest from Fayal in the Azores and on his return completed the discovery of the Azorean archipelago by finding the westernmost islands, Flores and Corvo. It was also said that Teive then sailed on, far into the North Atlantic, beyond Ireland, and that he suspected land lay to the west when he turned back without sighting it, leaving some to later argue that he may have reached the Grand Banks.

Other Portuguese voyages, real and alleged, productive and otherwise, followed. Goncalo Fernandes de Tavira made a 1462 voyage to the northwest of Madeira on which he was said to have seen land, but there was nothing in that direction other than the known Azores, unless he had carried on all the way to northeastern North America. That same year, João Vogado went looking for two imaginary islands, Capraria and Lovo; he returned without any sightings. Although the Portuguese had not given up on finding the next volcanic peak in a trackless sea when Columbus arrived in Madeira, the profitable discoveries had diminished seriously, and the time had come to consolidate their holdings and defend their enormous maritime territory.

In September 1479, the Treaty of Alcáçovas with Spain granted Portugal the Azores, the Madeiras, the Cape Verdes, West Africa's Guinea coast, "all other islands which shall be found or acquired by conquest [in the region] from the Canary Islands down toward Guinea," and the fisheries of the adjacent waters. The Canaries, where a conquest of islands still held by the indigenous Guanches had begun in 1478, were Spain's sole possession among the known Atlantic islands, and Spanish vessels could not sail south of them without Portugal's permission. Portugal's treaty rights were then encoded for all of Christianity in *Aeterni Regis*, a papal bull, or writ, of 1481.

The year of Alcáçovas was a busy one for Columbus. He returned to Genoa to testify in the suit over the sugar contract. He also married around this time Filipa Moniz Perestrello, the daughter of a Portuguese noble, Bartolomeu Perestrello, who had been dead for some twenty years but had been the first governor of the island of Porto Santos in the Madeiras. The governorship was hereditary, and when Columbus married Filipa, it was held by her brother, Bartolomeu the younger.

A Genoese wool worker of limited education in 1472 had rapidly transformed himself into an experienced seafarer, then a representative for sophisticated merchants and bankers, then a husband of a woman from a Portuguese family so noble that Filipa's cousin Isabel secured the Castilian crown of Spain through the Treaty of Alcáçovas just as Columbus was marrying. In short order, he would be a promoter of a voyage scheme who was said by an ardent supporter to have mastered classical knowledge of geography and astronomy. The shape-shifting was breathtaking in its diversity of mobility: social, geographical, intellectual. John Cabot would provide a convergent example of how during the Renaissance someone from northern Italy could remake himself so ambitiously. Men were redefining themselves according to the opportunities they were creating.

Still, it was one thing to improve oneself through industry and ambition; it was another level of achievement altogether to make a dizzying ascent through the social strata by a spectacularly improbable marriage. If Columbus was a Madeiran factor of a merchant as prominent as Antonio Spinola, his status could have made him somewhat attractive as a spouse. But Filipa Moniz Perestrello's family on both her mother's (Moniz) and father's (Perestrello) sides were of such nobility and courtly power that Columbus's acceptance almost defied logic. The fact that Filipa's father was of Genoese descent (or failing that, had been dead twenty years) might have allowed a low-born foreign commoner like Columbus to breach the family's ranks.

But the main reason Columbus was accepted could well have been timelessly prosaic: The couple's only child, Diego, apparently arrived in 1479, the same year the wedding is thought to have taken place. If Filipa was pregnant, legitimizing Diego would have required a marriage. On such a union of necessity the history of the world turned.

WHILE CHRISTOPHER COLUMBUS was making his way as a Genoese merchant's representative in the Portuguese Atlantic realm, John Cabot was residing in one of Europe's great cities of trade and culture. The republic that Venice ruled included the Italian cities of Padua and Verona, holdings on the Dalmatia coast and at Crete and Cyprus, and an Aegean portfolio that included the fortress town of Lepanto on the historically strategic strait of the same name. The diarist Marin Sanudo would boast in 1493 that his city "takes pride of place before all others, if I may say so, in prudence, fortitude, magnificence, benignity and clemency; everyone throughout the world testifies to this. To conclude, this city was built more by divine than human will."

Cabot was probably born before 1450, which made him slightly older than Christopher Columbus, because on March 20, 1470, he was accepted into San

Giovanni Evangelista, one of Venice's four Scuole Grandi, or great religious confraternities. Founded in 1261, it was a prestigious lay group located in the *sestier,*
or district, of San Palo on the island of Rialto, and would have had perhaps five to
seven hundred members.

The scuole were charitable organizations that looked after their own members,
many of whom were as poor as others were rich. They delighted in civic processions, particularly on Corpus Christi Day, when all the scuole, grand and minor,
turned out to parade with candles and in costumed extravagance. The largest of
them, the Scuole Grandi, were known—and criticized—for spending lavishly on
their headquarters, and San Giovanni Evangelista featured art by Tinteretto and
Carpaccio and housed a piece of the true cross acquired in 1361. During Cabot's
time in Venice, his scuola added an unusual outdoor atrium and gateway designed
by Pietro Lombardo that was completed in 1485. But if Cabot was able to avert his
attention from the conspicuous and indulgent splendor of the art, architecture, and
processions, he would have found himself within a stone's throw of considerable
intellectual enrichment, even inspiration.

Near the adjoining church of San Giovanni Evangelista was a bell tower, where
the hours were struck by two male figures bearing hammers controlled by a system of counterweights. At the foot of the remarkable tower, as Sanudo explained
in 1493, "lectures are given in philosophy and theology, both in the mornings and
afternoons, to whoever wants to go and listen; they are paid for from the funds of St.
Mark's." If these lectures were being delivered during Cabot's time in the Signoria,
a free education would have been available to him rivaling that of the university in
nearby Padua, which was also underwritten by the republic.

Cabot's membership in a scuola as prestigious as San Giovanni Evangelista
suggests he was well ensconced in Venetian society a half-dozen years before he
secured citizenship. He had managed to join the confraternity when there was a
waiting list for new members from established Venetian families. He must have had
strong connections in order to enter its ranks since he was not a native-born citizen.
That said, he was not wealthy; he made a donation on entry of four ducats while
better-off entrants gave as many as ten. Surrounded by men of greater means and
accomplishments, and living at the heart of a trading empire that held the European
monopoly on the finest goods of the Orient through the Levant, Cabot can be forgiven for overreaching in whatever direction fate happened to turn him.

Cabot's Venice was built on sea power. The republic defended fiercely its stran-
glehold on the supply of the East's finest goods with a navy, built and equipped at
the Arsenal, that had all but driven the rival Genoese out of the eastern Mediterranean and battled the Ottomans to maintain Venice's domination of the European
trade. All shipping out of Venice was controlled by the state, but with its merchant
galleys, oversight was the most acute. These vessels held the Venetian monopoly
on the transport of precious goods. Essentially anything expensive and unusual—

Persian carpets, jewels, spices, rare books, elephant ivory—was consigned to their relative safety (and costly freight charges). Leased to merchants by public auction, the galleys serviced established trade routes in distinct flotillas. The flotilla known as the Flanders Galleys made an annual voyage north to Sluys in the Low Countries. England too had become an important destination for this northern flotilla. Southampton on the English Channel was first visited by the Flanders Galleys in 1319 and was chosen as the main English port for galley service following alarming riots against foreign merchants in London in the 1450s.

Venetian traders also sent out round ships, or carracks, that specialized in bulk commodities such as malmsey, the sweet white table wine sourced at Candia, Venice's fortified station at Crete. But the galleys presented a particular spectacle of sails, oars, and pomp. The commander of a galley flotilla, the *capitaneus*, or captain, was a noble elected by the republic's citizen assembly, the Great Council of nobles. The flotilla captain was served by what amounted to a seagoing court that included a priest, a notary, physicians, musicians, and personal servants. Constructed in the Arsenal, each vessel was manned by 170 oarsmen. Defense was provided by 30 bowmen (*ballestraria*), "impoverished gentlemen" or nobles, according to Sanudo, who were chosen by election. The crew, which numbered more than 200, included navigating officers, a purser and his assistant, a caulker, carpenters, a cook, and a cellarman. These ships were as resplendent in their accoutrements as the wares they conveyed, fitted out to serve as floating reception and banquet halls worthy of hosting monarchs and ambassadors. They were at once a form of commercial transport, trade fair, and diplomatic mission that was without equal in Renaissance Europe.

Venice was the perfect metropolis for an ambitious seafarer with new ideas of tapping the Orient's riches to arise. Yet in searching for hard evidence of nautical savvy in Cabot's formative years in Venice, one ends up finding for the most part a property developer. On September 27, 1482, he acquired for five hundred ducats a down-at-heels property, "certain houses of sergeants, partly habitable and partly ruined," in the parish of San Giacomo dell'Orio in San Palo. The name of the parish—St. James of the Orient—makes no sense. Many explanations would revolve around a corruption of the proper name—one of them, *de luprio*, which means a dried swamp and would be appropriate to the particular terrain before it was developed, figures in the Cabot property records. But it is apt nevertheless that a man who would one day set out to prove a nonexistent westward route to Asia had owned real estate in a parish whose church was dedicated to a nonexistent saint of the Orient.

A month later, on October 30, Cabot made additional property plays in the town of Chioggia, about fifteen miles away in the southwestern corner of Venice's laguna. He acquired two homes, one in the parish of San Nicolò dei Mendicoli, the other in San Nicolò de Chioggia, as well as "a stretch of meadow land and three salt works" within the town's boundaries.

On January 13, 1484, Cabot pledged these Chioggia properties as security for the seventy-five-ducat dowry of his wife, Mattea. He was about to renovate and flip the San Giacomo dell'Orio property in Venice. In December that year, he sold the property, now featuring a "newly built house," for sixteen hundred ducats, more than triple what he had paid for it about two years earlier.

The records for these real estate deals tell us he was the son of a merchant named Egidius (Giulio, Zilio), and had a brother, Piero, who had an interest in the San Giacomo dell'Orio property. We also hear about his Venetian wife, Mattea, and when Cabot sells the San Giacomo dell'Orio property on December 11, 1484, Cabot is identified as the "father of a family of sons." At least two of his three sons thus were born by then, and were probably toddlers.

Property deals were but one part of Cabot's entrepreneurial ventures. He was identified in a number of confraternity references as a *pellizer*, a trader in hides, which would have been mainly those of sheep and other domestic animals. But his dealings also could have extended to the furs that lined the somber Venetian cloaks and to wool, even English wool, as one 1482 record calls him more broadly a merchant, and the terms of his 1476 citizenship would have given him plenty of leeway in the sort of business he conducted. Venetian records also capture Cabot in October 1483 selling a female slave in the Venetian territory of Crete; he had purchased her somewhere in the sultanate of Egypt, which extended all the way to Lebanon and Syria. Slaves were common in Cabot's Venice. They were found serving as household servants and gondoliers, and in the case of women, they inevitably bore children to owners.

Property developer, hide dealer, slave owner: Nowhere in surviving documents on Cabot's life in Venice do we find professional mariner, let alone aspiring explorer. Even so, he could have been to sea regularly as a merchant, and there are indications that his life at home in Venice moved in the margins of seafaring. The purchasers of the renovated property he sold in San Giacomo dell'Orio in 1484 were the sons of Taddeo da Pozzo, who in turn witnessed the will of the wife of Alvise Ca'da Mosto (Alvise Cadamosto), a Venetian explorer and merchant still alive in Venice in 1488 who made voyages to West Africa under the Portuguese in 1455 and 1456 and may have been the first to sight the Cape Verdes. A number of sailors and artisans involved in ship construction joined the confraternity of San Giovanni Evangelista the same year as Cabot; the nobles of Cabot's scuola included Polo Balbi, whose brother Benedetto was close to the ship patron and cartographer Cristoforo Soligo.

Yet living as he did in San Palo, in the commercial heart of a major maritime trading center, and with a membership in an organization as large and as distinguished as San Giovanni Evangelista, Cabot probably can be linked to almost anyone interesting. At the same time, he unquestionably lived in one of Europe's most vibrant, prosperous, and knowledgeable centers of maritime commerce. Recalling his time in Venice as he waited to board a pilgrim galley so he could visit Jerusalem, our Spanish traveler Pero Tafur would write how "each day I went about seeing many remarkable and delightful things. Every hour there came news from all countries of the world, for the sea-borne traffic is very great, and ships are continually arriving from all parts, and if one desires to have news of any place it is only necessary to enquire of the ships."

And Venice had been the home of Marco Polo, who remained the most celebrated traveler in Cabot's time. His late thirteenth-century adventures in the Orient proliferated through manuscripts and found an even wider audience in the late fifteenth century through Gutenberg's printing press. Polo's story continued to be the main reference for Europe's knowledge of Asia's riches, rulers, and geography. More than a century after the Mogul khans had given way to the Ming dynasty, Europeans, Columbus included, continued to expect that an empire ruled by the Great Khan lay in easternmost Asia.

More recently, a Venetian noble and merchant, Nicolò de' Conti, who died in 1469, had traveled extensively in the Middle East, India, and Southeast Asia. He had spent his youth in Damascus and learned Arabic, and sometime between the late 1420s and the early 1430s, he had made an extensive journey by land and sea along Muslim trade routes that included visits to India, Ceylon, Burma, Java, Sumatra, and Borneo. In 1439 in Florence, the secretary to Pope Eugene III, Giovanni Francesco Poggio Bracciolini, interviewed Conti and set down his experiences. The Latin manuscript remained unpublished until the seminal year 1492, when Poggio Bracciolini's material was incorporated into the fourth book of Cristoforo da Bollate's *Varietate Fortunae* (vicissitudes of fortune). Bollate gave the Conti material the title *India Recognita* (Indies rediscovered); the dedication was dated at Turin on February 15, 1492, less than five months before Columbus set out to discover the Indies himself with a westward sea route.

Although Poggio Bracciolini's account of Conti's adventures perpetuated the idea that the Great Khan still ruled Cathay, it contained a wealth of information on the Indies, their peoples, and their riches. Columbus may have been influenced by this work, if not before setting sail in August 1492 then at least by the time of his second voyage in 1493. Cabot could have had his own worldview informed by word of the experiences of this celebrated Venetian long before Bollate committed the Poggio Bracciolini manuscript to print in Florence. Nevertheless, the only eyewitness account of an effort by Cabot to propound on the established trade routes to the East, set down by the Milanese ambassador in London in 1497, would leave a striking impression of a man whose knowledge base scarcely matched that of the average merchant wandering the Rialto.

The slave purchase and sale tell us Cabot had traveled at least as far as the Levant, the Venetian gateway to the Orient's riches. The Milanese ambassador's report gives ample cause to believe that if Cabot ever dealt in precious goods, he had a very poor grasp of how they reached him. Cabot's milieu nevertheless teemed with shipbuilders, chart makers, and merchants who traded as far away as England, and he could have ventured this far afield, as animal hides, not to mention wool, were a major export there, carried as haul-back items on the Flanders Galleys.

His trade as a pellizer linked him to a critical aspect of seafaring: cartography, the trade pursued by Christopher Columbus's brother, Bartolomé. Mariners relied on the one-of-a-kind charts called portolans that were drawn and painted on vellum. Similar to parchment, which was prepared from lambskin, vellum generally used calfskin, and was more robust and thus better suited to the harsh marine environment. Cabot might have supplied raw calfskin or prepared vellum for cartographers, and conceivably could have drawn portolan charts as well, as his future would contain evidence of his engineering and drafting skills, including an eyewitness reference to him drawing and painting a harbor plan.

Cabot developed a diverse résumé in Venice and was far from finished in expanding the limits of his interests and ambitions. This was an age of audacious polymaths. Leonardo da Vinci, who was roughly the same age, was working for the dukes of Milan from 1482 to 1499, producing paintings, the clay model for a massive equestrian statue, military engineering innovations, and the dome of a cathedral. To encourage innovation, the Venetian senate had passed the world's first known patent law, the Statute on Industrial Brevets, in 1474, which granted individuals a ten-year protection within the republic for any "new and ingenious contrivance." More than one thousand petitions were received by the Venetian government by the end of the sixteenth century, for inventions ranging from windmills, to poisons, to lasagna and meat pies.

The quantifiable, the measurable, were being harnessed by the imagination. Principles of geometry and mathematics transferred readily across disciplines. Construction required architecture, engineering, and surveying; surveying was a close cousin of cartography, which along with navigation shared with surveying the methodologies and tools of observation. A man who could work out the height of a building or point of land by knowing its distance and angle of elevation was working in the same discipline as a mariner using a quadrant or an astrolabe to determine his latitude at sea.

Acquiring and developing properties in Venice and Chioggia would have required in Cabot an expertise in construction in a marine environment, which in turn invited a facility with drafting and engineering. Cabot's coming civil engineering schemes would be far more crucial to his future as an explorer than his experience trading hides around the Mediterranean. Yet the skill Cabot demonstrated above all was hustle, a willingness to take considerable risks not so much with empty oceans as with what could prove to be empty promises. He was also a man not so much constantly on the move as on the run.

THREE

So MANY STORIES, spun by so many chroniclers, eyewitnesses, and ax grinders: The career of Christopher Columbus formed its own Sargasso Sea of weedy narratives, dense and intertwined, thrown together by contrary yet converging currents of belief, justification, revisionism, hagiography, nationalism, condemnation, and early commercial publishing's sheer love of storytelling. And as a legal battle began to rage in Spain and the New World in the early sixteenth century over his descendants' heritable rights to his discoveries, depositions accumulated in a cacophony of sworn truths and were piled upon anecdote, memoir, and courtly histories in rival nations. Truth became an interminable feud of opinions, memories, and agendas. One can hack at these narratives all one likes and never clear a single incontrovertible course through their entangled contradictions.

This much appears to be true: By 1478, Columbus was living at least part of the time in Lisbon, and after marrying into a powerful Portuguese family, he was determined to leverage his in-laws' connections at court—to turn himself into an explorer of an Ocean Sea that could not be boundless, that had to have an end to complement its beginning on the Lusitanian shore.

The Fernando Columbus biography avowed that Columbus inherited through his wife's dowry a haul of charts and even secret knowledge of lands to the west, across the Ocean Sea. The biography also served up a diverse menu of tales by mariners that supposedly influenced Columbus's convictions. To be sure, the Atlantic realm was full of stories of landfalls sighted but not quite reached over the western horizon and of evidence carried on ocean currents and washed ashore, ranging from tree branches to strange corpses with wide faces.

The tales of Columbus's foreknowledge of discovery opportunities accumulated and cross-pollinated within a few years of his death. The sixteenth-century Spanish chronicler of the Indies, Gonzalo Fernández de Oviedo y Valdéz, heard one Columbus tale while he was in Santo Domingo on Española in 1514. Near Columbus's home on Madeira, a pilot who was the lone survivor of a shipwreck struggled ashore. Columbus took him in, and the dying man confided that he had seen a strange land in the west, but his ship had been driven back by a hurricane before he could reach it. The story was repeated in the Fernando biography as well as by Bartolomé de Las Casas, who was an eyewitness to Columbus's activities. Las Casas emigrated to Santo Domingo in 1502 and produced the only version of Columbus's 1492 voyage log we have. Both these later accounts shifted the mysterious landfall far to the north, to the west of Ireland.

Among the men who would offer an opinion on Christopher Columbus's inspiration was John Cabot's son Sebastian. Years after both his father and Columbus had died, Sebastian carved an astounding personal trajectory. The renowned chronicler of Columbus's voyages, Pietro Martire, would write a sentence in his third *Decades,* published in 1516, that would have seemed inconceivable in the 1480s, while the Cabot family was still in Venice: "I know [Sebastian] Cabot as a familiar friend and sometimes as a guest in my house." In 1518, Sebastian was hired as pilot-major of Spain, overseeing all navigation to the new lands Columbus had found.

On December 31, 1535, Sebastian Cabot was asked at Seville to provide expert testimony in legal actions surrounding the hereditary rights to Columbus's discoveries. He stated that no, he had never met Christopher Columbus, but that he had known his son, Diego, a long time. Asked by the crown attorney, Francisco de Aguilar, what he knew of the inspiration for Columbus's discoveries, he explained what he understood of Julius Solinus, an early third-century geographer who relied on the wisdom of the Roman Pliny, "who says that from the Fortunate Isles, which are [now] called the Canary Islands, sailing westward for thirty days, there were some islands that were named the Hesperides, and that this witness assumes that those Hesperides islands are the islands that were discovered in the time of the Catholic monarchs don Fernando and dona Isabel, of glorious memory, and the witness has heard that don Cristobal Colón discovered them in the times of the Catholic monarchs [Fernando and Isabel]." Asked where he had learned this, Sebastian said: "[F]rom many people in this city of Seville, whose name he does not remember, and that it is public and well known."

Sebastian did not elaborate, but Oviedo, drawing on Pliny, Solinus, and Isadore of Seville, concluded that the Hesperides had been ruled more than three thousand years earlier by a Spanish king named Hesperus. Columbus thus had rediscovered what Spain already rightfully claimed: "God returned this lordship to Spain after so many centuries."

For his part, Sebastian Cabot shed no further light for the crown attorney on the impulse to sail west that gripped not only Christopher Columbus but his own father, John. It did not help that Sebastian in his own claims of exploration prowess would give no credence to the accomplishments of John. As far as the son's version of history was concerned, the father might as well have never lived.

THE DISCUSSIONS OF Columbus's motivations seemed, for the most part, hearsay, sailor's tales, and convenient recollection, with the occasional strange label on an enigmatic chart encouraging the idea that someone had gotten somewhere, sooner, only to have the details obscured by the haze of memory and oral tradition or locked away as state secrets for so long that no one still alive was able to recall what actually happened. But amid all of the rumor, conjecture, and discordant personal recollection was one elegantly simple explanation for Columbus's voyage plan.

In 1474, the Florentine mathematician, astronomer, and physician Paolo dal Pozzo Toscanelli sent a map to Fernan Martins, canon of Lisbon, at the request of Afonso V of Portugal. The map no longer exists, but in the letter, Toscanelli addressed a fundamental question raised by the long-standing Portuguese effort to hunt down more Atlantic islands: Since the world was well understood to be a sphere, what would happen if someone kept sailing west into the Ocean Sea as he sought these elusive landfalls?

Toscanelli proposed that a mariner would encounter Antilla (or Antillia), a quasi-mythical landfall or island group that had materialized on a nautical chart drawn by the Venetian Zuanne Pizzigano in 1424. This archipelago was sometimes equated with another quasi-mystical landfall, the Isle of Seven Cities—so named for the communities supposedly founded by seven Iberian bishops fleeing the expansion of the Muslim empire of the Maghreb in the eighth century. The Portuguese initially thought the Azores were Antilla, and finding the actual Antilla spurred on some of their voyage initiatives. In the Toscanelli scheme, Antilla was a midpassage stepping-stone to spices, gold, and jewels, halfway across the Ocean Sea along the Tropic of Cancer, west of the Canaries. Next came Cipango (Japan), before the mariner reached the Asian mainland.

At the time, the term *Atlantic* was used only occasionally to describe the ocean beyond the Strait of Gibraltar. For the most part, the name used was the *Ocean Sea*, and the land on its western side was not Asia per se but *the Indies*. The plural was used because what we now consider to be Asia was composed of three different forms of India. (The term *Asia* generally was reserved for the former Roman Empire territories of Asia Minor, although it occasionally cropped up in documents related to Columbus in the broader sense.) *India Sinus* was China; *India Magna* (or *Mayor*) described the Indian subcontinent between the Ganges and Indus rivers; and *India Parva-Ethyopis* consisted of all the lands and waters from Calicut on India's southwest coast westward to East Africa, and included Persia, the Arabian Peninsula, and the Indian Ocean.

No one expected North, Central, or South America to stand in the way of a mariner sailing west from Europe, and no one could agree on how far such a voyage might be. The dimensions of Earth were far from settled, and Columbus, who most certainly knew Toscanelli's map and his voyage proposition, relied on the estimation of the second-century A.D. Greek geographer Ptolemy. His findings cast the planet with a circumference about 18 percent smaller than it actually is, although Columbus advanced a circumference 25 percent too small. But where Ptolemy had squeezed the known and habitable world, or *oikoumenē*, into half of its total circumference—which meant one would have to sail halfway around the world, across the Ocean Sea, to reach Asia from Europe—Columbus expected to have to sail only about one-third of the way around this smaller globe to reach the Indies, and along the way he would have Antilla as well as Cipango as profitable way stations. Nothing better illustrated the optimism of the scheme than the fact that this version of the planet (drawing on Pierre d'Ailly's 1410 world map *Imago Mundi,* which crammed the entire habitable world into the Northern Hemisphere) placed Cipango 1,500 miles east of the Asian mainland, and only 2,400 miles west of the Canaries. Japan in fact is more than 10,000 miles west of the Canaries, with some considerable obstacles lying in the path of any intrepid mariner.

Toscanelli's ideas may have been known to Cabot even before they reached Columbus. In 1480, four years after Cabot joined the confraternity of San Giovanni Evangelista, Febo Capella became its *guardiano grande,* or principal official. Capella was a humanist scholar and ducal chancellor who had a lengthy posting as Venice's ambassador in Florence. Given his movement in cultural circles around the Medici family, Capella could have brought home gleanings from the work of Toscanelli, especially as Capella's brother Priamo was a celebrated mariner. The idea that you could reach the East by sailing west on the Ocean Sea may have been very old news to Cabot by the time he was in Columbus's milieu.

THE GENOESE CHRONICLER Antonio Gallo in 1506 credited Columbus's brother Bartolomé with impressing upon Christopher the logic and feasibility of a westerly route to Asia. Having settled in Lisbon as a cartographer, Bartolomé had absorbed the wisdom of Portuguese mariners in the Atlantic realm. He showed Christopher "that if someone steered a course into the open sea, leaving behind the southern shores of Ethiopia, and directed his course to the right towards the west, he would necessarily run into a continent eventually."

Bartolomé, Gallo explained, had "dedicated himself to making money by painting maps for the use of sailors, on which seas, harbors, shores, bays, and islands are shown with their correct outlines and proportions maintained." Bartolomé, in other words, was in the business of making portolans, the coastal charts that provided mariners with distances and bearings but did not yet have a geographic grid of latitude and longitude.

There was a major conceptual leap to be made from a portolan to a chart employing latitude and longitude. It required, for one thing, an actual need, and the average mariner of the fifteenth century concerned with coastal navigation could do fine with the typically regional information of the portolan. He depended as much if not more on the piloting notes he kept in a *routier,* or rutter, as the English called it. What ocean passages there were—to Iceland, to the Atlantic islands of the Cape Verdes, Azores, Canaries, and Madeiras—left mariners out of sight of land for only a few days. Their destinations provided such a large target (if not in sheer mass like Iceland, then in sprawling archipelagos or towering volcanic landfalls) that it was difficult to go entirely astray, provided the weather cooperated.

The grid of latitude and longitude, proposed by Ptolemy initially in his *Almagest* and most famously in his *Geographia,* organized the world into fixed points, whereas piloting based on rutters and portolans was a relativistic exercise, concerned with relationships between locations in distance and compass course. As exploration accelerated in Europe in the fifteenth century, the need to shift to a Ptolemaic system was plain: It was the only effective way to create a coherent picture of the globe as more of it was revealed to far-ranging vessels, and Columbus understood the use of a degree-based grid in explaining and exploiting Toscanelli's opportunity. The Portuguese in particular drove the necessity, as their voyages southward, down the West African coast, increased the known world as well as the demand for new means of navigation.

The work of Ptolemy was familiar to scholars from manuscripts, but Gutenberg's press and commercial publishing were required to popularize his views. The first printed version of a two-volume *Geographia* likely didn't appear until 1477, in Bologna. There was also little practical way for a seaman to make use of the Ptolemaic grid. The vertical meridians, or lines of longitude, that ran from pole to pole could not be readily determined by any accurate means of celestial observation at sea—or on land, for that matter.

It had long been known that latitude, the lines running east–west parallel to the equator between the poles, could be determined by measuring the angular elevation of the North Star, or polestar. But this was still a difficult exercise, especially at sea. Instruments were crude, and conditions on a rolling deck often made accurate results impossible. No surviving chart with a latitude scale is even known before 1502.

When the Portuguese progressed sufficiently south in their investigation of the West African coast in 1481 that they lost sight of the polestar, another means of determining latitude was needed, and the king, João II, created a commission to find a way to use the noon elevation of the sun. The complication of solar observation (beyond the difficulty of knowing when it is precisely noon wherever one happens to be) is that the height of the sun changes every day, as its trajectory through the heavens shifts with the changing seasons. Solutions were tested off Guinea in 1485, and simple solar tables that could be used to correct the measurement on any given day of a particular year (because every year requires a unique set of tables) were adapted from ones created by the Jewish astronomer Zacuto of Salamanca.

Christopher and Bartolomé Columbus thus were in the Portuguese realm at a critical time in both exploration of the Atlantic and the advancement of scientific navigation and cartography. But practical solutions still lay over the horizon, and the brothers would leave Portugal just as the royal commission was investigating the use of the sun for observations, or "fixes." The first printed nautical almanac featuring daily correction (declination) tables of sun sights, *Regimento do estrolabo e do quadrente* (regiment of the astrolabe and quadrant), was still a few years away; it may have first appeared in Portugal in 1495, but the earliest surviving edition is from 1509. Not only was knowledge of the world imperfect; so were the means to explore and describe it.

FOUR

IN THE YEARS following Christopher Columbus's death, no one could agree on when and where (or in what order) he made his voyage proposals in hope of securing royal favor. The arguments were literally all over the map.

The sixteenth-century Spanish chronicler Anton de Herrara thought he tried his luck in Genoa first, in 1482. True or not, Columbus took the idea to the Portuguese court of João II in the early 1480s, probably exploiting connections he enjoyed through his in-laws. Jerome Münzer, a Nürnberg physician and humanist scholar who latinized his name as Hieronymus Monetarius, would meet João II at his castle at Évora in late November 1494. Münzer was in the midst of a tour of France, Spain, and Portugal on which he served as an envoy for Maximilian I, the King of the Romans (the German states) and the Holy Roman Emperor. João II was thirty-nine then, and Münzer found him "a very cultivated man, full of wisdom in everything, who rules his kingdom in peace and calm. He is very affable and has great curiosity in many subjects. He listens attentively to everyone who approaches him and boasts knowledge of the arts of war, navigation, and other sciences, then will make verifications and research proofs, and if he finds what someone says is true and useful, he gives everything necessary to make it possible."

João II effectively had been ruling Portugal since 1477, after his father, Afonso V, retreated to a monastery during the war of the Castilian succession when his campaign began to falter, but the son was formally crowned only in August 1481.

He was not yet thirty when Columbus approached him early in his reign; with both the Treaty of Alcáçovas and the bull *Aeterni Regis* in his favor, João II was fully engaged in expanding the Portuguese empire down the West African coast. In 1482, the fortified trading post of São Jorge de Mina, the first European settlement beyond the Mediterranean (which Columbus had visited, according to the 1492 journal abstract) was established on the Guinea coast in what is now Ghana; that same year, Diego Cão discovered the Congo River. Returning in April 1484 to Portugal, Cão set out again sometime in 1485 to push farther south and accommodate the sun-sight experiments.

Africa was the first true New World for Europeans, as the Portuguese continued to explore southward along its coast and began to send expeditions inland. Columbus was arguing for exploration in an entirely different direction. João II relied on the wisdom of scholars in ruling Portugal, and Columbus was told to present his voyage plan to a subcommittee drawn from the council the king had formed to solve the sun-sight problem.

The sixteenth-century Portuguese chronicler João de Barros said that Columbus proposed to sail west to reach Cipango, Marco Polo's Japan, which the Venetian traveler's account had assured was ripe with gold, pearls, and jewels. Relying on Polo's estimations of distance and their impact on the Ptolemaic world, Columbus argued that Cipango was only one-quarter of the way west around the globe and the continental Indies one-third of the way.

João II was enthusiastic about the idea of a westward search for new landfalls. Licenses were issued periodically to adventurers from the Azores and the Madeiras, and Columbus probably knew about recent Madeiran efforts. One was the Martín Antonio Leme venture, which Fernando Columbus and Las Casas would say sighted three islands equated with Antilla around 1484 (although no royal concession survives). And in 1484, João II preemptively granted Fernão Domingues do Arco of Madeira the governorship of an Atlantic island that he intended to find.

The Las Casas abstract of Columbus's 1492 voyage account traded in stories of landfalls and elusive sightings. Columbus gathered from "many trustworthy Spaniards" on the island of Ferro (Hierro) in the Canaries that every year they spied land to the west, which was affirmed for him by residents on Gomera. Las Casas probably was referring to the Arco grant when he then noted how Columbus recalled that in Portugal in 1484, a man from Madeira approached the king of Portugal "to ask for a caravel to go to this land which he had sighted, and which he swore he sighted every year and always in the same way." Columbus recalled how in the Azores the same thing had been claimed, "with everyone seeing land in the same direction with the same aspect and the same size."

João II's subcommittee in any case rejected Columbus outright, deriding his knowledge. Relying on Barros, Las Casas recounted in his *Historia de Las Indias* how the subcommittee "perceived Columbus's words to be vanities, founded on imagination and stories of the isle of Cipango" derived from Marco Polo's travels. He was all but laughed out of court, an ill-educated fantasist who had managed to marry into the right family.

Columbus, dismissed as an unschooled dreamer, then fled Portugal for his life.

COLUMBUS WAS COMPELLED to flee Portugal by the terror arising from the Braganza conspiracies of 1483–84. João II was ruling with anything but the "peace and calm" Münzer would observe in 1494. The Duke of Braganza, Fernando II, was in legitimate succession to the Portuguese throne when João II had him executed for treason in 1483 after letters were intercepted between the duke and Isabel of Castile, asking her to intervene in João II's consolidation of power. João II then personally stabbed to death Fernando II's brother-in-law Diogo, Duke of Viseu, in 1484.

Columbus may have been left dangerously exposed to the king's wrath through his in-laws. Columbus's wife, Filipa, was a cousin of Isabel's, and Diogo Gil Moniz was a member of the murdered duke's household. The exodus to Castile was led by Don Alvaro de Portugal, brother of the Duke of Braganza and a cousin of Isabel, who became president of the Council of Castile and a close advisor to the queen. Many members of Columbus's wife's family sought refuge in Isabel's kingdom, and Columbus followed them. When Columbus left Portugal, Filipa likely was already dead of unknown causes. Las Casas volunteered that God took her from Columbus so that he would be free to do the work of the Lord in spreading Christianity.

Filipa's sister, Violante (Brigolanda) Moniz Perestrello, resettled in Huelva with her husband, Miguel Muliart, in 1485; they would relocate to Seville in 1493, when Muliart joined Columbus for his second voyage. With son Diego in tow, Columbus is believed to have arrived at the Franciscan monastery of Santa María de La Rábida around 1485 as well. La Rábida was part of the harbor complex at the confluence of the rivers Odiel and Tinto that included the towns of Palos (de la Frontera) next door, Huelva, across the Tinto, and Isla Saltés sheltering the estuary from the Bay of Cadíz. The monastery was well known to sailors who called at the Andalusian port from different nations and made donations to the Franciscans to pray for them.

Columbus had been "deprived of all human aid, and because of both the faithlessness of his associates and his desperate poverty, he fell on such hard times that he went to [Santa María de La Rábida]." So claimed Alessandro Geraldini, the humanist scholar who would provide crucial support to Columbus in his arguments for making a westward voyage during the debate that led to his initial capitulation, secured at Santa Fé in April 1492.

The Columbus timeline is contentious: He may not have been taken in at La Rábida until 1491, long after arriving in Spain. Nevertheless, the Palos physician García Fernández also would vividly recall the aspiring explorer's forlorn arrival at La Rábida "on foot with son don Diego. . . . And at the entrance he requested that they give the little boy, who was a child, bread and water to drink." The Franciscans were known for their love of learning, and according to Geraldini, the friary's cosmographer and astronomer Antonio de Marchena "took pity on Columbus there."

Marchena supported Columbus in his voyage ambitions, but the most important figure in this influential circle was Juan Pérez, prior of the La Rábida monastery, who had served as Isabel's accountant and then as her confessor after entering the Franciscan order. Pérez tended to the protocol of securing Columbus an audience with Isabel and would represent Columbus in the negotiations for his capitulations in 1492.

Notwithstanding Las Casas's idea that God took Columbus's wife away so he could do the Lord's work, Columbus found a new companion, Beatriz Enriquez de Arana, who bore him the illegitimate Fernando around 1488. Columbus evidently dealt in maps and perhaps books as well, perhaps alongside Bartolomé, while trying to convince the Spanish monarchs to back a voyage. The Venetian Angelo Trevisan, who met Columbus in 1501, recounted how Columbus "followed for a long time the most serene sovereigns of Spain wherever they went, seeking their help to fit out some vessels, for he offered to find islands in the west in the neighborhood of India, where there is an abundance of precious stones, spices, and gold, which could easily be obtained. For a long time the king and queen and all the prominent men of Spain made fun of the idea, but finally, after seven years and many hardships, they conceded to his will."

Columbus's voyage pitch apparently was focused on Isabel, his late wife's cousin. The Treaty of Alcáçovas of 1479, which had secured so much of the known Atlantic realm for Portugal just as Columbus was marrying into the Perestrello and Moniz families, had also concluded the war of the Castilian succession in Isabel's favor. She had been contesting the right to Castile with her niece Juana, spouse of Portugal's Afonso V and daughter of her half brother, the late Enrique IV of Castile. Enrique had been shopping Isabel all over Europe when Isabel took matters into her own hands and married Fernando, heir to the neighboring kingdom of Aragon, in 1469.

Isabel and Fernando ruled Spain as coregents, equally powerful, under the motto *Tanto monta, monta tanto—Isabel como Fernando* (as much as the one is worth so much is the other—Isabel as Fernando), while their kingdoms of Castile and Aragon continued to operate under their own laws and civil administrations. The duo sought every opportunity to expand their realm through conquest and diplomacy. In 1487, they were about five years into an intermittent ten-year military campaign to secure Al-Andalus, the emirate of Granada on Castile's southern frontier, and end the centuries-old *reconquista* to eliminate the Muslim presence on the Iberian Peninsula. They were also beginning to arrange marriages for their five children, to secure dynastic alliances with England, Portugal, and the Holy Roman Empire. Their eldest, Isabel, who was seventeen when Columbus had his first audience with the queen, had been betrothed as a child to the Portuguese crown prince, Afonso, son of João II, as a means of healing the Iberian rift.

Jerome Münzer would meet the queen Isabel at Madrid in January 1495. He judged her plump—an impression upheld by her wedding portrait—but with a handsome face, and while he thought she was forty-eight (she was actually forty-four), he decided she could pass for thirty-six. He praised her capabilities as a ruler in both peace and war, possessing almost all virtues, "beyond what one would expect to find in someone of the female sex." Like other commentators, he noted her devotion to Christ and generous support of churches and monasteries: "She is profoundly religious, very pious, full of indulgence."

Piety did not save her from suspicions of infidelity, which had caused such chaos in the succession schemes of her forbears. (Fernando himself was no shining example of fidelity, as he sired at least a half dozen illegitimate children, some of them before his marriage to Isabel.) "Up to now," Münzer observed after meeting Isabel at Madrid, "when the king was not here, she always slept in a common chamber with her young servants, male and female. But now, she sleeps with her children and several noble women, so as not to risk being stained by the infamy of adultery. It must be said that the people of Castile are very mistrusting and always think the worst."

Whether it was because of her personal inclination, the connections to her and the Castilian court that could be leveraged at La Rábida, the links between Isabel and Columbus's late wife's family, or the fact that Castile rather than Aragon fronted on the Atlantic, it was Isabel rather than Fernando who took the lead role in the Spanish monarchy's consideration of Columbus's plan.

Columbus would praise Isabel's support of his plan, to the exclusion of all others (including Fernando), in a letter in 1500: "In all men there was disbelief, but to the Queen, my Lady, [God] gave the spirit of understanding, and great courage, and made her heiress of all, as a dear and much loved daughter. I went to take possession of all this in her royal name. They sought to make amends to her for the ignorance they had all shown by passing over their little knowledge and talking of obstacles and expenses. Her Highness, on the other hand, approved of it, and supported it as far as she was able."

Juan Rodríguez Cabezudo of Palos, who would claim to have watched over young Diego while Columbus was away on the first voyage, recalled renting to Columbus a mule so he could send "a friar of St. Francis" to court to negotiate on his behalf. He testified how "many people made jest of the admiral about the enterprise he undertook in going to discover the Indies and they laughed about it and even reproached this witness because he had given the mule, and that publicly they made jest of him and held the enterprise as futile, which he heard many people say publicly in this town [Palos] and even outside it." Like others to give evidence, Rodríguez Cabezudo insisted "if the old admiral had not discovered what he discovered, no one would have gone to discover."

Dr. Fernández too recalled the mule. Secretly before midnight, the prior Pérez climbed onto the animal at La Rábida and headed to court to confer with Isabel, who soon assented to the voyage. The physician also recalled how Isabel sent twenty thousand maravedis "in florins" to Diego Prieto of Palos, to provide to Columbus "so he could dress respectably and buy himself a good mount and appear before her majesty" and secure his capitulation. Rented mules would not do.

Columbus had also sought a noble patron, attempting to insinuate himself with the dukes of Medina-Sidonia and Medinaceli, both of whom had coastal power bases in Andalusia. He may have joined the staff of Luis de la Cerda, first Duke of Medinaceli, who, like Enrique de Guzmán, the second Duke of Medina-Sidonia, was active in the war for Granada.

Although Columbus's 1492–93 voyage journal suggests that his initial proposal was made on January 20, 1486, he is believed to have appeared at the siege of Málaga in 1487 at the behest of Isabel, as the Castilians began the final push to starve out the inhabitants of the port city in Granada and sell the Muslim residents into slavery around the Mediterranean. The initial voyage discussions, however, amounted to nothing. A learned council similar to the one formed by Portugal's João II found Columbus's proposal full of conceptual faults, among them an Earth too small in diameter and an Asia too close to the West. In any event, the proposal could not be entertained properly until Spain had completed its conquest of Granada. And that was more than four long years away.

SOON AFTER CHRISTOPHER COLUMBUS fled Portugal and the wrath of João II, John Cabot too was on the run. He bolted Venice as an insolvent debtor at some point prior to November 5, 1488, when the Venetian government issued a license recognizing a fairly significant debt, of 212 ducats, before court costs, owed by Johannes Caboto and his brother Pietro (Piero) to Tommaso Mocenigo and Paolo Rizzardo. The license would allow agents of the creditors to pursue the Cabot brothers beyond the bounds of the Venetian republic.

Virtually nothing is known about Rizzardo, beyond the fact that he was a steward of the procurators of the *sestier* or district of San Marco in 1509. Tommaso Mocenigo had a more extensive and intriguing curriculum vitae. He may have been from the same branch of the Mocenigo family that spawned three doges, and he would be elected mayor and captain of Treviso in 1494, mayor of Padua in 1501, and serve as one of three procurators, or patrician administrators, of the foremost Venetian sestier, San Marco, during which duties he was served by Rizzardo, his co-creditor of Cabot from 1488. His family had been active in merchant affairs in England; about one-third of goods transported by the Flanders Galleys from England in the early 1480s were directed to Marin Mocenigo, the son of the creditor pursuing the Cabotos. In April 1486, Tommaso Mocenigo acted on behalf of his deceased son in a legal case involving business in London.

There is no clue as to how or why the Cabot brothers fell afoul of a Venetian noble as prominent as Tommaso Mocenigo, although it could have had something to do with trade in English wool or hides. Nothing further would be heard of Pietro Cabot, but John Cabot was in for even stormier weather. On November 18, a "letter of recommendation to justice" was countersigned by a notary of the Venetian court in the name of the doge, Agostino Barbarigo, in favor of another daunting creditor of John Cabot alone. The letter empowered local authorities beyond Venice to act on the creditor's behalf to bring the fugitive debtor to justice.

The letter was given to a young noble, Vincenzo Cappello di Nicolò, to carry to Milan on behalf of his father, Nicolò Cappello. The elder Cappello was an important figure in Venetian maritime affairs and trade. In 1480, he was caught up in a short-lived trade dispute between Venice and England. As captain of the Flanders Galleys, he had been barred from loading English wool at Southampton, when Edward IV tried to restrict the export to Florentine vessels. The surprising news generated a diplomatic protest to Edward IV from the Venetian doge, Giovanni Mocenigo, who was quite likely a relative of Tommaso Mocenigo, Cabot's 1488 creditor.

In May 1488, Nicolò Cappello was commissioned as one of two directors of the Venetian fleet at Cyprus under the captain-general of the sea, Francesco Priuli. He moved to the Aegean that October when Priuli was recalled by the senate, just before the letter was secured from the Venetian court to pursue Cabot for bad debts. His son Vincenzo, dispatched to hunt down Cabot, would be a captain of the Flanders Galleys in 1504 and a supplier for the Venetian fleet in the eastern Mediterranean in 1512.

Nicolò Cappello was claiming from Cabot a considerable obligation of 981 ducats, which included his court costs. The debt may have arisen from a business Cappello had helped form in September 1487, in which Cappello was obligated to import wool from a northern source, probably England. Cabot may have been an intermediary or a merchant expected to provide the wool, and the size of the debt would suggest he had received funds to make a purchase he did not actually complete.

Vincenzo Cappello was to present the letter to the Venetian ambassador in Milan, Ermolao Barbaro, to bring to the attention of the duchy's authorities. Should Cabot not be found within the duchy, an additional letter was to be taken to Turin to present to Charles I, Duke of Savoy (which didn't have a Venetian ambassador), in the event that Cabot had fled to his realm.

Above and beyond the specific debts owed to Rizzardo, Mocenigo, and Cappello, military unrest in the Levant already may have pressed Cabot into dire straits by forcing the end of his usual merchant activities or inflicted a debilitating financial loss. Although the Ottomans had withdrawn from a campaign into northern Italy in 1481, they were at war in the Levant with the Sultan of Egypt from 1485 to 1491.

The Scuola Grande of San Giovanni Evangelista was supposed to take care of members who had fallen on hard times. If he still belonged in 1488, Cabot was either above asking for such charity or beyond hope. He surely left the republic with his wife and children. His status as an insolvent, possibly bankrupt debtor made him liable to arrest and imprisonment and the confiscation of his possessions.

Being incarcerated in Venice could be less mortifying than in many European jurisdictions. The Holy Land pilgrim Felix Fabri of Ulm, who passed through Venice twice in the early 1480s, wrote of prisons that were "beneath the walkway of the [Doge's] Palace, looking out towards the public square, and are lit by open windows barred by iron grilles, through which the prisoners can look out." In one he saw "rich men of business confined, but dicing and playing chess, and their wives and maids and servants stood talking to them through the bars. . . . They deliberately guard many prisoners with less care and allow them the chance of flight, especially where they think the opposing party has been unduly harsh, and so they mind little when such people break out and make off—as a few years ago a merchant of Ulm broke through the vaulting and escaped from custody." In another he saw "imprisoned artisans sitting and working with their hands at their trades and earning money."

But unless you were the right sort of prisoner who had committed the right sort of crime, being locked up in Venice was nothing to be envied. In still another prison Fabri saw "more than forty poor creatures going about and crying out for charity; in another I saw poor women calling for alms." Cabot was not going to chance such a fate for himself or his family. The letters issued for his creditors suggest that he was believed to have escaped overland through northern Italy to the duchy of Milan, which also ruled the republic of Genoa, or to Savoy, on Genoa's frontier. But as early as 1490, John Cabot had moved on to Spain, specifically to Valencia, most certainly with his family. He surfaced in a letter written on September 27, 1492, as "Johan Caboto Montecalunya, the Venetian" (*johan caboto montecalunya venesia*) who "arrived at this city two years ago."

The name Montecalunya, which is otherwise unexplained, suggests that he had spent time in the neighboring region of Catalunya (alternately Calunya, or Catalonia), perhaps in the mountainous region of the Catalan Pyrénees, far from the reach of the merchants seeking to exact payment. He may have cooled his heels there in Roussillon, a disputed county of Catalunya that remained in the hands of French troops until it was returned to Spain through the Treaty of Barcelona in January 1493. And although Cabot may have moved down from Catalunya's high country to Valencia, his creditors did not lose his scent. Cabot the pelt trader and property speculator was being herded by his financial misadventures into Christopher Columbus's world.

FIVE

DISAPPOINTED BY the initial results of his audiences with Isabel and her advisors, Columbus wrote João II in March 1488 to renew his proposal, asking for a guarantee of safe passage in Portugal; in response, the king warmly invited him to return to Portugal to make his pitch. Whether Columbus actually did so, however, is unknown.

The Columbus narratives multiplied and defied reconciliation. Alessandro Geraldini would claim that Columbus had been turned down all over Europe before even arriving in Spain: He first went to France and then to Britain, and after being rejected by both kings, he tried João II in Portugal before heading to Spain.

Although the Geraldini timeline is unlikely, the Fernando Columbus biography would agree that Christopher tried his luck in England as well as France, but that Bartolomé made these efforts on his behalf. Christopher, so this version of the story goes, had dispatched Bartolomé to England, concerned that he might not succeed in convincing the Spanish monarchs to back him. But Bartolomé was waylaid at sea by pirates, presumably from France: "For which reason, and because of his poverty and the sickness which in those foreign parts assailed him cruelly, his mission, with which he was entrusted, dragged on for a long time until, having acquired a little competence from the maps which he was making, he began to make approaches to King Henry VII, father of Henry VIII who is now reigning."

Bartolomé showed Henry a world map he had made, and after the king heard "what the Admiral [Columbus] was offering, he accepted the offer with good will and had him sent for. But since God had reserved him for Castile, the Admiral had gone already and returned with victory in its enterprise." Later in the book the story was revisited, adding that Bartolomé was returning to Castile with a capitulation from Henry VII for his brother when he learned at Paris from Charles VIII that Columbus had already returned from the first voyage.

If any of this actually happened, Bartolomé must have set out on his mission to England around 1488 or 1489, with Henry offering to hire Columbus in 1492–93, while Bartolomé was in France. (The sixteenth-century English historiographer Richard Hakluyt would state that Bartolomé Columbus presented Henry VII with a world chart on February 13, 1488, but the source of this information is unknown, the chart has never been found, and the date seems too early, coming so close to Christopher Columbus's audience with Isabel at Málaga in late 1487.) Around the time of the proposal to Henry, Bartolomé apparently had become a cartographer in the service of France's regent, Anne de Beaujeu, who ruled in the name of her younger brother, the dauphin, until he formally took power as Charles VIII in 1492.

The contradictions in the Columbus story continued to gain momentum in Spain and eventually found additional strength among residents of the New World colonies his discoveries founded. The idea that Columbus relied on hearsay and rumor in formulating his voyage plan infuriated Alessandro Geraldini, who was appointed bishop of Santo Domingo in 1519 by Pope Leo X. Geraldini surely heard in Española the same sorts of local stories about Columbus that had reached the chronicler Oviedo when he was there a few years earlier, as the residents crafted their own foundation myth. Oviedo had found dubious their tale of the shipwrecked pilot at Madeira but would include it anyway in his history of the Indies. In 1522, Geraldini wrote Leo X a lengthy letter describing his voyage to Española, in which he dismissed such stories of Columbus's early fact gathering.

These "monstrous, unnatural men" had contended that Columbus had heard from Galician sailors that land had been seen to the west. Others who were "tossed by a mighty tempest" off the Canary Islands saw strange trees and also reported to Columbus that unknown lands were nearby. "These reports are ridiculous," Geraldini fumed. Columbus, he insisted, "was moved to undertake this long ocean expedition, not by the vain chatter of men or the experience of Galician sailors, but by sure reasoning and a sure [knowledge of the] orbit of heaven and earth."

Geraldini gave Columbus's ideas a more classical sheen. Columbus "was well-known for his knowledge of cosmography, mathematics, and techniques for measuring the sky and land, but was famous most of all for the greatness of his spirit." Columbus had deduced that "the lands of the equator, or the Antipodes" could be reached by sailing a long way across the Ocean Sea. Columbus had been informed about the Antipodes by Plato's *Critias,* and Geraldini implicitly equated them with the lost Atlantis when he wrote that Columbus refused to believe they could have sunk.

Whether Columbus actually could read the Latin of a work like *Critias,* the idea that he thought he could find (or would decide he had found) the Antipodes is not without support. On September 13, 1493, Pietro Martire wrote the Count of Tendilla and the Archbishop of Granada, saying "You remember Columbus [*Colonum*], the Ligurian, who persisted when in the camps with the sovereigns, that one could pass over by way of the Western Antipodes into a new hemisphere of the globe." Martire, who had met Columbus on his return from the first voyage, would persist in this idea that reaching the Antipodes had been Columbus's objective.

But Las Casas (who drew on Columbus's now-lost accounts of his voyages for his *Historia*) thought Columbus had been mainly influenced by Toscanelli's letter and map: "I think he based the whole scheme of his voyage on this letter." According to Las Casas, Columbus wrote Toscanelli and received from him a copy of the letter and the map that had been sent to Fernan Martins in 1474.

Yet as likely as Toscanelli appears to have been Columbus's chief inspiration—and for all that Geraldini was infuriated by tales of Columbus having been influenced by shipwrecked sailors and the allure of half-glimpsed islands—several eyewitnesses to Columbus's activities in the lawsuit testimonies insisted on his indebtedness to Pedro Vásquez de la Frontera, an experienced mariner who lived in Palos and claimed to have made a passage toward an unknown land to the west while in the service of Portugal.

Three residents of Palos testified that they saw Vásquez both at the La Rábida monastery and in his Palos home, discussing plans for the 1492 voyage with Columbus and Martín Alonso Pinzón, a prominent local mariner who commanded the *Pinta.* Most emphatic was Alonso Vélez, mayor of Palos, who swore in 1532 that Pinzón received information from Vásquez, who had participated in a Portuguese expedition to discover a distant land. It was only because of "timidity" that they had missed the landfall, and they had also been misled "by the grasses [Sargasso Sea] that they had found in the gulf of the sea." Vásquez advised Pinzón not to allow Columbus to turn back when they came upon these "grasses." Coincidentally, Fernando Columbus's biography and Las Casas's *Historia* featured a mariner named Pedro de Valasco; Fernando wrote that Valasco told Columbus in Murcia about seeing land, in this case west of Ireland.

The Fernando biography offered still another story of intelligence being imparted to his father from northern waters, this time from a one-eyed sailor at Puerto de Santa María on the Bay of Cádiz, who confided "that on a voyage he had made to Ireland he saw that land which at the time he supposed to be a part of Tartary [in Asia], that it turned westward (it must have been what is now called the Land of Cod) and foul weather prevented them from approaching it."

It was truly remarkable how many stories of Columbus's intelligence gathering compiled by early Spanish chroniclers involved landfalls not beyond the Canaries or the Madeiras but instead far to the north. Perhaps the bounds of Columbus's wisdom were being stretched post facto to accommodate the lands that in fact were discovered by Cabot. Yet the stories of a world to the west of Ireland were not isolated to the Columbus literature; they had engaged mariners long before Columbus ever sailed. For his part, Columbus may well have had reason to suspect that there was solid ground waiting to be discovered in northern latitudes before he departed Palos with the *Niña, Pinta,* and *Santa María* on August 3, 1492, to seek it in more temperate climes.

THE ASPIRING EXPLORER eventually joined the Castilian staff of Isabel and resumed his voyage bid in late 1491, with the conquest of Granada all but completed. Columbus was an eyewitness to the surrender on January 2, 1492. "I saw Your Highnesses' royal banners placed by force of arms on the towers of the Alhambra, which is the fortress of the said city," he recalled of the fall of the city of Granada, "and I saw the Moorish king [Boabdil] come out to the city gates and kiss Your Highnesses' royal hands and those of My Lord the Prince," the *infante* don Juan, who was four years old.

Boabdil handed over the keys to Granada on January 6, and Columbus got down to the business of finally securing his privileges for the voyage. The court's advisors still had good reasons to doubt his proposal. Rodrigo Maldonado de Talavera, a doctor of laws who served as a legal counsel to Isabel, would state in 1515 that Columbus had made his proposal to a learned council on which he sat. He recalled how "all of them agreed that what the admiral wished was impossible to be true and that the admiral persisted against the opinion of most of them in making the voyage." But with the Granada conquest out of the way, Columbus wore down their resistance.

Leaving aside the opinions emanating from ivory towers, the broad consensus in the maritime community was that Columbus's plan was deeply flawed if not potentially fatal. Martín González, a ship's biscuit maker at Moguer, just upriver from Palos and La Rábida, would watch Columbus outfit the first voyage and return successfully. He would testify that "many wise seamen said that running to the west from Cape Saint Vincent and by other winds they pointed out, they would never find land even if they traveled two years . . . all said that the hope of don Cristóbal Colón was futile and they made jest of him, saying that it was impossible [for] the admiral to find land."

The king and queen ignored dissenting voices and insisted on sending Columbus anyway. The most critical opinion seems to have belonged to Luis de Santángel, chancellor of Fernando's household and comptroller general (treasurer) of the kingdom of Aragon. Santángel was from a wealthy family of *conversos,* Jews who had converted to Christianity. He and his brother Jaume had made a tidy fortune in Valencia as "tax farmers"—monarchs like Fernando essentially sold their future tax revenues to the highest bidder, leaving it to the bidder actually to collect the funds.

According to Geraldini, Luis de Santángel "asked Columbus how much money and how many ships would be required for such a long voyage. When he answered that he would require 3,000 gold pieces and two ships, Santángel immediately stated that he himself wanted to undertake the expedition and would provide the money, and then Queen Isabella, because of her naturally lofty spirit, received Columbus and very generously granted him the ships, troops, and money for opening up a new world to the human race." Santángel's enthusiasm unquestionably was an important factor in advancing the voyage. It was said that he argued that Columbus's scheme, if successful, offered such extraordinary rewards that it was worth gambling the money on his little expedition.

The negotiations between Columbus (through his representative, Friar Juan Pérez of La Rábida) and the chancery staff of the royal courts resulted in an initial agreement executed on April 17, 1492, at Sante Fé, a town built by Spanish forces in 1490 to support their siege of the city of Granada to the east. This Santa Fé capitulation documented clause by clause the monarchs' approval of terms. A final capitulation was then agreed to on April 30 in Granada. Columbus had requested the Granada version mainly to have the monarchs reiterate their promise to award him with royal offices should the voyage be successful. The most difficult points were his demands that he be rewarded with hereditary administrative titles to any lands he discovered as well as with a hereditary position of admiral. This clearly was based on his own experiences in Portugal, as his wife's family held the hereditary title to the governorship of Porto Santos in the Madeiras. The Castilian royal staff was unhappy with the idea of granting Columbus hereditary title to what were civil service positions in the Spanish system, but he got his way.

The notion of Isabel pawning her jewels to fund the voyage is a myth, although she did borrow the money to make the voyage possible. On May 5, 1492, 1.14 million maravedis were loaned to Isabel and the Castilian crown by Santángel in his capacity as treasurer of the Sancta Hermandad, the national police force under the direction of Fernando and Isabel. The finances of Santángel and the Aragonose crown were densely intertwined, and the Sancta Hermandad post gave him access to proceeds from properties confiscated from Jews during their coincident expulsion from Spain—they were ordered to leave by May 1, 1492, or convert to Christianity by the end of July.

Empowered by his capitulation and with funds from the crown, Columbus headed to La Rábida and the town of Palos to mount the voyage. Within a year, he would return in triumph from his adventure on the Ocean Sea. But the spoils of discovery would see some of the leading citizens of this maritime community turn against his memory and in the process craft a counternarrative that cast into doubt his achievements and heritable rights.

BY THE SUMMER OF 1492, Christopher Columbus and John Cabot were both well established in Spain, as refugees of rather different sorts—Columbus of the Portuguese Braganza terror, Cabot of powerful and determined Venetian creditors. Cabot had wound up in Valencia: His experiences as a *pellizer* could have taken him there, as it was an important center on the Mediterranean coast for trade in Castilian wool and skins. It was also the financial and administrative capital of Aragon and one of Spain's more prominent and sophisticated cities. Some forty thousand people lived there by 1489, making it one of the largest urban centers in southern Europe. Its ships fanned out across the Mediterranean, while the port provided a stepping-stone to Italian traders reaching toward the Atlantic and northern European markets.

The city was situated in the *huerta,* some fifty square miles of rich alluvial fields with extensive irrigation canals, and was bordered by coastal lands dominated by *marjals,* swampy terrain so sodden that it eventually would be turned over to rice cultivation. It offered opportunities beyond the hide trade that a Venetian like Cabot who had made part of his living in construction would naturally have sought. Maintaining canals in an area with such a high water table was a constant engineering challenge. Cabot's landholdings and salt works in Chioggia were an interesting precedent; Chioggia's fields were on canal-pierced lands reclaimed around the mouth of the Brenta River, and the marjals around Valencia would have posed familiar issues of drainage, reclamation, and cultivation.

Valencia itself was a city of canals, which were used for water power as well as drainage. The main canal of Na Rovella ran through Valencia's heart, and two other major canals, Favara and Mislata, coursed around the city walls and delivered water into the city through secondary channels. The Na Rovella was a foul sewer, a conduit for human waste as well as the discharges of dyers, tanners, cloth finishers, and other trades, and posed its own engineering challenges. Valencia would have been a good place to apply any lessons Cabot had learned from construction in Venice's district of San Palo and satellite town of Chioggia.

Cabot would have found a thriving mercantile community of Columbus's fellow Ligurians. Nearly 600 Genoese businessmen appear in Valencian notarial records between 1450 and 1525; 200 were identified as merchants, and as many as 377 were prospering in what was broadly called the silk trade, most of those being classified as *velluters,* or velvet manufacturers. Cabot arrived soon after their self-governing community coalesced around a religious confraternity, as the Genoese began to build a chapel to host its activities in 1487.

Valencia was about two miles inland on the north bank of the river Turia, which emptied into the Balearic Sea of the Mediterranean. The city was enjoying a golden age of Renaissance prosperity and in 1482 began building a marvelous new complex, called La Lonja. Originally intended as an exchange market for oil, it expanded to include a silk exchange and a banking facility. La Lonja was a major project in the city core; the main Sala de Contración (contract or trading hall) and its tower would be completed in 1498, with the entire complex not finished until 1533.

It was during the construction of this ambitious facility that Cabot, in association with a Catalan merchant named Gaspar Rull, proposed a complementary one: an artificial harbor along the seashore at the mouth of the Turia River. His vision was taken seriously, and he possessed the drafting and engineering skills necessary to impress a monarch. In September 1492, the project was brought to the attention of the King of Valencia, who was holding court some 185 miles up the coast in the Catalunyan capital of Barcelona. As the kingdom had been part of the House of Aragon since 1238, the harbor scheme thus came before Fernando, who, with his wife, Isabel, had just sent Christopher Columbus off in search of a new westward route to the Orient with the financial help of Luis de Santángel, treasurer of the Sancta Hermandad, comptroller general of Aragon, and wealthy tax farmer of Valencia.

SIX

THE *NIÑA*, the *Pinta*, and the *Santa Mariá*, the most famous flotilla in the history of seafaring, departed Palos within sight of the monastery of La Rábida on Fri day, August 3, 1492, clearing the bar of Saltés at eight in the morning. Columbus planned to ride the trade winds some six hundred miles southwest to the Canary Islands. One hundred miles was a good day's run, and they made brisk progress, approaching the nearest of the seven main islands in the archipelago, Lanzarote, which is about fifty miles off the coast of Africa, on August 7.

Surrounded by the Ocean Sea, Columbus was awash in personal debt. The crown had arranged for the *Niña* and the *Pinta,* but Columbus had turned to a Florentine merchant and slaver in Seville, Gianotto di Lorenzo Berardi, to fund his charter of the *Santa María.* Berardi and Columbus may have known each other in Portugal. Las Casas would assert that when Columbus wrote to Paolo Toscanelli, he entrusted the letter to the care of a Florentine merchant in Lisbon named Lorenzo Berardo (the Fernando Columbus biography changed the name to "Girardi"), who was traveling back to Tuscany. Berardi began appearing in notarial records in Seville in 1486 and served as a local factor for the Medici bank.

Columbus's fellow Genoese formed the largest self-governing community of *extranjero* (foreign) merchants in the city. The Ligurians had been active in Andalusia since the twelfth century and were already established in its capital, Seville, when it was under Muslim rule, prior to the 1248 *reconquista*. In 1492, the Genoese Francisco de Riberol (Sir Francesco de Rivaroli), who would become one of Columbus's chief financiers, formed in Seville a *compañia* or partnership with two other men. One was the Florentine Berardi; the other was an Andalusian noble, Alonso Fernández de Lugo, a veteran of the subjugation a decade earlier of Gran Canaria in the Canary Islands. The trio was embarking on a conquest of lush La Palma, the most northwesterly island in the Canary archipelago, at the very moment Columbus was sailing in the same direction.

The Canary Islands had been assigned to Spain under the Treaty of Alcáçovas in 1479, but the islands of La Palma and Tenerife were still in the hands of the indigenous Guanches. Drained financially by the decade-long struggle to conquer Granada, for which they had borrowed from Genoese financiers like the Spinolas, the Spanish monarchs were content to privatize the acquisition of the remaining Canary Islands. Riberol and Berardi put up the cash, Lugo the military know-how. Each man had an equal share of the spoils, including a 700,000-maravedis prize promised by Fernando and Isabel if the conquest was completed within a year.

Riberol may have met Columbus in Granada in early 1492, as the terms of Lugo's La Palma conquest were being negotiated at the same time as Columbus was securing his capitulation for the first Indies voyage and arranging to borrow from Berardi the money for the *Santa María* charter. The relationship between the two enterprises may not have ended there. Columbus would be bound to the Canaries by the same circle of Italian financiers, by personal experience, and by one notorious lover.

THE CANARIES WERE FORMED by volcanism and are strewn across 250 miles of longitude. In the center of the archipelago is its largest island, Tenerife; the sparsely vegetated cone of El Pico del Tiede rises more than twelve thousand feet above the sea, and on clear days it wears a necklace of cumulous clouds well below its squat peak. Tiede was active in 1492, erupting from the northwest rift, Boca Cangrejo. Columbus "saw a great fire issuing from the peak of the island of Tenerife, which is extremely high."

Columbus's little fleet spent almost an entire month in the Canaries, from August 9 to around September 6, in a most curious layover. As the three ships approached the archipelago, the *Pinta* twice unshipped her rudder, which Columbus blamed on sabotage by her co-owner, Cristóbal Quintero, and another sailor, who allegedly didn't want to make the voyage. (Whatever Columbus's misgivings on the first voyage, Quintero would serve as the master of the flagship of the second voyage.) The *Pinta* was directed to the main island of Gran Canaria, where Columbus initially hoped to leave her behind and replace her with another vessel. Instead, he had her rudder repaired and her rig converted from triangular lateen sails to square sails, which were more efficient when running before the prevailing trades.

While the *Pinta* was being refitted, Columbus sailed (perhaps with both the *Santa María* and the *Niña*) one hundred miles to the west to Gomera, the small island between La Palma and Tenerife, the two landfalls still under the control of the Guanches that Lugo and his partners Berardi and Riberol were aiming to subjugate. Columbus reprovisioned at Gomera, taking on wood, water, and meat, but first had to sail back to Gran Canaria to collect the *Pinta* on September 2 before bringing aboard the supplies at Gomera. The flotilla at last departed Gomera on September 6.

The Las Casas abstract of Columbus's journal never explained why he chose to bide time at Gomera while the *Pinta* was being refitted so far to the east, as the distance needlessly complicated his communications and preparations for the coming ocean passage. The least seamanlike but most romantic explanation is that he was remaking his acquaintance with a lover.

Columbus would also call at Gomera in 1493 and 1498. His childhood friend Michele da Cuneo, who was along on the second voyage, would write in 1495 that they paused at Gomera in October 1493 "because of the lady of the place with whom our lord admiral had once been in love." At some point in the past, Columbus had conducted a passionate affair with the island's governor, Beatriz de Bobadilla.

Doña Bobadilla was a notorious beauty. Born at Medina del Campo in 1462, she joined the court as a lady of honor to Isabel at age seventeen and is said to have become a mistress of Fernando. Isabel got rid of her by arranging to marry her off to Hernán de Peraza, governor of Gomera, in 1482. Peraza had been summoned to answer charges that he was complicit in the death of Juan Réjon, commander of a Castilian flotilla that had been sent to conquer La Palma and Tenerife in 1481. The Duke of Medina-Sidonia brokered a deal: Peraza would not be held responsible for Réjon's death if he agreed to mount the conquest himself and to marry Bobadilla and take her with him, far from Fernando. The conquest failed to come off, and Peraza was killed in a slave rebellion in 1488, which he is said to have ignited by his advances on a Guanche woman. Bobadilla then governed Gomera in the name of their son, Guillén, who would become the first Count of Gomera. She would be remembered foremost for her tempestuous love affairs and her cruel treatment of the Guanche slaves who toiled in her sugarcane fields.

Columbus and Bobadilla could have first met at Santa Fé in early 1492, when Peraza's widow is believed to have been at court and both Lugo's invasion plans and Columbus's voyage scheme were being negotiated with the crown. If so, it was an encounter crowded with portent: Not only would Bobadilla become Columbus's lover, she would also marry Lugo in 1498, and her brother would bring Columbus home from the Caribbean in chains in 1500.

One can imagine the explorer all but consumed by the volcanic passions of Doña Beatriz at the Castillo in San Sabastián de la Gomera while Tiede spewed fire and ash to their east. But it is also an absurd explanation for how an expedition

Columbus had sought to mount for years could be waylaid for an entire month only days after getting under way. Feeding some ninety men and maintaining discipline for that long was a serious burden on the little expedition. Columbus would have been fortunate even to have a fleet to command after such a lengthy delay. Rerigging and repairing the *Pinta* on Gran Canaria could account for some of the layover, but whatever he might have been up to with Beatriz de Bobadilla, Columbus was at Gomera at precisely the time the Lugo invasion of neighboring La Palma was being mounted.

Alonso de Lugo raised a force of nine hundred, much of it in Seville, but he also found men in the Canaries. Lugo received his royal commission on July 12 and would have established himself first in the conquered islands of the Canaries before mounting the La Palma invasion, while Columbus was in the archipelago. On August 20, a number of men on Gran Canaria and Gomera—the two islands Columbus was moving between—were contracted as foot soldiers for Lugo's invasion force. Lugo is thought to have landed on the beach at Tazacorte on La Palma's west coast no later than the end of September—no more than a few weeks after Columbus resumed his voyage westward.

Columbus's venture shared many key figures with the simultaneous Canaries conquest. Isabel's accountant, Alonso de Quintanella, played a lead role in advancing both enterprises; so did Castile's treasurer, the Genoese Francisco Pinelo, who also administered with Luis de Santángel the Sancta Hermandad, the source of royal funding for Columbus in 1492. Given Columbus's close relationship with the financier Berardi (and the close partnership that would emerge with Riberol), the explorer likely was serving the invasion in an advance role when he paused at Gomera. Columbus could have gathered intelligence, even scouted the landing beach at Tazacorte, and attended to logistical matters at Bobadilla's Gomera, which became a base of operations for Lugo and a holding pen for captive Guanches. Columbus assuredly did not depart Gomera until the Lugo invasion force was prepared for the Tazacorte landing.

The Columbus expedition was a small-change venture compared to the invasion being mounted by Berardi and his partners in the Canaries. To Berardi especially, who was providing Columbus with private financing for the *Santa María* charter, the Columbus voyage might well have seemed a side trip for the sizable Canaries venture: the *Santa María* at least could pitch in with advance planning for Lugo's assault and then, having already sailed as far as the westernmost islands in the Canaries archipelago, strike out toward the setting sun with the *Niña* and *Pinta*. As the voyage journal would reveal, Columbus expected to make his first landfall within about a week, which was about as arduous as sailing from Spain to the Canaries. Even if Columbus found nothing, at least he would have been of help in launching the subjugation of La Palma. The Guanches would be enslaved, the sugarcane would be planted, the investment capital would multiply rapidly, and the profits would be able to seek new opportunities—perhaps, if Columbus proved successful, farther to the west.

Columbus departed Gomera on Thursday, September 6, and learned from a caravel arriving from Hierro (Ferro) "that three caravels from Portugal were cruising in the area with the intention of detaining him; it must have been due to the envy the King felt at his having gone to Castile," according to Las Casas.

Columbus was becalmed that day, between Gomera and Tenerife. The stillness lasted all night and into Friday. It was not until three in the morning on Saturday that the breeze returned and allowed the flotilla to clear the archipelago. The wind blew hard from the northeast, and heavy seas broke over the ships' bows as they struggled westward. No harassing Portuguese warships were spotted. Six months would pass before Columbus was heard from again, and by then, the fighting for La Palma was almost over.

CABOT COULD RUN, but he could not hide. The Venetian creditors he had been avoiding included merchants who conducted business in ports as far away as England; their sources were everywhere, among sailors, fellow merchants, diplomats, and bankers in their networks of European commerce. Valencia was a major trading center in the western Mediterranean, where the Venetian galleys sometimes called. Perhaps his face was recognized on the waterfront, directing reconstruction of a wave-racked wooden pier, or his name had raised eyebrows as locals chattered about this ambitious Venetian prowling the beach of Grao, making measurements and sketching a vision in cut stone.

However the word returned to the Rialto, the news spread that Cabot was no longer in Milan, Genoa, or Savoy—if he had ever been there at all. A fresh Cabot creditor appeared before the senate, securing a "letter of recommendation to justice" for Valencia on July 5, 1492. Cabot (Ionnes Gaboto) was identified along with a man named Giorgio Dominici as owing 130 ducats to Giorgio Dragan, another figure from Venice's maritime economy. Dragan was a merchant active in the Mediterranean who had a carrack delivering wine from Crete to Flanders and Sandwich in the late 1470s. In September 1493, he would turn up in records shipping artillery and munitions on the order of the Count of Veglia, a city on the Dalmatia coast of the Adriatic.

This debt was far less onerous than the two previous ones that engendered letters designed to bring Cabot to justice. And by the time Dragan had the letter in the hands of Valencia's ruling jurors, Cabot probably wasn't even around, doubtless having decamped to Barcelona with Gaspar Rull to patiently wait, for months if necessary, an audience with Fernando for his harbor scheme.

Two years later—and only weeks before his travels caused him to truly converge with Cabot's life and career—Jerome Münzer made his own September visit to Barcelona, the largest city in Aragon's principality of Catalonia. He was impressed by the walled city and its formidable battlements, laid out in a circle on the shore of the Balearic. But ever since the Catalonian civil war of the 1460s, Münzer observed, commerce had been leaving Barcelona for Valencia, which had become "the market of Spain. And now Barcelona is almost dead, compared to its previous state."

Barcelona nevertheless possessed what Valencia did not: a superb harbor. Since 1474, a mole, or breakwall, sheltering vessels from the open sea in a deeper an- choring area had been under construction; it would proceed fitfully until the mid- eighteenth century in defiance of the city's economic decline. Valencia may have been capturing Barcelona's wealth, but what Valencia needed was Barcelona's port facilities. Cabot proposed to deliver the latter. With Gaspar Rull likely along to fi- nesse the courtly introduction, Cabot had set out for Barcelona. In the process, he had given yet another creditor the slip, for the time being. Perhaps Cabot adopted the additional name Montecalunya in hope of shaking his pursuers.

Despite the change in the cities' fortunes, Fernando and Isabel still chose Bar- celona rather than Valencia as a home for their roving court, which moved between major centers in Castile and Aragon throughout the year. The palace where the monarchs stayed, Münzer related, was so beautiful, so admirable, as to be without equal. "All the rooms of the palace have floors covered with clay tiles baked with drawings in various colors. The ceilings are all covered with very pure gold, adorned with diverse golden flowers. What a superb palace!"

John Cabot would have made his presentation to Fernando amid this royal splendor. The monarch was then forty years old. After meeting him at Madrid a few years later, in January 1495, Münzer described Fernando as a man of medium height, in whose face cheerfulness and congeniality were mixed with a certain gravity. Por- traits depicted him with a long nose, a full if pursed mouth, cheeks ample to the point of jowly, and a weak double chin. "He acts only with great things in his heart," wrote Münzer. "He enjoys an excellent constitution." Münzer expected Fernando to continue to be fit for a long time because of his hunting pursuits. "Now that the king- doms are peaceful and everything has been returned to good order, he is concerned especially with religion, restoring ruined churches and founding new ones."

Fernando's life wasn't half as idle in early 1495 as Münzer suggested, but it would have been far more contemplative when Cabot met him in September 1492, nine months after the end of the lengthy and costly Granada campaign. Still, Fer- nando's recent decisions to evict all Jews who did not convert to Christianity from his kingdom and to sell Moors captured at Málaga into slavery spoke of a ruthless- ness that would account for the gravity Münzer later detected mingling with cheer- fulness and congeniality in his face.

Cabot laid out the drawings before Fernando and explained the concept. Un- fortunately neither the drawings nor a record of the presentation's details have sur- vived, although we can surmise what he had in mind. Valencia's shipping facilities were feeble for such a major economic center. The river Turia on which it fronted was too shallow for major ocean traffic, but earlier proposals to dredge it had been rejected. On May 28, 1483, the year after construction began on Valencia's new trading facility, La Lonja, a man named Antoni Joan secured a privilege from Fernando to develop the city's first coastal port infrastructure: a wooden pier on the beach of Grao (*la playa del Grao*) on the north side of the mouth of the Turia. The city further granted him the exclusive right to operate the pier, which became known as the Pont de Fusta (meaning in Catalan simply "wooden bridge" or "wooden deck"). The pier cost ten thousand florins to build and another six hundred florins a year to maintain. Exposed to the Balearic, it was soon in such disrepair that Joan wanted to fashion a replacement, and on March 17, 1491, he renewed his privilege with Fernando.

Antoni Joan's pier refurbishing seemed more than coincidental with John Cabot's arrival in Valencia about two years before September 1492 and his subsequent interest in creating an artificial harbor at the same beach. The foundations of Pont de Fusta have survived beneath the modern streetscape of Valencia and its extensive harbor works. The cribs of loose rocks corralled in wooden frames are the type of construction employed in building foundations in Venice. Cabot could have been involved with the construction of the new Pont de Fusta from the earliest days of his appearance in Valencia; if so, he would have recognized that this pier was doomed to repeated replacement unless it was adequately protected. Valencia needed what Barcelona was receiving: breakwalls. A surviving letter mentions "arms" as part of the Cabot plan, which indicates at least two breakwalls creating a sheltered harbor area. But another letter also mentions a jetty, which suggests a project in direct competition with Joan's modest Pont de Fusta. And Joan was noticeably absent from Cabot's proposal.

The royal response to Cabot's pitch was superlative. Fernando wrote the governor-general of Valencia, Diego de Torres, on September 27, 1492, three weeks after Columbus's fleet had departed Gomera for the western horizon. The same king who had renewed Joan's privileges for the Pont de Fusta eighteen months earlier was impressed by Cabot's presentation.

Fernando explained how

we have been informed by Johan Caboto Montecalunya, the Venetian, that he arrived at this city [Valencia] two years ago, and during this time he has considered whether on the beach of this city a port could be constructed, and on finding that the aforesaid port could be constructed very easily both on land and sea, he has designed and painted plans of them, and he has brought them to us; and, having seen them and heard the aforesaid Johan Caboto, it appears to us if the said port and jetty could be constructed in the sea just as in the plan he has brought here, it would be something which would result in a great benefit for the common weal of this kingdom.

Fernando asked Torres to form a committee to examine the specifics of Cabot's plan, which involved quarrying stone from Cap de Cullera, a coastal promontory twenty miles south, and moving it to the construction site by barge. It was a process Cabot surely knew from his Venetian experience: Stone used in construction in the Signoria was quarried in Dalmatia and ferried along the Adriatic.

The committee reported back to the king on October 25 with a list of issues it said needed to be investigated. The list included how much sand or clay was in the proposed beach construction site, the depths in the beach area where Cabot proposed to construct the arms of the harbor, the depths of water for barges, and the expense and logistics of quarrying the stone. Stone cutters would have to be sent to Cap de Cullera "to cut stone of the size which the said Johan Cabot will indicate, and to have a boat carry it over the said shore and to see more or less what it will cost to put a stone in the place where the said port must be constructed." Once they could calculate how many stones were required for the depths of the waters in which Cabot had chosen to build, they would "have some idea of what the said port and jetty will cost."

Torres praised Cabot's choice of stone from Cap de Cullera: "[I]t is of such a nature and so good for carrying and cutting that nobody could ask for so good a stone as it has been found, in price and expense, for progress in the said work." Torres was generally optimistic about the plan's prospects and fairly persuaded of the benefits: "[M]any have argued that the building of this port will ennoble and enrich this city and even the whole kingdom."

Compared to Columbus's exploration scheme, Cabot's harbor project was pragmatic in the extreme, a civil engineering works with indisputable benefits. But the poorly conceived and interminable breakwall project at Barcelona may not have encouraged broad and unquestioning enthusiasm for Cabot's claims of easy execution. And the sticking point was the same as it always had been for Columbus's voyage proposal: how to pay for it all.

Cabot meanwhile appeared to have given his latest creditor the slip; he was able to return to Valencia and leave again for Barcelona without apparent incident. He and Rull were en route to another meeting with the king, and as Torres explained in his letter (which Rull was carrying), they "will tell Your Highness orally some expedients for obtaining money for building the said port; when Your Majesty hears that, you will see which is most satisfactory and least burdensome for Your Majesty and least harmful for this city."

Torres advised Fernando to consult his general treasurer and the royal financial scribe, both of whom (as Torres reminded him) were in Barcelona. The general treasurer was Luis de Santángel. Indeed, as a Valencian tax farmer who had just masterminded the financing of the Columbus expedition, surely Santángel could figure out for Fernando how to pay for a long-overdue artificial harbor for such a crucial economic center.

These men, Torres counseled, "are very knowledgeable in the affair of this city and kingdom. From them Your Highness will be able to obtain a full relation of where the money can come from." Torres was concerned that the project would never proceed if the city's lieutenant-general and its ruling council, the jurors, were left to decide how to fund it: If they "had to see where [the money] had to come from, they would never agree, but only Your Highness can best see what is most satisfactory for your service and order it to be put into execution."

On the day Torres wrote the letter that Rull and Cabot were carrying to Fernando at Barcelona, Christopher Columbus was guiding his three ships through the low-slung islands of the Bahamas to deliver a letter of his own. He had been in the archipelago for almost two weeks and was steering for a group of "seven or eight islands in a line from north to south"—the Ragged Islands on the southeastern edge of the Great Bahama Bank. Columbus was carrying a greeting from Fernando and Isabel that he had every hope of presenting shortly to the Great Khan, ruler of Cathay.

SEVEN

"**D**AY BY DAY** more and more marvelous things are reported from the new world through Columbus the Ligurian," Pietro Martire wrote Giovanni Borromeo of Milan on October 20, 1494. Martire thus became the first person to apply to Columbus's discoveries the term that would come to define them: *orbe novo* in the original Latin of the letter—"new world."

Martire was a Milanese scholar, poet, and chaplain at the court of Fernando and Isabel who first met Columbus at Barcelona on his return from the initial voyage. In the same letter, Martire confided, "I have begun to write a work concerning this great discovery." Martire indeed became the first historian of Columbus's voyages. When he wrote Borromeo with news of a *new world*, he had been grappling for more than a year with the issue of exactly what it was the Admiral of the Ocean Sea had found.

As a poet, Martire was employing the term *new world* more in a lyrical way than in a strict geographic one. The term also had a popular precedent. In July 1492, in the widely read volume of human history, *Liber chronicarum,* the Nürnberg humanist and physician Hartmann Schedel had called Portugal's discoveries in West Africa in 1483 a "new world." The lands Columbus had reached truly were a *new world* to Martire, one of frightening cannibals and promised riches of gold, precious stones, pearls, cinnamon, pepper, and so much more, and a novel landscape of flora and fauna. The more concrete idea that Columbus's discoveries represented a radically new geographic fact, a place no existing cosmography could account for, was years away.

Columbus's immortal reputation as the discoverer of the New World was an achievement of historical hindsight. He had not expected to find any such place as we define it, and in fact he had not yet reached a new continental landmass. His worldview hewed to the essential Toscanelli scheme: Sailing west would deliver a voyager first to Antilla (alternately the Isle of Seven Cities), then to Cipango, and finally, beyond a curtain of innumerable islands, to the Indies of the Asian mainland. Columbus was determined to shoehorn his actual findings into that geographic scheme while overlaying them on a globe much smaller than it actually is.

The related notion that Columbus dared to challenge the seemingly limitless mystery of a vast and empty ocean was an artifact of his success. He never expected to spend what proved to be more than a month trekking westward from Gomera in the Canaries. Within a week of clearing the Canaries on September 8, 1492, the flotilla was hopeful of finding land, and took heart from clues such as clouds, rainfall patterns, birds, and clumps of weed. On September 18, Martín Alonso Pinzón, master of the *Pinta,* took leave from Columbus, aboard the *Santa María,* to chase after a flock of birds in hope that they would lead the fleet to land.

On September 25, Columbus asked Pinzón to return him his chart, which had been aboard the *Pinta* for three days. Las Casas stated that the chart "had certain islands depicted in that area of the sea," by which Columbus could only have meant Antilla. Martín Alonso agreed that according to the chart, they should have been among them. Columbus proposed that currents had carried them northeast and that they hadn't actually sailed as far west as their pilots had calculated.

It is a testament to Columbus's sheer determination that he did not lose hope, as others before him surely had, when experience defied his expectations. The voyage was also a tribute to his powers of persuasion—and conniving—in that he managed to convince the crews of three ships, some ninety men in all, to keep pressing westward. Rarely did a seaman of the late fifteenth century have to spend more than a week out of sight of land when making a passage, and even then he had a known destination. Columbus had to stave off mounting disquiet verging on outright mutiny over the lack of results. No one was worried about sailing off the edge of a flat earth, but they had genuine concerns that they would never see home again. The trade winds blowing so favorably from the east in sweeping them westward could prevent them from ever returning, as ships of this time could not make effective progress into the wind.

Daily at dawn and dusk, Columbus gathered the three ships so that everyone could scan the horizon together for signs of land in the low slanting light. By October 3, Columbus was sure that he was passing Antilla but was determined to reach the Indies without delay. Such a false milestone—of attainable land presumed to exist beyond sight—kept the flotilla pressing forward. Rather than being cast upon a vast, empty sea, they were united by a hallucination of coherent geography, with imagined options of steering for Antilla or hurrying on for the Indies. On

October 6 came a suggestion from Martín Alonso of a change in course to the southwest. Las Casas wrote that Pinzón had in mind an encounter with Cipango, but Columbus resolved to maintain his westerly heading.

Pinzón proposed a course change toward the southwest in order to chase after another flock of birds, to which Columbus agreed. Had the flock not crossed paths with the flotilla, had Columbus kept sailing west, he would have run into Florida, perhaps around Cape Canaveral or Daytona Beach.

Instead, on October 12, 1492, the grand delusion of the New World began. Having been driven forward by theory, Christopher Columbus now confronted the concrete experience of actual people and geography on a Bahamian beach. Coming ashore through aquamarine waters onto fine white sand, banners unfurling in an ocean breeze unimpeded by low barrier dunes guarding a brackish inland lake, Columbus surely believed he had achieved the geographic goal that had inspired the voyage. However wrong that preconceived idea would prove to be, it had provided him momentum when other men would have (and already had) lost hope and turned back. The promises of Antilla, Cipango, and the Indies had steeled his resolve, and they continued to shape his interpretation of the landfalls he encountered. The late thirteenth-century tales of Marco Polo, amplified by Nicolò de' Conti and Toscanelli, continued to reinforce the expectation that Columbus would encounter the Great Khan, as he carried the letter from his monarchs to the ruler of a Mogul empire that had not existed for more than a century; the Mings had been in power since 1368.

The actual experience of landing on what the local Arawakan people, the Lucayo, told him was Guanahaní, which he renamed San Salvador, did not discourage Columbus. ("This island is very large and very flat, the trees are very green, and there is much water; there is a very large lake in the centre," Las Casas quoted Columbus. "There are no mountains and it is all so green that it is a pleasure to see.") Geographers had littered the Ocean Sea on the perimeter of the Indies with a multitude of islands, and Columbus adjusted his expectations accordingly. He accepted the sand-skirted, low limestone shelves of the Bahamas, unadorned by civilization, as primitive outlands of the empire he sought, and pressed forward through them. A new voyage was beginning, in search of the wealth he was sure was close at hand.

From the moment of his arrival, however, Columbus was also imagining a harvest of a sort of wealth that had nothing to do with the Indies. He cast a predatory eye over the bodies of the Lucayo he met on October 12, noting "they are naturally the colour of Canary Islanders." The comparison was more than physiological: "They ought to make good slaves for they are of quick intelligence since I notice that they are quick to repeat what is said to them," Columbus added. Although Columbus also believed the Lucayo "could very easily become Christians, for it seemed to me that they had no religion of their own," he had revealed his essential conception of these people. They were one and the same as the indigenous

Guanches the partnership of Berardi, Riberol, and Lugo were at that moment enslaving back in the Canaries. The essential similarity would haunt the Arawaks of the Caribbean (and their Carib enemies and Ciboney neighbors) over the next few cruel and traumatic years.

Columbus had a dogged singularity of purpose and vision that had served him well. He had persisted with his quest to secure a royal privilege for this voyage for nearly a decade, and the voyage itself (regardless of what some Pinzón acolytes would allege) had reached the Bahamas because of his relentless determination to stay the course westward. But once in the New World, that dogged singularity became a hobbling impediment: He could interpret what he found only within the framework of what he had promised to find. It would have been remarkable for any man of his time to recalibrate his perceptions within days or even weeks of arrival, to come up with an alternate idea of a world's configuration that no respected geographer had yet put forward. But Columbus's delusion was not temporary; he remained faithful to his original conviction that he had landed on the edge of the Indies to the end of his life, even as the evidence mounted that he must have been somewhere else entirely.

The expedition had brought along samples of pepper, cinnamon, and other spices that reached the Mediterranean through Venetian galleys doing business at Beirut and Alexandria. The flotilla's men had never seen them growing, and hoped that showing these samples to natives, whom they had immediately labeled Indians, could lead them to more. There was much optimistic interpretation of plants and trees that affirmed the natural wealth of their landfalls and persuaded Columbus that he was indeed on the edge of the Indies.

The flotilla took on board Lucayan guides and picked its way through the Bahamas. Columbus resolved on October 23 to sail for "the island of Cuba which I believe must be Cipango, to judge from the signs which these people give of its size and riches." He struggled with how to interpret Cuba. Columbus had every reason to believe it was an island, as the Lucayo told him when he arrived on the north coast on October 28 that "in their canoes they cannot circle the island in 20 days." While he set aside the idea that it was Cipango, he still provisionally accepted that it was an island and named it Juana, for the young crown prince. On his first day there he somehow gathered from the local Arawaks "that large ships came there from the Great Khan, and that from there to the mainland was a journey of 10 days." As the Arawaks had in the past been in contact with the Maya and may have continued to trade with what is now Guatemala, Columbus likely misunderstood an attempt to tell him about the peoples of Central America and what is now Mexico, where the Aztec empire was at its zenith.

Martín Alonso Pinzón helped change Columbus's mind about Juana, telling him on October 30 (according to the Las Casas abstract) that he understood "Cuba" was the name of a city and that the so-called island "was a very large stretch of mainland which extends a long way to the N, and that the king of that land was at war with the Great Khan, whom they call Cami."

Las Casas also recorded the first latitude fix for the voyage: Columbus had determined he was at 42° north, which was wrong by some 20 degrees. The error was so enormous it defies belief, yet Columbus reiterated it on November 2 with an evening sighting of the polestar.

"It is certain, says the Admiral, that this is the mainland," Las Casas wrote for November 1. Columbus was forcing his exploration results into a Toscanelli scheme steeped in the Marco Polo narrative; Las Casas wrote that Columbus thought he was "near Zaytó and Quinsay, within a hundred leagues more or less of one or the other." Zaytó—or Zai Tun, as Marco Polo described it—was supposed to be around the Tropic of Cancer, which was Columbus's true latitudinal position. But Columbus was insisting he was much closer to a port city called Quinsay (now Guangzhou, or Hangzhou), which geographers placed around latitude 45.

Toscanelli had advised of his letter's accompanying chart:

> From the city of Lisbon straight toward the West there are on the said chart 26 spaces, each one of which contains 250 miles, as far as the most noble and great city of Quinsay, which is 100 miles around . . . where there are ten marble bridges. The name of this city signifies City of Heaven, of which many marvelous things are told in regard to the great genius of the inhabitants and the size of the buildings and the great revenues.

The Book of ser Marco Polo already had sung the praises of "the most noble city of Kinsay, a name which is as much as to say in our tongue 'The City of Heaven.'. . . the city is beyond dispute the finest and the noblest in the world."

Columbus dispatched two men to make contact with the rulers of what he was convincing himself was mainland Asia. Accompanying Rodrigo de Jerez was a *converso*, Luis de Torres, who "knew Hebrew and Chaldean and some Arabic." They were to press inland on Cuba with the assistance of local Arawaks and be back in six days. It was baffling that Columbus was not looking for the great commercial centers of Zai-Tun and Quinsay from the water rather than with a two-man shore party. If trade in pepper alone from Quinsay was one hundred times as great as what the Venetians conducted through Alexandria, as Marco Polo had claimed, surely the ocean would have teemed with large vessels that could guide Columbus there, much as one would expect if searching the eastern Mediterranean for Alexandria itself. Instead, despite reporting several times of hearing about great ships, Columbus only ever encountered dugout canoes powered by men wielding paddles that he said were "a kind of baker's peel."

Jerez and Torres never found Quinsay, Zai-Tun, the Great Khan, or any evidence of his kingdom. Columbus and his men continued to encounter only

Stone Age peoples in scattered villages—one of which was abandoned on his approach—amid tropical verdure, and the sea was empty of trading vessels. But Columbus's mind nevertheless began to harden around the idea that Cuba was the Asian mainland.

On November 12, Columbus allowed himself to be distracted from the search for the cities of the Great Khan to seek out an island to the east called Baneque (or Babeque). There, he understood from the Lucayo, "the people collect gold by candlelight at night on the beach and afterwards beat it into bars with hammers." But he did not rush toward it, and the flotilla was still tentatively coasting the northeastern shore of Cuba when Pinzón broke with Columbus on the night of November 26, slipping anchor and disappearing with the *Pinta*.

Pinzón had lost patience with the lack of progress in finding Baneque and its gold. But the rift coincided with an admission by Columbus that his latitude reading of 42° north was impossible. Columbus now blamed his quadrant and said he would stop using the instrument until they had reached land again and he could repair it. It is hard to imagine what could have been so catastrophically wrong with such a simple angle-measuring device, or why he did not double-check his observations with his astrolabe, which Las Casas mentioned him having on the voyage home.

Columbus either did not understand how to use the quadrant or the astrolabe or had been pursuing a fiction about his location in the Indies that could not withstand the skepticism and impatience of an experienced mariner like Martín Alonso Pinzón. The former is almost unthinkable. On the way home, Columbus claimed to determine an accurate latitude fix just by eyeballing the height of the polestar, when the weather was too rough to use the quadrant or astrolabe. This could not be the same mariner who had spent several days believing an error of 20 degrees with the simplest form of celestial navigation.

Columbus may have been spinning a fiction about his latitude at Cuba in order to persuade Fernando and Isabel that he was close to reaching the Great Khan, so they would send him out again. He also could have been lying to mislead the other members of the flotilla about where they actually were, to ensure that he alone knew how to find this place again. Insulted, and impatient to locate the much-promised gold, Martín Alonso had chosen to plot his own course to riches.

On the outbound voyage, Columbus had striven to maintain discipline and faith among his largely ill-educated crew by keeping his plotting chart mostly to himself and by lying about his progress. Every day he gathered from the pilots of the vessels estimates of their distance covered in leagues, and according to Las Casas, he routinely understated his own estimates: "[H]e always pretended to the men that he was making little headway so that the voyage should not seem long; so that he kept two reckonings for that voyage: the shorter was the false one and the longer was the true one." Columbus's record of daily leagues, if truly intended to mislead, actually may have been aimed at the educated men on board the *Santa María:* Pero Gutiérrez, who was Fernando's chamberlain, and Rodrigo Sánchez de Segovia, who had been assigned by the monarchs as comptroller for the enterprise. These royal representatives would have been especially concerned if the voyage was not unfolding as Columbus had promised and might have been amenable to turning back if others agitated to abandon an ill-conceived and potentially fatal quest.

Columbus would confess on the return voyage to additional deceptions: Las Casas observed how Columbus "says that he pretended to have sailed further [eastward] to mislead the pilots and sailors who were plotting the course so that he would remain master of that route to the Indies, as he in fact remains, because none of the others was certain of the course and none can be sure of his route to the Indies."

Keeping a double set of books to track his westward progress had been a clever way to overcome crew fears that doubtless had defeated previous Portuguese attempts to make westward discoveries. But the deception led Columbus into a complex strategy of misrepresentation and denial that would mark his entire career in the New World. He would have to work tirelessly to keep afloat competing realities in order to defend the privileges he spent years striving to secure. The 1492 Columbus voyage had established a prime operating principle of this new age of westward exploration: If it served your purposes, lie about where you had been. But in this hothouse of misdirection and misrepresentation, the lies expanded in all directions.

IN THE DECADES THAT FOLLOWED Columbus's discovery, there would be no consensus on what had transpired on the most famous, most consequential voyage in the history of seafaring. The most essential facts would be disputed vehemently in the ensuing legal battle over Columbus's heritable rights. The venture would defy agreement on who conceived of it in the first place, who sighted land after more than a month at sea, what that initial landfall even was, and who deserved credit for its various discoveries. It was as if, less than thirty years after the United States had sent a manned rocket to the moon, no one could agree on who had thought of the Apollo 11 mission, recruited the participants, paid its expenses, piloted the craft, overcame its adversities, and pressed the first footprint into the powdery surface of the distant satellite.

At the heart of the most famous voyage in exploration history had pulsed one of its great rivalries. There were plenty of men—both aboard the expedition's ships and back on shore in Spain, in and around the port of Palos from which they had departed—who believed that the true hero and visionary of the voyage was Martín Alonso Pinzón. Many would testify to that end, as the squabble over the heritable rights to Columbus's discoveries saw some two hundred witnesses on both sides of the Atlantic swear out depositions between 1512 and 1536.

The counternarrative was encouraged by crown attorneys, as a way to undermine the claims of the troublesome Diego Columbus to his father's discoveries. The
main dispute involved later finds along the Caribbean coast of South America, but
the depositions expanded into a vigorous assault on the credit Columbus deserved
for the original voyage's achievements. Men who were on board the ships, or who
had friends or relatives on board, or who personally knew the principal characters
in an increasingly bitter and resentful tale were prepared to diminish and demean
Columbus's role and instead place credit—some of it, all of it—with the *Pinta*'s
captain.

Some said the very idea of a westward voyage had belonged to Martín Alonso,
that he had copied, while on a trading voyage to Rome, a map in the Vatican that
dated to the time of Solomon. Some linked him to Pedro Vásquez de la Frontera,
who supposedly had already made a westward voyage for Portugal. Some said Martín Alonso had organized the ships and crews in Palos and that there was a written
agreement between him and Columbus to share the voyage's spoils. Some said that
it was Martín Alonso's skills as a mariner and a leader of men that had guided the
flotilla across the Ocean Sea, suppressing dangerous mutinies along the way. Some
said Martín Alonso and his men were the first to sight the white sands of the island
of San Salvador; some even alleged that Columbus had lost hope and had wanted to
turn back, or actually had turned back, when Martín Alonso's resolve gave him no
choice but to follow the *Pinta*. And some said Martín Alonso had been the one to
discover Española and, most important, its gold.

Typically forthright was Garcia Fernández, who sailed under Martín Alonso
as the *Pinta*'s dispenser, or steward; on a 1499 voyage to South America, Fernández
would serve with Vicente Yáñez Pinzón, Martín Alonso's brother, who had commanded the *Niña* in 1492. Fernández's testimony possibly was tainted by the fact
that Martín Alonso was his godfather. Nevertheless, as Fernández told the crown
attorney at Huelva, Martín Alonso "was an energetic man of great heart, and he
knows that if it were not for Martín Alonso giving [Columbus] the two ships, the
admiral would not have gone where he went nor would he have found people [to
sail with him] and the reason was because no one knew the admiral, and the admiral went on that voyage because of the esteem for Martín Alonso and because of
the two ships."

The Pinzóns unquestionably deserved more credit for their role in the first
voyage than is usually granted them. Whether they deserved virtually all of the
credit, as some depositions proposed, is another matter. The idea that Martín
Alonso initiated the voyage is unsupportable. The Pinzóns evidently became involved because Columbus had the power from Isabel to embargo the necessary
vessels, and the town council of Palos was ordered by the crown on April 30, 1492,
to provide Columbus with two ships for one year as a means of settling a penalty
from a court case.

The two vessels were secured from or through the Pinzóns; Martín Alonso also agreed to command the *Pinta* and Vicente Yáñez the *Niña*. For his flagship, Columbus went to the port of Sanlúcar de Barrameda at the mouth of the Guadalquivir; using money borrowed from Gianotto Berardi, he chartered a Basque não, or cargo vessel, which he rechristened the *Santa María*, from Juan de La Cosa, who commanded her under Columbus's authority as captain-general of the flotilla.

That said, Martín Alonso was a leading citizen of Palos, and the 1492 flotilla included two of his brothers and one of his sons. Two of the three ships were under their command, and the fleet included "many other men of esteem, friends and relatives" of Martín Alonso, according to the 1532 testimony by Palos's mayor, Alonso Vélez, who also agreed that when Columbus returned to Palos with his capitulation from the monarchs, he needed the assistance of the Pinzóns to mount the voyage.

The idea that the Pinzóns' connections, reputation, expertise, and enthusiasm helped make the voyage possible is entirely credible. Save his in-laws in Huelva and his supporters at the Franciscan monastery of La Rábida, Columbus had little standing in the harbor community, especially among its mariners. He was a poor foreigner, a Genoese transplanted from Portugal. Columbus relied on Martín Alonso's experience in preparing the voyage and consulted him on key decisions during it.

The Palos physician Garcia Fernández (not to be confused with the *Pinta* steward of the same name), who testified in detail to Columbus's preparations, was among those who swore that a formal agreement was struck between Columbus and Martín Alonso, which Fernández said included Vicente Yáñez. Columbus made his pact with the Pinzóns "because they were suitable and knowledgeable people concerning matters of the sea." Dr. Fernández and Columbus evidently were comfortable discussing with the friar Juan Pérez the finer cosmographic points of the proposed voyage, but the abilities to assemble a flotilla "were beyond [Dr. Fernández's] knowledge and that of don Cristóbal Colón." The Pinzóns "advised him and taught him many things that were beneficial for that voyage."

The voyage played out more like a joint venture between Columbus and Martín Alonso than an undertaking by an unquestioned commander and a useful subordinate. The three days on the outbound passage during which Martín Alonso had custody of Columbus's plotting chart suggests a period in which he had actual command. But in the end, there was not enough room in the enterprise for both of their egos, their ambitions, their avarice. The race to prove a westward route to the Indies turned into a race to be the first home in order to secure glory and benefits.

EIGHT

CHRISTOPHER COLUMBUS and Martín Alonso Pinzón were scarcely on speaking terms when the return voyage began. Columbus was on the verge of departing the north coast of the island of Española (modern-day Haiti and the Dominican Republic) for home on January 6, 1493, when Martín Alonso reappeared with the *Pinta,* sailing westward, not having been seen since November 26. Columbus turned back to lead Martín Alonso to the anchorage at Monte Cristi.

No log or journal would survive to explain exactly where the *Pinta* had been all this time, but after stealing away, Martín Alonso had first lighted on the Bahamian island of Great Inagua, which was thought to be Baneque, where there was no promised gold. He had then turned toward Española, taking shelter in an anchorage at the mouth of a river far to the east.

Pinzón loyalists would affirm that Martín Alonso led a shore party up this river, which he named for himself. The party was gone for three days. Arias Pérez Pinzón said his father "saw such signs of gold in this land that everyone was astonished and greatly pleased" and then led a second expedition inland at another location on the island. Once back at the *Pinta,* according to his son's version of events, Martín Alonso sent natives in canoes to notify Columbus. After being told of the gold, Columbus arrived at Española from the Bahamas. Six weeks had passed since he and Martín Alonso had separated.

Columbus had his own version of the insubordination, and it contained no summons to Española by Pinzón. The *Pinta* had holed up at his eponymous river for sixteen days and acquired gold mainly through trade with the natives, with Martín Alonso keeping half of it and his men sharing the other half. When Pinzón learned that Columbus too was on the north coast of Española, he concluded that an encounter could not be avoided and attempted to have his men swear that they had traded at the River of Martín Alonso only for six days.

If Martín Alonso returned to Spain without squaring matters first with Columbus, he risked losing his life or liberty for disobeying the commander of a royal expedition, whatever side agreement between them might have been the basis of this voyage. He must have decided it was better to make the best of his situation now. And so he had steered west, back along the north shore of Española, to seek out his erstwhile commander. Still, when he saw only the *Niña* on January 6, he probably thought he was about to be reunited with his brothers. Instead, he found himself back in the company of Columbus, as by then the *Santa María* had been lost.

Columbus's chartered flagship had been wrecked on the north shore of Española at midnight on Christmas Eve. The *Santa María* had come inside the reef east of Cap-Haitien and likely had gone aground off the beach at Bord De Mer De Limonade. Short of room for all of his men aboard the little *Niña*, Columbus decided to establish a fortified post, La Navidad (the nativity), which was thrown together from the salvaged remains of the ship. Left behind there were almost half of the men in the three-ship expedition, thirty-nine in all. It was placed under the joint command of three men, the royal representatives Pero Gutiérrez and Rodrigo Sánchez de Segovia, and Diego de Arana, the second cousin of Columbus's companion, Beatriz Enriquez de Arana, with orders to venture into the countryside and find gold. Columbus had then transferred to the *Niña* with the remaining men for the return voyage.

Martín Alonso came aboard the *Niña* at Monte Cristi and "made his excuses, saying that he had become separated from [Columbus] against his will, giving reasons," according to the Las Casas journal abstract, "but the Admiral says that they were all untrue and that he had acted out of great pride and greed on the night that he had gone off and left him. And the Admiral says that he had no idea where he had got the arrogance and disloyalty with which he had treated him on that voyage."

Francisco Medel, a town councilor in Huelva, would testify that Martín Alonso Pinzón had found both Española and Puerto Rico (which was initially called San Juan), and attributed Columbus's anger to prideful resentment that Pinzón had discovered and marked these landfalls before he could. Medel said Columbus told Pinzón that "he should obey him in conformity with the powers of the king." Medel was among deponents who alleged that Columbus had tried to turn back on the crossing when Pinzón insisted on carrying forward and had Pinzón reply, "According to your wishes we would already have returned and not found land. I have discovered and marked it in the name of king. Let us go to Spain and they will judge us." When Columbus threatened to "have him hanged on his door," Pinzón replied, "Do I deserve that? For having placed you in the honor that I have placed you, do you say that to me?"

Columbus believed Martín Alonso and his brother Vicente Yáñez "and others who supported them in their arrogance and greed" were bent on making their own claim to what had been discovered by the wayward *Pinta*—"that everything was already theirs, and not heeding the honor which the Admiral had done to them." The Pinzón faction moreover "had not obeyed nor were obeying his orders, but rather were doing and saying many unjust things against him."

Columbus was vulnerable to criticism for his own decisions, which could have tempered his displeasure with Martín Alonso. According to the chronicler Oviedo, Pinzón was appalled to learn that Columbus had left behind thirty-nine men at La Navidad and argued that it was wrong to abandon these Christians in this foreign land. Pinzón had good reason to fear their vulnerability to native attack, as the *Pinta* had suffered a fierce assault while anchored in the River of Martín Alonso.

While Columbus would not be dissuaded from his decision to leave the men behind at La Navidad, he also chose to accept Martín Alonso's return without inflicting punishment or promising to have him judged once back in Spain. "The Admiral decided to turn a blind eye," reiterated Las Casas in the journal abstract, "so as not to give Satan a chance to do his evil deeds by hindering the voyage as he had done up till then." He "suffered in silence" Pinzón's disobedience "to bring his voyage to a successful conclusion." Columbus also feared some of the sailors, calling them "bad company" and "rabble."

Yet Columbus was not planning to turn the other cheek indefinitely. As Las Casas quoted him from the journal entry for January 9: "I will not suffer the deeds of evil men of little worth who presume to have their own way with scant regard for him who gave them that honor."

Columbus and Pinzón would have made for miserable, wary company, each in command of his own vessel, each deeply displeased with the behavior of the other, yet each realizing that it was in their own interest to return together. It was impossible to say how severely one might turn on the other when they were home, and there would have been a mutual desire to keep track of a rival. But on February 14, 1493, by accident or intent, Pinzón again slipped away from Columbus.

SO CLOSE TO SUCCESS, and everything was about to be lost. Christopher Columbus's quest for fame and fortune—his very life—was in utter peril. After almost a month at sea since departing Española, working northeastward to the latitude of the Azores and Portugal's Cape St. Vincent, Columbus feared he would never be able to deliver the news of his triumph: The voyage he had spent upward of a decade trying to mount had proven, as promised, a westward route across the Ocean Sea to the wealth of the Indies.

The two ships were raked by a ferocious North Atlantic storm. Fearing the worst, Columbus composed a long letter on February 14, 1493, describing his discoveries, making at least two copies. One, which he dated February 15, he would send to the treasurer of Aragon, Luis de Santángel, should he actually survive; the other was sealed in a barrel and tossed overboard. Columbus concealed from his crew the barrel's contents, letting them understand that he was making a religious offering in hope of sparing them from the tempest.

If the *Niña* went down, this barrel's wanderings in currents and waves might deliver—somewhere, somehow—some word of his accomplishments. Fernando and Isabel still could learn that their faith in him had not been misplaced, that his critics were wrong to have argued that the voyage scheme was both illogical and impossible. The physical evidence of his success—gold especially, and seven Indigenous people, at least some of whom he had abducted—might go down with him, but his words would endure, and so would his name. A forty-two-year-old Genoese merchant's representative who had started out as a simple wool worker would be remembered as the most heroic voyager of this or any other age.

As the wind shrieked and the barrel splashed into a voracious sea, Columbus lost contact with the *Pinta*. The two ships had no choice but to run before the wind during the worst of the storm, and in the night, the *Pinta* had outpaced the *Niña* and disappeared altogether, even though Columbus had kept flares burning to allow the vessels to maintain contact. In the morning, Columbus found his life had been spared but that he also had the sea to himself. The *Pinta* had either gone down or was now making her own way home. The possibility that the *Pinta*'s captain, Martín Alonso Pinzón, was still alive and would reach Spain before he did might have been the worst of the two outcomes for Columbus.

Columbus had ample reason to be concerned that Martín Alonso would beat him home to Spain and be the one to report not only on what they had found but what had happened. There might be nothing left for Columbus but a substantial debt to a slaver for a lost ship and a litany of shame.

COLUMBUS COULD NOT CHASE down Martín Alonso after they were separated by the storm. Land was sighted the next morning, and Columbus desperately needed to pause and reballast the *Niña*. There was much argument over where they were. Columbus claimed some of his men thought they were off Madeira while others said they were approaching Lisbon. He was confident they were in the Azores, and he was right: The speck of land ahead proved to be Santa María, the most southeasterly landfall in the archipelago.

Columbus had nearly passed the Azores altogether, and it might have been to his advantage to do so. When most of his crew went ashore on Santa María, they were seized by locals who feared Columbus might be another ravaging pirate, and the acting governor, João da Castanheira, tried unsuccessfully to lure Columbus ashore in order to capture him as well. Outraged by the reception, Columbus had to make for São Miguel, about forty miles north, under a skeleton crew and plead for the return of his men. Between securing their release, reballasting, and reprovisioning, Columbus was not under way again until February 25, only to be met by yet more calamitous weather.

WHILE CHRISTOPHER COLUMBUS made his historic if fractious and geographically bewildered cruise of the northeastern Caribbean, John Cabot's plan to create an artificial harbor for Valencia slowly advanced. Fernando and Isabel and their advisors, however, were awash in other pressing issues, not the least of which was Fernando's health. He was still recovering from an assassination attempt in November 1492. A crazed man named Cagnamarc from a village near Barcelona was convinced he would become king if Fernando died, and did his best to arrange that with a knife.

In addition, the monarchs' diplomatic file was fairly bursting. On January 19, 1493, Fernando and Isabel concluded the Treaty of Barcelona with a new figure in European politics, Charles VIII of France. The only son of Louis XI technically had been in power since ascending to the throne in 1483 at age thirteen, but control of the state had remained with a regent, his sister Anne de Beaujeu (who as noted might have employed Bartolomé Columbus as a cartographer), until her brother's marriage in 1491 to Anne de Bretagne.

By 1492, the twenty-two-year-old Charles was fully in charge, albeit to the perturbation of many. He was physically frail—the right side of his body appeared stronger than the left—and one diplomat noticed that his hands trembled constantly. He was perhaps too well read, as he seemed given over to romantic notions of chivalrous quests. A Florentine ambassador reported that he was incapable of dealing with serious matters. "He comprehends them so little, and takes so little interest in them, that I am embarrassed to say it." As a Venetian envoy summarized, "I hold for certain that, whether in body or in spirit, he is worth little." Charles's imminent military misadventures in Italy would induce a fresh paroxysm of diplomatic maneuvering throughout Europe that helped dictate the course of John Cabot's erratic career.

The Treaty of Barcelona was one of Charles's first major foreign policy initiatives. Determined to establish amicable relations with the rising power of the united Spain, Charles returned to Spain the frontier counties of Roussillon and Cerdagne in the Pyrénées—quite possibly where Cabot had been holed up before appearing in Valencia. The counties had been pawned by Fernando's predecessor, Juan II, to Louis XI in order to finance his actions in the Navarrese civil war and had been occupied by French troops ever since.

Next up for Fernando and Isabel was a proposal that March by England's Henry VII to reratify the 1489 Treaty of Medina del Campo and with it the agreement that his son and successor, Arthur Tudor, would wed Fernando and Isabel's youngest child, Catherine (Catalina) of Aragon, in England in late 1498, when Arthur was twelve and Catherine thirteen. Henry's effort to resuscitate a lapsed agreement provided Fernando and Isabel a fresh opportunity to strengthen Spain's strategic alliances through dynastic marriages. But they were lukewarm to the overture. They had what they wanted in diplomacy foremost from the Treaty of Barcelona in mending fences with France and no longer needed a dynastic alliance with England to threaten Charles VIII. Henry was left dangling.

At the same time, the Spanish monarchs were awaiting news from the Ocean Sea. Alonso de Lugo, Gianotto Berardi, and Francisco de Riberol were close to wrapping up their conquest of La Palma in the name of Fernando and Isabel and soon would be inquiring after their 700,000-maravedi reward. And there was the matter of what had become of Christopher Columbus and his three ships.

But Fernando did not forget about Cabot. On February 26 and 27, the king issued orders to Valencia's governor-general, Diego de Torres, to begin construction of the artificial harbor. Columbus had just departed São Miguel in the Azores, on what hopefully would be the final leg of the return voyage to Spain. Fernando's royal priorities were about to undergo a profound change.

A SQUALL ON MARCH 3 forced Columbus to reduce the *Niña* to bare masts after his sails were torn: The winds and seas "devoured them from opposite directions" according to Las Casas as rain and lightning filled the night sky. Columbus was certain they would perish, but in the morning as the weather eased he spied the Rock of Sintra marking the approach to Lisbon's harbor.

Of all the ports a storm could offer for salvation, Portugal's main naval base surely was the most daunting. Columbus already claimed to have learned at São Miguel that if João da Castanheira had been able to seize him at Santa María, he never would have been released, as there allegedly had been orders from the king, João II, to capture him if the opportunity arose. The *Niña* anchored initially off the beach at Restelo, on the north shore of the river leading into Lisbon's capacious and superbly sheltered harbor.

Columbus was promptly accosted by the captain of a massive Portuguese warship anchored nearby. The naval officer turned out to be Bartolomeu Días, who had proven that southern Africa could be rounded to reach the Indian Ocean in 1487–88. The Portuguese effort in establishing such a route to the Indies had stalled since then. At Restelo, Días brusquely demanded that Columbus turn himself over to the warship. Columbus refused to do so, but he provided his letter of commission from Fernando and Isabel.

Columbus wrote two letters on March 4. One was to Fernando and Isabel describing his triumph: "That everlasting God who has given Your Highnesses so many victories has now given you the greatest ever given to any monarch. I have come with the fleet that Your Highnesses gave me from the Indies, to which I crossed in thirty-three days after departing from your kingdoms."

The other was addressed to João II, requesting permission to move the *Niña* into the harbor proper. Columbus informed the Portuguese king "how the Monarchs of Castile had ordered him not to be afraid of entering His Highness's ports to buy whatever he needed." Columbus asked the king's permission to move his ship into Lisbon's harbor "in case some villains, thinking that he was carrying a lot of gold, and seeing him in a deserted harbor, should take it into their heads to commit some act of villainy, and also so that the King might know that he had not come from Guinea but from the Indies."

Columbus's letter to João II seemed to be saying: *I have a lot of gold on board, but I didn't get it from your West African territory—I have just returned from the Indies with it.* He was almost delighting in the opportunity to tweak the Portuguese king for not having employed him in his Indies scheme when he had the chance, confident that no harm could come to him with Fernando and Isabel as his protectors. But Columbus also may have been hedging his bets. Fearful of the reception awaiting him in Spain if Martín Alonso had beaten him home, Columbus could have been using this landfall to test the waters with João II, to see how he would be received and how interested the Portuguese might be in employing him going forward, if it came to that.

Columbus's behavior would arouse suspicions in Spain, which he was still protesting in 1500 in a letter to Juana de La Torre, who had been governess of the household of Crown Prince Juan. "I think your Ladyship will remember that when, after losing my sails, I was driven into Lisbon by a tempest, I was falsely accused of having gone there to the King [João II] in order to give him the Indies. Their Highnesses afterwards learned the contrary, and that it was extremely malicious."

In his letter written to Fernando and Isabel at Restelo, Columbus had condemned Martín Alonso's behavior while eliding the less complimentary details of his own performance. He explained how he had departed Española with "only one caravel, for I had left my flagship with the men in Your Highnesses' town of Navidad, where they were establishing a fortress, as I shall later report." Not a word about actually having *lost* the *Santa María*, which veritably had *become* La Navidad. As for the fate of his other vessel, the *Pinta,* "someone from Palos, whom I had put in charge of it, expecting loyal service, made off with it, thinking to help himself to great amounts of gold from an island about which an Indian had given information. I thought I would do with him later what seemed best." Although Columbus had not named Martín Alonso, he had made clear Pinzón's insubordination and had every intention of exacting revenge once back in Spain.

WHETHER BY DIPLOMATIC POUCH or Genoese trader, two Columbus letters—the one written to Santángel while at sea and the one to Fernando and Isabel

of March 4—were quickly delivered. Martín Alonso Pinzon had not yet rematerial-
ized in the *Pinta,* and so Columbus was able to get first word of his discoveries to the
Spanish monarchs. The court was then seated in Barcelona, and news propagated
from there with blistering speed. On March 9, a Genoese merchant at Barcelona
named Annibale De Zennaro relayed word to his brother in Milan of the discoveries, mainly drawing on details in the letter to Santángel that had only just arrived.
On that day, as word of Columbus's discoveries raced on to Italy, the explorer was
making an unplanned rain-soaked pilgrimage to Santa Maria das Virtudes, some
thirty miles to the northeast of Lisbon.

The entire sojourn in Portugal was beginning to look like a serious miscalculation. João II had retreated to Santa Maria das Virtudes, a sanctuary for the Portuguese monarchs since 1434, to avoid an outbreak of the plague. Although Columbus allegedly was reluctant to make the trip, he was politely but firmly informed
that the weather was too poor to allow him to sail from Lisbon anyway and his
presence was commanded by João II.

To hear Columbus tell it, the audience nevertheless came off splendidly, if a bit
stickily. "João II seemed to be very pleased that the voyage had been undertaken and
had ended successfully, but that he understood that according to the treaty between
the Monarchs and himself, those conquests belonged to him." The king was referring to Alcáçovas. Columbus professed ignorance, alleging he had neither seen this
treaty nor knew anything about it, which could not have been the case. He allowed
only that Fernando and Isabel had ordered him not to go near São Jorge de Mina or
anywhere else on the Guinea coast.

"The King graciously replied that he was certain that there would be no need
for third parties in this matter." On the contrary, there would be considerable diplomatic haggling over the rights to Columbus's discoveries. And while Columbus had
survived the audience and was treated respectfully, he could not make a ready retreat from Portugal. On the way back to Lisbon, at the monastery of San Antonio in
Vila Franca, there was another audience, with the queen consort, Eleanor of Viseu.
The meeting delivered Columbus back into the political treachery that had caused
him and members of his late wife's family to flee Portugal. Eleanor was powerful
in her own right as consort, and her immediate kin had been at the heart of the
Braganza conspiracy. João II had murdered Eleanor's older brother, Diogo, Duke of
Viseu; her sister Isabella had been the wife of the executed Duke of Braganza.

In order to mend fences with Portugal, Spain's Fernando and Isabel had arranged the 1490 wedding of their eldest child, Isabel, to Eleanor and João II's only
child, Crown Prince Afonso. In 1491, Afonso (then sixteen, five years younger than
his bride) was killed in a horse-riding accident, plunging the Portuguese succession
into disarray. João II had an illegitimate son, Jorge de Lencastre, whom he was determined to advance as his heir, but Eleanor for one would not stand for it. While
visiting Eleanor, Columbus met with her younger brother, Manoel, not yet twenty-

four, who had replaced their murdered older brother Diogo as Duke of Viseu. It was Manoel who would come to rule Portugal on the death of João II in October 1495.

Columbus finally set sail again on March 13, nine days after fetching up like some storm-tossed petrel at Restelo. At sunrise on March 15, the *Niña* arrived off the bar of Saltés marking the entrance to her home port. Columbus waited for high tide at noon to carry him over the bar and back into the greater harbor community of Huelva, Palos, and the La Rábida monastery.

While Columbus had been making his whirlwind of audiences with the present and future Portuguese monarchy, the *Pinta* had cast up 230 nautical miles north of Lisbon, in the port of Baiona in Spain's province of Galicia. Martín Alonso Pinzón sent word to Fernando and Isabel of his return; they directed him to return to Palos. There was no way for him to avoid another difficult reunion with Columbus, and the *Pinta* reappeared at the bar of Saltés within hours of Columbus's own arrival.

Yet evidently the two men never met. Almost forty-three years later, Martín Alonso's cousin, Hernan Pérez Mateos, would testify at Santo Domingo as to what transpired: "Martín Alonso did not join up with don Cristóbal Colón because, this witness learned, Martín Alonso was afraid of him, for what reason he did not know, except that he heard that if don Cristóbal Colón could capture Martín Alonso, that he would do so, and would take him with him as a prisoner before a court."

Like others who testified, Pérez Mateos also said that Martín Alonso was quite ill. Wading in the waters of the River of Martín Alonso in search of gold, it was believed, had exposed him to some terrible pathogen. He retired to an estate he owned outside of Moguer, Pérez Mateos explained, without ever actually setting foot in the town of Palos on his return. The illness worsened, and some of his kinsmen arranged to have Martín Alonso moved to the care of the Franciscans at La Rábida. Columbus's most worrying rival to his discovery claims was dead within a few days.

Lost was the most credible contrary source as to what had actually happened on the voyage. As another deponent, Pedro Arias of Palos, would attest, Martín Alonso "could not go to kiss the hands of their highnesses," and in his absence, "no advocate appeared on behalf of Martín Alonso to tell their highness the truth." Columbus alone would be able to define what had been found and to reap the benefits in partnership with Fernando and Isabel.

Yet as one rivalry expired at La Rábida, another was being born from within Columbus's plan to turn La Navidad into a trading colossus.

NINE

WHEN LUIS DE SANTÁNGEL received his letter from Columbus posted at Lisbon on March 4, he quickly provided it to a Barcelona printer so the voyage account could be widely disseminated. A near-identical version, addressed to Gabriel Sánchez, Ferdinand's treasurer (which may have been a case of mistaken identity by the printer and simply a variant on the Santángel letter) also began circulating in Europe. Both began appearing in print in April 1493, including in Cabot's native Venice.

Meanwhile, Columbus—who must have known of Martín Alonso Pinzón's death—had traveled from Palos to Seville, where he would have broken to his financier Berardi the good news of his discoveries as well as the bad news that the *Santa María* was a total loss. But there seemed little question that Columbus would be good for the debt, given the scale of his claims, and Berardi was soon securing the provisioning contract for the follow-up voyage.

The monarchs wrote Columbus at Seville on March 30, inviting him to Barcelona to report firsthand on his discoveries and to plan the next voyage, which they wanted him to make immediately. ("As you know, summer has begun and the season for the return trip already may be passing.") Columbus's claim to have reached a half-dozen islands on the perimeter of the Indies had opened a new frontier of expansion and prosperity that was assigned to the old kingdom of Castile and specifically to its capital, Seville, to administer.

Although it has long been considered possible that Cabot met Columbus in Valencia in early April 1493, when the explorer would have passed through town on the way to meet Fernando and Isabel, it is far more likely that the two men actually met at court in Barcelona in mid-April. Columbus's return had coincided with a serious setback for Cabot and Fernando on the harbor scheme. On March 28, Valencia's council had decided it would not fund the project. But the proposal had not died entirely. Even with the logistics of the Columbus venture on his plate, the king found time to make a last-gasp attempt on April 16 to revive interest in Valencia in financing Cabot's harbor scheme by writing a letter suggesting that civic leaders consult the Santángel brothers.

The dying moments of the harbor project strikingly coincided with the birth of Columbus's Indies trade and colonization venture in partnership with Fernando and Isabel. Cabot may well have been in Barcelona in April conferring with Fernando and his advisors (including Luis de Santángel) on how to get the Valencia harbor development back on track, even as Columbus's venture was making such profound demands on the court. Cabot would have been in close proximity to virtually every key figure in the courtly and bureaucratic support of the first and second Columbus voyages and the development of Seville as the Spanish operational center for the Indies.

The connections to Seville were not trivial where Cabot was concerned, because he would next surface in the documentary record in that city on September 15, 1494. He was hired then by Seville to oversee another significant marine engineering project of interest to the Spanish monarchs: a fixed bridge across the Guadalquivir River to the island of Triana, the heart of Seville's maritime activities. The hiring record indicated Cabot already had been in the city for three months attending to the bridge project, which was a crucial build-out of infrastructure for Columbus's Indies venture.

That Cabot turned up in Seville around June 1494 for the bridge job is not in itself a curiosity. The project was consistent with his earlier proposal to build an artificial harbor for Valencia, which through no fault of his own had failed to move forward, and Seville was a powerful attractor. All roads of commerce in Andalusia led to Seville, and surviving records for bills of exchange also stress the close relationship between the Genoese merchant communities in Seville and Valencia, where Cabot was last encountered in the documentary record.

But as simple as it might seem to send Cabot along the trail of money and opportunity leading from Valencia to Seville, that still left the question of what he was up to for fourteen months, between the last mention by Fernando of the Valencia project in April 1493 and the Venetian's appearance in charge of Seville's bridge project around June 1494.

The most logical, if extraordinary, answer is that he sailed to the Indies with Columbus when the armada of the second voyage departed Cadíz on September 25, 1493.

ONE CLUE TO JOHN CABOT'S 1493–94 experience of the Indies lies in a striking observation in a March 28, 1496, letter from Fernando and Isabel to their London ambassador, Dr. Roderigo Gondesalvi de Puebla. The monarchs were replying to news Puebla had sent on January 21 of Cabot's proposal to Henry VII to make a westward voyage to the Indies for England.

"With regard to what you say," they advised, "that the one like Colon went there to get the King of England into another affair, like that of the Indies, without causing any damage to Spain or Portugal, if he helps him as us, the one from the Indies will be quite at liberty."

Although his actual name was never used, this letter unequivocally was about John Cabot. It remains the earliest evidence of Cabot's exploration ambition, which was such a radical departure from his known activities as a property renovator and a would-be harbor engineer and bridge builder. Neither Puebla nor the Spanish monarchs apparently were aware of exactly who was making the pitch to Henry— only that in being "the one like Colon" he was another man with a yen to prove a westward route to the Orient. Puebla also may have led the monarchs to understand that Cabot too was an Italian. Had Cabot's name been stated in the lost Puebla letter, we would expect Fernando to have remembered him from the Valencia harbor development and the Seville bridge project—and perhaps even from the second voyage of Columbus.

The final clause especially of that sentence leaves us wondering about the letter's meaning. We will address the full content of this letter later. For now, its most interesting aspect is the way it appears to grant Cabot experience of the Indies. Based on what Puebla has told them, Fernando and Isabel think Cabot has actually been there, for he is both "the one like Colon" (*uno como Colon*) and "the one from [or "of"] the Indies" (*lo de las Yndias*). There is no sensible candidate for "the one from the Indies" other than Cabot in this sentence, or indeed in the whole letter. To call Cabot *lo de las Yndias* was to link him explicitly with Columbus's finds and activities.

The letter is not the only clue that Cabot had asserted to Henry that he had already been to the Indies. Such a boast would have given the English king confidence that the Venetian actually could find his way across the ocean to the Orient and would help explain what we otherwise cannot: how Cabot managed to secure an extraordinarily generous letters patent when the rest of his known résumé is so lacking in accomplishments that would recommend him to Henry.

A letter by an unknown correspondent in London to the Duke of Milan (likely written by one of the Spinolas in England) on Cabot's return from his first successful voyage for Henry VII to the New World in 1497 described Cabot as "a very good mariner" who "has good skill in discovering new islands." The writer may have been basing this characterization solely on Cabot's accomplishments on the voyage he had just completed, but it did rather sound like a testament to the depth of his experience. If Cabot had proven skills in discovering new islands (let alone enough sea experience even to qualify as a "very good mariner"), he could have gained them only on one of Columbus's voyages to the Caribbean.

It was impossible for Cabot to have been on the first Columbus voyage. Beyond the fact that the participants in the three-ship enterprise have been thoroughly studied and his name has never come up, Cabot was in Valencia during that voyage. However, not only was it possible for him to have participated in the second voyage, which discovered a plethora of new islands as it cruised through the Leeward chain after arriving at Dominica in the Caribbean; it was entirely logical. As circuitous as it appears, sending Cabot to the Caribbean on the 1493 Columbus voyage on business of the crown is as persuasive an explanation as one can find for how Cabot managed to get from Valencia to Seville, lose more than a year of known activity in the process, and also account for Fernando and Isabel's reference to Cabot as "the one from the Indies" in their March 1496 letter to the ambassador Puebla.

The second Columbus voyage departed Cadíz on September 25, 1493. Although Columbus himself did not return to Spain until June 1496, twelve of the armada's seventeen ships departed Española in February 1494 and arrived back at Cadíz on March 9. This return passage would have left time for Cabot to reappear in the evidence trail in Seville in June.

Once Cabot had come to the attention of Fernando in September 1492 and impressed him with his Valencia harbor plan, he apparently stayed active for more than two years within the milieu of marine infrastructure that was of priority to the Spanish state. Between the Valencia harbor project and the Seville bridge project was a state-sponsored initiative that cried out for the expertise Cabot had demonstrated to Fernando in his Valencia scheme: the envisioned royal trading center on Española.

THE CONVERGENCE OF SIGNIFICANT figures at Barcelona in April 1493, beyond Columbus and the Spanish monarchs, was exceptional. On hand was Luis de Santángel, who was central to both Columbus's exploits and Fernando's efforts to secure financial support for Cabot's Valencia scheme. Also appearing was Juan Rodríguez de Fonseca, Archdeacon of Seville and Bishop of Badajoz, who was assigned the task in May of organizing the fleet for Columbus's second voyage and who then administered trade and colonization efforts for the Indies at Seville.

The return flotilla of early 1494 would be under the command of Antonio de Torres, a member of Isabel's household staff. His sister, Juana de La Torre, was governess of Prince Juan's household; as we have seen, she would receive a letter from Columbus in the autumn of 1500 protesting his treatment as he was shipped back to Spain in irons to face charges of mismanagement of the Española colony. Both Antonio and Juana likely were related to Don Diego de Torres, governor-general of

Valencia, who had dealt with Cabot on the harbor project on behalf of Fernando in 1492–93.

With Columbus's second voyage, the Spanish monarchs were determined to create a state-owned trading facility in Española, with staff and settlers on the royal payroll. Spending significant royal funds on a new harbor in Valencia clearly was out of the question, but the monarchs were in immediate need of another new harbor—at La Navidad.

Based on Columbus's report from the first voyage, Española was thought to be located on the perimeter of the Asian mainland. La Navidad was to be a Castilian royal property, governed by their business partner, Columbus. Fernando and Isabel were sending Columbus back to the rough-and-ready refuge that had been thrown together with materials salvaged from the wreck of the *Santa María* to transform it into a properly stocked and fortified royal trading post, with a town and farms to support it. Fernando and Isabel envisioned their own version of São Jorge de Mina, Portugal's fortified trading post in West Africa, but the Venetian stations in the eastern Mediterranean, supplied by local farmers attuned to their needs, and with which Cabot would have been familiar, were also considered exemplary. They were sovereign enclaves on the frontiers of great mercantile opportunities, which was precisely the situation thought to exist in Española.

The public works project of the royal trading post in Española demanded skilled civil engineering, above all a harbor facility capable of managing the vast amounts of trade envisioned. Engineers did go along on the second voyage to plan the trading center and its supporting settlement and to oversee construction, some of it marine-related. In the earliest days, they dug, for example, a canal—a task that would have made someone with construction experience in Venice and a background in Valencia rather useful. We don't know the names of any of these engineers—in fact, we don't know the names of most of the people on the voyage, except for the sailors on three ships that explored the southern coast of Cuba with Columbus in 1494 and signed affidavits. The *Libros de Armada,* the official Seville records of the Indies voyages, did not begin until the relief flotillas of 1494. That Cabot might have been one of the engineers tasked to the Española outpost, after so impressing Fernando with the plan for an artificial harbor at Valencia, is entirely plausible. If Cabot was along, Columbus and Fonseca had to be aware of him, as the pair approved every participant.

If Cabot did in fact visit the Caribbean in association with Columbus in 1493–94, it would be an extraordinary change in our understanding of the New World's discovery and exploration. An alternative explanation is that Cabot merely *claimed* to have made the voyage.

Cabot had opportunities to learn details about the first two Columbus voyages while in Spain, particularly inside knowledge of them while in Valencia and especially in Seville, and could have passed himself off in England as someone who was just back from discovering new landfalls. Seville teemed with individuals, from common sailors and minor nobles (some two hundred of whom are thought to have been from Seville) who participated in the second Columbus voyage and returned with Antonio de Torres in March 1494. There were also numerous Italian merchants and financiers in Seville on the fringes of the grandiose scheme to turn Columbus's Española settlement and Seville into two nodes of a new trading colossus. And Cabot could not have been responsible for a project as critical as the Sevillan bridge without encountering Juan Rodríguez de Fonseca, the logistical supervisor of the new trade and colonization enterprise.

Saying you actually had been somewhere was much more persuasive than voicing informed opinions about how hypothetically to reach a distant place. Travel narratives of the time already were mixtures of fact and fantasy. As we shall see, another eyewitness account of Cabot in England in 1497 would reveal the Venetian's assertion that he had once been to Mecca, an extremely dubious claim.

Cabot would not have been the only explorer, would-be or actual, to pad his résumé in hopes of either securing royal favor or inflating his reputation. Amerigo Vespucci, a Berardi partner whom Cabot could have met in Seville in 1494, is an enduringly controversial figure who may have invented for himself a voyage to the New World in 1497, although he did sail to South America in 1499 and 1501. The sixteenth-century French royal geographer André Thevet would claim to have made a New World voyage that was more than likely pure fantasy and shamelessly plagiarized other writers. More pertinently, John Cabot's son Sebastian would play so fast and loose with facts that he claimed his father's voyages as his own; it is difficult to be confident about much of anything Sebastian would assert in the way of his New World voyages or his own past, beyond one documented expedition to South America he made for Spain in 1526 that ended in folly.

On balance, though, the case for John Cabot actually having participated in the second Columbus voyage is reasonably persuasive. He would have been along as an engineer, not as a de facto explorer, although it was the latter role that the Venetian most certainly would claim for himself at Henry's court in proposing his own voyage plan. The more one studies John Cabot, the more he appears to be a Columbus doppelgänger: someone who was not only inspired by the Genoese explorer, and probably was associated with him, but who was determined to pass himself off as a version of him and to replicate his essential Indies plan in more northern latitudes for another European monarch.

THE SEVENTEEN-SHIP ARMADA that sailed from Cadíz on September 25, 1493, was of truly incredible scale, eclipsing the dozen ships Portugal had sent out to create São Jorge de Mina in 1482. Columbus was taking more than three hundred settlers with him and an estimated twelve hundred people in all. Many of those extra bodies were young nobles out for an adventure, veritable tourists who were eager to see for themselves what Columbus had found across the Ocean Sea. Their departure turned into a festival of civic, maritime, and religious dimensions.

"The sailors carried out their most solemn rituals, those departing kissed their loved ones, the ships were all draped in tapestries and the ropes wrapped with fringed banners," according to the Pavian doctor of arts and medicine and professor of philosophy Nicolò Scillacio, to whom Guillermo Coma, one of the Spanish nobles in the flotilla, wrote an eyewitness account. "The royal standard decorated the sterns of all the ships. Flutists and guitarists held even the Nereids, Nymphs, and Sirens themselves rapt with their melodious tunes, and the shores rang with the blare of trumpets and cornets, while the deep sea resounded with the roar of the bombards."

As it happened, the Flanders Galleys under the command of Tomasso Zeno had put in to Cadíz en route to England. The Venetians joined in the exuberant salute of Columbus's armada, led by his new flagship, the *Maria-Galante:* "[F]ollowing the example of the Spanish fleet, with similar ardor and enthusiasm, [the Venetians] participated in the nautical rites, offering prayers to the ships setting out toward the Indies."

What a strange experience this must have been for the men of the Flanders Galleys. The sheer spectacle of this maritime event was contagious for any sailor, without parallel in the age of exploration. And yet they were cheering on what was supposed to be the beginning of the end of the Venetian trading monopoly to the Orient through the Levant, a monopoly that filled the holds of the very galleys that had paused in the harbor of Cadíz en route to Sluys and Southampton. We can well suspect that looking back at Zeno, the young nobles of the *ballestraria* and their crossbows, the navigating officers, priests, physicians, musicians, and the rest, was a Venetian who was on his way to Española to help Columbus build the trading center that would undermine his own Signoria's wealth and privilege.

The reception awaiting the armada in Española would be far less exuberant and joyous.

TEN

ON SEPTEMBER 25, 1493, the day Columbus's seventeen-ship armada departed Cadíz, Pope Alexander VI issued the bull known as *Dudum siquidem*. It was the fourth such writ that the pope, the Spaniard Rodrigo Borja, had issued dating back to May 3 that addressed the rights of Fernando and Isabel to Columbus's discoveries.

Borja had two illegitimate children, and as Alexander VI, he proved to be fixated on securing a heritable territory for his offspring in Italy. For Fernando and Isabel—and through them Columbus—Borja managed to use his papal authority to bestow a heritable territory of literally immeasurable dimensions, as the technical capability to define its globe-girdling expanse was beyond the grasp of the interested parties.

Collectively, the first three bulls are generally called *Inter cetera*. Under the premise of spreading Christianity to the heathen, the pope had agreed to reserve for the Spanish monarchs all lands on the western side of a meridian drawn from pole to pole, "whether mainlands and islands are discovered and yet to be discovered towards India or towards any other region whatsoever." This line of demarcation was to be drawn one hundred leagues beyond "any of the islands which are commonly called the Azores and Cape Verde, provided that all islands and mainlands found or yet to be found, discovered or yet to be discovered, from the said line to the west and south were not possessed in actuality by any Christian king or ruler, up to the day of Christmas last, from which the present year 1493 begins."

Inter cetera was hugely problematic in lumping the Azores and Cape Verde Islands into one island group for measuring purposes. The two island groups are separated north to south by some thirteen hundred nautical miles, and they also lie on different lines of longitude. The westernmost islands in the Cape Verde group, São Antão and São Vicente, lie around 25° west; Flores, the westernmost of the Azores, is around 31° west. In addition to this six-degree difference in the measurement starting point (which cosmographers at the time had no accurate means of knowing), measuring west from these places in leagues to determine a particular meridian where Spanish rights began would produce two very different results because of their latitude differences.

Another complication was that the rights assigned to Spain were said to be "towards India or towards any other region." In other words, the rights didn't include "India"—whatever that geographic term actually meant; the papacy may have added this phrase in order to placate Portuguese objections.

Inter cetera scarcely settled the matter of who could claim what. As Portugal already had rights through *Aeterni Regis* of 1481 to any undiscovered islands in the Ocean Sea in latitudes south of the Canaries, with no westerly limit specified thereto, there was naturally a diplomatic dispute over how the papal bulls of 1481 and 1493 converged. The language of *Inter cetera* also seemed to acknowledge that it applied only to waters south and west of the Canaries as defined by *Aeterni Regis,* despite the fact that the Azores were being used as a measuring point for the meridian. Portugal had already sent an ambassador to the Vatican in early May 1493 to contest Spain's claims; this diplomatic mission could have been in direct response to the debriefing Columbus gave João II on his return from the first voyage in March.

On September 25, 1493, came *Dudum siquidem,* issued by Alexander VI as a rough plaster job on some of the gaping cracks in *Inter cetera* as Columbus departed on his second voyage. *Dudum siquidem* acknowledged that "it could happen that your envoys and captains or vassals sailing toward the west and south might steer to eastern regions and find islands and mainlands which had been or were [discovered]," which appeared to be a nod to Portugal's earlier efforts to find a route to India from the opposite direction, around Africa. It went on to elaborate Spain's territorial rights by incoherently extending them to "regions of the West or the South or the East or of India." Still, where *Inter cetera* had granted rights only *towards* India, *Dudum siquidem* now included "regions . . . of India." Columbus personally may have demanded this, because according to his worldview, he already was *in* the Indies with what we know actually to have been Caribbean discoveries.

Dudum siquidem and *Inter cetera* were a muddle, and it would be left to Portuguese and Spanish diplomats to better define their spheres of authority through a treaty, which would take until June 1494 to settle. In the meantime, Columbus had sailed with the Spanish pope's assurance that whatever he had already encountered—and had yet to encounter—one hundred leagues beyond the Cape Verdes or the Azores was his alone to claim and also to exploit as Spain's governor and viceroy of Española and Admiral of the Ocean Sea.

THE CROSSING WAS LESS benign than had been the trailblazing one of 1492, as Columbus's fleet was lashed and scattered by a storm about a dozen days beyond the Canaries. But all seventeen vessels survived the passage and, perhaps because of the storm's wrath, arrived in the Caribbean well below the latitude of the first voyage's landfall.

Columbus's friend Michele da Cuneo said they made initial landfall on November 3 at Dominica, followed by Maria la galante (Marie-Galante) and Guadeloupe. The armada then sailed north through the Leeward Islands chain and also visited the Virgin Islands before reaching Puerto Rico, en route to Española.

This necklace of unprecedented landfalls (which could have given the unknown author of the August 1497 letter, which was sent from London to the Duke of Milan, the confidence to state that Cabot "has good skill in discovering new islands") was full of colorful and salacious encounters with natives to which the eyewitness accounts gave considerable attention. The cannibals only speculated about in Columbus's first-voyage report were now breathed to life as a ferocious people, the Caribs.

We know that the Caribs and the Arawaks had originated in South America, with the Arawaks arriving first and establishing themselves foremost in the Greater Antilles of Cuba, Jamaica, Española, and Puerto Rico, in the process reducing the original colonists, the Ciboney, who had come from Florida, to a territory in western Cuba. Arawak tradition held that the Caribs who followed them from South America had forced them out of the Lesser Antilles. Although the Caribs may well have been warlike and raided the Arawaks, the truth as to their cannibalism has been enduringly controversial. Nicolò de' Conti's experiences on his Indies travels, which by then had been published in Florence, could have fueled an expectation of such bestial savagery. Of the Andaman Islands, Poggio Bracciolini said Conti reported: "The inhabitants are cannibals, no travelers touch here unless driven so to do by bad weather, for when taken they are torn to pieces and devoured by these cruel savages." Poggio Bracciolini moreover seemed to foreshadow explanations of the Caribs in saying the inhabitants of an island called Batech "eat human flesh, and are in a state of constant warfare with their neighbors."

Some of the evidence of human bones and heads from the second Columbus voyage could have been inspired by funeral rituals and ancestor worship and inflated as literary entertainment. Participant Diego Alvarez Chanca, physician to Fernando and Isabel, who wrote a voyage report for his sovereigns, traded in some of the more gruesome details. Recounting how they rescued some of the Caribs' captives, Dr. Chanca wrote luridly of a systematic abduction and consumption of

Arawaks. "These women also say that the Caribs use them so cruelly that it appears incredible: that the children to whom they give birth are eaten and they only rear those they have by their native wives." Captured men were taken alive to Carib villages and slaughtered for food. "They cut off the genital member of the boys they capture and make use of them as servants until they become men, and then when they wish to make a feast they kill and eat them, because they say that the flesh of boys and women is not good to eat. Three of these boys came fleeing to us, all three having the genital member cut off."

On November 14, Columbus skirmished with Caribs at Santa Cruz—St. Croix in the Virgin Islands—losing one of his men, a Basque, to an arrow. A canoe was rammed and its three occupants, two men and a woman, were brought before Columbus. "One of them was wounded in seven places, and his insides were falling out," related the Sicilian Nicolò Scillacio in an account that drew on the letter written to him by "a very noble Spaniard," the voyage participant Guillermo Coma. "Since it was believed that he could not be healed, he was thrown overboard. However, he bobbed to the surface, and by kicking his feet while holding his guts in place with his left hand, he swam spiritedly to shore." The ferocity of the Caribs was both awe-inspiring and unnerving.

Columbus had dispatched to Española an advance party in a caravel, apparently before the main armada had even reached Dominica. It supposedly was sent out to circumnavigate Española, but most certainly its main task was to make contact with and relieve La Navidad, where thirty-nine Spaniards had been left to their own devices for more than ten months.

No mention survives of what became of this reconnaissance. Columbus meanwhile paused at the harbor of Monte Cristi on November 27 rather than proceed directly to La Navidad, which was only some fifteen miles to the south-southwest. Poor weather kept them pinned down at Monte Cristi, according to Cuneo, but in Dr. Chanca's recollection, Columbus had decided to halt there to scout for a new town site nearby, even before reaching La Navidad, "as the place where the Admiral had left the Christians to make a settlement had not appeared to him to be healthful."

When Columbus sent men ashore, they began to find bodies: "two dead men on one side near the river, one with a rope on his neck and the other with one on his foot," Dr. Chanca recalled. "This was the first day. The next day following they found the bodies of two more dead men farther along than the others. One of these bodies was in such condition that it could be seen he had been heavily bearded. Some of our people suspected more evil than good and with good reason. The Indians are all beardless as I have said."

They arrived off La Navidad a few days later. Lombard cannons were fired to signal their arrival. There was no response from the cannons that had been left behind, nor could any smoke be seen from cooking fires, or even signs of settlement.

La Navidad had been obliterated. "A certain strong house somewhat forti-fied by a palisade where the Christians had dwelt was burned and destroyed," Dr. Chanca reported, "and they found certain cloaks and clothing which the Indians had brought and thrown into the house." Other possessions were found in a nearby settlement the Arawaks abandoned on Columbus's arrival—"a very pretty Moor-ish garment which had not been unfolded by those who brought it from Castile, and trousers and pieces of cloth and an anchor belonging to the vessel which the Admiral had lost there on the first voyage and other things." The Spanish seriously doubted that the items had been traded away.

The entire contingent of men Columbus had left behind, to Martín Alonso Pinzón's distress in January 1493, had died or disappeared, and no one knew exactly how or why.

Ten or eleven bodies were then found on November 28, overgrown by grass. They had been dead, it was thought, for anywhere from fifteen days to three months. Cuneo said the bodies were missing their eyes. "We thought the islanders had eaten them, for as soon as they have killed anyone, they immediately gouge out his eyes and eat them." The bodies were "hideously disfigured by decay," according to the Coma account, "covered with dust, discolored by blood, and wearing a fierce expression. They had lain neglected, unburied almost three months beneath the sky . . . too disfigured for recognition."

Columbus understood precious little about the people in whose company he had left behind the men of La Navidad. The Arawaks of Española were far from ignorant, simple primitives. They lived in towns with central plazas and well-appointed homes of the ruling elite, called the Taino, from whose ranks were drawn the *caciques*, or heads, of the island's chiefdoms. The Taino nobility ruled over a broad population of common people who produced food and paid tribute to their rulers; beneath the common crowd was a class of dispossessed people who acted as servants to the Taino. Columbus understood at least that the society was led by caciques, and he turned to the local ruler, Guacamarí (or Guacanagarí), for an ex-planation of what had become of La Navidad and its men.

A terrified Guacamarí blamed a raid by rival caciques. Cuneo related how Guacamarí "with tears falling upon his breast (and likewise all of his men) told us that Caonabó, the lord of the mountains, had come with 3,000 men and had killed them, as well as some of Guacanagarí's own men, and had robbed them in order to vex them. We found nothing of what the lord admiral had left. Hearing this, we believed him."

According to Dr. Chanca, Columbus was also told that some of the Spaniards had succumbed to disease. Still others had gone to the land of that other cacique, Caonabó, to find a gold mine and were killed there. The people of Caonabó and another chief, Mayrení, had then come to La Navidad and killed the rest of the Christians while also assaulting Guacamarí's people. The Coma account likewise blamed Caonabó for the actual assault, based on what Guacamarí related, and said that Guacamarí and his men tried to defend the Spaniards. The cacique himself said he had been wounded in the arm, but when Columbus first met him and found him in bed, claiming to have been injured, he thought the claim doubtful.

Clearly, there was more to the story. As Dr. Chanca wrote, "[I]t began to appear that one of the Christians had three wives and another four, from which we believed that the evil which had befallen them had come from jealousy." Dr. Chanca seemed to suggest the Spaniards had turned on each other over women, but the Coma account elaborated on this differently:

> The incitement to hatred and the cause of the war was the excessive lust of the Christians for the Indians' women. Each Spaniard had taken five women for his pleasure, I presume in the hope of offspring, but the women's husbands and male relations were unwilling to accept this at any cost. The barbarians conspired together to avenge the insult and erase their shame (for no spirited race is free from jealousy), and rose up against the Christians in a great mob. The Christians were unable to hold out for long against their massed legions, and though they fought valiantly to the last man, they were still miserably cut to pieces.

The men of La Navidad probably had made themselves magnificently unpopular in the countryside as they roamed in search of gold. Taking female captives from distant tribes in the process could have ignited the fateful assault, although some of the women could have been from Guacamarí's people. Columbus spent about ten days trying to get to the bottom of the disaster. He gave the dead a proper Christian burial and had the ground of the burned La Navidad dug up, as he had instructed the party left behind to bury any gold that was found.

The day after the ten or eleven bodies were found, ships were dispatched to the east and west, to find a new location for the Castilian trading center, to be called La Isabella, after a local survey found no other satisfactory site. Columbus worried, with good reason, about disease in swampy terrain. But as much as he strove to reaffirm good relations with Guacamarí and his people, he also likely wanted little to do with the local Arawaks, as he was not fully persuaded of their innocence in the destruction of La Navidad and the loss of what amounted to almost half the men from the first voyage.

Columbus already had a solid prospective location for the trading center: the River of Martín Alonso. Located about forty nautical miles east of Monte Cristi, its superbly protected, Y-shaped harbor would become renowned as a hurricane-hole for sailors on the north coast of Española, which otherwise offers so little in the way of sheltered waters. Columbus had visited it with Martín Alonso Pinzón on the way home in January 1493.

Columbus had called it Río de Gracia, hoping to wipe Pinzón's name from any map. The name Río de Martín Alonso nevertheless would persist. The Coma account said that a search party in fact inspected "Puerto de Gracia," calling it "a very beautiful retreat," but did not explain why Columbus failed to choose it for his town site, especially when Pinzón already had proved that it gave access to the gold resources of the interior. Logistics may have had nothing to do with the decision. It allegedly was too associated with Martín Alonso Pinzón for Columbus's liking or pride.

One of the deponents in the Columbus suits, Gonzalo Martín of Huelva, spoke at Palos in 1532 to Columbus's refusal to consider this location for the trading center. Martín had sailed with Columbus on his third voyage and had also visited the River of Martín Alonso. He had been told "that Cristóbal Colón, from annoyance that Martín Alonso had discovered the island [Española] and the river first, had not wanted to settle there but three leagues farther down at the place now called La Isabela. Asked from whom he heard this, he said that it was publicly discussed in the Indies by most people who were there whose names he does not recall, but that what he has said was held there as a certain and a well known thing."

Columbus instead had selected a location about eight miles west of the River of Martín Alonso. The new town of La Isabella was sited on a squat bluff facing westward near present-day Cambronal. The entrance to a lazy, meandering river, the Bajabonico, whose mouth today is cleaved into two branches, was close at hand. Cuneo praised it as an "excellent harbor." True, the curve of the coast provided shelter from the prevailing easterly winds, but the location otherwise was totally exposed and there was no real harbor to speak of, only an anchorage.

Columbus can be excused for not knowing at the time that there was any such thing as a hurricane. But this didn't change the fact that the Cambronal site would provide no protection to an anchored vessel if the wind blew from the north or west, unless that craft could be safely moved into the Bajabonico. At the least, La Isabella would require harbor infrastructure to be viable as a major, long-term trading center. Protective breakwalls, such as the ones that framed the harbor of Columbus's native Genoa and of Barcelona, and that Cabot had so recently proposed for Valencia, would have been an early consideration. Cabot would have had his work cut out for him. One can imagine him beginning to envision the breakwalls that would make La Isabella the Valencian port he never got to build and estimating how much of the stone Columbus soon was using to construct buildings would be required to create it.

The anonymous engineers and laborers debarked and set to work erecting a Castilian town. Dr. Chanca (who curiously gave the new colony the name Marta) wrote of it approvingly, explaining in his letter home it was being built on the bank of this large river so near that the water marks its boundaries in such a manner that half the city is surrounded by water with a ravine of cleft rock so that there is no need of any defence on that side. The other half is surrounded by so dense a grove that a rabbit could hardly get through it. This grove is so green that fire could not consume it at any time of the year. A canal has been commenced from the river which the engineers say they will put through the centre of the place and construct upon its banks wind-mills, sawmills, and whatever mills can be operated by water.

Cabot would have been kept busy helping plan and executing these waterworks and performing preliminary surveying for a proper harbor facility.

Parties of men meanwhile struck out overland to seek gold, returning on January 20 and 21. "The one that went to Cibao found gold in so many places that a man dare not tell it," Dr. Chanca explained, "but truly they found gold in more than fifty streams and rivers and outside the rivers on land. So that they say that wherever they wish to seek for gold in all that province they will find it." Dr. Chanca promised that Fernando and Isabel "can consider themselves the most prosperous and richest Princes in the world, for no such thing has been seen or read of before in the world. Truly when the ships return on another voyage they can take away such a quantity of gold that whoever knows of it may wonder at it."

Yet the news from these overland expeditions of stupendous amounts of easily harvested gold was the worst possible sort for a settlement that expected several hundred newcomers to toil at menial labor and produce food on the Castilian payroll. The only force more destructive for La Isabella than the avarice the gold rush soon would unleash was the power of one of the Arawaks' most fearsome gods. His name was Huracán. The Spanish would feel his wrath twice in 1495.

DR. CHANCA'S LETTER was consigned to the care of the twelve-ship return flotilla under Antonio de Torres, which departed the nascent trading center on February 2, 1494. Sending most of the vessels back at this early date had not been the original plan. Dr. Chanca noted that the ships had sailed "on account of the great amount of sickness which had been among the people." The mysterious pathogen that already had felled Martín Alonso Pinzón and cost some lives at La Navidad evidently was spreading among the newcomers as well. They died in droves, and the ill were being shipped back to Spain, along with young nobles *cum* tourists who raced home before the epidemic could claim them as well.

The flotilla was back in Cadíz on March 9. No later than three months after that, John Cabot surfaced in Seville. If he had in fact just returned from La Isabella, then he had seen, done, or suffered enough. He would prove to be one of the most timid men in the history of exploration when it came to making contact with Indigenous peoples. Was he filled with fear by secondhand tales from the second Columbus voyage of the massacre at La Navidad and fierce cannibals, augmented perhaps by the reports from the actual Indies of the Venetian traveler Nicolò de' Conti? Or was it firsthand experience on that voyage—dead Spaniards with their eyes gouged out, terrified Arawaks who fled Carib captors and made Columbus's men understand that their children were raised as castrated foodstock—that instilled such profound apprehension in Cabot when his own ship came upon a foreign shore and its emerald-green woods stood before him in shadowed mystery?

Columbus would not reappear in Spain for another two years. In his absence, the quest to prove a profitable westward route to the Orient changed profoundly. The world was moving beyond scandalous tales of cannibals and gleaning more useful data about where Columbus had been and what he had found. That intelligence helped spur on fresh initiatives. By the time Columbus steered home for Spain, Cabot too would be on the Ocean Sea, steering in the opposite direction.

ELEVEN

AFTER COLUMBUS returned from the first voyage in early 1493, there was no consensus on where he had been and little practical information in circulation to support a particular interpretation. Although his letter to Luis de Santángel had been published in April, it contained precious little geographic data. Columbus estimated distances along and around the main islands of Española and Juana but offered no crucial distance for his discoveries in longitude or leagues west of either Europe or the known Atlantic islands. Of latitude, he only allowed: "[I]t is true that the sun is very fierce there, although it is twenty-six degrees north of the equator." He gave no indication of which of his landfalls the latitude of 26° north applied to. And there was no map of his landfalls in circulation, nor would there be during Columbus's lifetime.

Surely the Spanish court was given some idea of where he had been in order to secure the papal bulls of 1493. Yet Isabel herself had to prod Columbus to provide more concrete details. "Right away send me the navigation chart that you were supposed to make, if it is finished," she wrote him from Barcelona on September 5, 1493, a few weeks before the second voyage's departure. As Isabel also informed him: "No agreement has been made on the business of Portugal."

Spain was deep into the negotiations that would turn the rights secured through Alexander VI's inelegant and confusing bulls into a formal treaty with Portugal that would divide the world, discovered and undiscovered, along a meridian far out in the Ocean Sea. The bulls had granted Spain territories beginning at a meridian placed one hundred leagues west of the Cape Verdes and/or the Azores. Portugal wanted to divide the undiscovered world between the two nations along a meridian much farther west than that. Without an accurate chart of Columbus's discoveries, the Spanish were negotiating in the dark and at risk of giving away what he had already found.

We have no idea if Columbus managed to provide the chart Isabel requested before he departed in September 1493. Rather incredibly, Fernando and Isabel nevertheless proceeded to conclude the terms of the Treaty of Tordesillas without essential information from Columbus. Las Casas in his narrative of the third voyage would note how Columbus in his now-lost journal "mentions how the Sovereigns sent for him that he should be present at the meetings in regard to the partition" but that a grave illness contracted while exploring Cuba prevented him from returning to Spain from Española. This excuse seems dubious, as Columbus did not leave on that expedition until April 25, 1494. Still, without any direct input from Columbus, the treaty was signed on June 7, 1494. On August 16, Fernando and Isabel were still trying to get details out of Columbus on his latest discoveries—discoveries he had made in their name almost a year earlier in the Leeward Islands. He had sent back reports with the Torres flotilla that reached Spain in March 1494, but information obviously was lacking.

"Having seen all that you wrote to us, it is a great joy and delight to read [your letters] because you talk about things at such great length," Fernando and Isabel wrote. "Nevertheless, we desire that you write something more about how many islands have been found up to now. Of those islands you have named, what name has been given to each, because in your letters you give the names of some but not all of these, the names that the Indians call them, how far it is from one to the other."

Tordesillas at least was less ambiguous than the problematic bulls that inspired it. Portugal agreed to limit its territorial claims in the Ocean Sea to the east side of a meridian that it had been able to persuade Spain to shift to 370 leagues west of the Cape Verdes. (The treaty also eliminated the problematic inclusion of the Azores in the papal bulls of 1493.) The third voyage's narrative would relate Columbus's understanding that João II suspected profitable lands lay somewhere to the south and west of the Cape Verdes. Portugal's demand to move the meridian so far west has long raised suspicions that it already knew South America, particularly Brazil, was out there and that much of it would fall within its territory. In any event, any lands to the west of the meridian would be left to Spain.

Although the 1493 bulls strongly implied that the rights granted to Spain applied only to waters south of the Canaries as per Alcáçovas of 1479 and the bull of 1481, Portugal and Spain agreed in Tordesillas to cleave the world between themselves from pole to pole along the defining meridian. But all the challenges of determining the location of the dividing meridian remained.

Determining a degree of longitude accurately was so far beyond the abilities of mariners, geographers, and astronomers that cartographers could place new discoveries on whichever side of this dividing meridian suited a monarch's purposes, as proving otherwise was next to impossible. Fernando and Isabel sent a copy of the treaty to Columbus with the August 16, 1494, letter, asking him or his brother Bartolomé—who had recently joined him at Española—to mark the position of the dividing meridian on a chart for them. "It seems to us that line, or border, that is to be made is an extremely difficult matter requiring great wisdom and trust."

Spain plainly had agreed to the Portuguese insistence that the crucial meridian be shifted to 370 leagues west of the Cape Verdes without actually knowing precisely where it would end up in relation to Columbus's finds, especially his most recent ones. In the hands of enterprising Portuguese cartographers, the meridian would continue to shift westward toward Columbus's Caribbean discoveries. And far to the north, Cabot's finds soon would create a new frontier of dispute over who had a right to a novel shore, based on the meridian along which Spain and Portugal had agreed to divide the undiscovered world.

THE TREATY OF TORDESILLAS called for a joint Spanish-Portuguese surveying expedition to depart from the Cape Verdes within ten months of the treaty's signing in order to agree on the meridian's location. There is no evidence that any such expedition took place, although the Portuguese could have sent out vessels of their own to investigate Columbus's finds. Columbus meanwhile truly did his utmost to keep the details of his discoveries to himself.

His published and widely circulated letter to Santángel addressed his suspicion that Cuba, which he called Juana, was the mainland, but on balance he seemed satisfied that it was in fact an island, as he went on to write in that letter: "I can say that this island is larger than England and Scotland together." But before leaving on the second voyage, he had decided Cuba was a peninsula of the mainland. Pietro Martire wrote to Ascanio Sforza in Milan on September 13, 1493, shortly before Columbus departed Cádiz, and in sharing news of the original discoveries he referred to the Golden Chersonese, or Malay Peninsula. Martire's letter was the first indication that Columbus was advancing Cuba as this peninsula. A year later, Martire firmly made Cuba the Golden Chersonese in an October 20, 1494, letter to Giovanni Borromeo, based on Columbus's own conclusions: "[Columbus] declares that he has pushed his way from Española so far toward the West that he has reached the Golden Chersonese, which is the farthest extremity of the East."

Most of the sailors who accompanied Columbus on his coasting of the south shore of Cuba on the second voyage thought he was wrong in insisting that the apparent island was part of the mainland, according to Michele da Cuneo, who was along for that cruise. Nevertheless, to enforce his views, Columbus made the participating sailors, masters, and pilots swear aboard the *Niña* on June 12, 1494, that Cuba was indeed part of the mainland. Recorded the notary Fernand Perez de Luna: "I placed them under a penalty of 10,000 maravedis and the cutting out of the tongue for every time that each one hereafter should say contrary to what they should now say: and if it shall be a ship's boy or a person of such condition, that he should be given one hundred lashes and have his tongue cut out."

But Columbus could not control the minds or tongues of learned men back in Spain (and elsewhere in Europe) or relieve the widely held skepticism that had greeted his scheme before he had even sailed in August 1492. Martire captured that persistent skepticism in a letter written on October 1, 1493, to the Archbishop of Braga, Petro Inghirami.

> A certain Columbus has sailed to the Western Antipodes, even, as he believes, to the very shores of India. He has discovered many islands beyond the Eastern ocean adjoining the Indies, which are believed to be those of which mention has been made among cosmographers. I do not wholly deny this, although the magnitude of the globe seems to suggest otherwise, for there are not wanting those who think it but a small journey from the end of Spain to the shores of India; however this may be, they declare that a great thing has been accomplished.

Drafting the first volume of his *Decades*, which he may have begun working on as soon as the following month, Martire (who otherwise admired and celebrated Columbus's achievements) was firmer in his own skepticism. "He [Columbus] says that he has discovered the Island of Ophir," a source of Solomon's adornments for the temple of Jerusalem, according to the Old Testament's Kings III; in Columbus's time, Ophir was considered to be in the Indian Ocean, south of the Ganges. However, Martire cautioned, "if we take into account the teachings of the cosmographers, those islands are the Antillas and other adjacent ones."

Columbus did his best to dictate the geographic lexicon. In a letter drafted November 20, 1493, while he was at Puerto Rico, en route to Española on the second voyage, he called the series of islands he had just discovered the "East Indies." Columbus's term "Indies" would endure (albeit as the *West* Indies), but "Antilla" had momentum of its own. The Leeward Islands chain that he had just sailed through also would become known as the Lesser Antilles, and Cuba, Jamaica, Española, and Puerto Rico the Greater Antilles. Even in some Spanish commercial records of 1497, the Indies discoveries were called *las islas de Antilla*. Columbus was officially referred to in one Spanish document in 1497 as *almirante del mar oceano de las yndias de Antilla* (Admiral of the Ocean Sea of the Indies of Antilla).

In her letter to Columbus of September 5, 1493, Isabel had more indulgently called him "her admiral of the Ocean Sea and viceroy and governor of the islands newly found in the Indies." Fernando and Isabel may not have believed he actually had reached the Indies, as he claimed, but it didn't matter, so long as whatever he had found teemed with its own promised riches and provided a base for a trading station on the edge of the Orient. Columbus persisted in arguing that his discoveries were where he said they were. By early 1494, however, the first hard intelligence of the actual location of his finds began to leak out. Not only did it suggest that he had not reached the Indies as claimed; it indicated that some other enterprising individual could still find them.

IT WAS IMPOSSIBLE for Columbus to suppress all details of his discoveries after twelve of the 1493 armada's seventeen ships and an untold number of its estimated twelve hundred participants returned to Spain in March 1494, while he remained behind in the Indies. Even so, surprisingly little seemed to escape into the wider world—and his own monarchs would be begging for details the following August.

Over the next year or two, a few gleanings of useful if occasionally confused geographic data emerged. It was understood from the published Santángel letter that Columbus's finds involved an observation of latitude 26° north but, as noted, the letter did not explain what specific discovery fell along this line. The more critical issue was how far west his finds lay, above all if there was any reason to believe that he had sailed as far as the Indies.

Giambattista Strozzi, who was probably a merchant from the Florentine Strozzi family, wrote a letter from Cadíz on March 18, 1494, a surviving copy of which ended up at the court of Francesco II Gonzaga, Marquess of Mantua. Florentine interest in the Indies went beyond a curiosity in travelers' tales. Florence was where Toscanelli wrote his crucial letter and drew his (lost) map in 1474. It was also where Conti's true Indies experiences were set down by the papal secretary Poggio Bracciolini in 1439 and were published in 1492, in a volume dedicated to Pietro Cara, who was departing on a journey of his own to India by traveling east as Conti had done along the Muslim trade routes.

The Torres flotilla had arrived at Cadíz on March 7, and Strozzi had availed himself of the usual commodities of Columbian hyperbole. "They brought with them gold worth about 30,000 ducats, according to what they say; much cinnamon, but white like Arabian ginger; pepper in pods like the broad bean, very strong but not substantial like that from the Levant; logs which they say are sandalwood, but white; parrots like falcons and red like pheasants." The gold and the parrots were the only authentic items the flotilla would have possessed.

Noting the ships had returned from "the said islands of the Antilles," thus reiterating the general wisdom of where Columbus had actually been, he then wrote: "They place the said island[s] more than forty-three degrees [west], [from] 26 degrees to/within 31 degrees, below the Equator, according to report."

Strozzi's latitude figures were perhaps the result of deliberate disinformation. But his mention of "more than 43 degrees" can be only a westward measure of longitude. A span of forty-three degrees of longitude west of the Cape Verdes (which was in the process of being adapted exclusively as the reference point for Tordesillas) is an excellent result for Española. The accuracy is a testament to the skills of pilots of this era in dead reckoning, by which progress was measured by observing compass course and estimating ship speed with a trailing log line. By the time this information reached Strozzi at Cadíz, there had been five separate ship crossings (three there, two back) in 1492–93 and twenty-nine more crossings (seventeen there, twelve back) in 1493–94: a tremendous amount of dead-reckoning data that pilots could compare.

On December 29, 1494, Pietro Martire touched on the dimensions and location of Española in a letter to his friend Polonius Laetus. By then Martire had received a letter from Columbus, which must have been carried home on a supply flotilla that returned that November.

"This island of Española is in shape like the leaf of a chestnut tree: it is situated in twenty-six degrees of latitude on its northern side and twenty-one on its southern," Martire wrote. Those figures were off by several degrees. Latitude 26° it would turn out was an excellent result for Columbus's initial landfall in the Bahamas, but the north coast of Española lay along latitude 20°, and the south coast around latitude 18°. Martire also said the island was 49 degrees west of Cadíz. The latter measure brings to mind Strozzi's "more than 43 degrees," but Columbus would never have said Española was as close to Cadíz as 49 degrees. Apart from being significantly wrong—the actual span is more than 70 degrees—the figure would have seriously undermined Columbus's claim to having sailed about one-third of the way around the world in reaching the Indies. Martire's mention that the figure came from "those who have accurately measured it" suggests that his sources were mariners returning on one of the flotillas. The number Martire had offered also was likely inspired by Tordesillas and actually referred to a distance in degrees west of the Cape Verdes.

The apparent accuracy of the Strozzi and Martire longitude measures west of the Cape Verdes was a problem for Columbus. The figures indicated that Española was not much farther than one-sixth of the way around the world. Little surprise that so many believed Columbus had only reached Antilla.

To resolve the debate, a way to more directly determine degrees of longitude was needed. It wouldn't matter then how large or small the circumference of Earth was and how far around it men thought they'd sailed in leagues based on dead reckoning. If it could be shown that two places on Earth were separated by 120 degrees of longitude, for example, then they were separated by one-third of Earth's circumference, regardless of the actual leagues involved.

As it happened, when Martire wrote his friend Polonius Laetus in late December 1494, Columbus had recently conducted the most scientific effort yet to determine the longitude of Española. The solution to the problem probably had already struck the astronomical experts soon after Columbus returned from the first voyage; they just needed the celestial opportunity to apply it.

BECAUSE THE WORLD ROTATES once every twenty-four hours, every degree in 360 degrees of longitude is equal to four "clock minutes" of rotational time. Thus when Columbus wrote in July 1503 of having sailed westward for "nine hours" in reaching Cuba in 1494, he was referring to total longitude covered. The distance across the Ocean Sea to the Indies, he was arguing, spanned 135 degrees of longitude from Portugal's Cape St. Vincent, or three-eighths of the way around the globe.

The rotating Earth is also a kind of clock that allows local times to be used to calculate differences in longitude. Astronomers understood that if a celestial event is observed from two different locations, and the local times of the event are precisely recorded, the time difference could be converted into the separation in longitude of the places of observation. If an event occurs at 1:00 P.M. local time in one place and at 7:00 P.M. in another, the six hours of difference for an event observed simultaneously translates into 360 minutes of time, or 90 degrees of longitude. The observers are one-quarter of the way around the world from each other.

But few celestial events were available to a late fifteenth-century observer that could be seen without a telescope (which would not exist for more than a century) and also occurred frequently enough for coordinated observations in two widely separated locations to be readily made. A person also had to be able to predict an event so that observations could be planned and coordinated. Fortunately, the Nürnberg astronomer and mathematician Regiomontanus (Johann Müller) had published in 1474 his *Kalendarium,* which provided tables of unprecedented accuracy forecasting eclipses until 1525. Using the *Kalendarium*'s data, which predicted dates and times of eclipses in Europe (with a table of time adjustments for different cities), Columbus could work out a longitude based on a single observation in the Indies, although a precise observation in Europe as well would be needed to confirm the result.

With no useful solar eclipse forecast, the only alternative was a lunar eclipse, which takes place when Earth passes between the sun and a full moon, casting the moon into shadow. The *Kalendarium* had predicted one for April 1, 1493, and that night, with Columbus en route from Seville to Barcelona for his audience with Fernando and Isabel, the full moon turned a rusty crimson in the Spanish night sky. If the lunar eclipse solution had not occurred already to Spain's astronomers, then it surely came to mind as Columbus arrived at court in Barcelona to report on where he had been on the first voyage.

The *Kalendarium* promised two lunar eclipses in 1494, on March 21 and September 14; there would not be another one until January 18, 1497. With Columbus preparing to return to the Indies in September 1493, the 1494 eclipses presented timely opportunities to settle the matter of how far around Earth, toward the presumed location of the Indies, Columbus's discoveries actually lay.

Columbus appears to have made sure he was at La Isabella on March 21 to observe the first 1494 eclipse, pausing there between a twenty-nine-day overland expedition he had made on Española in search of gold and embarking on his survey of the south coast of Cuba on April 25. But the eclipse was of no use because it began shortly before seven in the evening at La Isabella, as the moon rose from the sea to the east; the shadow's initial appearance would have been impossible to see at dusk. The next eclipse, September 14, 1494, would be the last chance to attempt a longitude fix by celestial observation for more than two years.

Columbus had just inspected the entirety of the south coast of Cuba and had also visited Jamaica for the first time, where the reception had been hostile and his men killed about two-dozen Arawaks with crossbows and lombards. As the eclipse forecast by Regiomontanus approached, Columbus found himself a place of observation: an island on the southeastern tip of Española. He made a gift of it to Michele da Cuneo, naming it La Bella Saonese in honor of Cuneo's home of Saona; today it is known as Isla Saona. Cuneo extravagantly claimed the island had thirty-seven settlements and at least thirty thousand inhabitants. He went ashore and busied himself making improvements, clearing brush and cutting down trees, erecting a cross as well as a gallows as symbols of his righteous authority. After playing at being lord of La Bella Saonese on this cruise, Cuneo would never see it again.

Columbus left Cuneo to his feudal fantasies and waited for his eclipse. Timing the precise moment of its beginning, or of its full state, would have been a terrific challenge. A Nürnberg locksmith, Peter Henlein, had invented in 1490 the coiled mainspring, which allowed the introduction of small tabletop clocks for portable timekeeping, but the minute hand would not appear until 1577 in a clock created for astronomer Tycho Brahe. Once the eclipse began its own clockwork motion, however, Columbus would have recognized that his ability to insist Española was anywhere close to the edge of the Indies mainland was in an astronomical race against time.

If Española was one-third of the way around the world and it could be successfully observed in darkness, then the start of the eclipse would not be observable back home, as an eight-hour difference in the local time of observation meant the sun by then most likely would be up and the moon would have sunk below the western horizon. If, however, observers in Spain or Portugal could see the start of the eclipse—before daybreak, before the moonset—then Española had to be much closer to Spain than Columbus contended if he too witnessed it. By the same token, if the eclipse did not start early enough at Saona, Columbus would know, based on the event's predicted time for Europe, that he was far closer to Spain than he had been arguing.

On September 14, the full moon began to rise from the Caribbean Sea virtually due east on the horizon from Isla Saona shortly before 6:00 P.M. Twilight gathered; the moon continued to climb. Ten minutes before midnight, Earth's satellite began to dim from the upper left quadrant, and by 2:00 A.M. it was in full eclipse. It was not the result Columbus was hoping for.

In the manuscript of religious writings that would be published long after his death as his *Book of Prophecies,* he wrote that the eclipse told him the difference between Isla Saona and Portugal's Cape St. Vincent was *cinco oras y más de media*—five and more than one-half hours of longitude. Las Casas would give this as precisely five hours and thirty-three minutes. That was about 25 percent larger than the actual measure of about four and a half hours, but it nevertheless placed eastern Española less than one-quarter of the way around the world.

Using the data in Regiomontanus's published eclipse predictions, Columbus worked out his five-and-a-half-hour estimate of the longitudinal separation on the spot. He could not expect the result to improve in his favor through an observation in Spain: The eclipse had started too late at Saona for it to have been visible at home if he was anything like one-third of the way around the world.

As pilots in relief flotillas refined their dead-reckoning results, Columbus could not continue to defend the idea that Española was on the far side of the world. His initial solution was to grossly exaggerate the east–west dimension of Española, stretching the island like saltwater taffy in order to extend his discoveries farther west, beyond Isla Saona and in particular La Isabella, where the ships called. The Martire letter of December 29, 1494, said the island spanned 19 degrees of longitude, when it actually covers less than 7.

But as Española became better known to mariners and colonists, a wild inflation of its westerly dimensions could not be sustained. Columbus instead had to grossly exaggerate Cuba's westerly sprawl, in order to extend net progress toward the Asian landmass while continuing to defend his portrayal of Cuba as a large peninsula of that landmass.

Columbus doubtless suppressed his observational result of the eclipse at Isla Saona. Michele da Cuneo recounted how Columbus actually prevented a cleric who disagreed strongly with his geographic views from returning to Spain with Cuneo in early 1495. The man was "an abbot of Lucena, a very knowledgeable and very rich man who came alone to these regions for his pleasure, to see new things. This man is a good astronomer and cosmographer." The abbot disagreed that Cuba was mainland and said it was "a very big island. The majority of us, considering the course of our voyage, agreed with this opinion. For this reason the lord admiral did not want to let him return to Spain with us, since if he were asked his opinion by his majesty the king, he might with his answer cause the king to abandon the enterprise. The admiral will keep him there."

The abbot appears to have accompanied Columbus and Cuneo on the controversial coasting of Cuba's southern shore, which led directly to the lunar observation at Saona Island. If the abbot was as capable an astronomer and cosmographer as Cuneo asserted, he would have been one of those men who assisted in—or actually conducted—the observation (for as the Genoese notary Antonio Gallo wrote in 1506, Columbus's eclipse calculation was made possible "by the observation of

his men") and would have been additionally dangerous to Columbus as an eyewitness to the results. Columbus could hardly threaten such a man with the loss of his
tongue, but he could prevent the cleric from leaving the Caribbean and loosing his
tongue in Fernando and Isabel's presence.

In 1506, Gallo would further state: "[Columbus] said that, by the observation
of his men, when an eclipse appeared in the month of September, in the year of our
Lord 1494, it had been seen in Hispaniola four natural hours earlier than in Seville.
From this computation, one can gather that the island is four hours distant from
Cadíz in Spain." Columbus had at some point compared his Saona data with an
actual observation in Spain and achieved a more accurate result that was even more
damning when it came to his claims that he had reached the Indies.

As the moon, glowing orange as if burning from within, sank from view in the
west on September 15, 1494, a new day dawned in Seville. The ruling council of the
city gathered. Within hours of the eclipse that held an essential truth about Columbus's discoveries, these leading citizens hired "Johan Caboto, Venetian, inhabitant
of this city," to build a new bridge across the Guadalquivir to its maritime district
of Triana.

TWELVE

ON NOVEMBER 4, 1494, Nürnberg's Jerome Münzer ascended the bell tower of Seville's Cathedral of the Virgin Mary. It had been built in the late twelfth century as the minaret of Seville's great mosque, when the city was the capital of the Muslim empire of the Maghreb, which included North African territories from present-day Libya to Morocco. Seville had fallen to the Christians in the *reconquista* of 1248, and while the minaret was spared, the mosque, which had been damaged in an earthquake, was torn down to make way for the cathedral, the greatest Gothic structure in Europe. Its construction had begun in 1420 and was still proceeding when Münzer visited, attracting talent from across Spain as well as from Flanders and Germany as the city center was transformed into one of the world's greatest work sites of the fifteenth century. Christopher Columbus would be buried in it.

Münzer took in the panorama of "the most celebrated town of the kingdom of Andalusia" from more than ninety yards in the air. Seville retained "an infinity of monuments and old things from the time of the Saracens." It was built on a typical circular plan and located on flat ground on the eastern shore of the Guadalquivir. The city's riverside fortress, the Alcazar, dated back to A.D. 712 and had become a royal residence after the reconquest, with a palace constructed within its crenellated walls in the mid-fourteenth century during the reign of Peter the Cruel.

"The Sevillans hope that the king will come to live with them, and they are also smoothing the streets in macadam and undertaking many works," Münzer remarked. Fernando was "repairing the old crumbled walls [of the Alcazar] and preparing three apartments, for himself, his children, and the queen, apartments of exquisite style, built with art, of the kind that will never be found again."

Before Münzer was the Guadalquivir, "a very beautiful river, navigable and large." Ships of up to 150 tons, he wrote, called at Seville. "Outside the city and beyond the bridge on the Guadalquivir, which has been built to pass atop boats, there is a long suburb called Triana." Münzer found time to negotiate the contraption of anchored hulls lashed together with cable and surmounted by boards known as the Puente de Barca, or Bridge of Boats. An assessment of Seville was incomplete without a visit to Triana's waterfront district, the Barrio del Mar in the parish of Magdalena. This was the thriving center of maritime activity for a city serving as the administrative and logistical heart of the envisioned overseas trading center that Columbus was creating in the Indies.

In Triana, Münzer would have moved among some of Spain's most accomplished and entrepreneurial seafarers, divided into brotherhoods largely organized along family lines called *comitres*. The members were wealthy and powerful members of Seville's society, the equivalent of nobles, who were exempt from taxation. The strict laws on comportment allowed them to carry arms, dress in silk, and adorn themselves in gold and silver. As merchant sailors, they ranged as far as the Canaries, Flanders, and England, banding together in financial partnerships that sometimes included participants from Seville's considerable Genoese merchant community. Columbus's discoveries were giving Triana's merchants a new destination; many of the ships chartered for the new Indies service belonged to its comitres. Some people even insisted that the sailor who first sighted the New World on October 12, 1492, was a local man aboard the *Pinta*, Juan Rodriguez Bermejo, also known as Roderigo de Triana. Just one example of the local spin-off benefits was the provisioning contract for the second voyage's armada, granted to Seville's Gianotto Berardi, the Florentine creditor of Columbus from the first voyage. Berardi was paid to supply a vessel laden with between 200,000 and 300,000 pounds of ship's biscuit, an order that kept well stoked the ovens of Triana's *bizcocheros*, or biscuit makers.

Seville also held the leading role in the ongoing conquest of the Canary Islands and the expansion of its sugar industry. Between 1470 and 1515, trade involving the Canaries accounted for 70 percent of mid-Atlantic region voyages by vessels chartered in the port. The city's dominance of Andalusian trade was magnified by the declarations of Fernando and Isabel in May 1493 that Cadíz, whose commercial life was so closely linked to Seville, would be the hub of the Barbary trade as well as the designated Spanish seaport (under Seville's authority) for the Indies. A tight network of ports—Cadíz, Sanlúcar de Barrameda, El Puerto de Santa María, and the smaller ports of Palos, Moguer, and Lepe—was linked to and dependent on Seville, which also served as a key staging area for Italian shipping in the Flanders trade.

Triana was flourishing, with shipyards, ship's riggers, shops, and tavernkeepers as well as moneychangers and brokers. Münzer marveled at the large clay containers being manufactured there for transporting wine and oil. Most, he said, could hold nearly twelve or thirteen amphorae of wine. "If I had not seen them, I would not have believed it." This commercial bustle was placing additional strain on the breakdown-prone Puente de Barca, which had spanned the Guadalquivir since 1171. Münzer's footfalls had been sounding on the floating bridge at the very time John Cabot was being entrusted to replace it with a fixed link.

THE RULING COUNCIL of Seville had agreed on September 15, 1494, to employ "Mr. Johan Caboto, Venetian, inhabitant of this city," in the construction of the fixed link. The bridge, like the Valencia harbor project, could have been Cabot's idea, although the assignment probably came to him because of his success in ingratiating himself with Fernando and leading court figures at Valencia in April 1493 who were also associated with the Columbus enterprise that was developing its logistical headquarters in Seville. The fact that Cabot was entrusted with a public works project so critical to the city indicates the high esteem in which he was held.

Cabot was to be paid for a total of five months, and records indicate he already had devoted himself to the job for three months—hence he had been in Seville since at least June. He was to receive a fee from Seville of three reales and three maravedis per day. The city further released fifty Castilian doubloons, or 7,300 maravedis, for the construction of the "city bridge of brick," for which a brickworks on Triana would have supplied material, although stone was mentioned as well. The costs appeared trivial, compared to the expense the city was shouldering just to maintain the floating bridge. Since 1488, the care of the Puente de Barca had been contracted to a prominent comitre member, Luis Rodríguez de la Mesquita, who was also a tax farmer for Triana and some other towns under Seville's authority. The maintenance contract paid him an astounding 225,000 maravedis per year, which was the equivalent of more than four pounds of solid gold. Little wonder that Seville's civic leaders, enriched by the conquest of the Canary Islands and flush with the idea of the economic prospects awaiting them as Española was developed by Columbus, thought by mid-1494 that they needed and could well afford a more robust and reliable link.

Beyond noting the fact that the Sevillans were "undertaking many works," Münzer made no specific mention of the key infrastructure project Cabot was being paid to build. Regardless, Münzer and Cabot were in Seville and Triana, walking the Puente de Barca, during the same critical period in November 1494—a time critical not only in their own lives and careers but in the increasingly precarious Columbus enterprise.

Cabot would prove to be more than a builder of bridges. And Münzer already was more than a Renaissance German tourist.

JEROME MÜNZER WAS NO ordinary traveler, and this journey was no ordinary pilgrimage. In addition to being a physician trained in the Lombardy region's city of Pavia, Münzer was an envoy of Maximilian I of the Austrian house of Hapsburg, the new King of the Romans and Holy Roman Emperor.

Münzer and his three traveling companions, Gaspar Fischer and Nicolas Walkenstein of Nürnberg and Anton Hewart of Augsburg, had been wending on foot and horseback (or muleback) through Europe since August 1494, passing through Switzerland and southern France before arriving in southern Spain on September 19. The journey through Catalunya, Andalusia, and the recently conquered kingdom of Granada had strung together monasteries and villages within an itinerary that took in every major place of interest: Barcelona, Valencia, the city of Granada, and then Málaga, where they paused overnight on October 29 before heading for Seville.

Münzer probably imagined publishing the Latin travelogue he left behind, which never happened, but there was far more to the journey than his lightly detailed if engaging account conveyed. As an envoy of Maximilian I, he enjoyed audiences with the rulers of Spain, Portugal, and Navarre and conversations with other leading figures of the day, about which he related very little. He invested considerable time in significant locations, without accounting for all of his activities or revealing the names of everyone he met.

Münzer was keenly interested in geography, particularly the geography of opportunity that had lured Columbus westward. The year before he undertook this journey, Münzer had been promoting a new idea for reaching the Indies by sailing westward across the northern reaches of the Ocean Sea. There is every reason to believe that the scheme was still very much on his mind as he undertook his journey, that Columbus's alleged success had in no way suppressed his enthusiasm.

Seville was especially intriguing for him. Having arrived on November 4, he did not leave until November 11, and that week of respite and exploration produced little more than a tourist's description of landmarks, with intimations of great changes afoot. Münzer said not a word about the fact that Seville was the new headquarters of Spain's Indies enterprise, although he was perfectly aware of Columbus's activities and would be intimately informed about the many foibles of Española before his journey was over.

Münzer was an exploration advocate whose convictions and ambitions, far from having waned, could only have been reinvigorated by this Iberian tour. Five days after leaving Seville, where Cabot was supposed to be building his bridge, Münzer was at Évora in Portugal, dining with João II four times and enjoying unelaborated conversations; soon after Münzer was in Lisbon, staying in the home of the father-in-law of a fellow Nürnberger, Martin Behaim, whose participation in Portuguese exploration, friendship with Columbus, and precise role in the New World's discovery would dog historians for centuries. Through these two Nürnbergers the essential mystery of John Cabot's career—of how he went from being a bridge contractor in Seville to an explorer in England—approaches a coherent explanation.

JEROME MÜNZER WAS AN ENABLER and a facilitator for his friend Martin Behaim, an exploration figure whose stock has risen and fallen as violently as any speculative issue. At its greatest heights, Behaim has been hailed as the true discoverer of the Americas; at its most pronounced depths, he has been dismissed as a lying self-promoter. Behaim may well have claimed for himself loftier achievements than he was entitled to, but he was unquestionably an authentic figure in late fifteenth-century exploration.

Behaim was born in 1459 in Nürnberg, the center of the German Renaissance: prosperous, intellectually sophisticated, a hive of printing and precision instrument design and manufacture. The family's roots may have been in Bohemia, which would explain the name, but the Behaims had been leading citizens of Nürnberg since the early fourteenth century. Behaim's father, Martin the elder, was an affluent merchant and city counselor whose business dealings took him to Flanders in the north and Venice in the south.

Martin the elder died in 1474, and in 1476, the younger Martin was sent to Mechelin in what is now Belgium as part of the family trading business. A June 1479 letter found Behaim in Antwerp, contacting his uncle Leonhard in Nürnberg, to report having spent three hundred florins provided by his mother on English cloth at the fair at Bergen-op-Zoom. Seven years later, Behaim had achieved an ascent that the older Christopher Columbus, who knew him and was no stranger to upward mobility, could only have envied. Behaim was poised to make the very westward voyage in search of the Indies for João II that Columbus had failed to persuade the Portuguese king to support.

Behaim's spectacular progress presumably began with fortuitous connections he made in the Low Countries as a young merchant. Most of what is now the Netherlands, Belgium, and Flanders formed the prosperous yet politically volatile northern part of the duchy of Burgundy, which had come into Maximilian I's possession through his first marriage. The Burgundian Netherlands, as the historic region is known, had close relations with Portugal through trade as well as dynastic alliances, which extended Flemish influence far into the Atlantic realm. Isabella of Portugal— daughter of João I and sister of Prince Enrique (Henry) the Navigator—had been Duchess of Burgundy, and around 1460 she received a grant permitting her Flemish subjects, who were seeking relief from the privations of the 100 Years' War, to colonize the Azores. Immigrants from Flanders so dominated their settlement that they were commonly known as the Flemish Islands.

In 1466, a Flemish noble, Joss van Huerter, whose family had a seigneural holding in Wijnendale, began to settle the Azorean island of Fayal. Huerter was awarded the hereditary title of *captain donatorio* for Fayal in 1468; this captaincy, which granted the right to settle the land, was extended to neighboring Pico in 1482. Huerter did not spend all his time in the Azores. Known in Portugal as Joz d'Utra or some variant thereon, he maintained a splendid residence in Lisbon and would have returned to Flanders occasionally on business.

Behaim likely encountered Huerter around 1479–80 and followed him from northern Burgundy to Lisbon, although German merchants also were well established in the Portuguese capital. There was a close dynastic relationship between Portugal and the German states of the Holy Roman Empire: Frederick III's queen consort—and Maximilian's mother—was Eleanor of Portugal, sister of Afonso V and aunt of João II. (The Portuguese were also very fond of German gunpowder and artillery expertise.) Behaim would marry Huerter's daughter, Joana de Macedo, between 1486 and early 1489; in the meantime, Huerter's standing in both Lisbon and the Azores would have been crucial to Behaim's ascent.

By 1484, Behaim was a leading member of João II's learned council charged with solving the sun-sight problem, and his contributions included drawing up the required declination tables. Huerter must have advanced his candidacy, which was founded on Behaim's claim to having been a student of the great Nürnberg astronomer and mathematician Regiomontanus, who had produced the celestial almanac Columbus used in observing the lunar eclipse of September 1494.

Behaim was said to have provided a new astrolabe design for the Portuguese. It may have been based on the work of Regiomontanus, who created a number of improvements in observational instruments. Behaim also could have been a commercial conduit to Portugal—and ultimately even to Columbus—for the scientific instruments (including mariner's compasses) being produced in Nürnberg.

Behaim made a voyage to West Africa in the 1480s, supposedly in concert with solving the sun-sight problem, although it's not clear when. In July 1493, the massive *Liber chronicarum,* a copiously illustrated world history also called the *Nürnberg Chronicles* that was one of the great books of the Renaissance, was published in Behaim's hometown after five years of preparation. Compiled by Jerome Münzer's fellow physician and humanist scholar Hartmann Schedel while Behaim was back in the city, it claimed that João II dispatched "certain galleys" around 1483 down the coast of "Ethiopia"; Behaim was captain of one vessel while Diego Cão ("Jacobus Canus") commanded the other. The text described them observing longitude and latitude according to the Ptolemaic scheme and asserted that they crossed the equator, discovering lands that had been searched for in vain by the Genoese. If Behaim actually made a voyage with Cão, it was unlikely he was given command of a vessel. Behaim also had to have been back in Portugal in order to be made a knight of the Order of Christ by João II on February 18, 1485. It's more likely he sailed on a 1485–86 voyage by Cão in association with João Afonso de Aveiro, as part of the experiments to solve the sun-sight problem.

Behaim would have been in Lisbon, active as an esteemed member of a royal junta on navigation, at the very time Columbus was there, trying to advance his proposal for a westward voyage to the Indies. The Spanish chronicler Antonio Herrera y Tordesillas asserted that Behaim was a friend of Columbus and shared his views on exploration opportunities. Indeed, they must have known each other in Portugal, as Columbus strove to work his own courtly connections through his wife's family to advance his voyage plan.

One version of the Columbus story holds that four members of the sun-sight junta were tasked to hearing his voyage proposal. Behaim's name was conspicuously absent from this subcommittee, and he could well have been excused from hearing out Columbus because he lacked impartiality. In any event, Columbus's voyage plan was soundly rejected, and he left Portugal for Spain, fleeing João II's ruthless response to the Braganza conspiracy. Behaim then sailed to West Africa on the 1485–86 voyage to conduct sun-sight experiments. It was the apparent end of the relationship between these two ambitious men.

The biographies of Behaim and Columbus were remarkably similar: Both were foreigners who came to Portugal through mercantile activity involving textiles and sugar that was based on sea trade; both were familiar with the Atlantic islands; both ended up marrying daughters of a prominent figure in a Portuguese Atlantic colony; both claimed expertise in navigation; and both were interested in a westward voyage to Asia based on the Toscanelli scheme.

Of the two, Behaim was far better positioned to make the desired westward voyage and inadvertently discover the New World in the process. He was the younger man, well connected at the Portuguese court when there was a strong commitment to exploration, and he boasted a superior pedigree in astronomy and navigation. Through Huerter, Behaim had access to a departure point, the Azores, much closer to the anticipated landfalls than any other Portuguese locale or Spanish possession. In 1486, with Columbus an impoverished guest of the Franciscans of La Rábida—and with John Cabot still in Venice, many miles and career changes removed from making his own westward stab—the opportunity for Behaim to make that voyage arose.

THIRTEEN

ACCORDING TO THE sixteenth-century Portuguese chronicler João de Barros, one of the Portuguese junta members who had dismissed Columbus's voyage proposal soon had a change of heart. The bishop of Ceuta now argued for such a westward probe by João II. A naturalized Fleming named Fernâo Dulmo (possibly Ferdinand Van Olm, or Olmen, by birth) from the Azorean island of Terceira was awarded a royal patent for a voyage of discovery on March 3, 1486. Thus was born one of the most intriguing exploration initiatives of Columbus's and Cabot's era, a shadowy precursor of both men's efforts to reach the Indies. And while Terceira occupied less than 150 square miles of the Atlantic Ocean, it teemed with characters who proved central to the quest to find a westward route to Asia. The cast was bound together not only by the geography of that tiny landfall but by intertwining kinships and links to Portugal's royal family.

Dulmo held the captaincy of the district of Quatro Ribeiras on Terceira. His 1486 voyage patent spoke of a familiar Terceiran desire for acquiring greater slabs of real estate. Terceira had been awarded back in 1450 to a Fleming named Jacome de Bruges and was governed by his lieutenant, Diogo de Teive, who allegedly struck out in search of new lands and found the Grand Banks in 1452. In 1474, Teive's son, Joam, a resident of Terceira, was awarded a patent with Fernão Tellez that granted them the captaincies of any islands they might find, up to and including the Seven

Cities. They presumably returned without result, and now it was Dulmo's turn to try. His voyage was supposed to reach the Isle of Seven Cities (*ilha das sete cidades*). The objectives beyond it were described only as "the grand island or islands or main- land." Dulmo agreed to make the discovery voyage at "his own costs and expenses," as royal spending was focused on the southerly push down the West African coast.

Dulmo surely never sailed under the initial patent, as four months later a new plan emerged. On July 12, Dulmo formed a partnership with Afonso do Estreito, a resident of Funchal on Madeira, to exploit together the patent rights, with Estreito putting up the money. On July 24, the king issued a new patent for a two-ship voy- age by the pair. This new patent also mentioned an unnamed *cavaleiro alemam*, or German knight. It is impossible to come up with any logical candidate other than Martin Behaim, who had been knighted by João II about eighteen months earlier.

When Dulmo secured his exploration patent, Behaim would have just returned from the 1485–86 voyage to the Guinea coast as part of his sun-sight duties, with either Diego Cão or João Afonso de Aveiro. He also entered the picture only when the Dulmo venture included Afonso do Estreito, so Behaim may have been respon- sible for attracting the Madeiran's participation—and money. Madeira was a major production center for sugar and wine, and merchants from the Burgundian Nether- lands, including Behaim's father-in-law, Huerter, held a leading role in the trade. We know that Behaim represented Huerter in business activities, including sugar deals, and that Behaim's duties took him to Madeira.

Behaim would have provided Dulmo and Estreito with a chart based on the lost Toscanelli original. The patent held the unnamed German in such esteem and so independent of the command of either voyage partner that it granted him the right to choose the vessel on which he would sail. The arrangement suggests that Behaim was attached to the voyage at the pleasure of João II himself.

The expedition was to depart Terceira by March 1, 1487. Behaim was superbly positioned to discover the New World, even if that wasn't what he had in mind. In Terceira, he had a departure point 1,000 nautical miles west of Palos, from which Columbus would sail in 1492; some 2,200 nautical miles due west was the entrance to Chesapeake Bay, but only 1,000 nautical miles to the west-northwest was the Tongue of the Grand Banks. Yet the whole expedition was brought to a halt by care- less royal favors.

Dulmo was called away to Lisbon in the very spring the expedition was sup- posed to sail, in an effort to settle rival claims of captaincies that were confounding settlement of Terceira. Two other captaincies had been granted in 1474, which over- lapped with Dulmo's older one for Quatro Ribeiras. One of them, for Angra, had been assigned to João Vaz Corte-Real; the other one, for Praia, had gone to Antao Martins (also known as Alvaro Martins Homem). The late sixteenth-century Por- tuguese chronicler Gaspar Frutuoso would assert that around 1472 to 1474, Corte- Real and Martins had made a voyage from the Azores to the northwest and discovered Terra do Bacalhau, the "codfish land," in return for which they were awarded the captaincies in Terceira, but nowhere in the awards are discoveries mentioned. Frutuoso's account nevertheless inspired dubious claims that Corte-Real and Martins had discovered Newfoundland in the early 1470s.

Because of the captaincies dispute, the Dulmo-Estreito expedition never seems to have sailed. But through the star-crossed 1486 patent, Martin Behaim had tipped his hand to his interest in striking out westward as an explorer, with the same objectives as Columbus, six years before the Genoese managed to clear harbor on behalf of Spain.

The terms of the Dulmo-Estreito patent were so close in several aspects to the capitulation Columbus received from Fernando and Isabel in 1492 that more than coincidence must have been at play. Did connections back in Portugal allow Columbus to apprise himself of the 1486 Dulmo-Estreito patent and use it as the model for his 1492 Spanish capitulation? Or was the Dulmo-Estreito patent based on a rejected proposal Columbus had made to João II around 1484?

What has entirely escaped notice is how the patent John Cabot and his sons would secure from Henry VII in 1496 so closely mirrored the details of both the 1492 Columbus capitulations and the 1486 Dulmo-Estreito patent that included mention of a German knight presumed to be Martin Behaim. No less curious was how several Terceirans connected to the interminable captaincies dispute took to seeking Asia by sailing west after the results of John Cabot's successful 1497 voyage were known. Among them were two sons of João Vaz Corte-Real, Gaspar and Miguel, who were linked to Behaim through marriages to offspring of Joss van Huerter.

The cat's cradle of relationships Behaim enjoyed on little Terceira was anything but trivial where royal favor and exploration were concerned. João Vaz Corte-Real's disputed captaincy of Angra had been assigned to him by the widow of the late king Afonso V's brother, Fernão, Duke of Viseu; Corte-Real had served Fernão as *porteiro mor*, or high bailiff. Huerter's own connections were made clear enough by the sumptuous home he maintained in Lisbon on royal property. As for kinship bonds, Huerter's son and heir, Joss the younger, was the husband of João Vaz Corte-Real's daughter, Izabel. Huerter's daughter, Joana, was married to Behaim. Thus Martin Behaim and Gaspar and Miguel Corte-Real (brothers of Izabel) were kin through the Huerters.

Terceira's connections to westward exploration did not end with Behaim and the Corte-Reals. Two other Terceirans would secure a Portuguese voyage privilege following the news of Cabot's success for England. One of them, Pero de Barcelos, happened to become entrapped in the legal quagmire of local captaincies. The other, his partner João Fernandes, would join with Bristol merchants in the wake of Cabot's voyages to secure a letters patent of exploration from Henry VII in direct rivalry with the Portugal efforts of the Corte-Reals. Behaim's exploration ambitions, the Dulmo-Estreito patent of 1486, and the intrigues of property rights on little Terceira were anything but a dead end in North America's discovery.

IN 1489, BEHAIM CAME into a considerable inheritance from his mother and returned to Nürnberg around 1490 to settle the estate, leaving behind on Terceira his wife, Joss van Huerter's daughter Joana, and a new son, Martin III. Flush with the inheritance, Behaim indulged in several leisurely years in his hometown.

Behaim had returned to Nürnberg as Schedel was completing the *Liber chronicarum* and plainly provided the information about his supposed 1483 voyage with Diego Cão. Behaim knew Jerome Münzer well, and Münzer too is thought to have been involved in the *Liber chronicarum;* a map of northern Europe, and the accompanying text, appears to have been Münzer's handiwork. Münzer also became allied with an ambitious local project led by Behaim to create the world's earliest surviving terrestrial globe. Its implications for exploration, for Behaim, even for John Cabot, were profound.

There were likely a few other globes around this time, but Behaim's is the only one that survives. Toscanelli in his 1474 letter had advised that a globe was the best way for the King of Portugal to envision the advantage of sailing west to the Indies. Although the letter implied the existence of a such a globe, it didn't say Toscanelli actually possessed one: "Therefore, although I know that the world, as it is, could be shown to him with the sphere in hand, and he could be made to see it; nevertheless, I have decided to show the said route by a map similar to those which are made for navigation." Las Casas asserted Columbus had a globe, made by his brother Bartolomé. But the Las Casas abstract of the 1492 voyage journal indicates that Columbus at that time did not have one, rather that he had seen examples. The abstract quoted Columbus on October 24, 1492, as he departed Española for Cuba: "On the globes which I have seen and on the world maps Cipangu is in this area."

Apart from emphasizing the extreme rarity of globes in the late fifteenth century, Behaim's globe project also emphasized that they were a considerable technical achievement. The *Erdapfel* ("earth apple") was sponsored by five leading Nürnberg families, including the Behaims. Martin Behaim was the project's prime mover and may have conceived of it as a prop to support a new westward voyage—to realize the globe that Toscanelli said would best show the advantage of sailing west. A team of artisans was enlisted to construct it, and Behaim's paid contributions were limited to a world map used as a guide.

The *Erdapfel* was more than a map in three dimensions; it featured extensive blocks of text relating knowledge of the world from various sources, including Behaim. The inscriptions, for example, stated that Behaim had made his Guinea voyage in 1486. But the cartographic details were frozen in the mid-1480s: there was no recognition of Bartolomeu Días's 1487 rounding of Africa's Cape of Good Hope. Errors in the configuration of the West African coast cast some doubt on how closely Behaim had been involved with making actual experimental celestial observations. And if Dulmo and Estreito ever did get away from Terceira with Behaim, nothing they found to the west informed the innocent vision of the Nürnberg *Erdapfel*.

Still, with its depiction of Antilla, Cipango, and a generous scattering of islands along the coast of the Indies, the globe encapsulated the Toscanelli vision that had inspired Columbus as well as Behaim in the 1480s. Although it also drew on other sources, it may be the closest thing to a surviving version of the lost Toscanelli concept. The map Behaim provided (which no longer exists, but in the early nineteenth century was known to consist of two sheets of vellum) could well have dated from the Dulmo-Estreito enterprise.

When the globe was completed, Behaim was thirty-three years old, comfortable in his inheritance. A letter from his brother Wolff, then based in Lyon, to their cousin Michael in Nürnberg on December 5, 1492, captured concerns that Martin was doing little more than putter in Michael's garden while the rest of the family industriously pursued mercantile opportunities. "I am sorry to hear that my brother Martin is still with you, leading such a singular life," Wolff bluntly apologized. "I wish we were entirely rid of him."

Putting him on a ship and pointing him at an empty ocean might have seemed the best solution. Martin Behaim's life otherwise had expended all forward momentum. The six-year head start he had once enjoyed on Columbus in stumbling on the New World had vanished. On the day Wolff Behaim wrote their cousin Michael, Martin Behaim's old friend Columbus was sailing east from Cuba on the *Santa María* and sighting Española for the first time. And in Valencia, Cabot was emerging from the entrepreneurial froth of the Mediterranean, awaiting word from the court of Fernando at Barcelona on whether his harbor scheme would move forward.

Behaim's listlessness lasted another seven months. The first edition of the *Liber chronicarum* was published on July 12, 1493. Two days later, Behaim's friend Jerome Münzer wrote a letter to Portugal's João II that promised to pry Behaim out of his cousin's garden, return him to the forefront of exploration, and in the process shift the search for a profitable new ocean route to Asia into northern waters. It was through this enigmatic plan that John Cabot's voyages for England and his discovery of North America evidently found momentum of their own.

COMPOSED AS A RECOMMENDATION from Maximilian I, the July 14, 1493, letter by Jerome Münzer advised the Portuguese king to assign Martin Behaim to a discovery voyage as a special envoy of the German monarch. Although the letter was maddeningly vague on practical details, it nevertheless made clear that Münzer and Behaim were thinking of an ocean passage far to the north of the route Columbus had just used. But the letter gives no indication that Münzer and Behaim were aware that Columbus had embarked on his voyage of discovery in August 1492, let alone that he had returned in triumph in March 1493. No mention is made of Co-lumbus at all, which suggests that the two Nürnbergers were hopelessly in the dark four months after Columbus had reappeared in Europe.

The duo—and Maximilian I—did seem on first glance regrettably if perplex-ingly obtuse, as Columbus's letter describing his discoveries had been published in April and copies of it had spread rapidly in northern Italy. A version would not be published in Maximilian's realm until October 1493, at Basel, but by July, Spanish and Portuguese diplomats and the Vatican were well into the negotiations for the treaty that purported to divide the world between them along a meridian west of the Cape Verdes. Columbus moreover had debriefed João II and other Portuguese court figures within days of his return; there were such close links between Portugal and the realm of Maximilian I, particularly through the Burgundian Netherlands, that it is surprising word of the discovery had not filtered back to the German court or to a center of humanist thought like Nürnberg by the time Münzer composed his letter.

Although it is possible that Münzer, Behaim, and Maximilian I truly were ig-norant of Columbus's achievement, Münzer instead may have chosen to ignore it in his letter, just as he declined to address the Venetian monopoly on trade through the Levant or the promise of a round-Africa route raised by the 1487–88 Días voy-age. The letter was meant only to serve as a diplomatic preamble to Behaim's full presentation to João II of the voyage's specifics.

Münzer's letter never spelled out *exactly* what the duo were proposing. It in-stead mainly flattered João II and assured him of his ability to execute the plan Be-haim would present. "You also have in abundance the resources and wealth and you have the very knowledgeable sailors who also desire to win immortality and glory. O what glory you will obtain if you [show] that the habitable East was known to your West! And also what profits the trade will give you." When the envisioned voyage was achieved, Münzer promised that João II and his knights would be "celebrated forever."

The letter did overwhelmingly imply that Behaim was going to encourage João II to establish a sea route to Asia in northern waters, for its language and perspective were entirely aligned with higher latitudes. Münzer wrote cryptically: "Already you are praised as a grand prince, [by] Germans, Italians, Ruthenians, Poles, and Scyth-ians, who live beneath the arid star of the Arctic pole, as well as [by] the grand duke of Moscow." Münzer then remarked how it had not been more than a few years since, beneath this star, the grand duke had discovered the great island Grulanda, three hundred leagues long, on which there was a large colony under his rule.

The identity of Grulanda has long been a puzzle. Münzer may have recognized an early Russian discovery of Spitsbergen (Svalbard) or Novaya Zemlya; in either case, it was a high-latitude landmass. This mention probably was a preamble to a point Behaim planned to make at court: Russian experience showed that a royal trading colony along the lines of Portugal's São Jorge de Mina or Columbus's Española base could be established successfully in northern latitudes on the Asian side of the crossing.

Münzer went on to praise the skills of mariners of the Azores who "fear neither the cold nor the calms, as they navigate toward the shore of the East with moderate temperatures of air and sea." He also said that the voyage's destination was Cathay, which was considered to be a northern province of the empire of the Great Khan. Münzer's preamble pointed at a voyage proposal by Behaim for northern waters, a realm Columbus steadfastly shunned.

Columbus had a pronounced aversion to seas not much farther north than what most people would consider pleasantly temperate, even subtropical. The Las Casas abstract of the 1492 voyage contained numerous references to "cold" conditions by Columbus, none of them inspiring. Foremost was Columbus's strange misadventure with the allegedly faulty quadrant, in which he insisted for several days on the coast of Cuba in November 1492 that he was at latitude 42° north when he was actually at 22° north. Columbus was persuaded of his northerly location "by the sea which has a different character from the way it has been hitherto, and yesterday when I was going NW I found that it was cold."

In the journal abstract entry for November 12, 1492, when Columbus was still on the north coast of Cuba, Las Casas wrote how "[Columbus] also says earlier that it was somewhat cold and that for this reason it would not be a good idea to sail north to discover in winter." On January 21, 1493, only five days after leaving Española on the voyage home, Columbus "found the winds colder and thought, he says, that he would find them colder by the day the further north he went, and also because the nights were longer because of the shape of the Earth."

Columbus was so averse to higher-latitude sailing that he was squandering the chance to discover continental North America, which had been achingly close at hand on the first voyage. One has to wonder how much experience he had of waters above mainland Portugal and if a single voyage to England around 1477 had caused this son of the sun-dappled Mediterranean to swear off such passage making in the future.

A quick glance at the *Erdapfel* showed that Cathay's great city of Quinsay was thought to be around 45° north. This was the city Columbus had argued he was near during the bizarre quadrant malfunction episode in November 1492. Marco Polo had promised it featured a "port on the sea-coast celebrated for the resort of shipping, loaded with merchandise." Reaching Quinsay by an even moderately more northern route than the subtropical one Columbus clung to would have been a logical goal of Münzer and Behaim.

And the *Erdapfel* would have demonstrated clearly the advantages of a northern sea passage. Not only did the globe show that a major destination like Quinsay was only a few degrees of latitude higher than the Azores; it showed in a way anyone could grasp how a westward route closer to the top of the world would be much quicker than the one Columbus had employed near the equator—provided Columbus had even reached the Indies.

Because lines of longitude become more closely spaced as they move away from the equator and converge at the poles, sailing halfway around the world requires a vessel to cover a much shorter physical distance at higher latitudes. A map drawn on a sphere makes this obvious in a way that a flat, two-dimensional chart, with its problems of projection, generally does not. And like Columbus, Behaim and Münzer thought the world was much smaller than it actually is. The two Nürnbergers also proposed there was far less sea than land. Münzer's letter echoed Pliny in stating that six-sevenths of Earth's surface was land.

Münzer was advocating a northern route across the Ocean Sea when he assured the king that a voyage to Cathay could be accomplished in only a few days. Not even Columbus had been that optimistic; he had expected to take about a week to reach Antilla from the Canaries before pushing on to Cipango and finally the Asian mainland.

Portuguese chronicler João de Barros would write that Behaim made a globe for João II. If he did, it no longer exists, but Behaim would have brought a smaller, less lavish version of the *Erdapfel* to Lisbon in 1493, so that he could show João II the wisdom of his voyage strategy in three dimensions. Behaim's work seems to have inspired a copy, the so-called Laon globe, an inscribed metal sphere less than seven inches in diameter discovered in 1860 in a shop in Laon, France. Possibly Portuguese in origin or inspiration, it is thought to have been part of an astronomical clock.

Given Münzer's praise of the mariners of the Azores in the letter to João II and the kinship ties between Behaim and the Corte-Reals of Terceira through Huerter, the Corte-Reals may well have been enlisted in the scheme. A prime candidate for helping advance Behaim's cause at court was Vasqueanes, the elder brother of Gaspar and Miguel. Vasqueanes was born in mainland Portugal, possibly in Lisbon or Tavira. Despite inheriting João Vaz's Terceiran captaincy in 1497, he would never visit the Azores, leaving it to Gaspar to administer his disputed holding. Ensconced in Lisbon, Vasqueanes would serve as *vedor*, or intendant (an administrative official), to João II's successor, Manoel I, and would also help fund his brothers' explorations. As no surviving material explains whom Behaim and Münzer thought would actually put to sea for Portugal, the Corte-Reals may have been expected to secure the royal patent and command the expedition on which Behaim imagined himself being assigned as an envoy of Maximilian.

But all the preparation by Behaim and Münzer—the presentation, the endorsement of Maximilian I, the entire *Erdapfel* project—was for naught. The window of opportunity had firmly closed in Portugal. João II's ambitions for reaching the Orient by any direction had waned. There had been no follow-up voyage to the one by

Días in 1487–88 that showed Africa could be rounded to the south. The king may have quietly dispatched a few ships to investigate what Columbus had found, but by the time Behaim made his presentation around the autumn of 1493, the treaty being negotiated with Spain was going to divide the world from pole to pole. Based on what the *Erdapfel* itself contended about the nature of the world, Behaim would only end up discovering a route to lands that belonged to Fernando and Isabel. After the fiasco of the Dulmo-Estreito enterprise, there would be no second chance for Behaim in João II's realm. And the Corte-Reals would have to wait for a new king of Portugal, and word of Cabot's stunning success for England, for the opportunity to mount their own explorations.

About a year after Behaim made his pitch to the Portuguese king, Dr. Münzer rode into Seville. The quest to prove a northerly sea passage to Asia that would rival the more tropical one pursued by Columbus was very much alive.

FOURTEEN

FERNANDO AND ISABEL were disturbed by reports of the many failings of Columbus's efforts emerging from La Isabella in 1494. True, there was gold at Española, as Columbus had promised—Antonio de Torres brought home thirty thousand pesos' worth in the February 1494 flotilla. Columbus also pursued stories of rich mines he called Las Minas de San Cristóbal in the southern part of the island. Their location eluded the Spanish. Gold was gathered from the Arawaks and otherwise was alluvial, washed out of river sands and the earth. There was enough to make some men rich but not to sustain many years of commercial production. And despite reports of precious commodities, such as pepper, ginger, sandalwood, and cinnamon, no riches of the Indies as Columbus had itemized existed, save a dyewood on the south side of Española.

Problems had been mounting before the Torres flotilla had left for Spain in February. Preliminary news carried home persuaded the monarchs to issue a mandate they sent back with the four-ship relief flotilla commanded by Torres in August 1494, beseeching settlers to obey Columbus: "[W]e order all of you to carry out, execute [his orders], and cooperate with him, doing and carrying out all that he orders you to do on our behalf. Do this as if we commanded it in person, under pain of whatever penalties he imposes or orders imposed in our name."

The colony was a disaster. Settlers were more interested in prospecting for gold (or wresting it from the Arawaks) than in hoeing fields and planting crops. Columbus himself had wasted little time in turning to seeking gold, disappearing on a twenty-nine-day expedition into the Española interior after the Torres flotilla left in February 1494. A fortified post called Santo Tomás was built in the mountainous gold region of Cibao, according to Michele da Cuneo, who was along on the expedition. It was one of a series of fortified posts built in a chain across the island to enforce the Spanish rule of law. But Columbus's own men posed disciplinary headaches. He was unable to prevent some of his party from making private trades for gold: "[T]here were other deals, secretly made, against our rule and statute, for the value of about 1,000 castellanos," Cuneo related. "As you know, the devil causes one to do ill, then lets it be discovered; also, as long as Spain is Spain, there will be no shortage of traitors. One man betrayed another until they were all discovered, and those found guilty were well flogged, and this one had his ears cut off and that one his nose, such that it was a pity to see."

Columbus's brutal justice could not rein in the avarice or the excesses it encouraged even when the activities were sanctioned. And when he returned from his expedition, he found efforts to grow European crops failing, despite the hyperbole of the early reports of La Isabella's fecund soil. The Arawaks were well provided by their own staple crop of maize (corn); the Europeans were in danger of starving to death.

When the first council of La Isabella met on April 24, 1494, the young colony was facing ruin because of crop failure. Columbus refused to release food reserves stored in a royal warehouse. Some of the colonists moved farther away from town; some simply joined the Arawaks. Columbus meanwhile pursued a policy of demanding that the Arawaks pay regular taxes or tribute in gold. Every native over the age of fourteen in the presumed gold-producing regions was expected to provide a hawk's-bell full of gold every three months. Hawk's bells (which were tied to the legs of tamed hawks by the Spanish) had been introduced to the Arawaks as trade trinkets. Now their volume measure was a tool of servitude. The native reaction was predictable; having already obliterated La Navidad, they rose up against these grasping newcomers who were determined to become their feudal overlords.

As news of the reality of the settlement made its way across the ocean, Columbus's Indies scheme began to lose traction with important and influential figures back in Spain. At the same time, Cabot's bridge project was close behind it in sliding into disgrace.

SOMETHING HAD GONE seriously awry with Cabot's bridge project—so awry that Seville's ruling council of nobles had to meet on December 24, 1494, to decide how to proceed.

The minutes recorded how the council "have been entrusted to give, and have given to Johan Caboto, Venetian, fifty Spanish doubloons from the city, plus an additional three reales for each day for five months that he was in the city, so that an order should be given to build the bridge on this river with bricks." The work, however, "has not been carried out."

The council was informed on its dealings to date with Cabot by an alderman, Lorenzo Zomeno, using a report from Luis Méndez Portocarrero, who was an intriguing link to Columbus's world in Seville's dealings with Cabot. The aristocratic Portocarrero family had a lengthy history in Seville, and the report's author probably was Luis Méndez de Haro y Sotomayor, a son-in-law of Pedro Portocarrero. Virtually nothing is known about this son-in-law, but Pedro Portocarrero was a former governor of Seville who held the hereditary lordship of Moguer, one of the key maritime communities around Palos that had been involved in mounting the first Columbus voyage. Don Pedro's name surfaced in association with goods for a relief flotilla that departed Seville for Columbus at La Isabella around mid-October 1494, when Cabot was supposed to be building the bridge.

Also participating in the council meeting was one Don Alonsó de Guzmán, identified as the *mayor* of Seville. This must have been thirty-year-old Juan Alonsó Pérez de Guzmán y Afán de Ribera. A noble of tremendous stature in Spain, Juan Alonsó was Lord of Sanlúcar, Count of Niebla, third Duke of Medina-Sidonia, Marquis of Gibraltar as well as Cazaza, and commander of Castile's coastal defenses. On May 2, 1493, Fernando and Isabel wrote Guzmán, thanking him for passing along word that he understood the Portuguese were planning to send ships west to investigate Columbus's discoveries.

Luis Méndez Portocarrero's report stated: "[I]t was required and is required that no more money must be given to [Cabot]." Alternately, Fernando and Isabel should be approached, "asking that they give permission for that which has been agreed to be carried out." The council evidently thought the monarchs should have the option of continuing to employ Cabot, at their expense. Portocarrero's instructions suggested that the bridge project, and Cabot, had been of royal interest from the beginning. The floating bridge Cabot was supposed to replace spanned the Guadalquivir right outside the gates of the Alcazar, home to the new royal apartments that Jerome Münzer noticed being fashioned for the royal family. Fernando quite possibly had convinced the Sevillans to pay for a Cabot marine infrastructure project, having failed to persuade the Valencians to fund Cabot's harbor plan in 1493.

Portocarrero also advised that the council notify Don Juan de Silva, Count of Cifuentes, who served as the royal judge of Seville from 1482 to 1500. The count coincidentally had issued safe-conduct passes to Jerome Münzer and his party for their further travels in Castile when they arrived in Seville that November. Two councilors, Fernando Ruiz Cabeza de Vaca and Lope de Agreda, joined Alonsó de Guzmán in agreeing with and confirming Portocarrero's instructions. Lorenzo Zomeno further agreed with Portocarrero's guidance: The Count of Cifuentes should be "apprised of this [the situation with Cabot] so that [the count] negotiates in order that the city might not be caused loss." The city's civic leaders apparently were looking to this judicially powerful count from Toledo to get their money back from Cabot. Of all the creditors Cabot's various misadventures had harvested, this group was easily the most daunting.

All in attendance voted that Lope de Agreda "should go speak with the Count." But there was one dissenting voice, that of the absent councilor Fernando d'Esquivel—another name linked to Columbus. His signature is found on a 1489 certification of a copy of the decree appointing Alfonso Enríquez the admiral of Castile; Columbus studied this admiralty award in arguing for his own hereditary rights as Admiral of the Ocean Sea. A possible relative was Juan de Esquival, who probably was born in Seville around 1480 and sailed with Columbus on the second voyage. If Cabot was on that voyage, he may well have known Juan de Esquival, a rising star in the Columbus firmament who participated in the subjugation of Española's rebellious natives and in 1509 founded Sevilla Nueva (New Seville) on the north coast of Jamaica as the island's first governor.

Fernando d'Esquivel's response to Cabot's nonperformance on the bridge project was the harshest of all. Unable to attend the meeting, he had provided a statement that made clear his disgust, saying "he had always thought that the Venetian should be paid that which he was owed and that he should be dismissed from the city, and that the bridge should not be built; this is what he asks for and pleads for it by testimonial."

Nothing survives to tell us if the count was ever approached or if the council instead took Fernando d'Esquivel's advice and ran Cabot out of town without bothering to consult the judge. But Cabot may not even have been in Seville when the council convened to decide what to do about their nonexistent new bridge and the exasperating Venetian they had paid to design and build it.

WHO KNOWS WHAT CABOT did with the bridge money—perhaps he simply absconded with it, his life having turned into an ever-escalating Ponzi scheme: gaming new creditors to satisfy the restitution of old ones. But he had likely spied his next opportunity before squandering or abandoning the latest one, pocketing money from a phantom bridge as he was captivated by the possibilities of a fresh scheme beyond the limits of ports and their infrastructure.

There was a certain grandiosity emerging in Cabot's methods, an inclination to reach for initiatives with a manner that bordered on bald nerve, given the increasing gap between what he proposed or agreed to do and what he actually achieved. With no known track record in Spain as a productive marine civil engineer, Cabot was about to reinvent himself as an explorer—despite no known experience as a navigator or commander of ocean voyages.

The times, however, promised opportunities at scales previously known only to conquering monarchs, with seemingly little or no previous experience required. A single inspired man could propose and pursue objectives that were transformative on a global scale. Columbus was a shining example of what ambition (along with the right connections) could achieve in a largely feudal world. Cabot may have abandoned the bridge—an assignment that he would have been delighted to secure only a few months earlier—because it was beyond his abilities actually to execute (or because the Guadalquivir proved to be much more difficult to span with a fixed link than had been thought) but also because something so much larger loomed before him. He was now after a prize that with the same application of time and energy as the bridge could yield a lifetime of prosperity and secure the futures of his three sons as well. A few months of sailing with the right commission could change everything. And men like Columbus and Cabot did not have to be grizzled, veteran mariners to become explorers. They just had to hire the right people to manage the ship or fleet under their command.

A legitimate sense of opportunity for Cabot must have emerged from what had previously been envy. Cabot's Valencia scheme had failed just as Columbus had returned in triumph from his first voyage. Indeed, Cabot had some reason to blame Columbus for his harbor project's failure. Had Columbus not come along with his stunning claim of an Indies landfall, Fernando might have been inclined to pour some of the royal treasury into the Valencia project rather than dedicate funds to the Española trading center.

If Cabot did not find a place in the infrastructure build-out of the Indies project in 1493 with an engineering role in the second voyage, then he had unquestionably secured it by June 1494 with the Seville bridge job. But even as Cabot's project collapsed so ignominiously, Columbus's enterprise was attracting alarming dissension. Opportunities for others in Spain to horn in on his monopoly loomed—provided the object of the monopoly itself didn't become devalued to the point of disinterest.

BY LATE 1494, Seville was becoming disenchanted with the Indies project, at least as it was being conducted by Columbus. A Sevillan named Dr. Francisco de Cisneros wrote a petition to the king and queen, rejecting the idea that Columbus's discoveries were in the Indies and arguing they were instead the fabled Hesperides in *el mar oçeano atlántico ethiopico*. He called for a new Spanish expedition toward the Indies free of the authority of Columbus. The date of the petition is unknown: September 1497 has been proposed, but it may have dated to the time Cabot was in Seville, so the Venetian could have been aware of Cisneros's proposal. But the disquiet was much broader than that.

The papal legate Bernard Buyl, who had been assigned to Columbus's second voyage by a bull in June 1493, was back in Seville in the latter part of November 1494—a letter by the monarchs at Madrid on December 3 mentioned his return.

Columbus quite rightly feared what Buyl might say about him once back in Spain. Buyl was scathing in his criticism of the affairs of Española and the administrative mismanagement of Columbus. Momentum was building toward a major change in the crown's policy where Columbus's exclusive rights were concerned.

It was amid this ferment of disquiet that John Cabot failed to perform the work for which he had been paid on the fixed bridge. It was also precisely when the wandering German humanist Jerome Münzer passed through Seville en route to Portugal before turning back into Spain in early 1495, along the way amassing a series of encounters with key figures in the Indies scheme that seems almost divinely blessed in its good fortune and incalculably valuable to anyone considering a westward voyage of their own.

MÜNZER POSSESSED AN UNCANNY ability to turn up in the company of an improbable array of figures linked to Columbus's activities. He had already devoted a week of his journey to Seville, where the number of significant people he could have met was near infinite. Five days after departing Seville, he was at the royal palace at Évora, enjoying an extended period of hospitality from João II.

The Portuguese king was so graciously accommodating that he knighted Münzer's traveling companion Anton Hewart of Augsburg. Over the course of ten days at the palace, Münzer enjoyed his four dinners with João II. The knot of relationships by then was Gordian in its firmness. The previous year, Münzer had written the letter for Martin Behaim, conveying Maximilian I's recommendation to João II that Behaim be tasked to a westward Portuguese voyage of discovery aimed at Cathay. João II already had been served by Behaim on the sun-sight committee; Behaim in turn had been favored by João II in the Dulmo-Estreito voyage patent. Columbus too had pitched João II on the westward voyage plan, and when he actually completed it for Fernando and Isabel, he ended up debriefing João II first when he made landfall in Portugal on his return.

Münzer and João II certainly had much to discuss of joint fascination in their dinners together, up to and including Columbus, Behaim, and Tordesillas, but Münzer divulged no details. The king, he allowed, "spoke with me of diverse things, and showed himself very cultivated." He otherwise noted the king's general desire to learn from visitors more of "the art of war, of navigation, or other sciences."

From Évora and his dinners with the king Münzer headed for Lisbon, some sixty miles west, where he spent three days at the home of Behaim's father-in-law, Joss van Huerter. ("We arranged lodgings in a very grand and very beautiful royal residence, in the home of the father-in-law of the lord Martin Behaim, the lord Judocus de Hurder, of Bruges, nobleman and captain of the islands of Faial and Pico. . . . This home was found in a very grand place, in a very vast flat space, near the monastery of St. Dominic. We were treated there excellently.") If Behaim was there as well, the often-taciturn Münzer didn't mention it. But the lodging arrangement showed that Behaim and Münzer remained closely allied.

From Lisbon, Münzer and his companions wended through Portugal and back into Spain, making for Madrid, where the Spanish court was then based. They arrived on January 17, 1495, and remained for eight days. Münzer enjoyed several incredibly fortuitous meetings, above and beyond his audience with Fernando and Isabel on January 24, at which he expressed his delight and astonishment at having encountered in Seville some baptized natives Columbus had brought from the Indies. Seville, he told the monarchs, "presented to our eyes an extraordinary spectacle. We saw there men of a new species, unknown in our world, arrived from the islands of the Indies that were discovered on your command." Later in the same address, Münzer mentioned "the unknown peoples of the Indies, that you have shown into the unity of our faith." The encounter with baptized natives strongly suggests that Münzer had met in Seville the archdeacon and bishop Juan Rodríguez de Fonseca, who was also chief administrator of the Indies venture.

"There was at Madrid a very wise poet, Pietro Martire of Milan," Münzer further noted in his journal. This poet educated many young and prominent nobles, Münzer explained, "and he invited me to one of his lessons." Münzer thus met Pietro Martire d'Anghiera, who knew Columbus personally and had only recently set his mind to producing his history of Columbus's exploits. "I have begun to write a work concerning this great discovery," he had confided in a letter to Giovanni Borromeo of Milan on October 20, 1494.

Martire remained in touch with the explorer while cultivating other sources on his voyages and continued to write historically crucial letters reporting on what had been discovered on the first and second voyages as he composed his history. The letters were intensely detailed and demonstrated superb (if not always reliable) access to information. The latest one had been written to his friend Polonius Laetus on January 10, only five days before Münzer arrived in Madrid. It conveyed a considerable amount about Española, including its supposed latitude and longitude.

As an aspiring geographer with his own ideas about how to reach the Indies, Münzer would have been pleased to engage Martire in conversation about Columbus's finds and the state of his enterprise. Martire could be overly generous: He allowed (to his regret) Angelo Trevisan, secretary to the Venetian envoy Domenico Pisani during the latter's embassy to Spain in 1501, to copy part of his treatise on Columbus's voyages, which ended up being published in Venice before Martire could bring out his own work. Whether Münzer was able to read any of the Martire manuscript is something we will never know.

Next came his almost improbably fortunate encounter with Bernard Buyl. Münzer had turned up in Seville too soon to meet Buyl there, but at Málaga, Münzer had visited a new monastery of the Minorite order, "at the head of which is found the Aragon brother Bernard de Boil," his account explained. "He had been sent as a true explorer to the shores of the islands of the Indies." At Madrid, in the presence of Fernando, Münzer had the astonishing luck to encounter Buyl.

Buyl was far more than a priest. He had been a warship captain for the young king Fernando, leaving his naval duties on the Mediterranean to serve as Fernando's secretary until 1481. After entering the priesthood, he had withdrawn to a Benedictine monastery near Montserrat. Buyl served Fernando as an ambassador to France for the negotiations that secured the Treaty of Barcelona in January 1493. He had then headed to Española as a legate of the pope on the second Columbus voyage.

"He was very intimate with me. . . . He spoke with me of the islands." That was all Münzer cared to say, but Buyl would have conveyed to him a far more caustic, eyewitness account of Columbus's activities than that provided by the generally enthusiastic and awestruck Martire. What a tale Buyl must have told: of Columbus's administrative incompetence, the bad behavior of the colonists of Española, the suffering and hostility of the natives, and not the least the serious doubts that Columbus's discoveries were anywhere near the actual Indies.

Münzer was returning home with the experience of his dinners with João II that surely touched at some point on Tordesillas and exploration if there was any discussion of "navigation." He had also developed an exceptional grasp of how the Spanish enterprise in the Indies was unfolding and what had actually been found. This was at the very time John Cabot had gone missing. He would not be seen again until he resurfaced at the court of Henry VII in England no later than January 1496, seeking permission to mount the voyage that Münzer and Behaim had proposed to João II.

FIFTEEN

WHEN CABOT'S bridge project collapsed in December 1494, the councilor Fernando d'Esquivel saw no reason to continue it without him. Indeed, the breakdown-prone Puente de Barca would endure until 1852. The fact that there was no urgent call to replace it with a more robust and reliable structure suggests that the councilors were responding to the reality that the trading bonanza Columbus had promised was not materializing. Friar Buyl had just returned from Española in November 1494 with his damning news, and any further investment in public works related to the Indies trade surely would have seemed like so many maravedis tossed into the Guadalquivir.

Cabot left the greater Indies enterprise less than gracefully, but he had abandoned what must have seemed like a ship that was leaking badly if not actually sinking. As Columbus struggled to keep his head above water, the Venetian marine engineer struck out for fresh opportunities even as he fled his latest troubles with powerful men. That he was able to get himself to sea with another monarch's generous blessing just eighteen months after the bridge project debacle is one of the wonders of the annals of exploration.

It seems that like some Pied Piper of oceanic opportunity, Jerome Münzer had paused in Seville long enough to capture Cabot in the eddies of his wake. Münzer had earned his medical degree in the Ligurian city of Pavia in 1479 and had traveled to Rome in 1484; presumably no language barrier separated this German

envoy from a Venetian bridge contractor who probably was born somewhere between Liguria and Naples. As the crisis with the bridge project proved, Cabot's work
associated him with some of the most powerful citizens and nobles of Seville, even
of Castile, and Münzer was accustomed to meeting with the political and social
elite during this diplomatic pilgrimage. Münzer's and Cabot's lives would have had
ample opportunity to intersect, before Cabot's own relations with Seville's elite im-
ploded in December.

And after their time in Seville in late 1494, both Münzer and Cabot turned up
in Lisbon.

ON JULY 25, 1498, Pedro de Ayala, the Spanish ambassador to the court of Scotland who had relocated to London, wrote Fernando and Isabel with news of John
Cabot's third voyage for Henry VII, which had already departed Bristol. He had
only just heard of Cabot, whom he said "has been in Seville and at Lisbon seeking
to obtain persons to aid him in this discovery."

It made sense for Cabot, in fleeing Seville—and Spain—in late 1494, to have
crossed over into Portugal, regardless of his relationship with Münzer. His travel
options otherwise were narrow. Unless he had satisfied the demands of his Venetian
creditors with misappropriated bridge funds, he could not have risked showing his
face in the Rialto plaza. And while sea lanes still would have been open, the land
route back toward Venice through northern Italy was so fraught with peril as to be
mad to consider for himself, his wife, and three sons.

France's Charles VIII had begun massing his troops at Lyon in June 1494 for
his march on Naples, determined to lay claim to the throne that in his mind became available with the death of its king, Ferdinand, that January. Once Naples was
rightfully his, the young king imagined a crusade against the Ottoman Turks to
retake Constantinople. Charles's army was through the Alps and at Asti, just outside Genoa, on September 9. A naval force had already secured Genoa as a logistics
base. For five months, Charles's army moved up and down northwestern Italy with
speed and terror: Lorenzo de Medici handed over Florence on November 25, French
forces reached Rome on December 31 (a week after the Sevillan councilors met to
decide what to do about Cabot and his wayward bridge project), and Naples was
finally entered on February 22. The glorious crusade for Constantinople was forgotten. Diplomats were hastening to shape the Holy League, a multistate alliance
determined to drive Charles out of Italy altogether.

By necessity as well as design, then, Cabot had turned west for Lisbon. Where
Columbus had once fled Portugal for Spain, Cabot now fled Spain for Portugal.

Cabot must have been in the Portuguese capital soon after Münzer, who after
his ten days at Évora was in Lisbon from November 26 to December 2 (and in
nearby Santarém on December 3 and 4). The Venetian would have needed time to
pursue voyage opportunities there and then reach England with enough time to

secure an audience with Henry VII and have his activities at court noticed by the Spanish ambassador Roderigo de Puebla in January 1496.

Cabot may not have had the opportunity, much less the means, to secure an introduction to João II in early 1495 before racing on to England; in any event, no evidence survives for such an audience with the Portuguese king. But if Ayala's intelligence was correct, Cabot had only sought "persons to aid him in discovery" in Lisbon. This suggests that he was trying to contact individuals who could be of practical assistance rather than attempting to secure royal favor. Besides, anyone from Seville with the slightest knowledge of Columbus's Indies enterprise and Tordesillas would have known that Portugal was a doubtful option as a sponsor of a westward voyage. Cabot's Lisbon sojourn instead would have entailed making contact with the Huerter-Behaim circle, with or without a personal introduction from Münzer, whom he would have so recently met in Seville between November 4 and 11. We otherwise have no idea whom he would have known in Lisbon, to welcome him and his family and aid him in his radical career change.

Cabot's apparent appropriation of Münzer's and Behaim's northern passage concept could have been a case of the Venetian becoming aware of it as it gained circulation in Seville through Münzer's appearance there. But the circumstantial evidence asks us to take seriously the likelihood of an actual relationship among Cabot, Münzer, and Behaim. Throughout the northern passage-making gambit, Münzer was a facilitator for Behaim. Cabot, as an insider of the Columbus enterprise who was again on the lam and desperate for another fresh start after his serious misadventures with leading nobles of Spain, was a suitable candidate for the role Behaim needed fulfilled in England: a partner, a front man, a Columbus doppelgänger. Behaim himself apparently had already tried and failed spectacularly to make the northern passage pitch to Henry VII himself after being rebuffed by João II.

REJECTED BY JOÃO II, Martin Behaim was not prepared to give up on his vision of a westward route to Asia's riches and leave all the glory to his old friend Columbus, who by most accounts was making a hash of profiting from the Toscanelli scheme. Behaim was back at sea before the end of 1493, departing Lisbon on a strange voyage to the Burgundian Netherlands that landed him for three months in England in early 1494—the very place John Cabot would soon turn up, trying to persuade Henry VII to sanction a westward voyage of his own in northern waters.

On March 11, 1494, Martin Behaim wrote his cousin Michael in Nürnberg, trying to explain to this long-suffering relative what had become of him since departing Nürnberg for Lisbon in the latter half of 1493. Behaim had resurfaced in the county Brabant and was probably in Antwerp. He offered a terribly confused tale of alleged diplomacy gone awry.

The letter (in German) read: "Now in this year I was again sent by the King here in Flanders, to the King's son. On this journey by sea I was captured and transferred to England and kept for three months with all my servants and money for provisions that easily came to 160 Gulden, because of the young King from England who is now with the roman King because he has a hearth and home there."

Behaim was claiming he had left Lisbon for the Burgundian Netherlands under a commission from Maximilian I ("the king here in Flanders") to confer with Philip, Archduke of Burgundy ("the King's son"), who was at Bruges. Although the purpose of the diplomatic mission wasn't explained, Behaim had already gone to Portugal, bearing the Münzer letter, as a special envoy of Maximilian, and he had long-standing family and business connections in the Burgundian Netherlands. The fact that he was captured and held against his will in England for three months was consistent with someone traveling under diplomatic credentials of Maximilian: Relations between Henry VII's England and Maximilian's Holy Roman Empire, including Burgundy, were positively venal.

The reason for the poor relations (and Behaim's detention) was the matter of "the young King from England who is now with the roman King." Behaim was referring to the notorious pretender to the English throne, Perkin Warbeck, whose support by the dowager duchess Margaret of Burgundy and her son-in-law Maximilian, King of the Romans, was bringing Henry and Maximilian to the brink of war.

The issue of the pretender Warbeck was a central crisis of European relations in the 1490s. John Cabot's strange transformation from marine engineer in Spain to English explorer may never have happened without it. Cabot's exploration career ultimately was a by-product of vexatious matters of trade, diplomacy, and war that had nothing to do with finding a continent no one suspected even existed.

HENRY VII'S CLAIM to the English throne was achieved by the sword, through his victory at Bosworth Hill over the usurper Richard III in 1485. Henry's claim to royal blood, however—a link to Edward III through the house of Lancaster courtesy of his mother, Margaret, Countess of Richmond—was dodgy. Henry tried to quell dissent and unite the Yorkists and Lancastrians by wedding Elizabeth of York, eldest child of Edward IV, who was the elder brother of Richard III. The plan of 1489 to have Henry's heir, Arthur, eventually marry Fernando and Isabel's daughter, Catherine of Aragon, was another strategic move to legitimize the Tudor claim on the throne: Catherine's namesake was her great-grandmother on her mother Isabel's side, Catherine of Lancaster, who was a granddaughter of Edward III.

The reign of Henry VII was under constant threat from Yorkist forces—the White Roses of the War of the Roses—that used intrigues of pretenders in an attempt to overthrow him. The inspiration for these pretenders was the (still) unknown fate of two brothers of Henry's wife, the princes Edward V and Richard, Duke of York. Placed by their uncle, Richard III, in the Tower of London in 1483 as he seized power, no one had seen the boys since. It remains uncertain when and how they died, and whose hands were bloody.

The first imposter, a child of about ten named (we think) Lambert Simnel, was marketed by conspirators as Edward Plantagenet, Earl of Warwick, a simpleminded son of Richard III who was in fact being held in the Tower of London by Henry VII. Simnel was defeated and captured at the Battle of Stoke Field in Lancaster in June 1487. Henry treated the hapless pretender kindly. The child was given a job in the royal kitchen and then promoted to falconer.

Perkin Warbeck was less straightforward to deflect. He surfaced in 1490 in Burgundy, where Margaret, the dowager duchess of Burgundy, who was a sister of Edward IV and Richard III, embraced him as her missing nephew Richard, Duke of York. Margaret of Burgundy had already funded some fifteen hundred German mercenaries for the Simnel misadventure. She surely knew that Warbeck was an imposter, and in a confession eventually wrested from him, he purportedly admitted he was a Burgundian Fleming, the son of a French official in Tournai.

Maximilian I was Warbeck's most blatant supporter, after Margaret of Burgundy. His first wife was the dowager duchess's stepdaughter, Mary, who had become Duchess of Burgundy on the death in battle in January 1477 of her father, Charles the Bold. When Mary died in 1482 after breaking her back in a horse-riding accident, Burgundy was to be ruled by Maximilian as protector of their child, the duke in waiting, Philip. This went over very badly with the largest cities (or states-general) of the Low Countries, Ghent, Bruges, and Ypres, which rejected Philip's governorship and signed the Treaty of Arras with France's Louis XI in December 1482. The treaty turned over Maximilian and Mary's daughter, Margaret, to Louis XI, along with a portfolio of territories that included Artois and Franche-Comté; she was to be raised at the French court and eventually marry the dauphin, the future Charles VIII. So poorly did Maximilian fare in his power struggle with the states-general that although he was made King of the Romans in 1486 at his father Frederick III's behest, he was imprisoned by the citizens of Bruges in 1488 and cut off from both his children.

Maximilian managed to extricate himself from his imprisonment in 1489 and by 1492 was able to regain control over his Burgundian affairs. The French dauphin meanwhile had shunned Maximilian's daughter Margaret and instead wed Anne de Bretagne, Duchess of Brittany, in 1491. Outraged, Maximilian sent an army in December 1492 into Franche-Comté.

The dauphin, who had assumed power that year as Charles VIII, had already been rattled by an invasion by Henry VII in October. Henry wanted to press a claim to Brittany, which had been given over to France by the marriage of Charles and Anne de Bretagne, and to express his displeasure that France was harboring the pretender Warbeck. Henry's bold aggression alarmed the twenty-two-year-old Charles into suing for peace. By the Treaty of Étaples, in exchange for Henry relinquishing any claim of his own to Brittany, Charles agreed to evict Warbeck and to pay Henry 745,000 crowns in semiannual installments of 25,000 crowns.

Charles made peace with Maximilian through the Treaty of Senlis of 1493, by which the jilted Margaret was returned to her father, along with the dowry that included Artois and Franche-Comté. It was further agreed that Philip would assume his powers as Archduke of Burgundy when he turned sixteen in July 1494. Following the death of his father, Frederick III, in 1493, Maximilian was confirmed as Holy Roman Emperor by the unwieldy assortment of nobles and civic and religious authorities that comprised the empire's electoral diet.

Having settled his outstanding grievances with France, Maximilian immediately sullied his relationship with England's Henry VII, as Perkin Warbeck was able to find fresh shelter in Burgundy under the dowager duchess. Maximilian then invited Warbeck to his father's funeral in the autumn of 1493, going so far as to recognize him as Richard IV, the English king in exile. That Behaim, writing from Brabant in early 1494, so unquestioningly called Warbeck "the young King from England" showed how readily his legitimacy was accepted in the Burgundian Netherlands, from which Warbeck actually happened to hail.

Behaim had departed Lisbon for the Burgundian Netherlands sometime in late 1493. The mission presumably had something to do with the imminent ascent of Philip, who was at Bruges, to the dukedom of Burgundy. Maximilian had not set foot in the rebellious Low Countries since freeing himself from Bruges in 1489 and would not reappear there until August 1494. Still, Behaim did not explain why Maximilian would have expected him to travel all the way from Lisbon to confer with Philip at Bruges on the king's behalf, when Maximilian easily could have sent someone overland from his own court to do so.

Behaim moreover was traveling in the midst of the most aggravated relations between Henry VII and Maximilian I because of the Warbeck threat. Henry retaliated against Maximilian's and the dowager duchess's support of Warbeck by shutting down shipments of English wool to Burgundy: On September 21, 1493, the English merchant adventurers were ordered by Henry to relocate their staple, or designated market for wool and other goods, from Antwerp to Calais, England's remaining stronghold on the French coast of the English Channel. Back in England, Flemish merchants were deported and their property was seized. For at least two years, trade between England and the Low Countries of Burgundy fairly dried up.

It was in the midst of this sometimes-violent economic war that Behaim—possibly traveling on a Flemish vessel and in any event with papers from Maximilian, and also intending to conduct business for his Flemish father-in-law in the Burgundian Netherlands—was detained in England.

Behaim complained of a fever so severe while being held in England that he twice "took the candle in hand to await Extreme Unction." He had then made his escape with the aid of a French pirate—or alternately had been abducted by a French pirate while sailing from England, forcing him to secure his freedom by paying his own ransom. The letter wasn't at all clear on this point. The fever had almost passed in Brabant, and he was waiting to conclude a sugar contract for his father-in-law before returning to Portugal, by the Pentecost, he hoped. He advised that anyone wishing to write him in Lisbon should address the missive to the Portuguese factor in Bruges or Antwerp.

But before Behaim could send the letter, his plans abruptly changed. He was hurrying by sea back to Lisbon, where the letter would finally be sent with a post-script. He offered no explanation for the rapid about-face, but he must have taken fair measure of the severity of the trade war and beat a hasty retreat. As the post-script revealed, Behaim was now happily in the Lisbon home of Huerter, where he would stay until the Pentecost. He planned next to be in Genoa, then would return to Lisbon before moving on to Madeira and finally to the Azores.

"Doctor Jeronimus will not fail to give you my news," Behaim advised. What-ever news Behaim imparted to the good doctor Münzer to share with his family in Nürnberg is lost to us, but the advice indicated that the two friends were in close contact.

Behaim's letter was so ambiguous on so many levels that he seemed to be fudg-ing the truth of what actually had happened. A deliberate visit to England to seek support for the voyage plan that João II had just rejected made as much if not more sense than the cockeyed tale of diplomacy, captivity, and piracy that Behaim spun for a relative who would have hoped he had been productively engaged in com-merce. Given that Behaim had in mind a northern passage scheme, it made sense for him to have attempted to pitch it next to the English crown, which also enjoyed long and amicable relations with Portugal.

More to the point, England was not a party to the Treaty of Tordesillas, negotia-tions for which were concluding. Its terms had quashed any idea of João II support-ing Behaim's voyage plan. While Spain and Portugal imagined the treaty cleaving the world between them along a meridian drawn pole to pole, Henry could not be considered beholden to it. As a faithful son of the church, Henry would have had excellent reason to believe that he was limited in his actions only by how *Inter cetera* of 1493 arguably modified *Aeterni Regis* of 1481 and so only divided the *southern* waters of the Ocean Sea, below the Canaries. *Inter cetera* had no bearing on naviga-tion and discoveries in northern latitudes.

But any effort by Behaim to secure an audience with Henry was a traumatic failure. He probably had departed Lisbon before word arrived of Henry's open-ing salvo in the trade war of September 21, 1493. By the time he reached England, political and economic relations with Maximilian's realm were approaching their nadir over the Warbeck crisis. Behaim would have been treated harshly as an enemy alien, a subject of Maximilian who had been doing business in the politically explo-sive Burgundian Netherlands since the age of sixteen, was married to the daughter of a prominent Fleming noble, and was planning to serve in the Low Countries as a commercial agent for his father-in-law on this journey. Behaim would have been swept up in the detention of Flemings, seizure of their property, and deportation to the Burgundian Netherlands—in his case, with or without the aid of a French smuggler.

The strange letter of March 11, 1494, with its Lisbon postscript, is the last shred of evidence of the life and career of the man who should have been Columbus. He died in poverty in Lisbon in 1506, leaving behind debts for which creditors were still seeking redemption from his son in 1519. Behaim somehow had vaporized a substantial inheritance from his mother and squandered whatever advantages he had enjoyed from his personal and commercial relationship with his prosperous father-in-law.

The standard denouement of Behaim's story is that he retreated to the Azores, as an inscription on the *Erdapfel* stated that it was his plan to retire there. But there is no proof that he did so. It is hard to believe that the ambitious, vainglorious Behaim did nothing worth mentioning with his life after the March 1494 letter, as westward exploration soon experienced a boom in Spain, Portugal, and England; there also had to be an explanation for how he ended up in a pauper's grave. Something had consumed his time, his passion, and all of his money.

BEYOND THE ESSENTIAL SIMILARITY between Cabot's voyage plan and the proposal Behaim had made to João II with Jerome Münzer's help, foremost among the issues that suggested Behaim became directly, even intimately involved with Cabot in the English voyages was a December 1497 report from London by the Milanese diplomat Raimundo di Raimundis that placed a globe in Cabot's hands.

Raimundis encountered Cabot several months after the Venetian's return in August 1497 from his first successful voyage for Henry VII. "This Messer Zoane has the description of the world in a map, and also in a solid sphere, which he has made, and shows where he has been." Raimundis thus believed Cabot had fashioned the map and globe after completing the 1497 voyage, to illustrate his discoveries.

Cabot's marine engineering project at Valencia indicated he could draw detailed plans, so we cannot dismiss the possibility that he was capable of creating a globe from scratch. But other aspects of the Raimundis report would give ample cause to question Cabot's truthfulness (and for us to admire the Milanese ambassador's sheer credulousness on matters of exploration and trade with Asia). Cabot was perfectly capable of passing off the map and globe as his own handiwork.

It didn't seem possible that Cabot had the time to craft a globe after his return from the 1497 voyage in August and before Raimundis encountered him at court that December. His days would have been a whirlwind of audiences and preparations for an ambitious, multiship follow-up voyage, with travels between Bristol and London. He probably merely updated the geographical props he already possessed when seeking the letters patent from Henry VII in 1495–96. *The Great Chronicle of London*, an early-sixteenth-century work attributed to Robert Fabyan, would state how Cabot had used "a caart [chart]& other demonstracions Reasonable" to persuade the king to support his explorations.

Cabot still would have had to know how to fabricate a globe in 1495. It is highly questionable that he could have done so, at least not without expert advice. To appreciate the sheer challenge of making one, bear in mind that England's first domestically produced globe would not appear for another century; this landmark Molyneux globe, completed in 1593, was a team effort involving some of the finest navigational minds and cartographic experts in what had become a significant maritime power with burgeoning exploration experience.

As noted, sources like the Toscanelli letter and Las Casas indicate that a select few terrestrial globes existed in Europe in the late fifteenth century and that Columbus himself at some point possessed one. But the only person in Europe at the time of the Cabot voyages that we can unequivocally say had supervised the complex task of making a globe—which included drawing a world map from which a globe could be made—was Martin Behaim. And he was able to do so only with aid from the expert team of craftsmen he assembled in Nürnberg, a Renaissance center renowned for its mathematics and precision instruments. The Cabot globe was such a novelty that Raimundis couldn't come up with a term for it beyond "solid sphere."

Cabot's globe would not have been as lavishly illustrated as the Nürnberg *Erdapfel* of 1492, but it still would have been a daunting technical challenge to create. To begin, a perfect sphere had to be fashioned. The Nürnberg craftsmen began by creating a clay ball about twenty inches in diameter, over which linen was laminated. This linen shell was then cut in two, the clay form removed, and the hemispheres rejoined with a wooden band. A parchment skin was then applied, and on top of that they glued a layer of paper in six segments with two caps for the polar regions. Simply creating the hollow sphere had been a substantial undertaking by German craftsmen who knew their materials and methods.

As with the Nürnberg *Erdapfel,* there was an obvious and necessary link in the Cabot case between the two-dimensional world map and the three-dimensional globe: The first determined the second. Transferring a map drawn in two dimensions to a spherical surface—which is to say, drawing a map so that it *can be* transferred to a sphere—is a feat of geometry, as it raises significant headaches in cartographic projection. And cartographic projection was so new that an example of a chart displaying latitude (let alone longitude) isn't known before 1502. Translating a surface between two and three dimensions invites a command of spherical trigonometry, a then-abstruse brand of mathematics that would not enjoy the benefit of logarithms until John Napier invented them in 1594. A globe capable of impressing a monarch and his court, in short, was not a project that anyone could slap together in a quiet corner of a rented house.

Cabot's globe and map may well have come to him ready-made, directly or indirectly, from Behaim. They would have been artifacts of Behaim's efforts to work out the tenaciously difficult task of converting a two-dimensional world map on the Toscanelli model into a three-dimensional illustrative surface applied in eight pieces for the *Erdapfel*. Behaim would have taken them with him to Lisbon, to use in his 1493 northern voyage pitch to João II, as the so-called Laon globe appears to have been modeled on an example Behaim brought to Portugal that year. As Cabot was about to pitch Henry VII on a voyage scheme that originated with Behaim and Münzer, he could do worse than use Behaim's own props. The globe and map together thus could have been acquired by Cabot while he was in Lisbon or copied directly from Behaim's examples. We also know from Behaim's March 1494 letter from Lisbon that he was planning to be in and out of Lisbon for the next while, between visits to Genoa and Madeira.

What is more, the actual creator of the "world in a map" and "solid sphere" that Raimundis saw Cabot flaunting at the English court in December 1497 may have been standing right next to Cabot: a mysterious unnamed Burgundian companion noted by Raimundis alone.

For someone like Raimundis, it would have been easy to identify Behaim (whose name he evidently did not catch) as a Burgundian, as since his teens Behaim had spent so much of his life and business activity in the Burgundian Netherlands and was married to the daughter of a prominent Flemish Burgundian. This Burgundian had sailed with Cabot on the triumphant 1497 voyage, for as Raimundis noted: "He wants to go back." And this Burgundian wanted to go back because Cabot "has given him an island." He was also so knowledgeable that Raimundis corroborated with him everything Cabot said.

This *Burgundian*, then, was not some common sailor. He was allied with Cabot with high expectations of personal reward—a cut of the privileges at the level of nobility, as according to Raimundis, he was already fancying himself a count. By equipping Cabot with the theories, props, and intelligence that could secure a patent from Henry VII, Behaim would be able to match and even exceed the rewards that Columbus, his old friend from Portugal, had secured through the Spanish crown.

SIXTEEN

DURING JOHN CABOT'S time in Seville in late 1494 and in the months immediately following his dismissal from the bridge project, Christopher Columbus's Indies scheme experienced rapid and dramatic changes. The Andalusian push-out into the Atlantic realm was stuttering, lurching, regrouping, and becoming more restrictive even as it widened its opportunities within Spain.

When Antonio de Torres arrived at La Isabella with a relief flotilla in the autumn of 1494, Cabot was supposed to be building the fixed bridge to Triana in order to accommodate the boom in trade that was to pour in from the Indies. Torres expected to return to Spain with the panoply of valuable Oriental goods Columbus had been promising. Only there weren't any. Columbus compounded his administrative and financial failings by sending home instead a cargo capable of shocking a queen who made no objection to enslaving the men, women, and children of Muslim Málaga.

Columbus had already assured Fernando and Isabel that the Indies offered "as many slaves as they may order to be shipped, and who will be from among the idolaters" in his letter published in April 1493. In February 1495, he made good on that promise, regardless of the fact that his monarchs had never taken him up on the offer. Columbus gathered at La Isabella 1,600 captive Arawaks, men and women; the 550 finest specimens were chosen to send back to Seville with Antonio de Torres, to be sold not to enrich the crown but to address Columbus's personal debt from the first voyage to the slaver Berardi for the charter of the lost *Santa María*. Of the remaining captives, the colonists were told they could help themselves to however many they wanted. When this second culling was completed, 400 were left for whom no one had any use. Among them were women so terrified that they dropped their nursing infants on the ground and fled, so far into the forest that the Spanish considered they would never be captured again.

At least one of the Taino elite had seen this terrible day coming, to judge by the *Relación* of the Anchorite friar, Ramón Pané, who had traveled to Española in 1494 on Columbus's arrangement to gather more about the beliefs of the people of Española. Having learned the Arawak language, Pané heard how a fasting cacique once had been visited by their supreme being, Yocahu. The god "announced to the cacique that those who succeeded to his power would enjoy it only a short time because there would come to his country a people wearing clothes who would conquer and kill the Indians, and that they would die from hunger." The Arawaks initially thought Yocahu had been referring to the Caribs, but later, "reflecting that the cannibals only robbed and then went away, they decided he must have meant some other people. That is why they now believe that the idol prophesied the coming of the Admiral and the people who came with him."

Among the 400 Arawaks left unclaimed in the culling were a cacique and two of his senior men. Columbus decided that the best thing to do with them was to have them executed with arrows the next day, and so they were shackled in preparation. In the night, the three men gnawed at each other's feet until they could cast off their iron restraints, and they followed the mothers who had abandoned their children into the forest enclosing La Isabella on every side except the squat bluff that overlooked the sea.

Returning with the cargo of slaves was Columbus's childhood friend, Michele da Cuneo, to whom Columbus had earlier made a gift of a young woman. "I laid my hands on a gorgeous Cannibal woman who the lord admiral granted me," Cuneo recounted in a letter to Geralamo Annari, a Savonese noble, after his return. "When I had her in my quarters, naked, as is their custom, I felt a craving to sport with her. When I tried to satisfy my craving, she, wanting none of it, gave me such a treatment with her nails that at that point I wished I had never started. At this, to tell you how it all ended, I got hold of a rope and thrashed her so thoroughly that she raised unheard-of cries that you would never believe. Finally we were of such accord that, in the act, I can tell you, she seemed to have been trained in a school of harlots."

The ships in Torres's flotilla were battered and delayed by storms, and food ran short. "By the time we had reached Spanish waters," Cuneo wrote, "approximately 200 of the Indians had died—I believe it was because they were unaccustomed to the air which is colder than theirs—and we cast them into the sea. The first land we sighted was Cape Spartel [in Morocco], and very soon after we reached Cadíz, where we unloaded all of the slaves, half of whom were sick. For your information, they are not men made for work, and they fear greatly the cold and do not live long."

When the Indies administrator Fonseca put the miserable survivors up for sale in Seville's slave market in April, Isabel halted the auction. The queen considered the Indigenous peoples, the one certain if odious export item Columbus had identified in the Indies, to be her subjects. Rather inconveniently, the bulls of 1493 that granted Fernando and Isabel the exclusive right to Columbus's discoveries were predicated on the notion of Spain carrying Christianity to the idolaters, not on carrying the idolaters home as a bulk commodity.

The appearance of the Torres flotilla with its dying captives hardly could have improved Columbus's standing. But as the court received news of the arrival of the four vessels only on April 12, the flotilla had not returned in time to have influenced the monarchs' decision, issued two days earlier, to introduce sweeping changes to the Indies enterprise. The gross spectacle of the aborted auction and news of how the Arawaks had come to be captured nevertheless would have reaffirmed convictions that Columbus should not retain absolute oversight of all Indies activities beyond Seville. Columbus would attempt to adjust his human harvesting accordingly, categorizing captives alternately as prisoners of war and as subhuman cannibals, but Isabel's prohibition on his planned Indies slave trade remained firm.

In the new permissions for the Indies, issued at Madrid on April 10, 1495, Fernando and Isabel avowed how Columbus, "our admiral of the Ocean Sea, has reported to us that we should issue a writ stipulating the following terms." On the contrary, Columbus was unhappy to learn of their unilateral initiative, and would protest it on his return to Spain in 1496.

Granted, in a letter to Fernando and Isabel believed to date to 1494, Columbus had sketched out fresh proposals for organizing settlement on Española, although most of the letter was concerned overwhelmingly with gold, especially how any gold found should be shared among settlers, the crown, and the colony's governor, namely himself. He wanted 1 percent to be set aside to support the local church; the division of the rest he thought should be left to him to decide, although he suggested that the finders and the crown should share in it equally.

Instead, Fernando and Isabella had crafted a sweeping new policy of their own on settlement, trade, and gold. So long as Spaniards traveled to and from Cadíz, they could acquire land and settle in Española without being on the royal payroll (as La Isabella was initially organized); they would be free from duties and taxes, and receive one year's support from the crown. They could keep one-third of any gold they found—not half, as Columbus had suggested—and nine-tenths of any merchandise or goods they acquired, with the remaining tenth going to the crown. There was no mention of a cut for the church, or for Columbus.

For Columbus and would-be explorers alike, the most noteworthy part of the new regulations was the provision that "any of our subjects or citizens who wish to do so can go to discover new islands and continents in the vicinity of the Indies and to trade on those already discovered and any others except the island of La Española." Columbus actually had recommended that exploration be liberalized in his letter: "In regard to the discovery of new countries, I think permission should be granted to all that wish to go, and more liberality used in the matter of the fifth [the 20 percent share on commerce due to the crown], making the tax easier, in some fair way, in order that many may be disposed to go on voyages." Although Fernando and Isabel did reduce the "fifth" to a tenth, the new regulations reserved only Española for Columbus where trade was concerned.

Columbus was still the Admiral of the Ocean Sea in the region of the Indies (to exactly what that entitled him and his heirs would be of considerable legal dispute) and the viceroy and governor of Española. The new regulations also still reserved for Columbus the right to send one ship out of eight bound for the Indies, and all voyages (and voyagers) had to be approved by Juan Rodríguez de Fonseca in Seville. But unless Columbus could assert exclusive authority under his admiralty, the new rules appeared to extinguish his exclusive trading rights to Cuba—which he insisted was mainland Asia—as well as Jamaica, the Bahamas, and the string of Leeward Islands discovered on the second voyage stretching from Dominica north and west through the Virgin Islands and on to Puerto Rico. Those islands were home to the people he portrayed as irredeemable cannibals and hoped could be profitably enslaved. In fact, he began calling this chain the Cannibal Islands rather than the East Indies.

The catch in the new royal permissions was that to take advantage of the fresh opportunities of exploration and trade, one had to be a Spanish "subject" or "citizen." A subject was a resident who had been born in Spain but did not swear an oath of loyalty to the monarchs because of their religious affiliations. Native-born Spaniards were citizens of their particular communities within the kingdoms of Fernando and Isabel.

A foreigner could become a naturalized citizen by meeting one of ten different requirements; among them were marriage to a citizen and a ten-year residency. Columbus never did become a citizen, remaining a Genoese until his death, but he clung to his Indies entitlements through his precious capitulations. Cabot for his part had not resided anywhere in Spain long enough to become naturalized and was already married to Mattea. In addition, his Venetian citizenship not only granted him its rights beyond the cluster of prosperous islands forming the republic's Signoria; it required him to identify himself as a Venetian when abroad and be subject to the administration of a consul should there be an organized expatriate community.

In any event, by the time the new Indies permissions were introduced in April 1495, Cabot was long gone from Spain. Had he not fled Seville in late 1494—even had he not given the city's powerful leaders cause to banish him—these permissions would have defeated any aspiration he had to pursue explorations of his own in the Spanish realm.

The new regulations affirmed a recent and unrelenting trend in Fernando and Isabel's dominion, of favoring citizens who were also loyal to their Catholic faith. Jews had been forcibly converted or deported in 1492; in 1499, the rights granted to Muslims under the surrender of Granada would be revoked and, in 1501, they would be subjected to compulsory conversion as well. Italian merchants in Andalusia, particularly the Genoese in Seville, had begun securing Spanish citizenship in record numbers. Although the Genoese had enjoyed self-governing privileges in Seville since 1251, these businessmen were drawing themselves closer to Spanish power and the privileges and opportunities that could come their way. Among them was Francesco de Riveroli, who was naturalized in 1492 as Francisco de Riberol and would become one of Columbus's key financiers. Riberol's partner in the Canaries conquest, the Florentine Gianotto Berardi, was naturalized (as Juanotto Berardi) in 1494. Berardi of course was already a Columbus financier from the first voyage and had secured the provisioning contract from the crown for the second one.

Money thrived on opportunity, and if fresh ones could not be found, then they needed to be created. Evidently the recently naturalized Italian financiers of Spanish expansionism—which included not only Columbus's Indies initiative but the conquest of the Canaries and the war for Granada, which had been underwritten with the aid of the Spinola family branch in Córdoba—had made known their desire to have the Indies made more available to exploitation.

The plan to exploit the new regulations was in place before the regulations themselves officially existed. The recently naturalized Berardi was awarded a flotilla contract under the revised terms on April 9, 1495, the day before the terms themselves were proclaimed. Berardi agreed to send three flotillas of four ships each, in April, June, and September. Two ships were to remain in Española for fifteen days, facilitating trade, while the other two would be free to explore.

These flotillas seem to have been Berardi's idea, as Fernando and Isabel wrote Fonseca the same day the contract was awarded, informing the head of the Indies enterprise in Seville that Berardi had offered to mount them and that he was to be paid 600,000 maravedis. Although Berardi's arrangement was generally in accord with what Columbus himself had proposed to Fernando and Isabel, it's not known if Columbus was aware of it, or if he approved. As Columbus had made no profits from the first two voyages from which to retire his debt to Berardi, the Florentine can hardly be blamed if his proposal to mount three separate flotillas helped initiate the new regulations that would so alienate Columbus.

Yet Fernando and Isabel's hopes to revive the Indies enterprise with the liberalized regulations of April 10, 1495, were, to say the least, not met. No ships under Berardi's contract to mount three flotillas for trade and exploration even sailed in 1495.

JEROME MÜNZER WAS JUST RETURNING to Nürnberg when the new Spanish regulations for the Indies went into effect in April 1495. Columbus was still in the Indies; he had embarked on a scorched-earth campaign against Española's rebellious Arawaks on March 24 with a force of two hundred foot soldiers, twenty-four horsemen, twenty dogs, and an arsenal that included muskets, crossbows, spears, and swords. Laying waste to native populations who dared resist his authority, and enslaving those who survived, kept him busy for about ten months. Española was now indistinguishable from Tenerife in the Canaries, where Alonso de Lugo was in the midst of his latest campaign to subjugate the indigenous Guanches with backing from the same small circle of Italian merchants in Seville who were allied with Columbus. La Palma had fallen in May 1493, shortly after Columbus made his celebrated appearance at court in Barcelona and began planning the second voyage. The partners in the conquest, Gianotto Berardi, Alonso de Lugo, and Francisco de Riberol, then turned down the 700,000 maravedi reward promised by the crown in exchange for the right to subjugate Tenerife, the largest island in the archipelago.

When Michele da Cuneo learned of the new liberalized regulations for the Indies on his return to Spain in April 1495, he considered them a sign that Fernando "does not think much" of the lands Columbus had discovered to date, as he explained in his letter to Annari. Cuneo reported that Bartolomé Columbus, who had been named by his brother *adelanto*, or lieutenant, of the lands already discovered, was supposed to be making a new voyage of his own from Española. "The Adelanto is planning to depart with two caravels and a small galley, built in Hispaniola, to go exploring during the entire month of April." Given the king's evident lack of enthusiasm for what Columbus had already discovered, Cuneo advised, "If [Bartolomé] does not find more than what we found in those parts . . . I fear it will be necessary to abandon them."

Bartolomé, who had not participated in the first or second voyage, had arrived at Española with a three-ship relief flotilla in June 1494. He now was slated to overcome his brother's aversion to higher latitudes and strike out toward the north—far to the north.

"We are fairly certain that the lord Bartolomé sailing 500 leagues to the northern regions will find land," Cuneo continued, "but he will also find bigger storms and worse weather than we encountered. The lord admiral [Christopher Columbus] says that he will find Cathay."

Cuneo allowed that this optimism was disputed by the same learned abbot of Lucena who in 1494 rejected Columbus's claim that Cuba wasn't an island and was prevented by Columbus from returning to Spain to share his opinions with Fernando. Cuneo advised that Columbus planned to detain the cleric in Española until Bartolomé had returned from his voyage and reported on what he had discovered.

Why, now, was Columbus determined to have his brother sail so far to the north? Had news of the northern voyage scheme of Münzer and Behaim, proposed to João II in the latter half of 1493, reached Española with Bartolomé, who had left Spain in May 1494? Or had the Torres flotilla that arrived in the autumn of 1494 carried word? However the plan came about, in the spring of 1495, Christopher Columbus intended to send Bartolomé directly from Española into distant northern latitudes, to see if Cathay lay in that direction.

Bartolomé never made that voyage. So much of the New World's history would have changed if he had. And any further opportunity to sail north soon evaporated, as Columbus paid dearly for having so obstinately chosen not to site the Castilian colony at the River of Martín Alonso.

That June, La Isabella was scoured by the first of two hurricanes. Spaniards had never before experienced a hurricane, and the folly of La Isabella was devastatingly exposed. All but one of four ships, the redoubtable *Niña*, was destroyed when caught in the exposed anchorage in the first storm. The second storm, in October, entirely demolished a four-ship relief flotilla that had arrived in September under Juan de Aguado, who was charged with investigating complaints regarding Columbus's administration. Columbus as a result had no means of conducting further explorations and would have to cobble together a ship called the *India* from the available wreckage to get back to Spain in 1496.

The June storm also produced a surge that flooded with saltwater the farmers' fields, which were already struggling to grow European crops in a Caribbean environment. The disaster multiplied the festering problems of La Isabella, damping whatever mercantile enthusiasm might have arisen from the April 1495 proclamation. Isabel's halting of the slave auction in Seville hadn't helped matters: Humans comprised the only crop that seemed to grow readily and could be harvested. But another reason for the waning enthusiasm was the widespread consensus among learned Europeans that Columbus's discoveries were nowhere near the actual Indies. Italian financiers would gladly put their capital to work in a venture that promised to deliver results in reaching Cathay by a different westward route.

ISABEL'S DECISION TO STOP the Seville sale of slaves who had arrived from Española on April 12, 1495, was surely a factor in the failure of any of the three contracted Berardi flotillas to sail as scheduled, as Berardi's main business was the slave trade. The "explorations" his ships planned to make surely would have been little more than hunting expeditions for fresh human chattel. A separate fleet, carrying the investigator Juan de Aguado, had instead sailed, only to be obliterated by the October hurricane.

Despite the ban on slave trading, on October 21, 1495, Berardi's associate Amerigo Vespucci received from Fonseca 38,700 maravedis on Berardi's account for ninety-five slaves from the Indies, who presumably were among those who had arrived on April 12 and must have been sold before the queen's edict put an end to the auctions. That cash influx seemed to do the motivational trick for Berardi, who finally began preparing the first contracted flotilla in November. Another 10,000 maravedis were turned over by Fonseca to Vespucci for Berardi on November 5, and 500,000 maravedis were given directly to Berardi on December 4. But preparations were disrupted when Berardi fell ill. His health declined so rapidly that he wrote a new will on December 5 and died on December 15.

Vespucci promptly assumed responsibility for the long-promised flotilla to the Indies. When the ships at last departed under Jorge de Sosa, the venture continued to be spectacularly star-crossed. One of the ships got into some sort of trouble while still in the Guadalquivir, and the fleet had scarcely left Sanlúcar de Barrameda on February 3, 1496, when a storm hurled it back, scattering wrecks from Rota, to the north, to the island of Tarifa at the entrance to the Strait of Gibraltar, to the south. So ended Fernando and Isabel's initiative of April 1495 to expand beyond Columbus the exploration efforts in the Indies.

The Canaries rather than Columbus's Indies became the focal point of Spanish expansionism out of Andalusia backed by Italian merchants. Berardi's place as an investment partner in the Canaries conquest was assumed by Francisco de Riberol's brother, Cosme, who had also been naturalized at Seville in 1492. The Guanches had very nearly triumphed, massacring four-fifths of Alonso de Lugo's army in the Acentejo ravine in 1494, forcing him to retreat to La Palma and regroup for a second invasion of Tenerife. Lugo completed the difficult and bloody Tenerife conquest in 1496, selling captives indiscriminately into slavery in an effort to settle his personal debts, just as Columbus had attempted with Arawak prisoners in 1495.

The Riberols, Spinolas, and other Genoese families in Andalusia became major landowners in the Canaries, dominating 90 percent of the sugar production and trade as they built a prosperous slave plantation economy. On the other side of the Ocean Sea, the Columbus venture teetered unhappily between a logistical miscalculation that invited yet another change in strategy and management and an absolute folly that should be abandoned altogether . . . or used as a negotiating chip in international diplomacy.

SEVENTEEN

JOHN CABOT'S timing in taking to England the idea of a north Atlantic passage to Cathay was flawless in capitalizing on catastrophe. The venal relations between England and Maximilian's realm had shut the door on any chance that Martin Behaim could make a pitch of his own. But the trade war arising from the maneuverings surrounding the pretender Warbeck proved to be only part of the complications necessary to turn Cabot into an English explorer. Cabot also needed England to be somehow denied the services of the Flanders Galleys and the Oriental luxury goods they carried. In 1495, that condition was fulfilled in spectacularly disastrous fashion.

In January 1495, two of the three vessels in the Flanders Galley flotilla, including the flagship, perished in a storm in the Bay of Biscay en route to England. Then in October 1495, the lone surviving galley, the *Bragadina,* and another Venetian merchant vessel, the *Zorza,* with which the galley was to return home in convoy, suffered a brazen attack by French pirates at Southampton. The Venetian consul in London, Almoró Gritti, was dining aboard the galley when the raiders struck at dusk. The crews were taken prisoner. The galley convoy's captain, Piero Bragadin (Pietro Bragadino), as well as Nicolo da Napoli, commander of the *Zorza,* each were tagged with a 550-ducat ransom; a nobleman's son, Francesco Donado, who was wounded in the thigh by a falconet—a small cannon that fired a two-inch-diameter iron ball—was held for an additional 150 ducats. They were all carried away to France to await payment for their liberation.

Venetians found it outrageous that English defenses had allowed this pirate raid to succeed. It fell to the Venetian doge, Agostino Barbarigo, to address by diplomacy. He was about seventy-five years old and had been elected for life in 1486 as chief magistrate and head of state of the republic. Henry VII was a familiar if problematic customer for Barbarigo. On one hand, the English king had goods, wool especially, that Venice desperately needed. On the other hand, he could behave like an unpredictable barbarian, moving ruthlessly to press an advantage. "I fancy he will always wish to have peace with France," the Milanese ambassador to his court would remark in December 1497, "though I think if he saw her up to her neck in the water, he would put his foot on her head to drown her."

In 1492, Henry had commandeered two of the Flanders Galleys so he could ferry an army to Calais during his spat with Charles VIII over Brittany, threatening the captains with death if they did not comply. Barbarigo had naturally protested then; beyond the high-handedness that delayed the galleys' return with desired English wool, loading these exquisite craft with the Renaissance military's version of an organized, armed mob did little for their state of finish, and damage was also incurred bringing them into Calais. Henry's action had been little more than state piracy.

From his station inside the Palazzo Ducale on the Piazza San Marco—which a doge was not permitted to leave except in the most pressing circumstances—an infuriated Barbarigo now expressed to Henry his dismay with an altogether different sort of hijacking, which he nevertheless laid at the king's feet. Writing Henry on November 9, 1495, the doge lamented the "infamous and detestable seizure, in your Majesty's port of Hampton, by certain French subjects of the captain of our galleys and of our consul holding office in London, together with two other noblemen of ours, and some of our sailors, as it caused us displeasure." It did not help his mood that the *Zorza* evidently belonged to the renowned shipbuilding family of his son-in-law, Zorzi Nani. The doge was confident this assault was also "most irksome to your Majesty, whose honour is chiefly wounded by the violation of your harbor." Barbarigo trusted that "everything which can be desired has been done" by Henry "for the release and indemnity of our said captain, consul, noblemen, and sailors who went thither under the royal security and safe conduct."

The doge was keen to make Henry understand how shabby this incident made his kingdom appear as a place to conduct business and how unlikely future trade might prove to be if the matter was not resolved to Venice's satisfaction. He reminded Henry of "the very infamous offence done to yourself, and also to us and our subjects, the great convenience and profit afforded by whose trade in your kingdom is perfectly known to you."

Barbarigo proposed that Henry take his own hostages to secure the return of the captive Venetians. He ought to "seize the persons and effects of the subjects of the King of France for the release of our said subjects, for then you will provide both for the safety of the prisoners, and for your own honor, whilst our other merchants will have greater cause to traffic in your kingdom, perceiving you prone towards their indemnity and security."

What Henry actually did in response isn't known, but on January 22, 1496, the doge issued orders to Venice's new consul in London, Piero (Pietro) Contarini, a former capitaneus of the galleys: Send the 150 ducats to free the young noble Donado, and go to Southampton and take command of the two pillaged Venetian ships. London's Venetian merchant community was further required to reimburse the ransoms and expenses of Donado and the two commanders as well as the costs associated with springing the clerk, bowmen, and oarsmen of the galley and presumably the abducted consul Gritti as well. Contarini also had been instructed, if his own business permitted, to command the *Bragadina* for the return voyage, but Barbarigo soon had more important matters for Contarini to attend to on the republic's behalf in England.

RENAISSANCE GEOPOLITICAL CRISES seemed to unfurl and ensnarl without beginning or end, but the state of affairs at the time of the Flanders Galley crisis, already complicated by the Warbeck affair, was particularly energized by the highly destabilizing decision of Charles VIII of France to march a massive army across the Alps into northern Italy in 1494 in order to seize the kingdom of Naples.

Ludovico Sforza, ruling Milan as regent in the name of his nephew Gian Galeazzo Sforza, had created a fine mess for himself. He had encouraged Charles VIII's notions of entitlement to the kingdom of Naples and provided Genoa as a naval base for the invasion. He had hoped that the French king would introduce a new political and military power to the Italian peninsula that would in part counter the weight of Venice. But when Charles helped himself to the republic of Florence while he was in the neighborhood and his army began to inflict atrocities on whoever got in its way, even Sforza began to worry about where the French king might turn next for easy conquest. (Sforza had also become the new Duke of Milan after the death that October of his nephew, whom he was suspected of having poisoned.) In March 1495, the doge Barbarigo had fashioned Milan, Venice, Spain, the Papal States, and the Holy Roman Empire into the Holy League, also known as the League of Venice. Its forces confronted Charles's army at Fornovo in July 1495, persuading the French to withdraw back over the Alps.

To further check Charles's ambitions, the league then courted Henry VII. The English king had shown interest in joining the league after it was formed, but he did not relish the idea of becoming an enemy of France in the process. Wars moreover were a drain on the treasury, and Henry (hailed as the wealthiest monarch in Europe) was proving himself adept at maximizing royal revenues while minimizing expenditures. A shrewd if cynical economist, he has been called the finest businessman ever to wear the English crown. It was said that he went to war to extort money from his subjects and secured peace to extract more of the same from his enemies. He levied customs duties on exports of England's much-desired wool amounting to one-third of its value to encourage domestic production of cloth and finished clothing for export, which were subject to only a 3 percent export duty. As raw English wool was in such demand in the Low Countries and northern Italy, he filled his coffers with the steep duties foreign merchants were willing to pay. He forbade gold and silver and specie in general from leaving the country (keeping armies fed and equipped in the field was particularly debilitating in that regard) and would not allow pewter craftsmen to take their trade to the continent.

Henry had requested that Venice and Milan send ambassadors in order to discuss his options with respect to joining the Holy League, but in the wake of the French pirates' assault at Southampton, the Venetians considered it too dangerous to do so. Instead, the doge on February 22, 1496, turned to Piero Contarini and a fellow Venetian merchant in London, Luca Velaresso, who were already working together on the Southampton pirate assault file, to serve as ambassadors-designate in persuading Henry to join the Holy League or agree to some similar new alliance against France.

Still seething over the Southampton assault of October 1495, the Venetians continued to withhold the Southampton service of the Flanders Galleys, giving Henry a profound impetus to please the doge and senate by joining the Holy League. Venice was not the only Italian state to trade with England, but where luxury goods were concerned, it was the dominant player. Without the service of the galleys, England was hard-pressed to secure precious goods that verged on necessities, as many of the items we generally call spices were valued for therapeutic properties. Saffron, for example, in addition to being used in cooking, was considered "a cordial, a pectoral, an anodyne, an aperient, and an antidote to poison and hysterics." England's apothecaries, kitchens, and artisans were being starved of precious Venetian commodities, and the country's exports of wool as well as tin and lead were seriously compromised as the haul-back service of the galleys was lost. And a king who could not ensure that his nobles (on whose capacity to raise armies and suppress domestic unrest he so depended) were provided with the essential spices, therapeutics, and fineries for their estates and families and mistresses and assorted hangers-on was a king who could not expect to rule profitably, if at all. Henry needed galleys.

But as diplomacy swirled around the absent galleys and the League of Venice, Henry suddenly found an opportunity to make alternate arrangements for accessing the Orient's riches, arrangements that would render the Flanders Galleys obsolete and turn England into the new Venice.

HISTORIANS HAVE LONG ASSUMED that Cabot went directly from Spain to Bristol, from which his voyages for England sailed, and then tried to figure out how he got there. The English port city had long trade connections with Spain (and Portugal), so some Iberian vector usually has been proposed. The English merchant community at Seville, and particularly at Sanlúcar de Barrameda, would have provided an exploitable connection. We can add to them the *comitres* of Triana who traded with England and imagine Cabot hailing the first carrack downbound on the Guadalquivir as he slunk away from Seville in flight or actual banishment. But in addition to the likelihood that Cabot first went to Lisbon, as the Spanish ambassador Pedro de Ayala stated, there is good reason to believe he then went to London rather than Bristol, if not solely as an Indies voyage promoter then partly as a merchant.

In a 1534 senate report by the Venetian ambassador to Spain, Marcantonio Contarini, Cabot's son Sebastian was described as the "son of a Venetian, who went to England on the Venetian galleys with the idea of searching for new lands." The Venetian chronicler Ramusio in 1550 would further assert that a "Mantuan gentleman" who had met Sebastian in Spain had been told that John Cabot, "having left Venice many years ago and having gone to England to trade, he took [Sebastian] with him to the city of London."

If Cabot truly arrived in England on the Flanders Galleys, he must have been aboard the *Bragadina*, the lone vessel in the three-ship flotilla to reach England in early 1495 before service was suspended. Such a conveyance was poetically appropriate; it was the attack on the *Bragadina* in Southampton Water in October 1495 that caused the Venetians to suspend all galley service to England and created the political and economic crisis that would persuade Henry VII to license Cabot to prove an alternate route to the Orient's riches. To be sure, as a Venetian merchant whose earlier dealings in hides and possibly wool already may have taken him to England in the 1480s, Cabot would have been well informed about the Flanders Galley service and been able to persuade Henry to adopt a plan that could turn an English port, Bristol, into the new Venice of the Asia trade.

There are connections between Cabot and men associated with the 1495 Flanders Galleys and the ensuing crisis. But placing Cabot on the *Bragadina* is not easy. Piero Bragadin was already in Southampton by January 31, 1495, when he wrote the Venetian senate with news of the disappearance of the flotilla's other two galleys in a storm in the Bay of Biscay. Although we don't know when the *Bragadina* departed Venice, it is a challenge to put Cabot on board at departure if he was still in Seville in late December 1494. Perhaps he had already absconded with his money from Seville before the city council voted to dismiss him from the project and considered the measure of formally expelling him.

The tradition that he arrived in England on the Flanders Galleys may be a slight elision of the truth: that Cabot arrived on a merchant vessel sanctioned by the Venetian senate, but not one of the actual galleys, whose service was suspended after the flotilla disasters of 1494–95. Either the *Zorza* or the *Malipieri,* another significant Venetian merchant ship that reached England in the summer of 1495, was a good candidate for Cabot's conveyance. And if Cabot did appear in Lisbon to seek support for his voyage scheme, as Ayala asserted, he would have been positioned to hitch a ride to England on one of the Venetian merchant ships, the *Bragadina* included, that sometimes called there en route.

A Venetian was one of the few foreigners who could hope to initiate a westward voyage pitch to Henry VII by the winter of 1495–96 because of the myriad diplomatic complications. No subject of Spain or Portugal could do so without treasonously advocating a breach of the Treaty of Tordesillas. For a subject of Maximilian (or his son Philip) like Behaim, the initiative remained out of the question. Relations between Maximilian and Henry were even worse in 1495, when Cabot made his way to England, than they had been when Behaim was waylaid there for three months in early 1494. In January 1495, Henry VII had renewed the ban on Flemish merchants in England and trade to the Burgundian Netherlands. In April, Maximilian belatedly retaliated by closing the Low Countries of Burgundy altogether to English merchants, specifically banning the importation and sale of English wool.

A connection made by Cabot in Lisbon to Behaim and his father-in-law, Huerter, could explain how Cabot ended up in London as a merchant, as neither Sebastian Cabot nor the chronicler Ramusio indicated what Cabot was trading in and, more important, whom he would have been trading for as an agent when he went there. In the face of the countervailing embargoes that had eliminated official trade between England and the Burgundian Netherlands, Huerter and Behaim would have welcomed the services of a commission agent with experience in English wool (as Cabot's debts to Venetians Tommaso Mocenigo and Nicolò Cappello have suggested) who enjoyed the protection and privileges of Venetian citizenship in the English capital.

And Maximilian's support of the pretender Perkin Warbeck only hardened over the summer of 1495. On July 11, Maximilian confided to two Venetian ambassadors that he had gone to great expense to support Warbeck, whom he insisted on calling the Duke of York or the "new king of England," and that an invasion was under way. Maximilian didn't yet know that Warbeck's amphibious assault on July 3 had been a catastrophe. Of perhaps 1,000 men, only 600 came ashore in Kent. About 170 men were captured; all were executed, most of them hanged in coastal ports. Already in January 1495, Henry had beheaded an assortment of English nobles found guilty of supporting the Warbeck cause. The invasion leaders, who included a Spaniard and a Frenchmen, had a brutal fate specially reserved for them, with their severed heads put on display on London Bridge. Warbeck, who never even got ashore, stole away to Scotland, to plot anew with his supporters, with Maximilian's approval. James IV of Scotland was so persuaded of Warbeck's authenticity that he arranged for the ersatz Duke of York to marry his cousin, Lady Catherine Gordon, that November.

There was no end in sight to this intrigue, unless Spain, which had already refused to give sanctuary to Warbeck, could engineer a diplomatic solution. That solution rested in the way Fernando and Isabel continued to strategically deploy their children to forge dynastic alliances. One of the most crucial matches was a double wedding arranged in 1495 between Maximilian's house of Hapsburg and the coregents of Spain. Maximilian's son and successor Philip, Archduke of Burgundy, would wed Fernando and Isabel's daughter Joana; Maximilian's daughter Margaret, shunned by Charles VIII, would wed Fernando and Isabel's son and successor, Juan. The dual marriages would bind together the Holy Roman Empire and the united Spain.

Fernando and Isabel were also able to unite the ruling houses of Spain and Portugal by persuading their daughter Isabel to accept another Portuguese marriage after the death of her husband, the crown prince Afonso, in 1491. Isabel agreed to wed Afonso's uncle, Manoel, who had assumed the Portuguese throne on the death of João II in October 1495, on the condition that Portugal follow the example of Spain and expel the Jews who refused to convert to Christianity. Manoel obligingly introduced the crackdown in December 1496, and the couple was wed in October 1497.

At the same time, Henry VII very much wanted to revive the marriage plans for his son, Arthur, and Fernando and Isabel's daughter, Catherine of Aragon, that had been promised by the Treaty of Medina del Campo in 1489. In attempting to renew the treaty in March 1493, Henry had been hoping to address the uncomfortable fact that in the Treaty of Barcelona two months earlier, in order to get back Roussillon and Cerdagne, Fernando and Isabel had promised Charles VIII to go to war against England if France required support to that end. But Spain no longer seemed to have much use for Henry's friendship. The wedding between Arthur and Catherine was effectively off.

Then Charles VIII had invaded Italy, which changed everything, although it should not have. By the Treaty of Barcelona, Fernando and Isabel had agreed not to interfere in any French military adventure into Italy, but treaties at this time were being shredded into a snowstorm of legal confetti as parties maneuvered for fresh advantages. The Spanish monarchs decided it was in their interest to suppress Charles VIII's adventurism and turned on him by joining the Holy League. Now they needed Henry, as much to secure England as an ally as to not have England become an enemy allied with France.

The Spanish monarchs understood that the promise of a renewed marriage agreement for Arthur and Catherine gave them tremendous diplomatic leverage with Henry. They also needed the enmity between Henry and Maximilian to end, in order to unite them all within the Holy League against France, with which Spain was now heading toward war. For that to happen, the Hapsburgs had to stop supporting the pretender Warbeck.

What this all meant for the cause of westward exploration was that European geopolitics were precariously, fantastically unstable with Warbeck still in play, and England remained a hostile territory for any German or Burgundian hoping to secure a royal favor well into 1496. A Venetian, however—especially one who could also access the resources of Italian financiers in London—had a legitimate chance of persuading Henry to mount a westward voyage in northern waters to reach the Indies, especially now that the Flanders Galleys were no longer servicing England with the Orient's riches.

That John Cabot—a man who had left behind a trail of prominent creditors in Venice, had no oceanic résumé to speak of, could not fulfill a promise to build a bridge at Seville across the Guadalquivir, and in the process had angered some of the most powerful nobles in Spain—became the focal point of such an ambitious English royal gambit is one of the true oddities of the Renaissance. Cabot needed every ounce of help he could muster to position himself for the extraordinary privilege he was able to secure through the letters patent from Henry. The London branch operations of Italian financiers, prepared to gamble on the possibility of opening a new route to Asia that might bring healthy returns instead of the losses and discouragements of the Columbus scheme, may have been part of Cabot's proposal to Henry from the beginning, or at least soon after the patent was in hand. And the very conception of the scheme, it should be clear by now, appears to have originated elsewhere.

Behaim may have been something akin to a silent partner; Cabot was the one who would front the plan to the English court. Behaim had the voyage concept and the cartographic details—much as he appeared to in the Dulmo-Estreito plan of 1486–87—but until Henry VII was brought into the Holy League as an ally of Maximilian, Behaim had the extreme liability of hailing from Maximilian's realm. Cabot, in his involvement with the Seville project and his possible experience on the second Columbus voyage as an engineer tasked to La Isabella, would have had some idea of the state of the Spanish enterprise. Behaim, through Münzer's impressively thorough fact-finding on his 1494–95 tour of Spain and Portugal, would have been especially well informed and able to share details of the Spanish misadventures that Cabot could use to impress Henry's court and help the English king see the advantage still to be seized on the Ocean Sea by employing the higher-latitude strategy Portugal's João II had declined to exploit with Behaim's assistance.

But when Fernando and Isabel learned of Cabot's proposal to Henry, the Spanish monarchs saw an altogether different scenario: a meddlesome intrigue hatched by the French.

ON MARCH 28, 1496, Fernando and Isabel dispatched an urgent letter from Tortosa, in southern Catalunya's province of Tarragona. Entrusted to a ship departing the Basque port of Fuentarrabia on the Bay of Biscay, the letter was a reply to news their ambassador Roderigo de Puebla had sent from London on January 21.

Puebla had been striving to advance Fernando and Isabel's demands that Henry VII join the Holy League and become an enemy of France in order to revive the proposed marriage of Arthur and Catherine. In a message to Puebla on January 30, 1496, in which Ferdinand and Isabel gave their ambassador the power to negotiate the renewed terms of the marriage, the Spanish monarchs stressed: "[W]hat is wanted is [Henry VII's] *immediate* declaration of war with the King of France. For this reason de Puebla must, without delay, procure the marriage, and the alliance between Henry and them, and between Henry and the Archduke [of Burgundy]."

Before that letter arrived, Puebla had sent news of the "one like Colon," the "one from the Indies" footloose in Henry's court, promising to undertake a voyage that would succeed in securing the wealth of the Orient, where Columbus, in the service of Fernando and Isabel, thus far had failed.

Puebla's January 21 message has been lost, but the March 28 reply from his monarchs recounted a long list of pressing diplomatic issues, all of them tied in some way to the effort to bring Henry into the Holy League. Westminster was crowded with diplomats and their intrigues. Individual treaties needed to be completed, one between Henry and Maximilian and another between Henry and Maximilian's son Philip, Archduke of Burgundy. The English king could then be welcomed into the Holy League. And once the Perkin Warbeck crisis was resolved, the planning for the wedding between Arthur and Catherine could accelerate.

The three marriages involving Spain, England, and the Hapsburgs were at the foundation of Fernando and Isabel's diplomatic ambitions. It was critical that all the royal households involved be united by treaty, in opposition to France, with Henry's armies in the field with their own. But so long as the pretender remained at large and was thought capable of mounting another invasion, Fernando and Isabel would never allow Catherine to travel to England and wed Arthur. And any wavering by Henry in particular in the face of overtures from Charles VIII could collapse the entire scheme.

The Spanish monarchs were concerned by news from Puebla that French ambassadors were at Henry's court, making promises about the pension due him under the 1492 Treaty of Étaples—apparently not all of the semiannual payments had been made. Fernando and Isabel were nonplussed to hear Puebla tell of unkind words spoken by the French ambassadors to Henry about themselves as well as Maximilian, and chided Puebla for not having already forcefully refuted the slanders. "[Puebla] will not keep his word any longer than is convenient to him," they ordered. "The alliance of England with Spain, the King of the Romans, and the Archduke must be concluded as soon as possible."

The French efforts to undermine Henry's confidence in other members of the Holy League brought Fernando and Isabel around to addressing the other matter Puebla had raised: the arrival there of the "one like Colon" who wanted to entice the king of England into "another affair, like that of the Indies."

THE AMBASSADOR PUEBLA'S lost letter of January 21, 1496, is the earliest known mention of John Cabot's ambitions to secure the support of a European monarch in challenging Christopher Columbus in proving a profitable new route to the Orient. Fernando and Isabel's response to it, of March 28, is difficult to understand. In addition to being written in archaic Spanish, it came from the pen of Fernán Alvarez de Toledo-Zapata, a wealthy member of a powerful Toledo family who served as the secretary of state of both Fernando and Isabel for decades. Drafts of communications to diplomats in England were written by Alvarez according to the instructions of the Spanish monarchs, who maintained firm control of their foreign policy. But Alvarez was not a particularly learned man. He was unable to write Latin, which was still the prevalent language of diplomacy.

In addition, one often has to possess privileged knowledge to fully understand what was being discussed in a diplomatic message, and in the case of the March 28, 1496, letter, it doesn't help that the Puebla letter to which Fernando and Isabel were responding no longer exists. Especially cryptic is the first sentence addressing Cabot's voyage plan: "With regard to what you say, that the one like Colon went there to get the King of England into another affair, like that of the Indies, without causing any damage to Spain or Portugal, if he helps him as us, the one from the Indies will be quite at liberty."

Alvarez's phrasing in the final clause ("if he helps him as us . . .") is so crude and ambiguous that it is a wonder Puebla even understood the instructions in their original Spanish. Nevertheless, the letter does appear to say that were Henry VII to agree to assist not only Cabot but Fernando and Isabel as well, then Cabot would be free to make the voyage. In other words, Fernando and Isabel would look the other way where their exclusive rights under Tordesillas were concerned if Henry VII gave them what they most fervently desired at that moment: a declaration of war with France in concert with joining the Holy League.

The Spanish monarchs were thoroughly discouraged about Columbus's Indies venture. Exasperated and humiliated by it, even. Not a maravedi of profit had been generated; the Castilian treasury continued to be drained. The final indignity of Jorge de Sosa's flotilla disaster in February 1496, in which the Ocean Sea dashed their ambitions to splinters against the Castilian coast, would have been fresh in their minds as they considered the news of Cabot's pitch to Henry.

Allowing Henry to have his own crack at the money-hemorrhaging Indies game with Cabot would have been a small price to pay to gain the enormous dividend of the English committing to a war with France. Fernando and Isabel nevertheless suspected French chicanery—that Cabot was some kind of fifth-column diversion, with Charles VIII covertly engineering an exploration venture that would spark a diplomatic incident between England and Spain and derail plans to bring Henry into the Holy League.

"Take care that you prevent the King of England from being deceived in this or in anything else of the kind, since wherever they can the French will endeavor to bring this about," they instructed Puebla. They further advised (in a subtle nod to their ongoing headaches with the Columbus venture) "things of this sort are very uncertain and of such a nature that for the present it is not seemly [for Henry] to conclude an agreement therein; and it is also clear that no arrangement can be concluded in this matter in that country [England] without harm to us or to the King of Portugal."

Implicitly invoking *Inter cetera* and Tordesillas, they expected Puebla to make Henry understand that he could not approve Cabot's venture without infringing on Spain's (and Portugal's) rights. By offering to accommodate Henry under Tordesillas in exchange for his declaration of war with France, Puebla would soon find out how serious Henry was about employing Cabot—and if Cabot was anything more than a ruse by Charles VIII to cause trouble between England and Spain.

But by the time Alvarez wrote Fernando and Isabel's reply to Puebla's news of Cabot's presence at court, it was too late for the London ambassador to act on their advice and instructions. Henry VII already had awarded John Cabot and his three sons their letters patent on March 5. The quest to reach the Orient was gaining several new players—not only the Cabots, but Henry VII as well—just as Columbus was preparing to return to Spain for the first time in more than two and a half years to defend his widely discredited performance and to solicit fresh support for his westward explorations.

EIGHTEEN

HENRY VII WAS IMPRESSED by the artful Venetian who had already talked Fernando into a harbor scheme for Valencia and assuredly had enjoyed the Spanish coregent's support in landing the Seville bridge contract. In taking his gifts of persuasion to England, one cannot discount how valuable it would have been to Cabot to hail from Renaissance Italy, as Henry relied on Italian advisors and was well informed on the peninsula's tediously complex, mercurial affairs. Properly equipped and coached, Cabot would have dazzled Henry with his insights and alleged experience while evoking the land of Michelangelo and Leonardo. There is no reason to believe that Henry would have any knowledge of Cabot's fairly obscure misadventures in Spain, especially the debacle of the Seville bridge project, let alone his earlier flight from Venetian creditors. Whatever truth there was about Cabot's participation in the second Columbus voyage, he struck Henry as someone with sufficient knowledge and experience to warrant the generous terms of the letters patent conferred on him and his sons. Cabot was entrusted to achieve what Henry evidently did not believe any Englishman could.

Although no record survives of the presentation John Cabot made to Henry VII, we can be certain that he employed the northern-latitude argument that had already been crafted by Münzer and Behaim and made to João II of Portugal in late 1493 and that he deployed the globe and chart he was reported in late 1497 to have possessed.

The concept of a passage to a major trading center like Quinsay in Cathay, in the northern reaches of the empire of the Great Khan, likely was new to Henry VII. Martin Behaim might have hoped to present it in 1494, but the atrocious relations between England and Maximilian's realm evidently got in the way. If we can believe the Fernando biography of Columbus, Bartolomé already had proposed a voyage to Henry, and Henry had been prepared to employ Columbus to that end in 1493, when it was too late to do so. But it is doubtful that any plan presented by Bartolomé would have involved sailing in northern waters, as his brother Christopher was consistently wary of attempting any passage above temperate latitudes.

England was ideally positioned to reach the Indies' riches by sailing west to a trading port in Cathay, thus freeing itself from having to deal with the bothersome intermediary of Venice, which was still denying Henry the Flanders Galleys service. Scholars have debated how much Henry knew about the foreign treaties and bulls pertinent to the Cabot plan that preceded his reign, but Portugal's exclusive right to southerly latitudes under the bull *Aeterni Regis* of 1481 had been made explicitly clear to Henry by the Penamacor affair. In 1488, Lopo de Albuquerque, Count of Penamacor, a Portuguese refugee of João II's brutal suppression of the Braganza conspiracy (his brother Pero was arrested, tried, and executed), turned up in London. He tried to persuade Henry to mount an English trading voyage to Guinea, in part as vengeance against João II. The Portuguese ambassador got wind of it and warned off Henry, as the initiative would violate *Aeterni Regis*. Henry obligingly tossed the count in the Tower of London, where he lingered for a few years until being released at the behest of Fernando and Isabel. As it happened, two of the count's children developed intimate links to Columbus's family and career.

The proposal by Cabot must have persuaded Henry that nothing further issued by the Vatican (namely the bulls of 1493) denied him the right to seek his own westward route to Asia north of the Canaries. We don't know what João II's attitude would have been to an English voyage, or what he might have expressed to Jerome Münzer about the bulls and Tordesillas during their series of dinners in December 1494. In any event, João II had died in October 1495, and it would be left to his successor, Manoel I, to respond to any news of Cabot's activities or discoveries.

Henry nevertheless showed he was sensitive to Portugal's rights, at least as far as he understood them to extend. The patent he awarded to Cabot and his sons was for "all parts, regions and coasts of the eastern, western and northern sea." There was nothing, in other words, about the *southern* sea. Henry was being careful to have the Cabots and their rights steer clear of southern latitudes that had been set aside for Portugal by *Aeterni Regis* in 1481.

But that still left the objections of Fernando and Isabel, who had thought a Cabot voyage sanctioned by Henry would intrude on the rights of Spain as well as Portugal. Through their letter of March 28, 1496, they expected Roderigo de Puebla to set Henry straight without delay, even use their rights to lever from Henry an agreement to go to war with France. It was, to be sure, a tremendously risky time for Henry to attempt such an official undertaking without Spain's blessing. He was already deep in negotiations with Spain over his entry into the Holy League and, above all, over the final terms of the on-again, off-again union between Arthur and Catherine. Fernando and Isabel were also virtually alone among the royal houses of Europe in categorically refuting Perkin Warbeck's claim to his throne as the supposed duke of York. And Henry needed the trade war with the Burgundian Netherlands to end, which Spanish diplomacy was helping to resolve by advancing his rapprochement with Maximilian and Philip IV.

Henry in short did not have a more critical ally than Spain at that moment. Yet by dispatching Cabot on a voyage of discovery, he was risking a breach with Fernando and Isabel, whatever they thought of Columbus's performance and the relative value of their exclusive hold on landfalls to the west of the Tordesillas meridian. Had Henry been properly informed about Spain's likely response, he presumably would have turned Cabot away, much as he did Penamacor after a Portuguese ambassador got to him. And if he was briefed by Puebla on *Inter cetera* and Tordesillas, as Fernando and Isabel had desired, after the Cabots had been granted the letters patent, Henry might have been expected to tear it up—even toss Cabot in the Tower of London, as he had with Penamacor.

That Henry did no such things suggests he was either grossly misinformed or informed all too well. The latter seems most likely; Henry was a shrewd ruler and diplomat. He was also acutely aware of the pain being inflicted on his kingdom by the suspension of the Flanders Galleys. The dour, even threatening message from the doge Agostino Barbarigo on November 9, 1495, about the peril of future trade in precious Oriental goods carried by the suspended galleys most certainly made him consider Cabot's timely scheme to be something beyond geographic fantasy and more like an economic necessity. And by early 1496, the world well knew Columbus had found something to the west, although whether it was actually the Indies or some intermediary landfall was wide open to debate.

To accept Cabot's scheme, and then not to cancel the patent under objections from Spain, Henry would have required reassurance that the venture wouldn't ruin his good standing with Fernando and Isabel. A learned legal opinion about the bulls of 1493 and Tordesillas that favored Henry and Cabot would not have been enough. Henry would have wanted to be comfortable knowing that whatever he did wasn't going to upset the Spanish monarchs. He could be entirely in the right, and the wedding between Arthur and Catherine could be canceled regardless; worse, his isolated allies in Spain denying Warbeck's claim to the throne would be lost.

Of all the people who could have assured Henry that he was both within his rights and not to be worried about the Spanish reaction, the most plausible was the Spanish ambassador, Dr. Roderigo Gondesalvi de Puebla.

PUEBLA WAS AN INTENSELY polarizing figure in the Spanish diplomatic corps. His own monarchs were sorely tried by him. By 1498, he would be an almost obscenely disreputable character by some accounts. He was also considered physically repulsive; his precise disfigurement is not known but may have involved a missing limb.

Puebla's greatest failing was said to be his lack of fidelity to Fernando and Isabel; he also served as an ambassador to Henry for the pope as well as for Maximilian I, which was known and accepted, but he was suspected of having Henry's interests at heart more than those of his own sovereigns. At the least, he was routinely remiss in not keeping his monarchs properly informed of significant events in England.

Puebla was castigated several times in messages from Fernando and Isabel: Their chiding in the March 28, 1496, letter that he had not more forcefully refuted the slanders of the French ambassadors was a mild example. Although many of his reports (including, unfortunately, the one of January 21, 1496, which mentioned Cabot) have gone missing, periodic rebukes by his monarchs showed that he could go long periods without informing them about anything and that sometimes when he did write, he declined to mention the most stunningly important developments.

And yet Fernando and Isabel continued to employ him. He was a doctor of both civil and canonical law, and his expertise must have been (or seemed) valuable in negotiating important treaties. He had first been employed as one of two Spanish ambassadors to Henry (a commission dates from April 1488) to negotiate the marriage between Arthur and Catherine. But he would also stumble badly when he took it upon himself to strike another dynastic marriage agreement, offering Scotland's James IV the hand of Fernando's illegitimate daughter, Doña Juana. Puebla knew James would never agree to the match if he knew the truth of her status, and tried to pass her off as the legitimate offspring of a secret marriage by Fernando that preceded the union with Isabel. When Fernando and Isabel discovered the unauthorized ruse, they were furious that Puebla would attempt something so clumsy and doomed to exposure.

Puebla had traveled with the English delegation to Medina del Campo, the walled Castilian city that was home to the Spanish monarchs during the great national trade fair, for the signing of the marriage treaty binding Catherine to Arthur in 1489. Puebla might never have returned to Henry's court, but for the fact that, for some reason, Fernando and Isabel's preferred choice as ambassador in 1494 could not or would not accept the posting, so Puebla was sent in his stead. The importance of reviving the marriage plans in concert with the Holy League alliance likely recommended him, for good or ill, to the assignment, as the endless negotiations would benefit from his legal expertise and familiarity with the intricate agreements relating to dowry and hereditary title.

But Fernando and Isabel were careful not to entrust Puebla with any further missions to Scotland's James IV; Pedro de Ayala instead was chosen to deal with

Scotland. Ayala ended up spending much time in London, beginning in September 1497, infuriating Puebla with his presence and an alleged conceit that he was an ambassador to Henry's court as well. Puebla hated Ayala, and the feeling was mutual. The men had nothing to do with each other, and each made it their goal to have the other one recalled from Henry's realm, in as much disgrace as possible.

Unfortunately for Fernando and Isabel, the man they should have had at Henry's court in early 1496 when Cabot and his voyage scheme surfaced was not Puebla but Ayala, because Ayala had been one of two Spanish delegates at the preliminary round of negotiations for Tordesillas in 1493. Ayala would have known the various bulls of 1493 and the issues of Tordesillas as cogently as anyone. But Ayala was then in Scotland, and the highly unreliable and unpredictable Puebla was at Henry's court.

Fernando and Isabel provided firm instructions to Puebla to dissuade Henry from accepting Cabot's scheme, or use their approval as leverage to get Henry to agree to go to war with France, but there is no evidence that he ever did a thing about it. Granted, the instructions came too late to prevent the patent being issued. One might give the much-maligned Puebla the benefit of the doubt and credit him with surmising that trying to dissuade Henry from supporting Cabot after the fact would only risk unhappy repercussions in the ongoing effort to draw him into the Holy League—both sides had something to lose in this diplomatic game.

Nothing further from Puebla survives with respect to Cabot's activities in 1496 and 1497. The ambassador seems to have decided that news of Cabot and his voyage plans—and eventually of his actual voyages—was best left unaddressed. It was assuredly in Fernando and Isabel's interest that they be informed, but apparently not in Puebla's own. As events would prove, his other allegiances may well have effectively if not literally bought his silence and convinced him to assure Henry that Cabot's enterprise posed no problems with Fernando and Isabel.

THE LETTERS PATENT (translated from the original Latin) was awarded to "John Cabot, citizen of Venice, and to Lewis, Sebastian and Sancio, sons of the said John, and to the heirs and deputies of them, and of any one of them." They were granted

> full and free authority, faculty and power to sail to all parts, regions and coasts of the eastern, western and northern sea, under our banners, flags and ensigns, with five ships or vessels of whatsoever burden and quantity they may be, and with so many and with such mariners and men as they may wish to take with them in the said ships, at their own proper costs and charges, to find, discover and investigate whatsoever islands, countries, regions or provinces of heathens and infidels, in whatsoever part of the world placed, which before this time were unknown to all Christians.

The patent Cabot and his three sons secured from Henry VII was almost charming in its simplicity when compared with the intensively detailed capitulations Columbus had negotiated with Fernando and Isabel in 1492 and renewed at Barcelona in 1493. Nevertheless, it was replete with unmistakable echoes of the writs Columbus secured from the Spanish monarchs.

Cabot had proposed to Henry to make much the same voyage as Columbus on essentially the same terms. The Columbus blueprint, which spanned from Seville to Española, only needed to be shifted north, and almost everything in Cabot's efforts for Henry proved to draw their inspiration from Columbus, to the point of bald mimicry. However, some aspects of the Cabot patent recalled the 1486 Portuguese Dulmo-Estreito patent that involved Martin Behaim. Whoever drafted the Cabot patent was quite familiar with Columbus's capitulations and also seemed to know of the Dulmo-Estreito patent. That said, we have already seen that it is unclear if the Columbus capitulations themselves drew on the 1486 Dulmo-Estreito patent, or if the Dulmo-Estreito patent instead had drawn on a proposal Columbus made to João II around 1484.

The Spanish monarchs had kept secret Columbus's original capitulations before he sailed in 1492; how well known the capitulations would have been after his successful return is a matter for debate. Cabot might have acquired his own verbatim copies of the capitulations while he was in Seville, the administrative heart of the Indies venture, but otherwise he must have apprised himself of their essential terms through word of mouth. Jerome Münzer, for that matter, could have gained knowledge of them during his week in Seville, out of ostensible diplomatic interest as an envoy of Maximilian.

The Cabot patent echoed the earlier Portuguese and Spanish grants in referring to titular awards and authority, stating that Cabot and his sons would serve as "our vassals, and governors lieutenants and deputies." As with the Columbus capitulations, these rights were hereditary in the Portuguese model used for the colonization of the Atlantic islands and exploration for additional suspected landfalls. The inclusion of Cabot's three sons by name in the patent suggests that at least one must have reached the age of majority (twenty-one) by then (thus creating the need to name all three), as neither the Dulmo-Estreito patent or Columbus's capitulations mentioned an heir by name. (Columbus's only legitimate heir, Diego, was about twelve years old in 1492.)

Cabot's patent addressed the discovery of "the islands and mainland" (*insularum ac terre firme*). The conjoined terms were central to Columbus's privileges and found throughout them (*las ylas y tierra firme*) and were repeated in the papal bulls of 1493 (*insulas et terras firmas*). They had a precedent in the Dulmo-Estreito patent and its objective of "the grand island or islands or mainland" (*grande ylha ou hylhas ou terra firme*). In Cabot's case, Columbus's capitulations were the probable source, although if Behaim and Münzer were involved with him, the concept could have been borrowed from whatever proposal Behaim had made to João II in 1493, building on his familiarity with the Dulmo-Estreito patent and knowledge of standard practice for Portuguese privileges.

There was similar language about conquering settled territories. The Granada capitulation referred to "all the cities, towns, and villages [of those kingdoms and domains] that you may conquer and acquire." Cabot and his sons were given the right to "conquer, occupy and possess whatsoever towns, castles, cities and islands by them discovered."

The activities of both Columbus and Cabot were expected to benefit a specific port. None was named in Columbus's 1492 capitulations, but as soon as he had returned with news of his discoveries, Cadíz was chosen, with Seville granted the administrative authority. Cabot was "bound and holden only to arrive" at Bristol, which was to benefit from all imagined trade from the Indies. Vessels could depart from anywhere presumably en route to the Indies but had to land their goods at Bristol. The use of staple ports already was well known to the English from other trade ventures, but the similarity of the roles of Bristol and Cadíz are still worth noting.

There were suspiciously familiar provisions for rendering assistance to the explorers. The Barcelona capitulation promised Columbus that "all citizens, residents, and other persons who are now and in the future may be on the islands and mainland" as well as those "who travel on the seas described above . . . shall give and cause to be given to you all the consideration and help that you ask of them and may need." Cabot's patent "strictly command[ed]" all of Henry's subjects "as well by land as by sea, that they shall render good assistance to the aforesaid John and his sons and deputies, and that they shall give them all their favour and help as well in fitting out the ships or vessels."

One clear similarity to the Dulmo-Estreito patent was that Cabot's entitlements to the lands he found or conquered were positively feudal. Fernando and Isabel in contrast were crafting a transoceanic extension of the Castilian state, notwithstanding Michele da Cuneo's claim in 1495 that Columbus gave him Isla Saona. La Isabella was being run by Columbus as a royal property essentially on the model of a Portuguese trading station. Under regulations drawn up in 1497, a renewed colonization plan would adopt the organizational model of Castilian towns, thus firmly denying the introduction of a seigneural system that had never been mandated.

According to the Milanese ambassador who met Cabot on his return in 1497, Henry had extended to the Venetian the most extravagant powers, including the ability to confer titles of nobility on men of his own choosing, including the unnamed Burgundian who was expecting a gift of an island (much as Cuneo said he received from Columbus) and already considered himself a count. Cabot, who would call himself a prince as well as a Great Admiral on his return from the 1497 voyage, was on the verge of establishing his own state with titled nobles within the suzerainty of England.

Where the Columbus and Cabot agreements differed hugely was in compensation. Columbus's activities were essentially left to others to fund: the Spanish monarchs, and merchants and financiers. Columbus had an option to invest but wasn't required to do so. The initial Santa Fé capitulation stated that Columbus was entitled to one-tenth of net proceeds from "any and all merchandise" in the resulting trade, in addition to whatever profits he generated from his own trading as well as from his titular and administrative duties. Columbus was further entitled to reserve one-eighth of all shipping to and from the Indies for his own activities (as the controversial April 1495 liberalization reaffirmed). Cabot in comparison was accorded 80 percent of the net profits and was further exempted from customs duties on goods landed at Bristol. Cabot was accorded a significantly higher reward than Columbus because he was assuming a significantly higher risk. Cabot was expected to mount the voyage at "his own costs and charges (*sui ... propriis sumptibus et expensis*).

This was a key condition found in the original 1486 Dulmo patent for the voyage to be undertaken with the German knight who could only have been Martin Behaim. Dulmo was to mount it at *sua propria custa e despesa*—his own costs and expenses, or charges. The condition of "own costs and charges" had already appeared in agreements for English royal privileges that had nothing to do with seafaring more than a decade before Cabot came along, with *propriis* sometimes erroneously interpreted as "proper" as well as "own," as in the case of standard modern English translations of the Cabot patent. Although Henry's court thus may have insisted on the condition, the author of the Cabot patent nevertheless could have been adopting the Portuguese voyage scheme with which Martin Behaim had been allied or, more concretely, the lost proposal Behaim had made to João II in 1493.

It is tempting to see the Cabot patent as a product not only of the Columbus and Dulmo-Estreito precedents but as a reflection at least in part of the lost proposal we know Behaim made to João II with Münzer's help, which then would have been refined for an English voyage through the ensuing activities of both Nürnbergers. After being rebuffed by the Portuguese king, Behaim had made his curious visit to England, which as noted reads as plausibly as a star-crossed attempt to sell the concept to Henry VII as it does a cockeyed diplomatic mission for Maximilian I gone awry. A patent proposal would have been prepared for Henry, even if Behaim never had the chance to present it. A few months later, Behaim's close associate Münzer was traveling through Spain and Portugal on what amounted essentially to a fact-finding mission on the Columbus enterprise. With the aid of Cabot, the elements of Columbus's capitulations would have updated and elaborated whatever Behaim had already proposed to João II in 1493 and perhaps had intended to pitch to Henry VII. There could well have been a side deal between Behaim and Cabot, entitling the old Columbus compatriot and chief architect of the *Erdapfel* to discovery benefits based on his contribution of the basic scheme and cartography. This would not have been unusual; English royal patents routinely involved licensing of entitlements to people never mentioned in the original document, and for that matter Columbus suit deponents insisted a deal had existed between Columbus and the Pinzóns to profit from the royal privilege the Genoese had secured.

Unfortunately for Behaim, Cabot proved to be an unnecessary complication. Persistently cursed by bad timing, Behaim would have seen Cabot nearing success in the English pitch just as trade and diplomatic relations between Henry and Maximilian began to thaw. Only a week before Cabot secured his patent, the countervailing embargoes between England and Burgundy were lifted with the so-called *intercursus magnus* of February 27, 1496. By July, with Henry formally welcomed into the Holy League, Maximilian and Henry were allies. Behaim could have safely initiated—or resumed—his own voyage proposal then. But Cabot was already at sea in his first attempt to prove the northern passage strategy conceived by Münzer and Behaim.

So little is known about the 1496 voyage that we cannot say if Cabot's Burgundian companion was along for the ride. Regardless of whatever agreement might have been struck between them, the rights for the English search were now in the unlikely possession of this fugitive Venetian hide trader and property speculator *cum* failed marine engineer.

Moreover, as Cabot sailed on his first voyage for Henry, Columbus returned to Spain and found himself hard aground, unable to secure the necessary backing or royal permission to resume his own explorations. Bartolomé Columbus's plans to sail far to the north from Española in search of Cathay had been firmly crushed by the two destructive hurricanes of 1495, and Fernando and Isabel's hope to encourage fresh explorations by liberalizing their regulations for the Indies had produced only one flotilla, which was destroyed in a storm soon after leaving Sanlúcar de Barrameda. The Americas, both north and south, were waiting to be discovered. A Venetian had emerged from within the logistical margins of Columbus's own enterprise to test for the English a northern passage-making concept that two Germans originally had intended to benefit the Portuguese.

NINETEEN

THE 1496 PATENT granted Cabot fabulous privileges, far beyond what Columbus had been able to secure. But as the Dulmo-Estreito venture of 1486–87 had proved, such a royal privilege was worthless unless the bearer actually could get an expedition off the dock. A voyage of even one ship, never mind five, would require money that Cabot himself didn't have. Given how Italians all but monopolized the banking system that made commerce function across Europe and how their family networks had extended their activities to the Indies enterprise of Columbus and the Canaries conquest of Columbus's associates, it should be no surprise that Cabot would have turned to a branch operation in London to fund his English voyages.

Without the clever bankers of Genoa and Florence and their innovations, such as bills of exchange, double-entry bookkeeping, and a fiscal sleight of hand that permitted loans to be made without violating the church's stricture that any sort of interest constituted usury, Renaissance commerce could not exist. London in particular had no bank of deposit and needed exchange bills for international trade to function. It's not certain whether even a handful of Englishmen in the late fifteenth century understood the banking and accounting systems northern Italian financiers pioneered and dominated. Henry relied on advisors, Genoese and Florentines especially, from the Italian merchant community. Arriving at Henry's court in September 1497, the Milanese ambassador Raimundo di Raimundis remarked on how well apprised the king was of Italian affairs and how "the merchants, more especially the Florentines, never cease giving the long advices."

Florentine bankers were vital to business in Europe, England included. Lombard Street, around which the Italian merchant community in London was organized, was named for Florence's Lombardy region of northern Italy. Florentine galley service to England had all but ceased by the end of the reign of Edward IV in 1483, leaving the Italian trade in precious goods to Venetian galleys and bulk goods largely to Genoese ships, but Florentine merchants were still active in London, moving goods on English vessels. They were sufficiently numerous for their community to be organized under a consul and were powerful enough to engineer a monopoly on English wool exports to Italy through a 1490 treaty, only to see it collapse under Venetian opposition a few years later.

Cabot secured at least some of his voyage financing through two managing partners in a branch operation off Lombard Street of Florence's House of Bardi, a family firm that had been active in England since the dawn of the fourteenth century. The Bardis had vied with their fellow Florentines the Peruzzis for bragging rights as Europe's greatest bank until both firms went bankrupt in the 1340s. The Bardis nevertheless carried on as bankers and merchants, and their name was suspiciously evocative of Gianotto Berardi, Columbus's banker.

Spellings of family names (as Cabot and Columbus well demonstrated) were extremely elastic at the time: Amerigo Vespucci, Berardi's associate in Seville, was called Bespuche in records relating to his assumption of responsibility for the ill-fated Sosa flotilla of February 1496. No other Berardi merchants or bankers are known, except for the Lorenzo Berardo whom Las Casas said carried Columbus's letter to Toscanelli to Tuscany, and who was most likely Berardi himself. Nor did the Bardis have a family member representing their business in the economically vital Seville during Berardi's years there. Francesco Bardi is the only family member to appear in Seville's notarial records, from 1504 to 1506. Berardi was a factor for the Medici bank in Seville until it collapsed in 1492, but the Bardi and Medici families intermarried, and it would not have been surprising that as a Bardi, Berardi would have tended to Medici business in the Andalusian capital.

If Gianotto Berardi was actually a Bardi, it is possible Cabot had already made connections with the Bardi banking network in Seville in 1494 before arriving in England in 1495. Having struck a flotilla agreement with Fernando and Isabel in early 1495 that may not have had Columbus's knowledge or approval, Berardi would have been open to the idea of Cabot pursuing a route to Asia to compete with the one claimed by Columbus and so passed him along to the family branch in London. Cabot's ability to secure Bardi financing could have been a key factor in Behaim and Münzer choosing to work with him.

Berardi certainly had had his fill of Columbus in 1495. In his deathbed will of December 5, he made a point of excoriating the Genoese for the heavy debts he left him bearing and even accused him of bringing on the end of his life. "To serve him," he declared, "I have . . . wasted my property and that of my friends, and have even sacrificed my own person, for if our Lord should take me from this world with this present sickness, it is the result of the travails and sufferings I have endured for the service of his lordship."

Cabot otherwise appears to have made his connection with the London House of Bardi through one of the partnership's clients: the deputy collector of papal revenues in England, the Augustine friar Giovanni Antonio de Carbonariis, who also seems to have been Cabot's champion at Henry's court. He surfaced as a Milanese envoy in 1489, conveying messages between Henry VII and Ludovico Sforza in association with Benedetto Spinola, one of that well-known Genoese merchant family's leading members in England. In late 1489, Carbonariis was attached to a mission to England as a "servant," or aide, to the Milanese ambassador, Francesco Paganus, who had come to England to secure a treaty of friendship. Paganus stayed in England only a few months and was back home by April 18, 1490. Carbonariis remained in England and became the proctor, or deputy, to the collector of papal revenues in England, Antonio Castellesi. When Castellesi left England for Rome in 1494 to serve as Henry's proctor there, he retained his rights as collector. Carbonariis continued to serve as Castellesi's proctor and took over the rental of his London house.

Carbonariis was at the height of his ascent in England when Cabot came along, and he was close to the king. Henry granted him a benefice of the rectory of Gosforth parish church in Cumberland on January 9, 1496, right around the time the Spanish ambassador Puebla took notice of Cabot's lobbying for his letters patent. Although it's not known how Carbonariis and Cabot met, Carbonariis apparently was advancing Cabot's scheme at court and could have served as his interpreter. Puebla was said to have cut corners in his domestic expenses by living in the Augustine friary in London, and so the Spanish diplomat must have known well a senior member of the order like Carbonariis.

As the absent Castellesi's deputy, Carbonariis oversaw the church's considerable income stream in England, which poured in as tithes and tenths and from various other sources from the faithful and church properties. The wealth of the English church impressed even Italian ambassadors, who marveled at the opulence of its churches and cathedrals. European monasteries traditionally had been a source of funds for merchant bankers, who routinely borrowed the money they loaned out themselves. As Henry forbade specie from leaving England, there would have been a tremendous amount of church revenue sloshing around the kingdom's economy, where it wasn't fixed in opulent reliquaries. Whether the funds Cabot was able to borrow to mount his explorations actually came from church revenues isn't known. Carbonariis could have used his banking connections at the House of Bardi to open doors for Cabot, as other members of London's Italian merchant community also may have extended support. The Spinolas, for that matter, could have been involved. But the relationship could have flowed in the opposite direction: Cabot using his Berardi/Bardi connection to link up with the influential House of Bardi client Carbonariis once in London.

The funds Cabot initially raised were not considerable. Having secured a letters patent from Henry VII in March 1496 that permitted him to mount a voyage of up to five vessels, Cabot was able to secure only enough money to outfit one in Bristol for that season. Henry could have selected Bristol in the patent negotiations and directed Cabot to organize his voyages there. As the second largest city in England and its major port on the west coast, facing in the direction Cabot proposed to go, Bristol made sense as a base of operations. Southampton was too far up the English Channel—and, as the 1495 Flanders Galleys incident underscored, was vulnerable to French pirates. Bristol thus would serve as Henry's staple port for the Asia trade.

But Cabot himself may have proposed he operate out of Bristol because mariners there already had some knowledge of a distant shore.

BRISTOL AT THIS TIME was as entitled as Madeira and Puerto de Santa María to dockside tales of storied landfalls over the western horizon. Southern Ireland was a principal area of trade for the port, a source of wool and fish; Bristol merchants also held rights to Irish salmon streams. The tales of the voyage of St. Brendan, the Irish monk whose fabled sixth-century wanderings may have held kernels of truth of distant Atlantic landfalls, possibly as far as the New World, would have been common currency, and St. Brendan's Isle was a regular feature of fifteenth-century charts.

As well, the Icelandic fishery and trade, and church postings there, would have provided ample opportunities for the English to have heard something of the Norse sagas recounting the discovery around A.D. 1000 of Helluland, Markland, and Vinland, which today are generally thought to represent in turn Baffin Island, the Labrador coast, and a more southerly, verdant land that at the least included Newfoundland. An Englishmen, John Williamson Craxton, was appointed Bishop of Hólar in Iceland in 1425. After first visiting his see in 1427 on a trading voyage, he appears to have lived in Iceland from 1429 to 1435. A learned man who also had extensive dealings with English traders, Craxton was in Iceland at the time the sagas were being written down for posterity. Other Englishmen had secured chiefdoms in Iceland by 1430 and would have been familiar with the stories, both oral and more recently as set down on vellum, of the discoveries made in centuries past to the west of Greenland.

Trade brought to Bristol Icelandic merchants as well as children who were alleged to have been abducted (or even sold by their parents). Early English voyagers to Iceland may have fished off Greenland and traded with its Eastern Settlement, which is thought to have endured to about 1450. Whether any of these English by accident or intent wandered across Davis Strait and the Labrador Sea and saw for themselves the lands promised by the sagas remains fertile ground for debate.

But in the years immediately preceding Cabot's appearance in Bristol, the main focus of the city's maritime curiosity was the elusive Brasil, sometimes called O Brasil or Hy Brasil, and not to be confused with the Brazil of South America. The name is generally believed to be Irish in origin, a corruption of the Celtic word *bras* or *bres*, meaning among other things "noble" or "happy." It has been associated with the Island of Delight, or Insula Deliciosa of the tale of St. Brendan. Brasil first appeared in a portolan chart drawn by the Genoese Angelino de Dalorto between 1325 and 1330, and was placed southwest of Ireland around latitude 52°.

"Brasil" proved to be a flexible concept. Its Irish Gaelic origins became confused with brazilwood, which probably originated with an Oriental dyestuff called berzin that the Venetians had introduced to Europe in the late twelfth century. On some maps that followed Dalorto's there were two different Brasils. The "new" Brasil was placed in the general region of the Madeiras and the Azores, and sometimes was associated specifically with little Terceira, where another dye, a reddish resin called dragon's blood, was extracted from the leaves and bark of the dragon-tree.

The fifteenth-century Spanish Basque chronicler Lope García de Salazar gave Brasil as the final resting place of King Arthur; his sister Morgain cast a spell on the island that made it almost impossible to find. He asserted the island "is 25 leagues off Cape Longaneas, which is in Ireland." Salazar's geography was confused: Le cap de Longaneos was the Basque name for Land's End in Cornwall. In addition, a distance of only twenty-five leagues hardly inspired visions of a New World discovery.

But Salazar's offer of corroborating contemporary evidence for Brasil's existence was noteworthy:

> And the English say that that island can be found if the ship can see the island before the island the ship, for a vessel from Bristol [*briscol*] found it one dawn and, not knowing that it was it, took on there much wood for firewood, which was all of brazil, took it to their owner and, recognizing it, he became very rich. He and others went in search of it and they could not find it. And sometimes ships saw it but due to a storm could not reach it. And it is round and small and flat.

As Salazar died in 1476, his undated account must have been written before then. He simply may have caught wind of an early Bristol landfall on Terceira, which was some eleven hundred nautical miles southwest of Land's End and equated with Brasil in some mid-fifteenth century portolans. It had not yet been settled in the 1460s or early 1470s and featured a kind of brasilwood (dragon-tree). With its low bluffs of volcanic rock along the north shore, Terceira also agreed with Salazar's description of the landfall being "round and small and flat."

Nevertheless, Salazar's account was testament to a Bristol curiosity in Brasil that was drawing its mariners farther into the Ocean Sea. A Bristol man named

William Worcestre, who died in 1481, recounted in an undated manuscript a voyage from Bristol in 1480 in search of the Isle of Brasil involving his brother-in-law, John Jay, Jr., in a ship of eighty tons burden under the master Thomas Lloyd, "the [most] knowledgeable seaman of the whole of England." The ship had departed on July 15; word was received in Bristol on September 18 that "the said ship had sailed the seas for about nine months but had not found the island." Rebuffed by storms, the ship had taken refuge in an Irish harbor.

The 1480 voyage of Jay and Lloyd clearly had been a failure. But the quest continued the following year.

On January 20, 1483, a "customer," or customs collector, in the port of Bristol named Thomas Croft received a pardon in a confusing case in which he had been accused by the crown of illegally landing fish in the port. In 1480, Croft had been one of three men to receive a license from Bristol to trade anywhere with two or three vessels, provided they did not exceed sixty tons. But because Croft was a port customer, he should have been barred from trading at all, which suggests that the license was intended to further exploration.

The crown showed Croft held a one-eighth share in two ships, the *Trinity* and the *George*, which had departed Bristol on July 6, 1481, each loaded with forty bushels of salt. The ships were naturally suspected of having embarked on a fishing expedition. Croft was licensed to trade, which was a different sanctioned activity from catching fish in the open sea and bringing them to port.

Croft was able to beat the charge. The salt, the crown agreed, had been aboard "for the reparation and sustenation of the said ships"—to salt down fish caught to feed the crew during the voyage. The salt moreover was not aboard "by cause of merchandise but to the intent to search and find a certain Isle called the Isle of Brasil as in the said Inquisition more plainly it doth appear."

The records of Thomas Croft's case did not say if the search for Brasil had yielded results. Croft may have successfully deployed the "looking for Brasil" defense to excuse what truly had been an illicit fishing expedition. Or perhaps he had been involved in a westward voyage in search of new fishing grounds that also happened to include a landfall Bristol sailors called Brasil.

The church's allowance of fish consumption on fast days, which included every Friday, created a massive demand that had made it worth the while of the English to sail all the way to Iceland to get cod especially. But for decades, English merchants out of Bristol and eastern ports, such as Lynn and Hull, had been embroiled in a vicious dispute over access to Iceland's bounteous cod. The range of adversaries included native Icelanders and the merchants of the powerful Hanseatic League of northern German cities, who wanted to keep the Icelandic fishery and trade to themselves. The crown of Denmark, which since 1397 had ruled Norway and in turn Iceland, tried to impose a ban on direct trade by the English with Iceland and alternately to enforce a licensing system, with Bergen in Norway serving as the staple town. In 1467, the Danish governor of Iceland was murdered by Englishmen as he tried to uphold regulations.

When Henry VII first visited Bristol in 1486 after wresting the crown from Richard III, he was greeted by a pageant that included an oratory by an actor portraying a legendary king, Bremmius, who by tradition founded Bristol. Through the actor's speech the local merchants made known their complaints about the decline in local trade: "That Bristol is fallen into Decay."

The herald's account of the visit noted that Henry VII took up this theatrical pleading. "After Evensong, the King sent for the Mayor and Sheriff, and Part of the best Burgers of the Town, and demanded them the Cause of their Poverty; and they showed his Grace for the great Loss of Ships and Goods that they had lost within 5 years. The King comforted them, that they should set on and make new Ships, and so exercise their Merchandise as they were wont for to do."

But the theatrical complaint had nothing to do with the Icelandic fishery, as has been often alleged. The only commerce it mentioned was "Cloth-making," which referred to the wool Bristol sourced from Ireland, in association with a decline in its merchant fleet, or "Navy." In 1490, prosperity had returned. A number of streets were "newly paved," and on a visit that year, Henry levied a 5 percent "benevolence" (essentially a loan he had no intention of paying back) on the "commons" of the thriving port.

The Icelandic fishery may have ceased to be a trade concern for Bristol merchants in 1490, when Henry entered a treaty with Denmark that secured English trade with Iceland and fishing in its waters. English ships were required to obtain a license from the Danish crown that was good for seven years and, when departing Iceland, would have to pay a fairly nominal fee of six shillings, eight pence. But the treaty was compromised when the ratifying Icelandic parliament struck the provision permitting direct trade by English ships. This meant English merchants could not trade at Iceland for "stockfish"—cod dried on land-based racks—but English fishermen were free to exploit the "green" fishery, which involved catching and salting down fish at sea.

Strife over access to this vital fishery might have encouraged Bristol sailors as late as the 1480s to search westward for an alternate grounds, perhaps in association with seeking the fabled Brasil. But because of the access to Iceland's green fishery secured in the 1490 treaty, there seems to have been little to no economic impetus to find a new fishery for a half dozen years when John Cabot secured his letters patent and mounted his voyages out of Bristol. The idea that Bristol sailors were exploiting a secret fishery discovered across the Ocean Sea also fails to hold water. If anything, men of the city might have found a distant landfall they recalled as Brasil at some point in the past, but by the time of Cabot's voyage, they had lost track of it.

The fundamental issues of Brasil—of who might have already found it, of where it was thought to be, and especially of what Cabot's contemporaries and

English associates then thought of his discoveries in relation to it—also became the fundamental issues of Cabot's English voyages. Having come north to prove a route to Cathay, he found himself entangled in a dispute not unlike the one in which Columbus saw his Indies discoveries dismissed as Antilla. And like Columbus, whose discovery claims would be further undermined by hazy stories of prior landfalls, Cabot's achievement faced concerted questions about its originality. There would be good reason to believe that the lands Cabot saw were not, as he would claim, Cathay and that they had, in fact, been known for decades in the port from which he departed.

TWENTY

L ITTLE IS KNOWN about Cabot's 1496 voyage beyond the fact that it was a failure. The weather was fierce and the food in short supply; the men were discouraged and contrary. Cabot's vessel (name unknown) skulked back into Bristol, his attempt to reach Cathay having bowed to the harsh realities of a westward passage in the north Atlantic.

Columbus's aversion to high-latitude sailing was not without justification. Storm tracks move from west to east on the jet stream, opposing the intentions of ships that could not make much progress toward the wind. Columbus practically could be blown to the Indies on the prevailing trade winds of the lower latitudes, then ride the westerlies home on a more northerly course. Cabot needed the right window of opportunity to sail to the west and then had to pray that it was not slammed shut a week or two out of port by the next low-pressure cell sweeping toward the British Isles.

While Cabot was away on his thwarted passage attempt, Columbus was crossing the Ocean Sea again, to set foot in Spain for the first time since September 1493. He had left La Isabella on March 10, pausing en route at Guadeloupe, where he claimed to tangle with Amazon warriors. He arrived at Cadíz on June 11 in command of the *India*, a vessel all too choicely named. Having been assembled from materials salvaged from the wrecks of the 1495 hurricanes, the ship symbolized the battered, patchwork state of Columbus's effort to secure for himself, his monarchs, and the merchants of Seville the promised wealth that lay to the west.

The Española colony continued to flounder, and more than a year after Fernando and Isabel had liberalized regulations for the Indies over Columbus's objections, not a single fresh voyage of exploration had occurred, owing to the disaster of the Sosa flotilla in February 1496. Returning at the same time as Columbus moreover was Juan de Aguado, who had been sent out by Fernando and Isabel to investigate the state of Española. The relationship between Columbus and Aguado had been prickly. Aguado's royal orders, terse in the extreme, instilled in him the presumption that he should serve as Española's governor while making his inquiries. Columbus had other ideas, and Aguado complained that Columbus waited five months before deigning to inspect the commission he was carrying from Fernando and Isabel.

Aguado returned aboard the *Niña,* and more than two hundred disgruntled colonists, brimming with complaints, also made the voyage on the two ships. Columbus was in another race home with a rival, and this time his adversary would not perish within days of regaining Spanish soil. Columbus would spend more than a year rebuilding his standing with his monarchs and shaping a fresh plan for his troubled discoveries.

Henry VII was in Bristol on August 12, 1496. The defeated Cabot would have been back in port by then, and the king could have learned firsthand from the Venetian what had gone wrong with his own quest to tap the riches of the Indies. The news would not have been encouraging, and Henry was not inspired to dedicate any of his own funds to a renewed effort. Back in March, when the letters patent was issued, Cabot's scheme may have promised a solution to the feud with Venice over the suspended Flanders Galleys, but by August, it was clear that Henry was going to have to press on with solving his trade headache by conventional diplomatic means.

In July, England's entry into the Holy League had been achieved, with the important proviso for Henry that he would not commit to going to war with France in defense of other league members. If ever Roderigo de Puebla proposed to Henry that Fernando and Isabel would condone a violation of the Treaty of Tordesillas by Cabot in exchange for Henry's military support against Charles VIII, the king had not thought Cabot's gambit worth the enormous cost of deploying an army and a navy in a continental battle. Henry ratified the treaty in September, and in November, his new allies in Venice chose an ambassador to his court, Andrea Trevisan. But Trevisan didn't actually depart Venice, as the Flanders Galleys remained canceled in the wake of the previous flotilla's multiple disasters.

Henry surely thought he had kept up his end of the galley bargain in signing on to the Holy League. In urging in early 1497 that these veritable treasure ships be sent once again, he also reminded Venice to send the promised ambassador. His kingdom had not received one from the republic on the Adriatic in almost a century, and he was anxious to discuss the affairs of the Holy League and the bewildering and highly fluid state of military and political affairs in Italy.

Venice's concern for the safety of the galleys was genuine—French pirates were making the passage far too dangerous—and it remained resolute about not sending them. But the republic would dispatch the ambassador. The senate summoned Trevisan on March 22, 1497, and told him to prepare to leave immediately. He would travel through the heart of Europe rather than risk death or capture at sea.

A member of Venice's Great Council of forty ruling clans since 1480, Trevisan had been chosen for the diplomatic post from the ranks of the republic's *curti,* or "new," noble families. The Trevisans had been involved in the English trade for at least eighty years. An ancestor, Lorenzo Trevisan, had traded out of Southampton in the second decade of the century, and the family had provided a London consul, Pietro Trevisan, in the 1480s. Although the exact relationship between them all isn't known, other Trevisans held other key posts in the Venetian diplomatic corps in 1497: Domenico Trevisan was the ambassador in Genoa, and Angelo Trevisan was secretary to the Venetian ambassador in Spain. It was Angelo Trevisan who would meet Christopher Columbus as well as Pietro Martire and write an account of the first three Columbus voyages that would be published in Venice in 1504. Andrea Trevisan, en route to England in the summer of 1497, was seemingly on his own collision course with a key figure in exploration history: his fellow Venetian John Cabot, who was not giving up on the northern passage project.

ON APRIL 3, 1497, the day before the Venetian senate resolved that Andrea Trevisan should travel to England with sixteen horses and two stirrup-men rather than twelve horses (to "go more honourably, as becomes the dignity of our State"), Christopher Columbus attended at Burgos the wedding of Prince Juan, heir to the Spanish throne, and Margaret, daughter of Maximilian I, who had been jilted by Charles VIII. Margaret's young life was unfolding as a series of unfortunate ordeals. Her sea passage to Spain had been so horrendous that she had tied an identification tag around her wrist, convinced she was going to drown. The marriage ceremony sealed the formidable double union that bound the houses of Aragon and Castile to the Hapsburgs, as Philip IV already had wed the princess Juana.

Almost ten months after returning from Española to answer his critics, Columbus was still in Spain, with no clear opportunity to reinvigorate his discovery agenda. But at least he had successfully defended his original capitulation rights.

Fernando and Isabel's profound dissatisfaction with Columbus's performance in Española had been surmounted by their dissatisfaction with the utter lack of response by Spanish citizens, subjects, and merchants to the liberalized conditions for Indies trade, exploration, and colonization they had created on April 10, 1495. Only Berardi had stepped forward with his flotilla scheme. Not only were the four ships wrecked in the only flotilla mounted under the contract, but Berardi had died

before they had even sailed, thus costing Fernando and Isabel the one Sevillan merchant who had been prepared to gamble money on Indies discoveries. Fernando
and Isabel also hadn't been able to bargain away some of their rights under Tordesillas to secure Henry's military support of their feud with France. Stuck with Columbus, they were now determined to salvage Española rather than abandon it and were
drawing a new blueprint for its development.

Fortunately, there were encouraging glimmers of promised wealth. Alonso de
Hojeda, a former *criado* (page or retainer) of Fernando and Isabel, had ably demonstrated his instinct for unscrupulous brutality during the campaign against the
Arawaks with Columbus in 1495 and in 1496 reported discovering a source of gold
in Española's interior. Columbus had also dispatched a party that found an alluvial
load in the rió Haina and its stream courses on the south side of the island. Here at
last Columbus was sure he had located Las Minas de San Cristóbal.

Beginning on April 23, 1497, and continuing through the next several months,
the crown began issuing a series of detailed writs on how colonization should now
proceed under Columbus. He was reaffirmed as Admiral of the Ocean Sea and governor and viceroy of the Indies, while Bartolomé, who had remained in Española,
was formally recognized as the colony's lieutenant governor.

The April 10, 1495, measures were revoked on June 2. Fernando and Isabel
acknowledged that Columbus "claims that our writ and everything stipulated in
it is prejudicial to the grants he holds from us and to the powers we gave him."
Unusually apologetic, their revocation stressed: "It never was and is not our intent
or desire that Sir Christopher Columbus, our admiral of the Ocean Sea, should be
harmed in any way, or that anything should violate or infringe on the contracts,
privileges, and grants that we made and conferred on him; rather, we intended to
confer on him additional favors in view of the services he has done for us."

The privileges he had secured in 1492 and 1493 were reinstated. But the plans
for Española were scaled back, and any further idea of enslaving the natives was
firmly rejected by instructions to convert them to Christianity. Colonists would
again be on the royal payroll, and Columbus was authorized to send 330 at the
crown's expense—500 if he could find the necessary funds from the colony's revenues. The terms for organizing and administering these pioneers were those of a
Castilian town, and Columbus was commanded to found a second settlement on
the south side of Española to take advantage of the "gold mine" the king and queen
had been told about.

Columbus was authorized to round up subjects and citizens of Spain who were
guilty of various crimes and have them pardoned and put to work in Española at their
own expense, doing whatever Columbus saw fit. "Those who merit the death penalty
will serve for two years, while those who merit lesser penalties not involving death
although possibly the loss of a limb shall serve for one year." He was also empowered
to gather men or women who "have committed crimes for which they merit exile to

an island, hard labor, or service in mines" and have them work the mines of Española for the benefit of the crown. Columbus was given the additional right to exile anyone in Spain "guilty of misdemeanors not carrying the death penalty but who justifiably could be given a sentence of exile to the Indies, depending on the nature of the offense." Those exiled by Columbus would have to remain on Española, "doing what the admiral orders for the time that seems appropriate to [him]."

The days in which colonists could seek out gold and keep a portion for themselves were over. Fernando and Isabel reverted to the traditional model of all precious metals in their kingdoms being theirs alone, and they hoped the mines of San Cristóbal would fill their coffers through the labor of pardoned convicts while colonists focused on founding a proper, self-sustaining agricultural colony. But in truth, there were no such "mines." The alluvial gold around the río Haina nevertheless set off a rush that depopulated La Isabella. Bartolomé Columbus saw no choice but to follow these rogue adventurers and relocate the colony to their squatter camp, thus founding the city of Santo Domingo. Although this satisfied the crown's orders to establish a second town on the south side of the island, La Isabella would fade away.

A relief flotilla was to depart for Española under Antonio de Torres in the summer of 1497. Columbus was remaining in Spain, as he had not yet secured permissions, or financial backing, for a fresh round of exploration. A third summer was slipping by without the Spanish expanding their very limited knowledge of what lay across the Ocean Sea.

DESPITE THE FAILURE of the 1496 voyage, John Cabot was able to amount another modest, single-ship venture for 1497. He departed Bristol sometime in May— as early as May 2, as late as May 20, depending on which secondhand account is believed. No log or journal from the voyage would survive and nary a word from Cabot himself would tell us where he went or what he saw.

There were eighteen to twenty men aboard the vessel, which was not large, about fifty tons. She might have been sixty feet long, a caravel not unlike the ones employed by Columbus, with high "castles" or raised deck areas at the bow and stern. One account called her a "ballinger," a corruption of the French term for whaler, *baleiner,* as Bristol ships were known to both fish and hunt whales in Iceland. She probably had two masts rigged with square sails, a bowsprit with a single square spritsail, and a third mast at the stern supporting a triangular lateen that was an aid to tacking, or turning the bow through the wind. She would have rolled horribly in a swell and been lucky to manage an average speed of four knots. Maurice Toby's so-called Bristol chronicle, which was probably written around 1565 and did not mention Cabot at all, said a ship called the *Mathew* was sent out by Bristol merchants on May 2 and discovered "the land of America." It is charmingly possible that Cabot had something to do with naming her, as *Mathew* (or *Matthew*) was as near as one could come in English to the name of his wife, Mattea.

We have little idea of who was with him, and if any of his three sons accompanied him; Sebastian later would remark on the voyage only so far as to claim it
as his own. Beyond the mysterious Burgundian and the Genoese barber-surgeon
that the Milanese ambassador Raimundis would meet in December 1497, the crew
ranks were fundamentally unknown, although we can be sure that they indeed were
"practically all English and from Bristol," as Raimundis would relate.

A recently discovered reward by Henry VII in January 1498 to a well-connected
Bristol merchant named William Weston strongly suggests that Weston accompanied Cabot on the 1497 voyage. Weston traded to the Iberian Peninsula, and in
1480, he shipped cloth to Madeira, possibly one of the earliest trading voyages there
out of Bristol, at a time when, coincidentally, Columbus was serving as a factor
there. Weston's father-in-law, John Foster, who died in 1492, had been one of the
great citizens and merchants of Bristol.

Cabot—or whoever was serving as his ship's master—would have directed the
Mathew westward to pass to the south of Ireland around latitude 51° before turning
north, up the open Atlantic, rather than sail north, up the Irish Sea. The latter passage would have carried the *Mathew* through the restricted waters between Ireland
and Scotland, culminating in the tidal rip where only a dozen miles separate Torr
Head from the Mull of Kintyre. Along the way, Cabot would have risked running
afoul of Scottish pirates when relations between Henry VII and James IV were especially poor; the Scottish king had been launching border raids, and his support for
the pretender Warbeck was well known. The southern passage, in contrast, would
have taken the *Mathew* safely clear of the conflict and through waters of the Irish
fishery that supplied the Bristol market. This passage agrees with the December
1497 account of Raimundis, who said Cabot departed Bristol and "passed Ireland,
which is still further west, and then bore towards the north, in order to sail to the
east [i.e., Asia], leaving the north on his right hand after some days."

The best Bristol mariners would have been skilled in pilotage, which is a very
different skill set from ocean navigation. Pilotage then was based overwhelmingly
on building up a knowledge base of local waters: how certain headlands appear
when viewed from certain approaches; how an island group would show itself; what
the depths should be for a channel; how far offshore a vessel would "come into
soundings" when approaching a landfall, as the deep-sea lead line began finding
the hundred-fathom contour; what the bottom composition—mud, sand, shells,
nematode worms—should be for that particular approach to land, based on samples retrieved by tallow smeared into the hollow of the bottom of the sounding lead
or by the wad of cloth stuffed into it if mud was anticipated. And on and on. These
pilots were far less dependent on charts than they were on the carefully compiled
personal notebooks they called rutters. In fact, they scarcely had use for charts at
all and were unlikely to understand the mathematical problems of plotting a course
on a two-dimensional representation of a three-dimensional orb, particularly when
the cartographers didn't necessarily understand the problems themselves.

Bristol sailors knew the sea route to Iceland, which lay above latitude 63°; after clearing southern Ireland, they needed to do little more than follow the compass north for about 750 nautical miles. Cabot probably sailed half that distance, seeking a latitude sufficiently high for his purpose of delivering on a promised shorter passage to Cathay. Somewhere between latitudes 55° and 59°, between the parallels marking northern Ireland and northern Scotland, he would have turned westward, as Raimundis described.

Cabot, who before 1496 had no known practical experience in commanding a vessel on any ocean, within or beyond the sight of land, was making his second attempt to persuade a ship's crew to defer to his conviction that Cathay would reward their collective persistence. The wind was favorable, from the east-northeast, and the seas were calm. It was a remarkably fortunate turn of the weather. In the early seventeenth century, English vessels were still swinging all the way south to the latitudes of Columbus's passages to cross the Atlantic before turning north, up the eastern seaboard, to reach landfalls in northeastern North America. They were striving to avoid the punishing headwinds that had confounded Cabot on his first attempt for Henry VII. This time, Cabot was able to still hold to a westward course more than a month after his Bristol departure.

THE VENETIAN SENATE had no ambassador in place in England to report on the latest purported threat to their domination of trade in precious goods from the Orient—this one from within the ranks of their own citizens. The delays and difficulties in Venetian shipping to England, which had been a major factor in Henry VII's decision to endorse Cabot's plan to sail west to Asia, had also conspired to prevent the Signoria from getting an ambassador to England in a timely manner. The rulers of Venice apparently had no idea of Cabot's letters patent, his failed 1496 voyage, or the renewed attempt he was now making to prove a westward route to Cathay, which if successful would undermine their trading monopoly in the Levant.

In fact, the Venetians had remarkably little knowledge of Columbus's ongoing activities. There was not a single mention of Columbus or the Spanish plans for the Indies in the diaries of Marin Sanudo, who had access to senate papers, after an abstract of Columbus's published 1493 letter describing his first voyage was recorded by the senate. The enormity of Venetian ignorance was underscored by the events that followed the return to Venice on May 17, 1497, of Francesco Cappello after a two-year stint as the ambassador to Fernando and Isabel. He had arrived in that post not long after John Cabot, the debtor of a likely relative, Nicolò Cappello, had left Spain under a cloud because of the Seville bridge debacle.

Francesco Cappello appeared in Venice with several gifts for the republic from the Spanish monarchs: two mules, a cloak tailored from cloth-of-gold, an assortment of parrots, and one human being.

The man was, as Sanudo recorded, "a dark-skinned king, or more precisely brown like a Canary islander, from those islands newly discovered by the king of

Spain." Sanudo further noted how "the said black king was presented to the Signoria, and he was well behaved, but did not know how to talk, although he had been caused to be baptized."

The *savii* of the Collegio, the steering committee of the senate, debated what to do with the black king. Some advocated re-gifting him to the marquess of Mantua, Francesco II Gonzago, who as a mercenary military leader, or *condottiero,* led Venice's army from 1489 to 1498 and had been commander in chief of the Holy League army against Charles VIII's force at Fornovo in 1495. But the matter was left unresolved. On May 25, the man was paraded through Venice as part of the celebrations of Corpus Christi Day, joining the religious confraternities in the procession of candles, floats, and costumes.

Despite the initial report that the black king could not talk, the Venetians managed to gather from him the opinion "that it seemed to him he was in Paradise." Cappello must have furnished what little was understood about his past, as related by Sanudo: "this one, as it is said, had 2,000 persons who ate under him, and in their country they eat human flesh, that is of executed criminals; and together with six other kings, he was brought to Castile by the caravels and troops of Spain, who went to conquer the lordship of the said islands; and it is said, that before they were captured, these chiefs made a stout defense."

The Venetians were terribly confused about the origin of the black king. It was commonplace to compare, as Sanudo had, the physical traits of Indigenous peoples of Columbus's Indies with the Guanches of the Canaries, as Columbus himself had drawn the comparison the moment he saw his first New World residents. Yet the particular scale of Venetian confusion was captured precisely in Sanudo's further comment on June 2 that Cappello had returned home with *il re di Canaria preso in le Indie*—"the king of the Canaries taken in the Indies."

Cappello had delivered gifts from two separate Spanish *conquistas,* but to judge by Sanudo's report, the Venetians thought the Canaries and the Indies campaigns were one and the same thing. On Columbus's way home in 1496, his men had looted a settlement on Guadeloupe, helping themselves to large red parrots they called *guacamayos;* these were probably some of the parrots "of diverse kinds and colours" Sanudo noted among the gifts borne by Cappello. Columbus had arrived at Cadíz with the parrots on June 11. No later than June 10, seven Guanche *menceys* or kings captured in the final stages of Alonso de Lugo's conquest of Tenerife in April and May appeared at Almazán. One of them had been chosen as a token of Spanish gratitude for Venice's friendship.

On June 2, 1497, the Venetian senate finally decided to send the black king twenty miles west, to Padua. There he could live in a house at the palace of the city's governor, Fantin da Pesaro. The state would provide the king five ducats a month for lodging and expenses as well as two ducats a month for a servant. He would also be given clothing "from time to time, as he had need."

On June 18, the black king entered Padua with Pesaro. Sanudo's mention of the relocation of this solitary Guanche chief from Tenerife whom the Venetians thought was from Columbus's Indies is the last time any word is recorded of him. The Venetian senate returned to its business, with the Rialto's warehouses still gorged with goods of the Orient and Columbus's Indies venture a nonexistent threat to their domination of the trade. Thousands of miles away on the Ocean Sea, a Venetian citizen was about to make his own terribly confused and confusing discovery in the cause of breaking the republic's grip on Asia's riches.

THE NORTHERN PASSAGE to the land of the Great Khan was turning out to be far more arduous than the weeklong jaunt that Münzer and Behaim had promised João II in 1493. But where Cabot's 1496 voyage had been battered by storms and foiled by an unhappy crew, on this second attempt he was able to press on, even when foul weather beset the *Mathew* for two or three days late in the passage.

The compass also began to behave strangely, indicating that north was two rhumbs, or points—about 23 degrees—more to the west than what the polestar told them. No one then understood the reason for the difference between geographic north and magnetic north, but the closer Cabot approached northeastern North America, the more pronounced this magnetic variation would have become, as the angle widened between the direction of the geographic pole and the north magnetic pole in what is now the Canadian Arctic. Had Cabot been relying fundamentally on the compass to guide him, the variation would have bent his course increasingly southward as he steered west. A crossing that may have begun as high as latitude 59° had been deflected to around latitude 52°.

That piloting error may have saved Cabot's life, preventing him from steering on south of Greenland into the Labrador Sea, where dangerous ice floes and icebergs are common in June. But his latitude likely also remained high enough to spare him the confusion of the Grand Banks.

Whoever was piloting the *Mathew* would have been deploying a deep-sea sounding line, probing for the continental shelf and the promise of landfall. Had Cabot approached North America as low as latitude 47°, he would have come over the hundred-fathom line of the Flemish Cap with Newfoundland's Avalon Peninsula still 350 nautical miles to the west. Cabot and his crew would have expected landfall within a day or two, based on the way they were accustomed to coming into soundings on European shores. (Approaching Portugal, a mariner came into soundings as close to land as forty nautical miles.) But after the banks dramatically shallow, hundreds of miles from shore, they deepen again as one sails west, before actual land is sighted—provided it can be sighted at all.

The Grand Banks are notorious for fog, as the warm Gulf Stream, coursing northeast, meets the cold flow of the southerly Labrador Current. The fog can be so thick that the bow of even a small vessel like the *Mathew* cannot be seen from the stern. It is easy to understand how would-be discoverers, whether Portuguese from the Azores or Bristol sailors seeking Brasil, could have in the past found the banks with a deep-sea line but not actual land beyond them, as they were compelled by subsequent increasing depths while enshrouded in claustrophobic fog to turn back and look for a landfall in the heart of the banks that wasn't there. All the while they would have been dismayed by the perplexing, increasing divergence between north as indicated by the direction of the polestar and the needle of their compass.

On June 22, Fernando and Isabel issued the writ authorizing Columbus to settle pardoned criminals on Española. Two days after that, Cabot made Columbus and his monarchs pay dearly for leaving the far reaches of the Ocean Sea unexplored for three years, as the empty horizon ahead thickened.

TWENTY-ONE

TWO SHADOWY FIGURES stole through shoreline woods, one behind the other. Animal? Human? The men of the *Mathew* could not tell, and they may have been too terrified to find out, too indoctrinated in the cannibal tales of the Indies to want to risk confronting strangers. In thirty days of coasting an unknown land, the crew followed their Venetian leader ashore just once. There was none of the imperious swagger normally attributed to explorers: armor gleaming, striding through surf to raise a flag and declare a sovereign's God-given dominion over the new land as well as its awestruck, gathered natives. A crossbow-shot was as far as these mariners were willing to venture inland in their only sortie ashore, remaining long enough to plant a cross and banners and cast nervous eyes over their surroundings.

They found remnants of a fire and an unstrung bow dyed red. Trees appeared to have been felled, and clearings suggested cultivation, but their anxious glances were only fueling their imaginations. They gathered snares and a needle they thought was for making nets. No one emerged to greet them, let alone inspect them from a canoe, a kayak, or an umiak. The wariness was deep and mutual. Only the running figures, too fleeting to resolve into man or beast, indicated any sign of life.

As far as John Cabot was concerned, he had found the land of the Great Khan. At least, that was what he was going to tell people when he returned.

IN THE SUMMER OF 1497—with Christopher Columbus in Spain negotiating new regulations for Española and trying to mount another voyage and John Cabot wandering an uncharted ocean and gathering the cast-off tools of an unseen and unknown people on a distant shore—Henry VII's troubles were converging danger-ously. The pretender Perkin Warbeck and his Yorkist supporters were planning an assault with Scotland's James IV. Meanwhile, in the southwest, a rebellion over new tax measures imposed by Henry to pay his military bills ignited a mob uprising of alarming dimension and determination.

Upward of twenty thousand angry rebels were soon marching out of Cornwall on London. So confused was the situation that a royal force that could have blocked their way, under the Earl of Surrey, instead wheeled north to deal with a coinci-dental Scottish attack in support of Warbeck. The road was left clear to the capital, where the rebels were determined to seize power and clean the treasures out of the Tower of London. A letter received by the senate and doge on July 15 from Venetian merchants in London advised that "the island was in commotion, both owing to these insurrections of the people who were desirous of a change, and because the King of Scotland, who favored the Duke of York, was also molesting the kingdom."

The Duke of Milan was no less concerned; a critical intelligence source on En-glish events was the Spinola family, which had been involved in English trade since at least 1303, with merchant banking branches in London and Southampton. The family was keen to grease the wheels of diplomacy where profitable relations be-tween England and the Duchy of Milan were concerned, assisting whichever side required their services.

Prominent among the Spinolas was Antonio, a banker and merchant who had joined the Genoese family's operations in Southampton in 1470. After becoming an English subject in 1475, he branched into diplomacy, serving three successive En-glish kings: Edward IV, Richard III, and now Henry VII. Henry made him surveyor of the royal customs at Southampton in 1489, and he seems to have spent most of his time there, occasionally appearing in London. In 1496, he had been dispatched as Henry's envoy to the Vatican. Before returning to England, he was empowered while in Genoa as an agent of the Duke of Milan.

Back in London in late June 1497, Spinola gathered from the royal court at Westminster an update on the convergent crises for the duke. The common people of Cornwall had risen in rebellion, he informed Ludovico Sforza, "because of the money which they have to pay to the aid of the king for the war of Scotland, and they came as far as Blatz [Blackheath], but the king routed them near Greenwich." The battle—remembered as the Battle of Deptford Bridge or the Battle of Black-heath—had occurred on June 17, four miles from the capital, Spinola further ex-plained. As for the situation to the north, Spinola got things roughly correct. The Scots had attacked the English border fortress at Norham on Tweed. But a planned coordinated assault by sea under Perkin Warbeck failed to materialize, and the Scottish siege fizzled. Warbeck was still at large—hiding from Henry's forces on the Irish Sea, in a barrel in the bilge of a ship.

At Bruges on August 5, Raimundo di Raimundis, the new Milanese ambassador who was en route to England with the new Venetian ambassador, Andrea Trevisan, wrote the Duke of Milan with news gathered on the fly from London: "[W]e learn that his Majesty is 50 miles beyond London towards Scotland, to prevent the White Rose [Warbeck] from taking root, and I gather that our coming is desired by his Majesty. Those affairs are in great travail." The following day, local tradition would hold that John Cabot and the *Mathew* reappeared in Bristol.

Henry VII was bracing for an altogether different arrival by sea. The king had been sequestered since July 28 at his manor at Woodstock, outside Oxford, about sixty miles from Bristol and fifty miles from London. Intelligence received from Waterford in Ireland on August 5 indicated that Perkin Warbeck had found refuge in Cork on July 25 and was expected to land an invasion force in Cornwall. Henry replied promptly on August 6, at the very time Cabot was reaching Bristol, thanking the mayor and citizens of Waterford for their diligence and proposing that they dispatch ships to capture the pretender.

Cabot was at Woodstock a few days later, reporting to Henry on his triumph. No account survives of the meeting, but what Cabot reported gave Henry some pleasure during one of the darkest periods of his reign. The king's household books noted for August 10–11 a payment of ten pounds—a modest initial reward—"to hym that found the new Isle." From there, Cabot was on to London, to spend some of his windfall, doubtless confer with his Florentine bankers and Giovanni Antonio de Carbonariis, and boast to the Italian merchant community about his spectacular find and his plans for the next voyage.

Cabot's voyage had proved to be perfectly timed to avoid the terror and chaos of the simultaneous rebellion and invasion of 1497. The initial plan of the Cornish rebels in fact had been to head for Bristol. Their leader sent word to the mayor, John Drewis, to prepare to feed and lodge two thousand men. Drewis replied that they would not be welcomed. "And then the Maire mustred and made redy to withstond the said rebelles, and garnished the town walles with men harnessed and with gonnes, and brought shippes and botes about the mersshe, garnished with men, artillery, and gonnes. And the said rebelles hereng of this chaunged theire purpose, and toke another wey."

Cabot headed for a capital that two months earlier had faced down the dangerous mob army that had chosen to march directly on London rather than make an initial appearance at Bristol. Approaching from the far side of the English Channel were the ambassadors from Milan and Venice. Raimundis and Trevisan reached Calais under escort to protect them from thieves on the road on August 8, where there were more delays in their protracted overland journey because of fears over hostile shipping. They did not expect to be able to cross until August 14. In fact, they were not able to sail from Calais to Dover until the twenty-third, due to delays regarding protocol and weather. There was then yet more waiting for the two ambassadors, as an escort of nobles and church figures arrived to welcome them and lead them to London, in a procession that grew to two hundred horses at Canterbury on August 26. The ambassadors would travel the seventy-five miles to the capital first and wait there until Henry was prepared to grant them an audience at Woodstock.

The repeated delays meant that neither Raimundis nor Trevisan—especially the Venetian Trevisan—was able to witness John Cabot's return from his momentous 1497 voyage.

TREVISAN WROTE TO THE senate a quick summary of what he had learned since arriving at Dover. The king, he reported, was in the field with his army, which wasn't literally true, although the king's army itself was certainly in the field. Henry had been at Woodstock, while the queen, as Trevisan correctly understood, was in London. Elizabeth and the two princes, Arthur and Henry, had taken shelter during the strife at the Tower of London.

The Duke of Milan also received two letters sent from England on August 24. Raimundis wrote one of them, at Dover, updating his whereabouts and plans and relating what little he knew about Henry's movements. The correspondent of the second letter plainly was much better placed than Raimundis to gather the latest court news. The identity of its author has never been settled, but the best candidate is one of the Spinolas. It may have been Antonio Spinola, who had already written a detailed report on the unrest in the kingdom in late June and would continue to be valued as an intelligence source in England by the Duke of Milan. Another candidate was Benedetto Spinola, who made his first appearance in Southampton records as a clerk in the family enterprise in 1458 and also spent time in London. On April 18, 1490, he had been empowered as an envoy to Henry VII by the Duke of Milan when Francesco Paganus ended his brief embassy in London. Still another candidate was Agostino Spinola, who would assume envoy duties in London for the duke in 1498.

The correspondent did his best to glimpse reliable facts amid the fog of rumor and outright panic, especially in London. He first reported that "by God's grace, the King and the whole court were in good condition" and were at Woodstock, where on July 14 "there had been firmly concluded and published the marriage of the daughter of the King of Spain to the eldest son of the King of England—that she was to come over next spring." The wedding news, however, proved premature. Perkin Warbeck had not been captured and was still dangerous, and Catherine of Aragon was going nowhere.

Next, he summarized what he knew about Henry's defeat of an invasion by the King of Scotland and "the individual who styles himself Duke of York." The correspondent didn't quite get all the details correct—for one thing, Perkin Warbeck had never put in an appearance—but it was close enough for now.

Next: "[T]hree of the leaders of the Cornwall rebellion had been beheaded and quartered in the city of London on the 28th June, many others being put to death; so that his dominion may be considered much strengthened and perpetual." That was fairly correct. Two of the Cornish leaders, An Gof and Thomas Flamank, were to be hanged (until not quite dead), then drawn (their entrails pulled out and burned before their blinking eyes) and quartered (chopped to pieces), but Henry demonstrated a particular Tudor sense of mercy by commuting their sentence to a less excruciating execution by hanging, followed by decapitation, on June 27 at Tyburn. On June 28, the third ringleader, Sir James Tuchet, Baron Audley, was led out of Newgate prison to Tower Hill mockingly dressed in a paper suit of armor and there decapitated; all three heads were then displayed on pikes on London Bridge and were waiting to greet Trevisan and Raimundis when they arrived in the city.

And then the writer had this to note, practically as an afterthought: "Also, some months ago his Majesty sent out a Venetian, who is a very good mariner, and has good skill in discovering new islands, and he has returned safe, and has found two very large and fertile new islands. He has also discovered the Seven Cities, 400 leagues from England, on the western passage. This next spring his Majesty means to send him with fifteen or twenty ships."

TWENTY-TWO

AS THE VENETIAN AMBASSADOR Andrea Trevisan journeyed on horseback from Dover to London in late August 1497, he was most struck by how thinly inhabited the English countryside appeared to be. He would gather the same impression from travelers who had been north to Scotland and west to Bristol and Cornwall: "The population of this island does not appear to me to bear any proportion to her fertility and riches." England's population had been devastated by plague and wars at home and abroad, but what the nation lacked in people it more than made up for in sheep. The wealth in wool was obvious to any visitor.

Arriving in the capital to await an audience with Henry VII, Trevisan likely was housed by the ambassador-designate Piero Contarini. His fine courtyard home had twelve bedchambers (some of which were probably used as offices), a stable, a larder house, and a garden house. It served as a place of business for the Contarinis and their Venetian partners and was well chosen for commerce. It was located on Buttolph (now Botolph) Lane, next to St. Buttolph's churchyard, in the heart of Billingsgate Ward, just downriver from London Bridge and next to St. Katharine's Pool, where shipping in and out of London anchored.

Trevisan would have found himself in the very heart of the London so recently frequented by John Cabot. A short walk north on Buttolph Lane could take him to Lombard Street, locus of Italian banking and trade in the capital and the source of Cabot's funding. To the north of Lombard, just inside the old city walls, was the friary of Giovanni Antonio de Carbonariis's Augustinian order. Among the vessels that called at London virtually within sight of the Contarini home in the summer of 1497 was the *Pasqualiga*, which the Venetian senate had chosen to provide haul-back service for much-desired English goods in lieu of the continued suspension of the Flanders Galleys. In late August, the ship had probably moved on to Southampton, where the senate had ordered it to wait three months before loading for the return voyage. Lorenzo Pasqualigo, who was minding the family's affairs in England, nevertheless was in London when he wrote his brothers Alvise and Francesco back in Venice on August 23, just as Trevisan arrived at Dover.

Pasqualigo's letter conveyed the first news from England of Cabot's return from the 1497 voyage, one day ahead of the letter to the Duke of Milan written in London. Both may have been penned around the same time in order to take advantage of a mail packet that was about to leave the city. Pasqualigo's account was far more detailed and evidently wasn't the first news of Cabot that he had passed along to his brothers. Although the letter noted that Cabot was now in Bristol with his wife and children, Pasqualigo's account suggested a firsthand encounter with the Venetian explorer during a visit to London.

"That Venetian of ours who went with a small ship from Bristol to find new islands has come back," he explained, "and says he has discovered mainland 700 leagues away, which is the country of the Grand Khan [Gram Cam]." Cabot had coasted this land for three hundred leagues and landed on it, and while he did not see any people, he had returned with some artifacts: snares for capturing game, a needle for making nets. Cabot had also seen felled trees, which he thought was a sign of inhabitants. "Being in doubt he returned to his ship; and he has been three months on the voyage; and this is certain. And on the way back he saw two islands, but was unwilling to land, in order not to lose time, as he was in want of provisions. The king here is much pleased at this; and he [Cabot] says that the tides are slack and do not run as they do here."

Pasqualigo understood that Henry VII promised to fulfill Cabot's desire to have ten armed ships for another voyage in the spring "and has given him all the prisoners to be sent away, that they may go with him, as he has requested; and has given him money that he may have a good time until then, and he is with his Venetian wife and sons at Bristol."

For once, someone actually took notice of this adventurer's name. "His name is Zuam Calbot and he is called the Great Admiral and vast honor is paid to him and he goes dressed in silk, and those English run after him like mad, and indeed he can enlist as many of them as he pleases, and a number of our rogues as well. The discoverer of these things planted on the land which he has found a large cross with a banner of England and one of St. Mark, as he is a Venetian, so that our flag has been hosted very far afield."

We can well imagine Lorenzo Pasqualigo's bemusement as he watched Cabot swan around London, using the king's reward to outfit himself with fine garments made from silk that Venetian ships brought to England. Gone was the somber black hooded cloak that Venetians wore in the Rialto. Cabot had taken to sporting the finery that his social standing also would never have permitted in Spain. The fact that he was being called the Great Admiral underscored his determination to re-make himself as a Columbus of the North. Nothing in the letters patent from Henry promised him such an exalted title, nor does any record survive of Henry conferring this honorific.

Cabot was shaping his next effort according to the parameters of Colum-bus's second voyage. He expected to have a considerable number of ships: Where Pasqualigo said there would be ten, the August 24 letter to the Duke of Milan prom-ised fifteen to twenty, which was essentially the size of Columbus's 1493 armada of seventeen vessels. Cabot also imagined establishing a colony along the lines of La Isabella and would need all the prisoners that Henry reportedly was willing to release to him to serve as labor. Columbus had been empowered to pardon crimi-nals for his first voyage, and had sprung three men from the jail in Palos to serve aboard the *Santa María* in 1492. But Cabot had not been granted a similar power in his 1496 patent. Pasqualigo's mention of prisoners being provided to Cabot for the next voyage instead evoked the decision earlier that summer by Fernando and Isabel to release criminals to Columbus as labor on Española; Cabot remained well informed about the latest developments in Columbus's enterprise and was incorpo-rating them into his own plans.

Andrea Trevisan was in London only four days after Pasqualigo wrote his brothers with the stunning news that the Signoria's banner of San Marco had been planted in the land of the Great Khan by one of their fellow citizens. Pasqualigo was also in close touch with Trevisan's contacts in London. The senate had called for the *Pasqualiga* to have at least 120 additional men for its protection and had ordered the new Venetian consul in London, Almorò Pisani, to call a muster roll on the ship before its return passage and send it home with the seal of Venice, so that the senate could be sure its manning orders had been followed. Failure to do so would result in heavy fines for the ship's masters and a suspension of their licenses for ten years.

It was thus altogether remarkable that after arriving in London to await an audience with Henry VII at Woodstock, Trevisan apparently heard nothing about John Cabot's exploits, so recently the talk of London's Italian merchant community, including its Venetians. Or if he did hear about it, he didn't think it worth sharing with the doge and senate. Only days after arriving in London, more urgent matters were before him.

ANDREA TREVISAN LEFT LONDON September 1 to meet Henry VII on Sep-tember 3 at Woodstock, which he found "a sorry village." He was joined there by his traveling companion, the Milanese ambassador Raimundo di Raimundis, for a shared audience. Henry knew how to stage a greeting, to impress with his wealth. They found him "in a small hall, hung with very handsome tapestry, leaning against a tall gilt chair, covered with cloth of gold," Trevisan reported. "His Majesty wore a violet colored gown, lined with cloth of gold, and a collar of many jewels, and on his cap was a large diamond and a most beautiful pearl."

When Trevisan and Raimundis arrived in England, war and rebellion seemed to belong to an unhappy if very recent past. They could concentrate on welcoming Henry into the Holy League and assessing progress on the new peace between England and Scotland that had just been brokered by Pedro de Ayala. Trevisan expected to confer again shortly with Henry when the king returned to London, but England suddenly was being plunged back into political and military turmoil. There was now nothing on anyone's mind but a fresh threat to Henry's reign. On September 8, Perkin Warbeck came ashore in Cornwall with a few hundred supporters, mainly from Ireland. Warbeck proclaimed himself the true king, Richard IV, and united with elements of the summer's tax rebellion. After laying siege to the gates of Exeter on September 18 and 19, the mob army several thousand strong had nothing to show for its efforts but a few hundred casualties among its own numbers. Warbeck remustered his force in Taunton, where the Cornwall rebels made a show of murdering the abducted proctor of Penryn in the marketplace; they "slewe hym pytuously, in such wise that he was dismembred and kutte in many and sundry peces." The proctor had been butchered for allegedly having been one of the commissioners in the country who gathered more money from the people than reached the king.

Warbeck then fled his own army with several chief accomplices, including a London mercer named John Heron, who had left the capital to avoid debts there. They took refuge in Beaulieu ("Bewley") abbey, a Cisterian sanctuary near Southampton answerable only to the pope. The rebellion was over. Giovanni Antonio de Carbonariis, Cabot's promoter and banking connection, raced to Exeter and kept Henry abreast of events. The king then rode for Exeter, and Warbeck's whereabouts were soon discovered.

The pretender and Heron agreed to come to Taunton and surrender there to Henry, who spared the lives of both men. Warbeck soon confessed to the ruse of his claim to be Richard IV and admitted to his humble Flemish origins ("ffirst it is to be knowen that I was born in the Towne of Turney, and my ffaders name is called John Osbek; which said John Osbek was controller of the Towne of Turney. And my moders name is Kateryn de ffaro . . .").

Trevisan secured an audience with Henry on the king's return to London in late November. Trevisan's reports were terse, in marked contrast to those of Raimundis, who made intensive inquiries about the uprising and wrote in detail to the Duke of Milan. Trevisan did not even report what he and Henry discussed at Westminster.

He had had his fill of Henry's kingdom and, on November 28, he wrote the Venetian senate for permission to return home, "perceiving that his stay in England is of no importance." His parents had died recently, and his relatives in the Signoria were agitating for the senate to approve his early recall.

Trevisan had never warmed to the country, or its people. In the report Trevisan would write for the senate and doge after returning to Venice the following spring, he found the English self-satisfied, convinced of their superiority. He begged to differ. "They are gifted with good understanding, and are very quick at everything they apply their minds to; few, however, excepting the clergy, are addicted to the study of letters; and this is the reason why anyone who has learning, though he may be a layman, is called by them a *Clerk*." The English were also uncouth, and he shuddered at how they shared one wine cup among three or four people.

He detected little loyalty to Henry VII: "They generally hate their present [king], and extol their dead sovereigns." He added: "The people are held in little more esteem than if they were slaves." Yet he assured the doge and senate: "From the time of William the Conqueror to the present, no king has reigned more peaceably than he has, his great prudence causing him to be universally feared."

On January 31, 1498, Trevisan again pleaded to be recalled. The senate acquiesced. In the meantime, he had missed altogether John Cabot's reappearance at Henry's court.

ONLY WHEN THE CORNWALL rebellion and Perkin Warbeck's easily crushed attempt to secure the crown had run their course could John Cabot resume his efforts to press for the king's support of a follow-up voyage. With Henry back in London, Cabot returned to court to pursue his vision of a large-scale venture modeled on Columbus's second voyage of 1493.

Cabot first secured a lifetime reward from Henry for his achievement. On December 13 at Westminster, the king "graunted unto our welbiloved John Calbot of the parties of Venice" an annual pension of twenty pounds, to be paid out of Bristol customs receipts "for the tyme beying" in two annual equal installments, at Easter and Michaelmas, with an initial reward to be backdated to the Feast of the Assumption on August 15. It was while Cabot was at Westminster, securing this reasonably generous stipend, that the Milanese ambassador Raimundo di Raimundis encountered him and his entourage. Raimundis listened with fascination as Cabot explained what he had found and what he hoped to achieve.

Raimundis may have witnessed a lecture Henry arranged for Cabot to give at court, but as the Milanese ambassador professed to having become a friend of the explorer, he also enjoyed private exchanges with Cabot and his small circle of associates. How Andrea Trevisan managed not to encounter Cabot or write anything about him is one of the oddities of both the Venetian explorer's career and the ambassador's tenure in England. Trevisan and Raimundis were at court together on December 14, the day after Cabot was awarded his pension, having been summoned to hear the king clarify his position with respect to France and the Holy League. It was most certainly around this time that Raimundis had the encounter with Cabot that provoked a voluble letter to the Duke of Milan on December 18.

But in addition to Trevisan's weariness of England and distraction of the deaths of his parents, which dulled his enthusiasm for the posting and made him yearn to quit the country, the Milanese ambassador had a circumstantial advantage over his Venetian counterpart: Most connections to Cabot in London revolved around the Duchy of Milan (and its protectorate Genoa) rather than Venice. There was Giovanni Antonio de Carbonariis, who was so prominent at court and also a link to Cabot's London bankers. Although those bankers were Florentine rather than Genoese, in the House of Bardi, the Duke of Milan maintained communications channels with England through Florentine merchants. Raimundis, in discussing how best to get letters to him on September 8, 1497, had mentioned both "the Genoa letter bag" as well as "such Florentine merchants as are in your confidence, as their correspondence passes through France without impediment and is but little searched." Florentines in London also would have had no time for the company of a Venetian ambassador, as they were still smarting from the loss of the lucrative English wool staple at Pisa arranged in 1490, after Venice crushed it through trade and duty countermeasures.

The Milanese sphere of Cabot's enterprise included the barber (surgeon) that Raimundis met, who was from greater Genoa. Even the mysterious Burgundian qualified, because the Duke of Milan had forged a close alliance with Maximilian and the Burgundian Netherlands by engineering with the aid of a massive dowry the 1494 marriage of Maximilian (a widower since the death of Mary of Burgundy in 1482) and his niece, Bianca Maria Sforza.

"Perhaps amid the numerous occupations of your Excellency, it may not weary you to hear how his Majesty here has gained a part of Asia, without a stroke of the sword," Raimundis wrote the duke.

There is in this Kingdom a man of the people, Messer Zoane Caboto by name, of kindly wit and a most expert mariner. Having observed that the sovereigns first of Portugal and then of Spain had occupied unknown islands, he decided to make a similar acquisition for his majesty. After obtaining patents that the effective ownership of what he might find should be his, though reserving the rights of the Crown, he committed himself to fortune in a little ship, with eighteen persons. He started from Bristol, a port on the west of this kingdom, passed Ireland, which is still further west, and then bore towards the north, in order to sail to the east, leaving the north on his right hand after some days. After having wandered for some time he at length arrived at the mainland, where he hoisted the royal standard, and took possession for the king here; and after taking certain tokens he returned.

Because Cabot was "a foreigner and a poor man," he would not have been believed in his discovery claims, "had it not been that his companions, who are practically all English and from Bristol, testified that he spoke the truth." The ambassador mentioned the world map and the globe that showed his findings. "In going towards the east [i.e., Asia] he passed far beyond the country of the Tanais"—in other words, far to the east of the river Don that empties into the Sea of Azov. "They say that the land is excellent and temperate, and they believe that Brazil wood and silk are native there. They assert that the sea there is swarming with fish, which can be taken not only with the net, but in baskets let down with a stone, so that it sinks in the water. I have heard this Messer Zoane state so much."

Cabot's English companions said

they could bring so many fish that this kingdom would have no further need of Iceland, from which place there comes a very great quantity of fish called stockfish. But Messer Zoane has his mind set upon even greater things, because he proposes to keep along the coast from the place at which he touched, more and more towards the east [i.e., Asia], until he reaches an island which he calls Cipango, situated in the equinoctial region, where he believes that all the spices of the world have their origins, as well as the jewels.

The fact that Raimundis had never heard of Cipango, made famous by Marco Polo, was an initial clue to his credulousness. He went on to relate an assured lie by Cabot: "He says that on previous occasions he has been to Mecca, whither spices are borne by caravans from distant countries."

Although a journey to Mecca was within the realm of physical possibility, the ratio of risk to reward was absurdly high. Cabot would have had to disguise himself as a Muslim to make a truly epic round-trip journey of about two thousand miles from the Venetian trade port of Alexandria. There was no mercantile purpose to visit the holy city near the Red Sea on the Arabian Peninsula, and if he was caught, he likely would never have seen home again.

No westerner is known to have visited Mecca covertly until a daring Bolognese, Ludovico di Varthema, began his journey there from Venice in 1500. Varthema first studied Arabic in Damascus before disguising himself as a Muslim in a Mamluk escort for a *hajj* caravan bound for the holy city in 1503. Varthema did find Mecca erupting with spices, silks, jewels, and other precious goods, but the supply chain of the European market through the Bab el-Mandeb Strait did not involve a detour through a city barred to nonbelievers fifty miles into the desert from the Red Sea. Cabot's visit to Mecca, if it was true—and he baldly claimed to have made more than one—would have been so extraordinary that he squandered the opportunity to publish a Renaissance bestseller about his experiences. As it happened, Varthema produced his own book in 1510.

There were, however, plenty of travelers' tales for Cabot to embellish as his own. Venice teemed with Holy Land pilgrims who were transported on the Signoria's galleys, and many endured the desert trek of some three hundred miles from Alexandria to Mount Sinai at the height of Cabot's activities in the Signoria. The German Dominican friar Felix Fabri made pilgrimages to Jerusalem in 1480 and to Mount Sinai in 1483–84, on both occasions traveling to and from Venice on a merchant galley. Fabri wrote about his experiences in the Holy Land, Arabia, and Egypt in the massive *Evagatorium in Terrae Sanctae, Arabiæ et Egypti peregrinationem,* which included an account of crossing the desert with Muslim guides to reach Mount Sinai as well as a purely imaginative rendering of a Muslim pilgrimage to Mecca. Cabot could well have cobbled together his Mecca adventure from Fabri's published account.

Most striking about Cabot's idiosyncratic championing of Mecca as a trading center through which Asia's precious goods flowed is that it echoed a notion Columbus expressed around the time of his own second voyage. In a letter written in 1500, Columbus recounted how his initial discoveries had promised to yield to Fernando and Isabel "just as much as would the traffic of Arabia Felix [southern Arabia] as far as Mecca, as I wrote to their Highnesses by Antonio de Torres in my reply respecting the repartition of the sea and land with the Portuguese." Not only had Cabot appeared to sail on that second voyage; he would have returned to Spain with Torres in the February 1494 flotilla that most likely was the one to deliver the letter Columbus later mentioned. The letter of 1500 was written to Antonio de Torres's sister, Juana de La Torre, and both were probably related to Diego de Torres, the governor of Valencia, with whom Cabot had dealt on the Valencia harbor project.

Cabot used his claim of a journey (or journeys) to Mecca to anchor his supposed sagacity on the sources of spices. According to Raimundis:

When he asked [at Mecca] those who brought them what was the place of origin of these spices, they answered that they did not know, but that other caravans came with this merchandise to their homes from distant countries, and these again said that the goods had been brought to them from other remote regions. He therefore reasons that these things come from places far away from them, and so on from one to the other, always assuming that the earth is round, it follows as a matter of course that the last of all must take them in the north towards the west. He tells all this in such a way, and makes everything so plain, that I also feel compelled to believe him.

The idea that Cabot had some special insight into the source of Asia's riches—and that Cipango was the source of spices—only emphasized Raimundis's own naiveté.

The general trade routes were fairly well understood by Cabot's time, and some of that knowledge had been gathered by two Venetian diplomats who had journeyed into Persia during Cabot's years in the Signoria. Josophat Barbaro had been sent to Persia as an ambassador in 1471 and met an ambassador from India at the court of the king, Assembei. Barbaro reported at length on the trade route through the Strait of Ormuz to the mercantile center Calicut and to points farther east where goods were sourced. Another Venetian ambassador, Ambrogio Contarini, also visited Persia on an exhaustive journey overlapping with Barbaro's embassy between 1473 and 1477.

In 1487, João II had dispatched overland expeditions through the Levant by Pero Covilham and Alfonso de Payva, whose orders included determining Venice's specific sources of drugs and spices in the East and gathering what they could learn about the possibility of reaching India by sailing around Africa. Payva was murdered, but Covilham reached Calicut and Goa. Once back in Cairo, he sent a report describing the trade at Calicut in cinnamon, pepper, ginger, and cloves and the feasibility of the round-Africa route.

The trade routes to the East were so well known that around 1494, a Genoese merchant named Hieronimo di Santo Stefano set out from Cairo on a business venture that took him all the way to India and beyond to Ceylon, Malaya, and Pegu in southeast Asia; after a number of ordeals, he resurfaced in Tripoli in September 1499. His sea passage from Aden to Calicut alone, requiring thirty-five days, was as long as those of Cabot and Columbus. While Santo Stefano's fellow Genoese Columbus was claiming to have reached the Indies, this intrepid merchant was actually there, taking note of pearls, jewels, coconuts, pepper, ginger, and sandalwood. Meanwhile, all Cabot could offer Raimundis in London was some vague and spurious insight, allegedly gathered from traders at Mecca, that their goods came "from places far away" and that he had deduced that because the world is round, he could reach these faraway places in the East by sailing west.

Either Raimundis was not a very attentive listener or Cabot was a fabricator who should have done more homework. Perhaps Trevisan was right, in that the English did not value schooling as much as his fellow Venetians, which had made Cabot the proverbial one-eyed king in the land of the blind where knowledge of the Indies was concerned. Raimundis's fascination with the purported novelty of Cabot's ideas was an embarrassing if inadvertent confession of his own ignorance, which would have been apparent to the Duke of Milan himself. Nicolò de' Conti's account of his travels as far east as Borneo, as set down by Giovanni Francesco Poggio Bracciolini, had been published in 1492 by Cristoforo da Bollate, a senator of the Duke of Milan, and dedicated to a senator of the Duke of Savoy, Pero Caro (Pietro Cara), who was embarking on his own journey to India and beyond. Raimundis was aware of Ludovico Sforza's curiosity regarding the voyages of Columbus; otherwise he never would have bothered writing to the duke at such length about Cabot. But Raimundis had shown himself as gullible to Cabot's pedestrian wisdom as any Englishmen far removed from the ferment of discussion in the most learned courts of Italy.

Henry VII too appeared to be easily dazzled by the Venetian's patter. "What is much more, his Majesty, who is wise and not prodigal, also gives him some credence, because he is giving him a fairly good provision, since his return, so Messer Zoane himself tells me." Cabot was decidedly optimistic about the level of support the king would provide, to hear Raimundis tell it.

> Before very long they say that his majesty will equip some ships, and in addition he will give them all the malefactors [imprisoned criminals], and they will go to that country and form a colony. By means of this they hope to make London a more important mart for spices than Alexandria. The leading men in this enterprise are from Bristol, and great seamen, and now they know where to go, say that the voyage will not take more than a fortnight, if they have good fortune after leaving Ireland.

But the king was not as captivated by Cabot as Raimundis—or Cabot himself— thought. The confirmation of Englishmen had been necessary to persuade Henry that Cabot had actually found a new landfall.

Raimundis then mentioned two unnamed Cabot companions. One was *sua barbero da castione Genovese*—his Genoese barber, who could have been from the community in London but was probably originally from Castiglione Chiavarese, a municipality of no more than two thousand souls about thirty miles southeast of the city of Genoa, which had been sold to the Genoese republic in 1276. The other was the intriguing Burgundian (*uno Borgognone*), with whom Raimundis spoke at length and who demonstrated considerable knowledge because he "corroborates everything." Each accomplice was expecting an award of an "island" on the next voyage. Cabot's cohorts "both consider themselves counts, while my lord the Admiral esteems himself at least a prince." A life of hustling, of dodging creditors, of fleeing angry nobles, had finally yielded an opportunity that made Cabot almost giddy with inflated self-regard.

"I also believe that some poor Italian friars will go on this voyage, who have the promise of bishoprics," Raimundis added. "As I have made friends with the Admiral, I might have an archbishopric if I chose to go there, but I have reflected that the benefices which your Excellency reserves for me are safer, and I therefore beg that possession may be given me of those which fall vacant in my absence, and the necessary steps taken so that they may not be taken away from me by others, who have the advantage of being on the spot." Raimundis was probably only half serious about taking Cabot up on the opportunity to be an archbishop, as he concluded, tongue firmly in cheek: "Meanwhile I stay on in this country, eating ten or twelve courses at each meal, and spending three hours at table twice every day, for the love of your Excellency, to whom I humbly commend myself."

Raimundis would pass on the opportunity to secure an archbishopric from Cabot and, in early 1498, was recalled by the duke to assume fresh duties in Italy, his position in London assumed by Agostino Spinola. But the duke was soon sending Raimundis back to London to deal with a profound crisis that may have made the ambassador regret not taking Cabot up on his offer to make him an archbishop across the Ocean Sea.

Charles VIII died on April 8, 1498, the result of a freak accident in which he cracked his head on a low door lintel, purportedly while playing indoor tennis. The French crown shifted to his cousin, the Duc d'Orleans, who became Louis XII, and a recent major political realignment was shattered.

On November 25, 1497, Charles VIII and Fernando and Isabel had achieved at Alcala, near Madrid, an extraordinary pact reversing their recent enmity, forming an alliance aimed at divvying up territories in Italy. The Duke of Milan had seemed relatively safe under the new alliance. But with Charles VIII's death and Louis XII's ascent, Ludovico Sforza was suddenly at great risk.

A veteran of the 1494–95 Italian campaign, Louis XII had a claim to Milan through his grandmother and was intent on seizing it. In a letter to Agostino Spinola in London on May 11, 1498, Sforza alluded to "this new French king who calls himself Duke of Milan." Raimundis was returned to England to drum up support to oppose Louis's designs on the duchy. He did not arrive until September 7, 1498. By then, it was too late for Raimundis to resume his acquaintance with John Cabot.

On February 9, 1499, France and Venice signed a pact that made Milan their joint enemy. Raimundis left England for Flanders on July 12, all diplomacy now futile; Sforza fled Milan for the sanctuary of Maximilian's domain as French and Venetian forces conquered the duchy in a campaign that lasted from August to October. Raising a force of his own, Sforza launched a counterattack in 1500 but was captured and removed to France, at one point being transported ignominiously in an iron cage sheathed in wood. He would die forgotten in 1508.

Raimundo di Raimundis, who had opened such an intriguing window onto John Cabot's activities, character, and aspirations in December 1497, never again wrote of the Venetian explorer. The Milanese ambassador was also the first and last eyewitness to the presence in Cabot's entourage of an unnamed Burgundian who corroborated his claims, expected title to part of the 1497 discoveries, and already fancied himself a count.

TWENTY-THREE

IT HAD TAKEN Columbus more than a year since his return to Spain in June 1496 to fend off his critics and recover his standing with Fernando and Isabel. The paperwork detailing his fresh terms for exploiting the Indies was essentially completed by late July 1497, but there was still no new voyage for him.

Columbus's efforts to move forward his exploration agenda were disrupted by a profound loss to Fernando and Isabel. Prince Juan, their sole male offspring eligible to inherit and unite the crowns of Aragon and Castile, died on October 4, 1497, less than six months after marrying Maximilian's daughter Margaret at Burgos. Margaret was pregnant but gave birth to a stillborn daughter on December 8. Not until December 23 were fresh items of royal business completed for Columbus, as authority was granted to him and Juan Rodríguez de Fonseca to contract for provisions for another voyage, and Columbus was permitted to use royal profits and assets in the Indies to cover costs there.

As Columbus waited to return to sea, a letter in Spanish signed by an Englishman named John Day arrived. Addressed to *el Señor Almirante Mayor,* it was written sometime over the winter of 1497–98, after John Cabot returned from his second voyage and before he departed on his third. Within that letter was the most detailed account known of Cabot's 1497 voyage to the New World as well as the only recorded mention of a previous voyage by Cabot in 1496. Pinned down in Spain and trying to organize a third voyage of his own, Columbus had developed an intelligence pipeline into Cabot's activities out of Bristol.

John Day was a merchant active in Spain who moved in the highest circles of Columbus's commercial associates. The English formed the second-largest merchant community, after the Genoese, in and around Seville, although most of them were downriver in Sanlúcar de Barrameda, where they enjoyed special privileges under the Duke of Medina-Sidonia. In a 1499 suit at Sanlúcar de Barrameda, Day gave power of attorney to another Englishman, "Pedro Albordin," a Bristol native, to settle a debt Day owed to Batista Negrón and Francisco Pinelo. To guarantee the payment of the debt, Day had pawned a shipment of English cloth that was being held by Sebastian Doria, another member of the Genoese merchant community of Seville.

"Batista Negrón" was probably Battista di Negro, a Genoese merchant active in Seville from 1486 to 1503; if so, he was from the prominent family that had employed Columbus in the 1470s. Francisco Pinelo was the Genoese royal treasurer of Castile, whose nephew Bernardo was treasurer of the Indies enterprise at Seville. Sebastian Doria was from still another prominent Genoese family in Andalusia. A relative, Francisco Doria, formed a partnership with Francisco Catanio, Gaspar de Spinola, and Francisco de Riberol (of the Canary Islands conquest) to begin bankrolling Columbus's activities in Spain in 1498, loaning him almost 200,000 maravedis to cover his expenses through 1501. These four Genoese partners in Seville also would form a partnership with Columbus to ship trade goods to Santo Domingo in 1500.

It turned out that "John Day" was an alias used in Bristol activities by a prominent London merchant, Hugh Say, who identified himself as a member of the mercers' company. Related by marriage to Lord Mountjoy, Henry VII's Master of the Mint, for whom he was listed as a "servant" in 1514, Say had been active in Bristol since at least 1492–93, when local customs records showed him importing oil and wine from Lisbon. He was granted membership in the Bristol staple in 1494 as "John Day of London, merchant."

Hugh Say apparently also had connections to Icelandic traders in Bristol and was related through marriage to Bristol merchants associated with Cabot. His family may have been embroiled in Yorkist plots against Henry VII, with a father or brother indicted for treason. This would explain why he died with such a guilty conscience, leaving a large sum in his will to go "towards the building of our mother church Saint Peters at Rome to have pardon for wrongs done which I know not how to make restitution." It also may explain why Say had removed himself to Bristol under an alias as the Warbeck crisis festered and why he took such care in his letter to Columbus not to communicate in any way that could be considered treasonous. Say had promised "when I get news from England about the matters referred to above—for I am sure that everything has to come to my knowledge—I will inform your Lordship of all that would not be prejudicial to the King my master."

Say began by acknowledging receipt of an unknown letter in which Columbus had questioned him about Cabot's activities. "I would be most desirous and most happy to serve you," Say replied—by which he assuredly didn't mean actually working for him but rather satisfying his curiosity. Say further acknowledged his promise to send Columbus two books. One was a "book of Marco Polo"; the other was *Inventio Fortunata*.

Say confirmed he was sending the Marco Polo book. Columbus already would have been familiar with Polo's exploits, but Say could have been the source of the abridged Latin version of *Marco Polo's Travels* printed at Antwerp around 1485 that appeared in an inventory of Fernando Columbus's books. As there was no price written down for the book by the fastidious Fernando, it may have been one of the books he inherited from his father.

Say apologized for not being able to find the promised copy of *Inventio Fortunata*. In fact, no known copy of fourteenth-century work survives. Secondhand references indicate it included an account of the northern wanderings of King Arthur, who after conquering the northern islands of Scotland in A.D. 530 crossed over to Iceland and then to Greenland, leaving behind colonists. Even though Say was unable to make good on his promise of a copy of *Inventio Fortunata*, both Las Casas and the biography attributed to Fernando Columbus held that Christopher Columbus was informed in some way of the lost work's geographic information. And while the manuscript was supposed to be concerned foremost with discoveries in high northern latitudes, Las Casas and the Fernando biography mentioned *Inventio Fortunata* in association with more southern landfalls. Fernando's biography said "Juventio Fortunata" spoke of floating islands south of the Cape Verdes. Las Casas asserted that St. Brendan visited "many islands" beyond the Canaries and Cape Verdes that were "always burning," and which he stated had been mentioned as well in *Inventio Fortunata*.

Say had further promised to send Columbus a map, but had not done so, "because I am not satisfied with it, for my many occupations forced me to make it in a hurry at the time of my departure." Say then mentioned "the said copy," from which Columbus "will learn what you wish to know, for in it are named the capes of the mainland and islands, and thus you will see where land was first sighted, since most of the land was discovered after turning back." And so with this "copy" Columbus already had a rough sketch of Cabot's discoveries.

Say's letter is the most authoritative surviving account of the 1497 voyage. It is not only the most detailed; it is also stripped of details gathered first- or secondhand from Cabot himself, which spoke of brazilwood, silk, and other Oriental riches—the very sort of hyperbole that Columbus himself traded in where his own discoveries were concerned. Say's geographic intelligence was divorced from Cabot's agenda, with a factual purity Columbus himself never managed to achieve.

Say did agree with earlier accounts in indicating that Cabot had reached both the Isle of Seven Cities and mainland beyond. From the sketch map, Say explained,

Columbus could see "that the cape nearest to Ireland is 1800 miles west of Dursey Head which is in Ireland, and the southernmost part of the Island of the Seven Cities is west of the Bordeaux River, and your Lordship will know that he landed at only one spot of the mainland, near the place where land was first sighted, and they disembarked there with a crucifix and raised banners with the arms of the Holy Father and those of the King of England."

The account left some confusion over where the "cape" was. At first mention it was near the initial landfall, from which Cabot had then coasted back along the shore toward England. But later Say advised that Cabot departed for home "from the above mentioned cape of the mainland which is nearest to Ireland." Although the exact location of the cape was problematic, the fact that the letter could have been a Spanish translation of a lost draft Say made in English is a possible source of the confusion. There was probably more than one cape, and it is best to set aside the cape issue and focus instead on the unfiltered information being conveyed to Columbus from Bristol's docks by Say.

Say's description indicated that Cabot first sighted land (thirty-five days after departing Bristol) at a place on the same latitude at Dursey Head, which is at about 52° north. This would have brought him to North America at southern Labrador or nearby at Cape Bauld in northernmost Newfoundland, coincidentally in the neighborhood of the only known Norse settlement in North America, at L'Anse Aux Meadows. Cabot evidently thought he had found the mainland of Asia. After going ashore for the first and only time and erecting the banners of the pope, Alexander VI, and Henry VII (there was nothing about a banner of San Marco for his native Venice, as related only by Lorenzo Pasqualigo), Cabot then had worked his way back toward home, south and east along the fiercely meandering north shore of Newfoundland. He would have been hoping to reach Quinsay, around latitude 45°, but the coast was trending mostly eastward and no great seaport of Cathay revealed itself.

He coasted Newfoundland to the point that he ran out of shoreline around the Avalon Peninsula. Here the coast turns sharply and trends westward into the Gulf of St. Lawrence at about 46½° north. Cabot had now gone as far south as the latitude of the *rio de bordeos*—the mouth of Bordeaux's river, the Gironde, is at about 45½° north. The 1-degree discrepancy is more than acceptable. First, the latitude shared with the mouth of the Gironde was only a general orientation offered by Say. Second, a 1-degree error was a very good result for a late fifteenth-century mariner. Columbus made errors of several degrees. The result was actually impressive if the crew made a celestial observation from the rolling deck of a moving ship, as they went ashore only once, after first sighting land.

Cabot enjoyed an extremely brisk return crossing, completing in fifteen days a passage that wandered too far south and raised the European coast in Brittany. The speed further suggested that he departed from the Avalon Peninsula, the most easterly location possible, for him to have completed a passage of nineteen hundred nautical miles in such short order in a ship of his day. Say's letter thus supported the opinion of Bristol mariners cited by Raimundo di Raimundis that the westward crossing could be made in a fortnight from Ireland if the weather cooperated.

By the "Isle of Seven Cities," Say might have been referring to Newfoundland, but it seemed to be considered part of the mainland, because in Say's confusing discussion of the "cape," he advised that Cabot had steered for home "from the above mentioned cape of the mainland which is nearest to Ireland" and his departure presumably was from around Newfoundland's Avalon Peninsula.

The answer seems to lie in the distances quoted in the different accounts. A common thread was a distance of four hundred leagues. The Pasqualigo letter said Cabot's landfall came on the mainland seven hundred leagues distant (but not from where) and that it was coasted for three hundred leagues. As Say's letter said the coasting was back in the direction of home, it would imply a return ocean passage of four hundred leagues for Pasqualigo's account. Say's letter gave a passage distance of eighteen hundred miles between Dursey Head and Cabot's point of departure for the return voyage. With four Roman miles (of five thousand feet) to a league, Say's distance from Dursey Head to the departure point thus was 450 leagues. The anonymous letter to the Duke of Milan on August 24, 1497, had Cabot discovering the Isle of Seven Cities four hundred leagues from England.

The entirety of Newfoundland would be depicted as an island archipelago by cartographers for centuries, including on a 1544 map printed at Amsterdam that has been attributed (not entirely persuasively) to Cabot's son Sebastian. But the Avalon Peninsula of eastern Newfoundland, rather than all of Newfoundland, may be the best candidate for the Isle of Seven Cities or Antilla, four hundred leagues from Dursey Head. Both Seven Cities and Antilla often were presented as a group of islands—in Columbus's case, the West Indies were called the Antilles. Cape Bonavista would have been the cape on the "mainland" from which the sail for home began. It would have been easy to presume the Avalon Peninsula to the south represented two islands, as mentioned by Pasqualigo and the unknown Milanese correspondent in London, and which doubtless were also the islands that the Burgundian and Genoese associates of Cabot expected in reward. Pasqualigo tellingly noted the two islands being seen on the way back, which was consistent with a coasting experience along the north shore of Newfoundland ending around Cape Bonavista. Cabot's last experience of eastern North America involved a passing glance at the headlands formed by the deep, broad indentations of Conception and Trinity bays, which convinced the crew they were passing a pair of islands.

Still, dragooning the Isle of Seven Cities into the role of the two "islands" glimpsed as Cabot departed easternmost Newfoundland was an imaginative reworking of the prevailing geographic order—although no less imaginative than the way Columbus coopted the Golden Chersonese to make Cuba serve as a peninsula of the Asian mainland.

Cabot's interpretation shifted Antilla far to the north of its presumed location and much closer to the Asian mainland. The Andrea Bianco portolan of 1436, the first to display an island called Antillia, had placed it in the middle of the Ocean Sea between about 32° and 38° north. It had since been slipping southward. Toscanelli put it west of the Canaries, around 28° north, and Martin Behaim in his Nürnberg globe fixed *Insula Antilia genannt Septe citade* down at 24° north. Were Cabot's find judged authentic, it would at least explain why no one had ever been able to find the Isle of Seven Cities in the locations cartographers promised.

Say's account was full of small, well-informed details. He explained that Cabot's ship was fifty tons, carried twenty men, and was provisioned for a seven- or eight-month voyage. He recounted the favorable winds from the east-northeast and the storm late in the outbound passage and how, as Cabot approached landfall, "his compass needle failed to point north and marked two rhumbs below." Say reported the two shadowy figures running through the woods, the fear of Cabot and his men to investigate more than a crossbow's shot inland, the length of wood with holes at both ends "and painted with brazil," which would have been an unstrung bow decorated with red ocher used by the Beothuk or "Little Passage" people of Newfoundland, or the Innu of Labrador. Leaving aside Cabot's timidity, it should not surprise us that he met no one; while he apparently coasted Newfoundland around the time of the Atlantic salmon's spawning run in July, which brought families to the coast, there may only have been five hundred to seven hundred Beothuk or "Little Passage" people living in all of Newfoundland at this time. Of the return voyage, Say recounted a dispute with crew members who said they were steering too far north, which caused them to steer too far south and raise the European coastline at Brittany.

Say also reported the voyagers' impression that the land they discovered was cultivated. They were sorely mistaken; their imaginations turned nervous glimpses of open ground into agricultural bounty. Cabot would have had to sail well down the coast of eastern North America, beyond Nova Scotia and Maine, to find semisedentary people practicing agriculture in cleared fields anywhere along the seaboard. Nevertheless, Say reported: "[I]t seemed to them that there were tilled lands where there might also be villages."

The appearance of the words *tierras labradas* (worked or tilled lands) in the original Spanish of Say's report is noteworthy, as it arises from the first known landfall that was in the general vicinity of what we call Labrador. Instead of a later Portuguese voyager having inspired the name Labrador, as often has been weakly proposed, Cabot's 1497 voyage would have introduced labels on maps now lost to us denoting the alleged tilled lands or, more particularly, the land of the "farmer," which in modern Spanish is *labrador* and in Portuguese *lavrador*.

Columbus had also wanted to know more about Cabot's 1496 attempt. "Since your Lordship wants information relating to the first voyage," Say obliged, "here is what happened: he went with one ship, his crew confused him, he was short of supplies and ran into bad weather, and he decided to turn back." To this day, that is the entirety of what is known about the 1496 voyage.

A fairly arresting part of Say's letter was his assertion that the land Cabot had discovered was already known to Bristol sailors and, moreover, that the earlier discovery was something Columbus himself knew about. "It is considered certain that the cape of the said land was found and discovered in the past by the men from Bristol who found Brasil [*el brasil*] as your Lordship well knows. It was called the Island of Brasil [*la ysla de brasil*], and it is assumed and believed to be the mainland that the men from Bristol found."

Say thus contended that an earlier landfall thought to be the island of Brasil turned out to be part of a larger mainland. His observation revealed the kernel of a serious dispute. Bristol interests were not about to concede that everything Cabot had discovered belonged to him and his sons under the letters patent, which had promised the Cabots the rights to lands "unknown to all Christians" and "newly found by them." Say also agreed with Raimundis that these waters were rich in cod and thus were a potential source of wealth that had nothing to do with Oriental silk or brazil-wood. "All along the coast they found many fish like those which in Iceland are dried in the open and sold in England and other countries, and these fish are called in English 'stockfish.'"

It wasn't clear what Say meant when he asserted a landfall known as Brasil had been discovered "in the past," as phrased in the standard translation. The original Spanish, *en otros tiempos* ("in/at other times"), could refer to an event (or several events) that had occurred within the past few years or several decades earlier. Say thus could have been referring to a successful recent search for Brasil, made sometime between 1481 and the early 1490s. Or he could have been alluding to a more distant event, a landfall in the 1460s or 1470s or even earlier that Bristol sailors had not been able to find again.

As for Say's assertion that this prior discovery of Brasil was a fact Columbus "well knows": How long had Columbus known this? Say might have been reiterating something he had already explained to Columbus in their last encounter or that Columbus had gathered recently from other English merchants around Seville or Sanlúcar de Barrameda. But it did rather sound as if Columbus had been aware of an English claim to a discovery of Brasil for some time.

Columbus could have heard of the search for Brasil by Bristol merchants when he first arrived at La Rábida around 1485. There was a compelling connection between the Franciscan monastery that sheltered him and helped secure his capitulations from Fernando and Isabel and Bristol voyages in search of the quasi-mythical landfall in 1480–81.

ON OCTOBER 18, 1480, an English merchant ship called the *Trinity* departed the mouth of the Avon downstream from Bristol on a trading voyage to Andalusia. This was probably not the same *Trinity* that would depart Bristol in search of Brasil the following summer. The *Trinity* of the Andalusia voyage was a substantial merchant ship of three hundred tons while the *Trinity* of the 1481 search for Brasil had to be much smaller, as the terms of Thomas Croft's trading license limited ships to sixty tons. Nevertheless, one of the three owners of the Andalusia-bound *Trinity* was John Jay, Jr. On September 18, 1480, an eighty-ton vessel backed in part by Jay had returned to Bristol from a failed search for Brasil, only a month before the *Trinity* cleared the Avon.

The crew of the three hundred–ton *Trinity* certainly could have carried with them to Andalusia word of the recent search for Brasil backed by her co-owner Jay. Some of them might have been participants in the search. An accounts book of the purser, John Balsall, showed there were even three crew members with Spanish names, which eliminated any possible language barrier in disseminating news of the 1480 search. What is more, the *Trinity* spent several weeks around Isla Saltés, by the monastery of La Rábida, mainly trading in English cloth with merchants from the local towns of Huelva, Palos, and Moguer. The Balsall accounts showed that the *Trinity*'s men visited La Rábida, recording a donation "paid to the friars at Our Lady of Rábida to pray for us."

In the weeks that the *Trinity*'s men (who included those three Spaniards) spent in the vicinity of La Rábida, there would have been plenty of time to share the news of the (failed) 1480 effort out of Bristol by the *Trinity*'s co-owner, Jay, to find Brasil—an effort that would resume under Thomas Croft soon after they were back in Bristol. Columbus was still about five years away from reaching La Rábida, but the Bristol mariners' stories of the search for Brasil could have reached the monastery's learned friars, who in turn would have shared them with Columbus as they spent years debating what lay to the west before his capitulations were secured. Bristol ships would have continued to appear in the harbor in ensuing years, and their sailors would have continued to give the Franciscans money to pray for them. And so there would have been many other opportunities to share scuttlebutt of a success unknown to us that came after 1481 and for that scuttlebutt to reach Columbus once he had appeared at La Rábida.

What Say foremost had done for Columbus was explain that the Bristol discovery of the Isle of Brasil, which the Genoese explorer already knew about, had proved to be something else altogether. Cabot's voyage had shown that the Isle of Brasil was actually part of a greater mainland. It remained to be determined what that mainland actually was, and who was entitled to it.

THE HUGH SAY LETTER never named the head of the English exploration enterprise out of Bristol, referring to Cabot several times only as "he." Presumably in a previous exchange Say had informed Columbus of the man's identity. If Columbus had already crossed paths with Cabot in Spain or knew him from his own second voyage and the preliminary engineering work on ill-fated La Isabella, the intelligence from Say must have been as infuriating as it was perturbing. Unable to mount another voyage of exploration, including the one northward to Cathay planned by Bartolomé in 1495, and having been unwilling to test northern waters himself, Columbus had allowed someone from within his own greater Indies enterprise to raise the banner of another monarch on a shore across the Ocean Sea.

Columbus's own claim that Cuba was a peninsula of the Indies mainland was widely doubted. So what of Cabot's claim of a mainland to the north of his finds: Was it Cathay, in the land of the Great Khan? Or had the Venetian found another troublesome slab of geography that had to be aggressively shoehorned into the general template of Marco Polo's travel narrative, Pierre d'Ailly's *Imago Mundi* and Toscanelli's letter and map? Say's letter notably declined to call the *tierra firma* Cabot had coasted Cathay or any part of the Indies.

Whatever it was, more would soon be known. As Say advised, Cabot was preparing a substantial follow-up voyage: "[W]ith God's help it is hoped to push through plans for exploring the said land more thoroughly next year with ten or twelve vessels."

Columbus needed to secure a Spanish claim to lands he had left unexplored before Cabot sewed up even more of them. Yet he was hobbled by his aversion to sailing in the cold and storms of northern latitudes. Say's letter, and the lost sketch chart, would have made clear an undeniable yet extremely misleading fact: The cape nearest to Ireland was 1800 miles, or 450 leagues, from Dursey Head. As the westernmost Cape Verdes, the starting point for measuring under Tordesillas, were thought to be about 35 degrees of longitude west of Ireland, Say's report made it fairly clear that whatever Cabot had found fell within the Portuguese realm, which extended westward to a meridian 370 leagues west of the Cape Verdes.

João II had more than likely declined Münzer's and Behaim's idea of a westward voyage in 1493 because, under Tordesillas, whatever Behaim found presumably would turn out to be Spanish territory. Cabot had now shown there was in fact a landfall to the west that was within the territory assigned to Portugal, and this provided a major disincentive for Columbus to dedicate a voyage to investigating the discovery.

Columbus didn't know that what Cabot had found was a geographic anomaly. Newfoundland may have been positioned far enough to the east to be considered at least partly Portuguese, but below and behind it was an entire unknown continent that by the terms of Tordesillas belonged to Fernando and Isabel. If Columbus failed to investigate Cabot's find and left eastern North America open to Henry VII to probe on succeeding voyages, a monarch who paid no heed to Tordesillas would be able to plant his banner all along the shore of a vast new land.

TWENTY-FOUR

THE NEWS THAT Cabot had been awarded a royal pension in December 1497 that was to be paid out of the customs revenue of Bristol was not as agreeably received in the port as Cabot would have hoped. There simply may have been a failure by Henry VII's clerks to generate the necessary paperwork, but Bristol customers had refused to pay Cabot. Henry VII had to issue a warrant ordering the twice-annual payments on February 22, 1498. According to the king's household daybooks, between January 8 and 12 Henry had already given "to a Venysian in Rewarde" 66 shillings, eight pence, which was the equivalent of five marks. It was probably to compensate Cabot for his travels and troubles in resolving the pension mess. Also in January, Henry awarded without explanation 40 shillings to "William Weston of Bristol." It may have been to compensate the merchant for expenses in preparing the next voyage or to reward him for corroborating Cabot's testimony as to what he had found.

Cabot also renewed his patent with Henry on February 3, 1498, with an additional conferral of rights that complemented the original patent of 1496 rather than replaced it. Yet the Venetian's grandiose promises to mount a flotilla on the scale of Columbus's second-voyage armada and establish a colony were not borne out. Henry granted "John Kabotto" (or Kaboto) the right to impress in the king's name up to six vessels as large as two hundred tons and pay for them out of his own pocket at the normal rates of the crown. Cabot was also allowed to take with him any of "our officers or ministers or subjects" who chose to go freely, as no one otherwise could leave his realm without his permission. But there was nothing about emptying prisons to provide the free labor Cabot needed to develop the colony, much less any mention of a settlement or trading post.

England clearly was not Spain. Cabot would have to make do with much less than Columbus. He would also have to turn a profit promptly from his claims of having reached the land of the Great Khan. Henry VII was not going to pour funds into Cabot's vision with the munificence or the patience of Fernando and Isabel.

Precious little is known about the ships or the men who accompanied Cabot. The king's household accounts for March and April 1498 include a series of payments to a Launcelot Thirkill of London in association with a man named Thomas Bradley for the press of a ship going to "the new Ilande." Evidence recently surfaced that the king also loaned Thirkill and Bradley money for this voyage. A reward was also made in April to one John Cair who was "goying to the new Ile," and this probably involved a ship press as well. William Weston presumably was involved, perhaps in the king's service. The Genoese barber and the Burgundian whom Raimundo di Raimundis had encountered surely were along. If Martin Behaim ever were to step forward and actually invest in the voyage scheme, either with a ship of his own or as a provider of trade goods, now would have been the time. Raimundis had also heard about "some poor Italian friars" who had their eyes on bishoprics.

No voyage log or journal would endure, but more than likely there were five ships. Despite the reports of great schools of cod from the 1497 voyage, no fishing was contemplated. The *Great Chronicle of London*'s account for the year September (Michaelmas) 1497 to September 1498 described how Henry was encouraged to "man and victual a ship at Bristol in search for an island which [Cabot] said he knew well and was rich and replenished with rich commodities." In this ship, paid for by Henry, "diverse merchants of London ventured in her small stocks," or trade goods, "being in her as chief patron the said Venetian, and in the company of the said ship sailed also out of Bristol three or four small ships freighted with slight and gross merchandise [such] as coarse cloth caps, lace point and other trifles. And so departed from Bristol in the beginning of May."

FOR HIS FIRST NEW voyage since departing Cadíz (more than likely with Cabot) in September 1493, Columbus needed to weigh two factors in choosing where he was about to sail. One was the startling discovery Hugh Say had credited to Cabot in 1497. The other was the renewed interest of the Portuguese in a sea route to the Indies around southern Africa.

The new king, Manoel I, had revived the quest to prove the round-Africa route to India that had lain dormant since the Días voyage of 1487–88. Three ships under Vasco da Gama departed Lisbon on July 8, 1497, and word of this initiative surely reached Fernando and Isabel. Were the Portuguese successful, there was bound to be a dispute over how the rights of Portugal and Spain converged in the Indies from opposite directions. With Columbus insisting that his discoveries to date included the Chersonese peninsula and islands on the perimeter of the Indies, da Gama's flotilla could wind up approaching Española from the west in 1498.

Columbus could not meet the disparate challenges posed by Cabot and da Gama in one voyage. Of the two, the threat posed by Cabot must have seemed the least dire. His discoveries seemed to be in Portuguese territory, and in colder, higher latitudes that Columbus had no desire to challenge. And the only riches Hugh Say had reported were stockfish. The last thing Columbus wanted to find was a new source of air-cured cod.

Columbus thus embarked on his third voyage with three priorities—at least as far as Fernando and Isabel were concerned. He needed to relieve and reinvigorate the struggling Española colony left under Bartolomé Columbus's care; confirm and consolidate the Spanish claim to his alleged Indies discoveries; and be prepared to rebuff any attempt by da Gama, using force if necessary, to overstep the territorial bounds of Tordesillas and the papal bulls of 1493 if the Portuguese flotilla happened to approach Española from the west.

Columbus left Sanlúcar de Barrameda on May 30, 1498, with six ships; Cabot's five ships were probably already at sea. Columbus's fleet paused twice in the Madeiras to take on supplies: on June 7 at Porto Santos, where his late wife's brother was governor, and then on June 10 at Madeira, where Columbus had once served as a factor for Genoese merchants.

During Columbus's Madeiran sojourn, affairs in Henry VII's England acquired one of their periodic, potentially explosive complications. Perkin Warbeck, who was living under house arrest, escaped on the night of June 9 through a window of the palace at Westminster. He was found the next day, hiding in a monastery a few miles away in Shene. After twice putting him on public display to endure ridicule, Henry removed the pretender to more closely guarded quarters in the Tower of London.

"I wrote a long while ago to your Highnesses, supplicating you to give your opinion and advice as to how the King of England ought to deal with Perkin," Roderigo de Puebla wrote Fernando and Isabel on June 12. "Your Highnesses have not to this day, no doubt for some just reason and impediments, sent a word in reply, or written anything. I say this because the said Perkin fled a few days ago, without any reason. Your silence causes much pain to me, because I am sure the King of England would do what your Highnesses might advise."

It was true that Henry had long been unsure of how to deal with Warbeck after sparing his life with a pardon and that the recent escape was demanding a firm decision. But Puebla had a habit of claiming that past messages never reached his monarchs, thus excusing his silences on weighty matters. Where Warbeck was concerned, Puebla had never even told them about the alarming uprisings in 1497. For Puebla to claim that his monarchs' silence now caused him much pain was galling.

A public feud between Fernando and Isabel's two ambassadors in London, Roderigo de Puebla and Pedro de Ayala, also had become a scandal for the Spanish crown. Puebla had been agitating against Ayala's presence in London since the initial peace with Scotland was secured in September 1497 and otherwise had been deriding and even undermining his performance. He had excoriated Pedro de Ayala's actions as ambassador to Scotland so persuasively that in early 1498 Fernando and Isabel had been compelled to send a new ambassador to Scotland, Fernán Pérez de Ayala (who never took up his post, as he perished in a shipwreck en route). But while Pérez was delayed in his fateful departure by bad weather, news had arrived from England of the recent "disturbances" there. At first, the monarchs doubted the report of the traumatic 1497 Scottish invasion, the Cornwall uprisings, and Perkin Warbeck's capture, "because De Puebla had not said a single word about it in his letters."

Puebla's silences were astonishing lapses, as Fernando and Isabel were preparing to have their daughter Catherine wed Henry's heir Arthur and had no idea the kingdom had been plunged into such chaos, and with such a serious threat to the rule of the house of Tudor. Puebla likely had also become far too close to Henry in regard to Cabot's enterprise. It was within the bounds of his character and his expertise as a doctor of civil and canonical law to have assured Henry in 1496 that Cabot's activities would not offend Fernando and Isabel or the terms of *Inter cetera* or Tordesillas. Perhaps he had interpreted the opaque letter from his monarchs of March 28, 1496, to mean that if Henry at least joined the Holy League, they would look the other way where Cabot and Spanish rights under Tordesillas were concerned. Once Henry had done so, even though he refused to agree to go to war against France, Puebla could have considered the Cabot matter closed. And the fact that Fernando and Isabel had then entered into the remarkable pact with France at Alcala in November 1497 obviated any concern that Henry had not fully complied with their earlier wishes.

Regardless, Puebla had never followed up on his initial January 1496 report on John Cabot's efforts to secure a patent from Henry, had never told his monarchs about the first voyage attempt of 1496 or, more important, the successful second one of 1497. It went without saying that he had reported nothing about the third voyage, which had already sailed when Puebla wrote Fernando and Isabel on June 15, 1498, to lodge another forceful complaint about Ayala, furious he was living in the capital and styling himself as the ambassador to both Henry VII and Scotland's James IV. Puebla had confronted Ayala, who showed him a letter from Isabel to Henry VII that supported Ayala's contention (as Puebla conceded) that "he has been furnished with letters and credentials." Nevertheless, London was not big enough for both of them. Puebla told Fernando and Isabel that they "must decide, from what he has written, whether all this be for the good of their service or not."

Puebla did not know it, but his reputation with the king and queen had plummeted in recent months as the news of his unhelpful silences emerged. Two Spanish diplomats, the knight commander Sanchez de Londoño and the subprior of Santa Cruz, Johannes de Matienzo, were en route to England. They had been dispatched to Flanders to deal with the disturbingly erratic behavior of Fernando and Isabel's daughter Joana, Philip IV's new bride. Under secret instructions, the envoys were first making a detour to London. "They are to inquire into the manner in which De Puebla conducts his business," the monarchs had instructed on March 7. "It is said that he is entirely in the interest of King Henry."

IN *ESMERALDO DE SITU ORBIS*, which was composed for Manoel I between 1505 and 1508, the Portuguese cartographer Duarte Pacheco Pereira stated: "Fortunate Prince, we know and we have seen how, in the third year of your reign, in the year of Our Lord 1498, your Highness ordered us to discover the occidental part, beyond the Ocean Sea, where was found a huge continent surrounded by many large islands." The word of Cabot's discoveries thus had reached Portugal, the other signatory of Tordesillas, and Manoel had ordered in 1498 a search for the lands Cabot had discovered.

The Portuguese picked up where they left off in their westward voyaging—in Terceira, which of course had been home to the voyages of the Teives and the scheme of 1486–87 that involved Dulmo, Estreito, and Behaim. Gaspar Corte-Real, son of João Vaz, who had been central to the captaincy dispute that thwarted the Dulmo-Estreito-Behaim enterprise, may have begun searching unofficially for what Cabot had found as early as 1498. As mentioned, Gaspar was the brother-in-law of Joss van Huerter's heir, Joss the younger, and thus part of the extended family of Martin Behaim, who had married Joss the younger's sister, Joana. The Corte-Reals had been prime candidates for playing a leading role in the stillborn voyage proposal Behaim made to Manoel's predecessor, João II, in 1493.

Although it would not be surprising if Gaspar in fact mounted an unofficial search for Cabot's 1497 discoveries at the first opportunity, particularly if his relative Behaim had been involved in the Bristol enterprise, the earliest surviving Portuguese exploration patent for these investigative voyages, dated October 28, 1499, granted a "Johan Fernandez" of Terceira the governorship of any islands he might discover. Fernandez (or João Fernandes) clearly was acting on news that Cabot's finds fell on the Portuguese side of the dividing meridian of Tordesillas, as his patent noted he "was desirous to make an effort to seek out and discover at his own expense some islands lying in our sphere of influence." Whether Gaspar Corte-Real was actively involved at this early date or not, the quest to find the Isle of Seven Cities was being reinvigorated on Terceira. Martin Behaim may have helped export the search to England, but the Terceirans wanted it back, along with whatever landfalls Cabot (with the aid of Behaim) might have claimed for Henry VII.

Fernandes pursued Cabot's finds with a partner named Pero de Barcelos. The search was thus drawn right back into the unresolved squabble with the Corte-Reals over the captaincy rights of Terceira that had confounded the earlier enterprise of Dulmo, Estreito, and Behaim. As a landowner embroiled in the squabble, Barcelos mentioned in the course of giving evidence in 1506 how "there was an order from the king our lord to go discovering, for me and for one João Fernandes Lavrador, on which discovery we spent three years." Fernandes and Barcelos likely had started this three-year quest in 1498, the year before Fernandes secured the known patent. But in all their searching, the statement of Pero de Barcelos implied, the duo found nothing.

Give Cabot and his Bristol companions their due: They had reached a landfall in the west that apparently had thwarted Portuguese investigations for decades and that continued to defy their investigations.

FROM MADEIRA, COLUMBUS PROCEEDED to the Canaries on June 16, arriving three days later at Gomera; the island's governor and former Columbus lover, Beatriz de Bobadilla, coincidentally married the Canaries conquistador Alonso de Lugo that year. There Columbus divided his fleet. Three ships would sail directly for Española, under the command of loyal men: Columbus's companion's brother, Pedro de Arana; a cousin from Genoa, Juan Antonio Columbo; and the governor of the city of Baeça (Baeza), Alonso Sanchez de Carvajal. Columbus would sail on with the three remaining vessels southward for the Cape Verdes.

Spanish vessels were not permitted to sail south of the Canaries through the waters off the West African coast without securing Portugal's permission, and presumably this had been arranged so that from the Cape Verdes, Columbus could steer west, doing his best to estimate through dead reckoning the location of the dividing meridian of Tordesillas relative to any known or new landfalls. Four years after the treaty was concluded, this would be Columbus's first opportunity to confirm that his previous discoveries lay on the Spanish side of the meridian.

Yet according to the voyage account seen by Las Casas, Columbus had an altogether different goal: "[H]e wishes to go to the south, because he intends with the aid of the *Sancta Trinidad* [Holy Trinity] to find islands and lands, that God may be served and their Highnesses and Christianity may have pleasure, and that he wishes to prove or test the opinion of King Don Juan of Portugal, who said that there was continental land to the south."

Columbus had gathered that João II thought Tordesillas would reserve for Portugal landfalls yet to be discovered to the southwest of the Cape Verdes. The late king "was certain that within [the Portuguese territory under Tordesillas] famous lands and things must be found." When Columbus paused with his three ships at Santiago in the Cape Verdes, "certain principal inhabitants" came to him and said "that to the south-west of the island of Huego, which is one of the Cape Verdes distant 12 leagues from this, may be seen an island, and that the King Don Juan was greatly inclined to send ships to make discoveries to the south-west."

Columbus admitted that his desire to investigate João II's suspicions had been a matter of contention between himself and Fernando and Isabel. His monarchs would have been interested in having him finally confirm the location of his existing discoveries in relation to the Tordesillas meridian, not find out what other landfalls existed in the Ocean Sea that might belong only to Portugal. But now that he had at last embarked on a new voyage of discovery, Columbus had his own agenda to pursue.

COLUMBUS MAY HAVE DECIDED not to share what he learned about Cabot from Hugh Say with his monarchs, as the intelligence could have had negative implications for his own claims about an Indies discovery. But as Say knew prominent men, such as Isabel's own Castilian treasurer, Francisco Pinelo, it seems unlikely the news of the 1497 voyage would have stopped at Columbus. As Say's intelligence had indicated that Cabot's finds were in the Portuguese realm of Tordesillas, Fernando and Isabel as well as Columbus may have thought it best to let this sleeping dog lie. No communiqué from Fernando and Isabel to either Roderigo de Puebla or Pedro de Ayala in London endures to suggest an effort by the monarchs to raise Cabot's activities with Henry VII.

As Columbus's third voyage unfolded, however, he proved to be intensely curious about undiscovered lands that indeed might belong to Portugal, albeit in southern latitudes rather than in northern ones. At least one item of intelligence gathered from Say would have helped dictate Columbus's course: *Inventio Fortunata* promised volcanic islands somewhere beyond the Cape Verdes.

Columbus departed the Cape Verdes on July 4 with his three ships. He ordered a course toward the southwest, "because then he would be on a parallel with the lands of the sierra of Loa [Sierra Leone] and cape of Sancta Ana in Guinea, which is below the equinoctial line [equator], where he says that below that line of the world are found more gold and things of value: and that after, he would navigate, the Lord pleasing, to the west." Columbus reasoned that lands along the same latitude, even if separated by hundreds of leagues, would offer the same resources. The English could have their cod in waters the Venetian had explored far to the north. Columbus wanted the gold of Portugal's Guinea Coast, and he was dearly hoping some new landfall to the west of them would yield that wealth.

SANCHEZ DE LONDOÑO and Johannes de Matienzo arrived in England on June 27 after "a very bad voyage." On July 5, the day after Columbus departed the Cape Verdes, Londoño and Matienzo had an audience with Henry VII, accompanied by Roderigo de Puebla. Matienzo reported to Fernando and Isabel that Puebla "showed great suspicion, standing there and watching them like a wolf." For the next thirteen days, the pair would assemble a fairly incredible dossier of Puebla's alleged crimes and misdemeanors. Cabot's fleet continued to sail on, its existence unreported by any member of the increasingly crowded and fractious Spanish diplomatic corps surrounding Henry's court. Its investigative energy was focused entirely inward.

On July 13, at latitude 5° north, Columbus made an authentic if miserable discovery: the Doldrums of the mid-Atlantic equatorial region. They were a cruel reward for his long-standing aversion to the cold of northern latitudes braved by Cabot. For eight days, "the wind deserted him and he entered into heat so great and so ardent that he feared the ships would take fire and the people perish. The ceasing of the wind and coming of the excessive and consuming heat was so unexpected and sudden that there was no person who dared to descend below to care for the butts of wine and water, which swelled, breaking the hoops of the casks: the wheat burned like fire: the pork and salted meat roasted and putrefied."

While Columbus and his men suffered in the equatorial furnace, Londoño and Matienzo wrote a report to Fernando and Isabel on July 18 that was devastating to the standing of the ambassador who had maintained a cone of silence around Cabot's activities for more than two years.

"The Doctor is in such a state of irritation with Don Pedro de Ayala that it has been the cause of many disagreeable scenes which are notorious in England," they advised. "There is no remedy for it. De Puebla cannot bear any other ambassador. He has been unable to conceal his fear and distrust towards them, though he had been told that [Ayala's] services are fully appreciated in Spain."

Although Londoño and Matienzo did not mention it, Ayala did give cause for concern. He was cutting a dangerous figure, with a retinue of servants that engaged in brawling. Of the dozen men employed by him since arriving in Britain, only three hadn't been killed or maimed by 1498: Four had fallen in border skirmishes between England and Scotland, two had been killed on the road in Scotland, and another three were incapacitated by wounds they had suffered.

Puebla would recount to his monarchs how one brawl erupted in London when Ayala was struck in the arm by a brick thrown from a window. One of his retinue, a Scottish cleric no less, had killed an Englishman in a street fight. Only an intervention by Henry VII spared the Scotsman from being hanged, and the corrupt English legal system soaked the clergyman's brother for an astounding two hundred pounds.

Regardless, in Londoño and Matienzo's estimation Ayala could do no wrong, and the feud between the two ambassadors was irreparable. "There is not a single person in England who speaks ill of the one, or well of the other. The quarrels between them are a public scandal. It is time to throw the baton between them."

Puebla was judged a shameful disaster as an ambassador. Londoño and Matienzo called him "a liar, a flatterer, a calumniator, a beggar, and does not seem to be a good Christian." The attestations they gathered recounted how he sponged meals off the royal household and lined his pocket as a legal fixer for Spanish and Italian merchants in the capital. He even lived in a whorehouse run by an English mason, where he took his meals with the prostitutes and covered up robberies committed by the mason against the brothel's clients. As scandalous as this may have seemed, the worst of it was Puebla's favoring of Henry's interests over those of Spain.

Addressing Puebla's complete failure to notify his monarchs of the dangerous uprisings and invasion from Scotland of 1497, Matienzo said he had informed Henry that "as soon as the news of disturbances in England had reached Spain, the Spanish fleet had been armed and kept ready to assist him, although the truth of the tidings was doubted, because De Puebla had not mentioned them." Because of his poor service, the Spanish had secured far less advantageous terms for the marriage of Arthur and Catherine than they could have, at a time when Henry had been under such duress.

Puebla was "a great partisan" of Henry VII and "a quarrelsome intriguer." Spanish merchants alleged he failed to defend their interests and was "more an agent of the exchequer of the King of England than ambassador of Spain. He is under such subjection to Henry that he dares not say a word, but what he thinks will please the King."

Especially damning was the opinion gathered from the privy councilor Pierre Le Pennec ("Pedro Pennec"), who was from Morlaix in Brittany. Like Puebla, he was a doctor of civil and canon law; like Ayala, he was a prothonotary of the church. In addition to being a clerk and councilor of Henry, he was also a political agent in Henry's foreign service. Puebla was said to have "conducted the business of Spain very badly." He had compromised treaties, delayed peace efforts, and sabotaged Ayala's diplomacy to the detriment of Spain's interests. There seemed to be no end to the failings of Puebla. Indeed, according to a testimony signed by a "Doctor Breton," who was assuredly Le Pennec, "It would require all the paper in London to describe the character of the man."

"De Puebla wished to ingratiate himself with Henry" was one of the many allegations in the statement by Dr. Breton. "For this reason he told Ferdinand and Isabella that things were very difficult which, in fact, were very easy. Henry makes use of De Puebla for his advantage, but he knows the man."

Puebla's instinct for graft, and his closeness to Henry VII, had already been noticed by Raimundo di Raimundis in a letter to the Duke of Milan on December 18, 1497, which was written on the same day that he described his encounter with Cabot. "The Spanish ambassador, a man much after this king's heart, sometimes throws out a hint that his sovereign might do something if he were assisted with money."

The sweeping condemnations of Puebla pointed to additional reasons the ambassador was compromised where Cabot's services to Henry were concerned.

Puebla's activities as a legal fixer for Italian merchants could have placed him in the company of Cabot's backers. It was also said he had cut corners on his living expenses by residing at the Augustinian friary in London. This was the order of Giovanni Antonio de Carbonariis, Cabot's champion at Henry's court and the link to his Florentine financiers in London. And Carbonariis had just sailed with Cabot on the latest voyage.

On June 20, Agostino Spinola, who had assumed the Milanese ambassadorship from Raimundo di Raimundis, had written the Duke of Milan from London, acknowledging receipt of several letters for Sforza's subjects in England. One was for "Messer Giovanni Antonio de Carbonariis. I will keep the last until his return. He left recently with five ships, which his Majesty sent to discover new islands."

Raimundis apparently had been on target when he informed the Duke of Milan the previous December that "some poor Italian friars will go on this voyage, who have the promise of bishoprics." Whether Carbonariis qualified as "poor," expected a bishopric, or had company from members of the Augustine friary in London or not, the pope's subproctor in England indeed had just sailed with Cabot's flotilla.

THE HEAT WAS SO INTENSE on July 19 that Columbus thought his men and ships would burn. That they did not he attributed to the direct intervention of God. "He succoured him by His mercy at the end of seven or eight days, giving him very good weather to get away from that fire: with which good weather he navigated towards the west 17 days, always intending to return to the south." On Sunday, July 22, they saw "innumerable birds pass from the west-south-west to the northeast: he says that they were a great sign of land. They saw the same the Monday following and the days after, on one of which days a pelican came to the ship of the Admiral, and many others appeared another day, and there were other birds which are called 'frigate pelicans.'"

One week after Londoño and Matienzo sent their devastating bundle of allegations regarding the performance of Roderigo de Puebla, and three days after Columbus's ships were visited by "frigate pelicans," the scandalous ambassador's rival, Pedro de Ayala, wrote his own detailed report on recent events for Fernando and Isabel. Most of the letter addressed Scottish affairs, but he also wrote at some length about Henry VII.

Apparently he was not as wealthy as people thought. "He likes to be thought very rich, because such a belief is advantageous to him in many respects." Royal revenues were dwindling in part because Henry's penchant for levying taxes was hurting commerce. Ayala further noted the "impoverishment of the people by the great taxes laid on them. The King himself said to me, that it is his intention to keep his subjects low, because riches would only make them haughty."

Ayala assured his monarchs that Henry's hold on the crown "is, nevertheless, undisputed, and his government is strong in all respects. He is disliked, but the

Queen beloved, because she is powerless." Henry was now forty-one and looked old for his years "but young for the sorrowful life he has led." Ayala took measure of his vanity, his desire to be regarded as a ruler of global consequence. "He likes to be much spoken of, and to be highly appreciated by the whole world. He fails in this, because he is not a great man. Although he professes many virtues, his love of money is too great."

Ayala also raised a fresh matter that had come to his attention. "I think your Majesties have already heard how the King of England has equipped a fleet to explore certain islands or mainland which he has been assured certain persons who set out last year from Bristol in search of the same have discovered," he began.

Leaving aside what they might have learned of Hugh Say's intelligence, Fernando and Isabel had heard nothing of the kind, at least not from Roderigo de Puebla, who by suspicious coincidence rushed a note to them on Cabot's voyage the very same day. Cabot's fleet was not only "equipped"; it had already sailed, and Ayala was furious.

TWENTY-FIVE

TWO AND A HALF years after Roderigo de Puebla had made his only known mention of Cabot's presence in England, he and his rival Pedro de Ayala were competing to deliver the first word by a Spanish ambassador in Henry VII's kingdom of the Venetian's activities. The intelligence failure had been atrocious. By this time, Cabot was already at sea on his third voyage, with a small armada determined to expand on his initial 1497 discoveries, trade for the riches of the Great Khan, and plant Henry's banners wherever they went.

Having only returned to London from Scotland in September 1497, Ayala had missed all the fuss arising from Cabot's own return the previous month. Ayala had then gone back to Scotland to promote a marriage between James IV and Henry's daughter Margaret, thus missing Cabot's appearance at court in December, which had inspired the lengthy report by Raimundo di Raimundis to the Duke of Milan. Roderigo de Puebla should have known about Cabot's achievements and plans but for his own reasons had apparently chosen to share nothing about them with his monarchs. And Puebla most certainly was never going to share anything about them with his hated rival, Ayala.

That Puebla chose to write a short note about Cabot to Fernando and Isabel on July 25, the very same day as Ayala and so soon after the unnerving investigation into his conduct by Londoño and Matienzo, suggests he was rushing to avert further humiliation. Ayala's report could only reveal Puebla's lengthy silence on Cabot's activities: Either Puebla had failed to inform his monarchs of important news he possessed, or had been so derelict in his duties as to not even have been aware of Cabot's voyages. While both diplomats would have had access to information about Cabot at Henry's court, Ayala's report seems to have been the source of the bulk of Puebla's note. Ayala made his comments as part of a lengthy assessment of affairs in England and Scotland, and Puebla likely was able to peruse and crib from it before it entered the diplomatic pouch.

"The King of England sent five armed ships with another Genoese like Colón to look for the Island of Brasil and the surrounding territories," Puebla wrote. His strategy thus was to not even acknowledge that Cabot had made any previous voyages, let alone achieved his 1497 success. Puebla's position was that this was a new initiative, aimed not at the Indies, which were so dear to Spain, but rather at the elusive mid-ocean island of Brasil. It was an indefensible position in the long term, but it would buy Puebla some time by sowing confusion over the truth of Ayala's version of events and hopefully thwart immediate condemnation from his monarchs for once again not having reported anything at all about a matter of considerable diplomatic importance.

Puebla's reference to Cabot, not by name but as *otro Genovese como Colón*, recalled how his monarchs, in their March 1496 letter to him, similarly called the unnamed Cabot *uno como Colón*. Puebla's note lacked any recognition that he was discussing one and the same explorer; his description of Cabot also was a verbatim repeat of Ayala's phrasing that day: "I have seen the map made by the discoverer, who is another Genoese like Colón who has been in Seville and at Lisbon seeking to obtain persons to aid him in this discovery." It is difficult to believe both men failed to refer to Cabot by name and independently arrived at the mistaken impression that he was Genoese. This reinforces the likelihood Ayala was the original source and that Puebla, who had probably turned a blind eye to Cabot's activities, repeated the "Genoese" error in filching from Ayala.

Puebla explained two of the ships had been provisioned for one year, whereas Ayala said all five ships were so prepared. "They say that they will have arrived [returned] for September of 1498," Puebla added, agreeing with Ayala's voyage timeline. Ayala's report however was considerably more detailed, and worrying. He made a startling claim: "For the last seven years the people of Bristol have equipped two, three [and] four caravels to go in search of the island of Brasil and the Seven Cities according to the fancy of this Genoese." Although it was impossible for Cabot to have been directing and participating in such a search for the past seven years, it was true that he had been making his voyages out of Bristol for several years. But had Bristol sailors been making voyages of their own, before Cabot came along, since 1491? Perhaps the Bristol discovery of "Brasil" had been very recent and been kept very quiet. Or Ayala may just have garbled the details of the treaty between England and Norway of 1490, which had permitted Bristol ships to engage in the Icelandic fishery through licenses that had to be renewed every seven years.

Ayala said he had spoken with Henry several times about the Cabot venture, and testified to the king's optimism. "He hopes the affair may turn out profitable." Puebla made a similar claim: "The King has spoken to me on occasion about it; he hopes to have a very great share." Ayala further advised that Henry had decided to send more ships westward this year "because last year sure proof was brought him they had found land." Ayala also had intelligence to share of the latest voyage's progress. "News has come that one of those, in which sailed another Friar Buil, has made land in Ireland in a great storm with the ship badly damaged. The Genoese kept on his way."

Ayala's "Friar Buil" was Giovanni Antonio de Carbonariis, whose participation had been noted by Agostino Spinola in his June 20 letter to the Duke of Milan. Cabot's mirroring of Columbus's second voyage now extended to the inclusion of a Bernard Buyl mimic. Carbonariis was no papal legate empowered by a bull, as had been the Minorite friar Buyl attached to Columbus's second voyage, but Carbonariis may have imagined himself fulfilling much the same role in representing the church and carrying the word of Christ to the heathen. More lucratively, he may have aspired to the bishopric (a gateway to personal wealth) alluded to by Raimundis the previous December. But according to Ayala's intelligence, Carbonariis's adventure had been interrupted if not ended altogether, with his storm-damaged ship limping into an Irish port.

As far as Ayala was concerned, Cabot's four remaining vessels were outward bound for a violation of Tordesillas. "Having seen the course they are steering and the length of the voyage, I find that what they have discovered or are in search of is possessed by your Highnesses because it is at the cape which fell to your Highnesses by the convention with Portugal." Ayala thus had traced Cabot's proposed course on a chart the Venetian had left behind and must have recognized "the cape" he was so confident belonged to Spain from whatever maps had informed his activities as one of two Spanish negotiators for Tordesillas in 1493. Puebla seconded Ayala on this point: "Seeing the course that they are taking to it, that which they are seeking is that which Your Majesties possess." Here, Puebla implied he had seen a map with Cabot's course, whereas Ayala was explicit about having inspected one. But Puebla was ambiguous about the provenance of what the English were seeking, for the Spanish monarchs "possessed" not only new lands but also more generally a (supposed) new sea route to the Indies.

Ayala reported that the distance to Cabot's discoveries was "not 400 leagues." Puebla was more circumspect. "I believe that there is nothing from here up to 400 leagues," he wrote, not admitting that Cabot and the English had already made a discovery, which of course he should have reported at the latest in late 1497. Puebla instead made it sound like there was no landfall between England and the anticipated discovery of Brasil, four hundred leagues distant.

The distance of four hundred leagues should have told Ayala the lands reached in 1497 were more than likely within the Portuguese realm. Ayala however was convinced Cabot was a bald liar, and had not minced words with the English king. "I told him that I believed the islands were those found by Your Highnesses, and although I gave him the main reason, he would not have it. Since I believe Your Highnesses will already have notice of all this and also of the chart or *mappemonde* which this man has made, I do not send it now, although it is here, and so far as I can see exceedingly false, in order to make believe that these are not part of the said islands."

Ayala had spent enough time in the Tordesillas negotiations to be quite familiar with the prevailing ideas of the world's configuration. The Cabot map struck him as a tissue of cartographic lies. The mention of "400 leagues" by both Ayala and Puebla recalled the general agreement in the various letters of 1497 that placed the Isle of Seven Cities that distance to the west of Dursey Head. Ayala must have seen a chart that moved the Seven Cities far to the north of where anyone had previously located this landfall or its equivalent of Antilla. To a Spaniard, for Cabot to have truly reached Antilla, he had to have visited the islands Columbus discovered and so had ventured far to the south of where his world map claimed. Perhaps "the cape" Ayala saw on the Cabot map made him think of eastern Cuba, which Columbus said was the Golden Chersonese, a peninsula of mainland Asia. The map thus to Ayala was "exceedingly false," a blatant distortion. The Venetian was trying to pass off his findings as another place altogether, with his map contrived to show that his discoveries had nothing to do with Columbus's finds. He had already intruded on Spanish territory and surely was on the way back to the Indies.

As for Ayala's assumption that Fernando and Isabel already knew about Cabot's enterprise and moreover possessed a copy of Cabot's map: perhaps Henry left Ayala with the impression he had already informed the Spanish monarchs of the Cabot venture. Perhaps Henry himself assumed that Puebla had long since told them about Cabot's activities—or had been led to believe by Puebla they had been so informed and there was nothing to worry about. But nothing survives to indicate that the Spanish monarchs were apprised of Cabot's journeys by any source in England after Puebla's letter of January 21, 1496.

It may be that Ayala was shrewdly sticking a knife into his hated rival Puebla's reputation: *Surely, Your Highnesses, Dr. Puebla has already informed you thoroughly on this matter,* his letter implied. And Cabot and his Bristol accomplices had been making these voyages for *seven years!* Would Dr. Puebla not have informed them about that as well? Should Fernando and Isabel reply to the contrary, only then would Ayala send a copy of the map. The proof would be unequivocal that on yet another matter of supreme diplomatic importance, Puebla had left his monarchs dangerously in the dark. Puebla's hasty note, written the same day and so seemingly derivative of Ayala's report, does read like an attempt to counter Ayala's revelations. Puebla could not afford to have Ayala forward news on Cabot before he did. His note was an exercise in personal damage control, and in refusing to acknowledge Cabot had already succeeded in reaching a distant shore, Puebla created confusion where Fernando and Isabel deserved clarity. And all the while, Cabot's flotilla sailed on.

ESCAPING THE DOLDRUMS, Columbus enjoyed seventeen consecutive days of good weather and, on July 29, was hoping to soon sight land, having been at sea without interruption since departing the Cape Verdes on July 4. In the intense heat, the seams in the hull had worked open; the provisions, for both his crossing and the Española colony, had begun to spoil. Two days later, he was running out of freshwater and felt he could no longer hold this course in search of landfalls João II had suspected and *Inventio Fortunata* had promised. He called for a more northerly heading. They would now try to reach Dominica or one of the other "cannibal islands" he had discovered on the second voyage and replenish the casks before they all perished from thirst.

At noon on the very day Columbus in desperation and disappointment ordered the course change, one of his servants, Alonso Pérez Nizzardo, climbed the rigging and spotted land fifteen leagues to the west.

"And it pleased our Lord," Columbus noted, "by his Exalted Majesty, that the first lands seen were three rocks all united at the base, I say three mountains, all at one time and in one glance." The sight was prophetically apt, for Columbus had been relying on the supernatural oversight of the Holy Trinity on his third voyage. In gratitude, he named the landfall *Trinidad.*

DESPITE THE FACT THAT he understood the Cabot flotilla was provisioned for a full year, Ayala expected it would be back by September and promised to tell Fernando and Isabel what he learned then. But there would be no additional report from Ayala or Puebla on the matter. Their July 25 letters were the last contemporary accounts of John Cabot's activities. The Venetian and his English ships might as well have sailed off the edge of a flat earth.

John Cabot's 1498 flotilla was the largest English expedition dedicated to exploration for almost a century. The scale of the effort did not save it from a most peculiar fate. If not actually lost to the Ocean Sea, it was soon lost to history. Not a single account of the voyage would endure. No contemporary chronicle or observer had a thing to say about it. When the *Great Chronicle of London* entry for September 1497 to September 1498 noted that the flotilla had left in early May, it concluded with the foreboding words: "Of whom in this mayor's time returned no tidings."

Only four years after the voyage, the scholar and cleric Polydore Vergil (Polidoro Virgilio) of Urbino arrived in England as Alexander VI's collector of papal revenues, replacing Giovanni Antonio de Carbonariis, who had vanished from the historical record along with the 1498 Cabot voyage. Vergil was commissioned by Henry VII to write an official history of England, an exercise largely devoted to burying the contentious nature of his claim to the throne, which Vergil worked on well after Henry's death in 1509. In a manuscript copy preserved in the Vatican was a paragraph devoted to Cabot written around 1512–13 that never appeared in the printed edition, which was first issued at Basel in 1534.

There was talk at about this time that some sailors on a voyage had discovered lands lying in the British ocean, hitherto unknown. This was easily believed because the Spanish sovereigns in our time had found many unknown islands. Wherefore King Henry at the request of one John Cabot, a Venetian by birth, and a most skilful mariner, ordered to be prepared one ship, complete with crew and weapons; this he handed over to the same John to go and search for those unknown islands. John set out in this same year and sailed first to Ireland. Then he set sail towards the west. In the event he is believed to have found the new lands nowhere but on the very bottom of the ocean, to which he is thought to have descended together with his boat, the victim himself of that self-same ocean; since after that voyage he was never seen again anywhere.

Vergil was not the most reliable scholar, but his unpublished account, even with its obvious flaws, would reinforce the idea that Cabot had been inspired by a prior discovery by Bristol mariners and would also support the general conclusion that persisted into the twenty-first century: Cabot had perished on the 1498 voyage.

CHRISTOPHER COLUMBUS SPENT almost two weeks in the vicinity of Trinidad in August 1498, nearly committing one of the greatest blunders in the history of exploration. He probed the large embayment on its western side that he called the Golfo de la Ballena (gulf of the whale), now called the Gulf of Paria. "He says that all that sea is fresh," Las Casas remarked, inspecting the admiral's lost journal. Columbus thought this gulf was enclosed by four islands and so could not fathom where such an enormous volume of freshwater could originate, "because it did not appear to have the flow from great rivers, and that, if it had them, he says it would not cease to be a marvel."

Columbus failed to grasp that all the land to the south of Trinidad, as well as the mountainous terrain enclosing the gulf to the west, was the mainland of South America. He examined the silt-laden gulf, so charged with freshwater, and compared it to the Guadalquivir at Seville yet did not accept that this was incontrovertible evidence of an enormous river nearby. He did not recognize that the entire shore of the gulf's south side was part of the great delta of the Orinoco River. The fourth largest river in the world by volume, after the Amazon, the Congo, and the Yangtze, it drained almost 340,000 square miles of land. The outflow was so enormous that in meeting the ocean tide, it set up a dangerous rip of standing waves in the two straits between the mainland and Trinidad that Columbus fearfully and respectfully called the Mouth of the Dragon.

Columbus left Trinidad and the gulf before he could properly determine what he had found. He could be forgiven his obdurate response to the overwhelming evidence of this coast's true nature because of his debilitated health. The illness he had first contracted while coasting the south shore of Cuba in 1494 had reerupted, exhausting and nearly blinding him as it filled his eyes with blood. But by pressing farther west, where he had already sent a ship to investigate, Columbus was able to avert his horrendous error of interpretation.

He reached Isla da Margarita, and behind it was a sweeping indentation he called the Gulf of the Pearls. He had refused to believe the mariners of the advance party when they tried to tell him what was there. Looking upon the coast of this gulf, there could be no denying what he was seeing even through blood-soaked eyes.

"I believe that this is a very great continental land, which until today has not been known," he wrote. He now accepted that a great river must be feeding the Gulf of Paria and that it was draining a continent. He further revealed what he never had before: that Indigenous peoples on Guadeloupe had once told him there was continental land to the south and that this had been affirmed by others on St. Croix and Puerto Rico, who also told them that much gold would be found there.

He reminded Fernando and Isabel how it had been said only a very short time ago that

> there was no other land known than that which Ptolemy wrote of, and there was not in my time any one who would believe that one could navigate from Spain to the Indies: about which matter I was seven years in your Court, and there were few who understood it: and finally the very great courage of your Highnesses caused it to be tried, against the opinion of those who contradicted it. And now the truth appears, and it will appear before long, much greater: and if this is the continental land, it is a thing of wonder, and it will be so among all the learned, since so great a river flows out that it makes a fresh-water sea of 48 leagues.

Columbus believed he had found more than a *tierra firma* Ptolemy could not account for. This was the Earthly Paradise, the home of the Garden of Eden, which was to be found at the end of the East. Through his perseverance and the blessing of the Holy Trinity, Columbus had come to the end of the East by sailing west.

He assured Fernando and Isabel: *Y vuestras Altezas ganaron estas tierras, tantas, que son otro mundo:* "And your Highnesses will gain these lands, so great, which are another world." Columbus came very close to deploying the words that would define his achievements for all posterity, *nuevo mundo*—"new world." He had not quite embraced them, as Pietro Martire so poetically yet presciently had in 1494, when he called Columbus's discoveries (in Latin) *orbe novo*. Columbus also would never relinquish the claim that he had reached the Indies. But his *otro mundo* spoke of a dawning recognition that there was more on the far side of the Ocean Sea than could be accounted for by a mind steeped in the writings of ancient geographers and philosophers.

TWENTY-SIX

AROUND NINE in the morning on May 19, 1499, John Arundel, Bishop of Coventry and Litchfield, turned to address Arthur, Prince of Wales, in the chapel of Bewdley Manor, the residence of the heir to the English throne. The bishop informed the twelve-year-old son of Henry VII that it was well known how much King Henry wished that the marriage between him and the Princess of Wales, as Catherine of Aragon was now to be known, should be contracted *per verba de præsenti*. The thirteen-year-old princess was still in Spain; she would not come to England until after Arthur had turned fourteen in September 1500. But the marriage was proceeding as a new treaty of friendship was concluded between England and Spain. Catherine had authorized a Spanish diplomat to appear in her stead at Arthur's side.

The bishop asked the diplomat if he possessed the necessary power to serve as Catherine's proxy. Roderigo de Puebla duly presented the power, and it was read aloud to the assembled group. Puebla and Arthur then clasped their right hands. The prince declared that he accepted Puebla in the name and as the proxy of Princess Catherine, and Princess Catherine in his person as his lawful and undoubted wife. Puebla declared, in the name of Princess Catherine, that she accepted Arthur as her lawful and undoubted husband.

Arthur and Catherine were now indissolubly united, although more than two years would pass before the newlyweds met. Puebla, clutching the prince's hand, had survived the withering assault on his credibility and loyalty in the evidence against him assembled the previous July by the investigating envoys, Sanchez de Londoño and Johannes de Matienzo. Puebla would still be serving as Spain's ambassador in London after Fernando and Isabel, after Henry VII—after even young Arthur—had died.

Only six days after the bundle of letters and depositions that seemed to doom Puebla's ambassadorship was sent in July 1498, Fernando and Isabel had conveyed to him their surprising decision to recall his hated rival, Pedro de Ayala. A grateful Puebla had replied on September 25 that he "kisses their hands and feet for the favour they have done him. . . . It is for their own good."

Where his failure to report critical events was concerned, Puebla had continued to insist that he did write regularly. The same day he expressed his gratitude for the recall of Ayala, Puebla professed he was "astonished that his letters to Spain have not arrived. Is always very careful in sending them; and if he be in fault, it is not from carelessness, but from too great zeal."

Puebla's career may have been spared by the profound distraction of a fresh tragedy in the lives of the Spanish royal family. Fernando and Isabel's daughter, Princess Isabel, had died on August 27, 1498. The princess had lost her first husband, the Portuguese heir Afonso, soon after their marriage in 1490 and had been persuaded to marry his successor, Manoel. Now Isabel had died giving birth to Miguel. Having also lost Crown Prince Juan in October 1497, Fernando and Isabel's plans to secure dynastic alliances through the marriages of their children were unraveling. Only their daughter Joana remained both alive and married, to Burgundy's archduke, Philip IV, but her behavior was so disturbing that the two envoys who had investigated Puebla's behavior in London before visiting her in Flanders had chastised her. "Told her, among other things, that she had a very hard and obdurate heart, and no piety—as is the truth," Matienzo reported to Isabel. A tongue-lashing proved not to be the required cure. Joana would be saddled with the pejorative *el Loco*—"the Mad."

After the loss of her daughter Isabel, Queen Isabel was virtually incapacitated by grief until the following March, when the proxy for Catherine's marriage to Arthur was issued. Having been involved in the negotiations for the marriage since the Treaty of Medina del Campo, Puebla was again considered indispensable, regardless of the litany of misbehavior gathered by the investigating envoys.

But Puebla did not entirely escape censure. He seriously mishandled the treaty renewing the friendship between Spain and England, overstepping his authority. Fernando and Isabel informed him on March 12, 1499, that they were "very angry and very much astonished to see in what manner he has concluded the treaty." The pact was supposed to exempt the Holy Roman Empire, Burgundy, and France from its provisions of mutual defense. If this went uncorrected, their and Henry's treaties with these other parties "would be directly dissolved, and the peace of Christendom endangered." They expected Puebla to negotiate a new treaty with Henry "without transgressing his instructions by a single word."

Because of his grave misstep, Puebla was compelled to accept an odious new condition for his posting. Pedro de Ayala, whom the monarchs initially had decided to recall, would now serve as Puebla's joint ambassador to Henry. In all matters except the renegotiations with Henry over the botched treaty, Puebla was to inform and involve Ayala. "For, as he alone has made the blunders," Fernando and Isabel reprimanded him, "he alone must mend them."

Ayala had been cooling his heels in London since notifying Fernando and Isabel of Cabot's activities in July 1498, awaiting new instructions. In the same letter that had carried news of Cabot's latest voyage for England, Ayala advised Fernando and Isabel that his hopes to secure a lasting peace between Scotland and England were foundering on the lack of a suitable dynastic marriage. He doubted Henry's daughter Margaret would make a match with twenty-five-year-old James IV: She was not yet nine years old, a tiny child. Ayala had suggested that Fernando and Isabel consider offering the hand of their eighteen-year-old daughter, Maria, instead. Catherine's marriage to Arthur would mean two Spanish sisters in the British royal houses could work to keep their husbands on friendly terms. But the death of Princess Isabel had made that impossible; Maria was required as a replacement wife for the Portuguese king.

With Ayala now empowered in England, there was some chance that the Spanish diplomatic corps would take proper note of Henry's ongoing interest in new lands across the Ocean Sea. But Ayala was instead busy brokering a lasting peace between Henry and James IV—Henry's daughter Margaret would have to serve as the Scottish king's bride, and they would marry in 1503, when Margaret was fourteen. We can only wonder if the months of bleak despair into which Isabel plunged following the death of her daughter contributed to the conspicuous diplomatic silence on the 1498 Cabot voyage. Yet the silence lasted much longer. After his brief and misleading note of July 25, 1498 to Fernando and Isabel, which reduced the third Cabot voyage to a search for Brasil, nothing further from Puebla survives on the matter of English exploration. As it happened, nine days before Fernando and Isabel ordered Puebla to accept Ayala as his co-ambassador and Catherine named Puebla her proxy for the marriage to Arthur, Henry took an unusual step to ensure his continued probing of the newly discovered lands. And John Cabot, contrary to the later assurances of Polydore Vergil, had not gone to the bottom of the Ocean Sea in 1498.

THE IDEA THAT JOHN CABOT vanished on the 1498 voyage would be reinforced by a letter written on October 19, 1501, by Pietro Pasqualigo—brother of Lorenzo, who had written from London with some of the first news of Cabot's 1497 voyage. As secretary to the Venetian ambassador to Portugal, Pietro was writing home from Lisbon to his brothers of the return of one of the vessels in a two-ship voyage by Gaspar Corte-Real.

Terceira continued to be the centrifuge of Portuguese voyages in search of lands across the Ocean Sea, spinning off one exploration effort after another. Gaspar Corte-Real made his first known attempt in 1500. His endeavor likely encouraged his fellow Terceiran, João Fernandes, who had secured a patent from Manoel I entitling him to discoveries in 1499 but probably had made his first in a series of voyages in 1498, to take his services instead to England, in the company of Francisco Fernandes and João Gonsalves, who were also from the Azores and were probably fellow Terceirans. The trio teamed up with three Bristol merchants in securing an exploration patent in 1501 from Henry VII. Those three merchants could well have been involved in the Cabot voyages.

On his first known attempt to locate Cabot's discoveries in 1500, Gaspar Corte-Real seems to have sailed so far north that he cruised up the east coast of Greenland. His second effort at last brought news of success for Portugal in reaching Cabot's landfall, but only one of his two ships had returned. Gaspar himself was never seen again.

The news carried by the surviving vessel indicated the Portuguese had seen a considerable amount of northeastern North America. The ship had also returned with seven captive natives; Gaspar was supposed to be on the way with another fifty, which suggests he thought he had found a new source of slaves. "In their land there is no iron," Pasqualigo reported, "but they make knives out of stones and in like manner the points of their arrows. And yet these men have brought from there a piece of broken gilt sword, which certainly seems to have been made in Italy. One of the boys was wearing in his ears two silver rings which without doubt seem to have been made in Venice."

Cabot's 1498 voyage was a logical source of the broken sword and rings, as the 1506 evidence of Pero de Barcelos indicated that the three years of explorations he undertook with João Fernandes, which must have been from 1498 to 1500, had been fruitless. The broken sword suggested a calamitous end to Cabot's 1498 voyage, which would have been consistent with the dire pattern then set by the Corte-Reals. After Gaspar vanished in 1501, Miguel set out after his brother in 1502; he was never heard from again either. When the eldest brother, Vasqueanes, attempted to mount a search expedition, Manoel I refused him permission as a key member of his staff to depart, having lost enough Corte-Reals already. But archival finds in England in 2009 indicate that, unlike the unfortunate Corte-Reals, the 1498 Cabot flotilla did not vanish, at least not entirely, and that Cabot himself returned alive.

It has long been known that the forty-shilling rent on Cabot's house in Bristol was paid for the year from Michaelmas 1498 to Michaelmas 1499. His pension was also paid for the same period out of Bristol custom revenues. His wife or one of his sons could have handled these transactions in his absence. After Michaelmas 1499, the known paper trail on Cabot's Bristol activities cease. But we now know he did return to England and was alive in May 1500, although he may have died that year in Bristol or London.

The details of the final voyage and of Cabot's ultimate fate remain unresolved. Henry VII's actions in the spring of 1499, as final preparations were made for the proxy marriage between Arthur and Catherine, only complicate the picture of what became of Cabot's last expedition and his ambitions to reach Cathay—and of who might have left behind a broken sword and rings on the far side of the Ocean Sea.

ON MARCH 12, 1499, Henry wrote his lord chancellor, John Morton, to order a stay of judicial proceedings in a suit involving two Bristol merchants, John Esterfeld and William Weston. Henry had already given Weston the forty-shilling award in January 1498 for services that must have been related to Cabot's 1497 voyage and quite possibly involved the king's personal interest in the voyage of 1498.

Henry VII ordered Morton to pause the legal action in order to free up the services of Weston, who "shall shortly with goddes grace passe and saille for to serche and fynde if he can the new founde land." It evidently was not to be a matter-of-fact return to a landfall that had already been visited but rather was an undertaking of considerable uncertainty. It was either a mission of rediscovery or a voyage intended to expand on what Cabot had previously found. Weston would receive a further reward from Henry VII in the year ending at Michaelmas (late September) 1500 that likely was for the successful completion of this 1499 assignment, although it could have been for a voyage that concluded in the summer of 1500.

Weston almost certainly had participated in both the 1497 and 1498 Cabot voyages. Precisely when the 1498 flotilla returned—either in whole or in part—and whether it remained intact or split up to pursue different prerogatives remain open questions. Some ships could have returned by the autumn of that year, while others remained in North America into 1499 or even reappeared in Bristol in the spring of 1500. If Weston participated in the 1498 voyage, he must have been back by the winter of 1498–99. Thirkill and Bradley must also have returned, if they accompanied the ships of theirs that were pressed, as a recently discovered suit by the king to recovered monies he loaned them in 1498 for a voyage to the "new isle" dates to June 1500.

As for what the 1498 Cabot voyage found, the evidence may lie in a landmark *mappa munde* that incorporated an original chart of the Western Hemisphere drawn by Juan de La Cosa, a respected Basque pilot and cartographer who had a long association with Columbus. After the Admiral of the Ocean Sea chartered La Cosa's *Santa María* (and wrecked it) on the 1492–93 voyage, in which La Cosa participated, the Basque went along on the second voyage as a cartographer. La Cosa joined Alonso de Hojeda and Amerigo Vespucci (the lone partner in Seville's House of Berardi after the 1495 death of Columbus's financier of the *Santa María* charter) for their 1499–1500 voyage. It was one of the first in a flurry of forays out of Andalusia to South America and the southern Caribbean inspired by Columbus's discoveries on his third voyage in 1498.

La Cosa drew the portion of the map describing the New World at Puerto de Santa María in 1500, on his return from the voyage with Hojeda and Vespucci. The map is full of surprises, among them Cuba shown clearly and rather accurately as an island, several years before it supposedly was first circumnavigated and six years after Columbus had threatened the mariners (including La Cosa) on his 1494 cruise with the loss of their tongues if they ever said it was not a peninsula of the Asian mainland. The map illustrates a dawning comprehension of a continental land-mass distinct from the true Indies, as not a single label on this western shore evokes Asia. It hints at a continuous continent running from the Caribbean coast of South America in a rough arc consistent with the Gulf of Mexico and extending north-ward and eastward. The uncertainty over an actual Central American connection between North and South America is cleverly cloaked by a portrait of St. Christo-pher, the patron saint of voyagers, carrying the infant Jesus across the waters, which strategically conceals where the coastlines promise to link.

What we now know to be North America is an enormous landmass overhang-ing Columbus's Caribbean, along which are planted five English flags. They begin at a cape in the east bearing the label *cauo de ynglaterra* (cape of England) and fol-low westward along a southern shore to an indentation labeled *mar descubierto par inglese* (sea discovered by the English). The coast's orientation cannot be considered reliable—indeed, the apparent latitudes of some well-known European features are significantly wrong. It is a tribute to the seductive vagueness of the map that ex-perts have alternately identified *cauo de ynglaterra* as Greenland's Cape Farewell and Nova Scotia's Cape Breton. Its revelations are in the eye of the beholder: The lands attributed to the English may include only Newfoundland and Labrador, or they may extend as far south as Florida.

In seeking an explanation for the details of La Cosa's map, historians have rou-tinely turned to the chronically unreliable and self-serving Sebastian Cabot, who created considerable confusion about his father's discoveries by claiming John's voyages as his own and merging them with a voyage he probably did make, in 1508–09, in search of the Northwest Passage. In his *Decades III* of 1516, Pietro Mar-tire published an account of a voyage by Sebastian, who he knew personally. Mar-tire had Sebastian ranging all the way south to the Caribbean, leaving Cuba on his left. Some historians concluded that this must have been his father's 1498 voyage. However, Martire in the first book of his *Historia dell' Indie Occidentali,* published in Venice in 1534, struck all mention of Sebastian having reached Cuba on this un-dated voyage. Instead, after Sebastian sailed as high as latitude 55°, he made his way down the coast "which runs at first for a while in the southerly direction, [and] then turns west." Although this still leaves it possible that Sebastian in 1508–09 or John in 1498 sailed all the way to the Caribbean, it also sounded like a voyage that made a westward jog farther north—below Newfoundland, into the Gulf of St. Lawrence, below Nova Scotia, toward the Maine shore, or below Cape Cod, toward New Jersey.

The La Cosa map has long been thought to depict Cabot's discoveries in 1497, with perhaps some knowledge of the 1498 voyage that made it home on a surviving ship. There is now good reason to believe that La Cosa indeed was informed of Cabot's 1498 discoveries, and perhaps of what William Weston saw, presumably in 1499, as the flagged coast suggests a different cruise than the one Cabot made in 1497 from around Cape Bauld to the Avalon Peninsula. The series of five flags implies shore parties that actually staked separate claims, and Cabot went ashore only once in 1497.

The intelligence reached Spain by unknown channels. Was Roderigo de Puebla actually doing his job? Did Ayala eventually send a map, as he initially promised in July 1498? Perhaps the helpful Hugh Say passed one along, as he had already given Columbus a sketch map showing Cabot's 1497 discoveries.

Leaving aside any possible presence of John Cabot in the Caribbean in 1498 or 1499, the map helps explain what concerned Fernando and Isabel when they drafted the capitulations for Hojeda's second voyage, on June 8, 1501. Hojeda was told by Fernando and Isabel to continue sailing westward from Coquibaçoa, the region around the Golfo de Venezuela and the islands of the Netherlands Antilles, along the South American coast "because it goes towards the region where it has been learned that the English were making discoveries; and that you go setting up marks with the arms of their Majesties, or with other signs that may be known, such as shall seem good to you, in order that it be known that you have discovered that land, so that you may stop the exploration of the English in that direction." The monarchs promised Hojeda a gift of six leagues of land on Española "for what you shall discover on the coast of the mainland for the stopping of the English."

La Cosa's cartography presciently suggested that the shore marked as having already been discovered by the English might be connected to the Caribbean coast of South America, and Fernando and Isabel had no doubt Henry VII would keep pressing in that direction. Henry was adamant that Tordesillas posed no restrictions on his own exploratory ambitions, and he was no longer so needful of the goodwill of Fernando and Isabel. The marriage of Arthur and Catherine had been secured, and on November 23, 1499, Henry had extinguished the most persistent threat to his throne, which had once made him so dependent on Spanish support. Perkin Warbeck was hanged, with his head then struck from his body and displayed on London Bridge.

To curtail Henry's activities across the Ocean Sea, Fernando and Isabel expected Hojeda in 1501 to continue pressing west, and then north, around that speculatively curving shore toward the coast bristling with English flags, and mark the land clearly so that the English would not extend their claims any farther south. The instructions, when paired with the La Cosa map, suggest that the English had not yet reached the Caribbean but were surely on the way. By 1500, however, the Spanish no longer had to be concerned that the English interloper would be John Cabot.

CABOT'S ABILITY TO MOUNT the five-ship voyage in 1498 indicated there had been some belief in his geographic notions—although not enough belief to fulfill his licensed quota of six ships. Certainly there had not been the enthusiasm to warrant a true mirroring of Columbus's second voyage, with enough ships equipped to establish a trading colony along the lines of La Isabella. Say had expected ten or twelve vessels would be sent, and he was not given to hyperbole. The idea that Cabot's discoveries represented Cathay was in serious doubt if not already firmly discarded. A Weston voyage in 1499 could have been born of the rift first hinted at by Hugh Say. Even before the 1498 flotilla sailed, Say's letter to Columbus had indicated a fundamental disagreement in England over what Cabot had found. The Venetian had been telling people he had reached the land of the Great Khan while Say's letter contended Cabot had shown that a landfall previously located by Bristol mariners called the Isle of Brasil actually was part of some mainland. Say's unwillingness to employ the terms *Cathay* or *Indies* further suggested Bristol skepticism that Cabot had achieved his goals.

Henry's letter ordering a stay of proceedings against Weston employed the words *new founde land,* which is the first known appearance of a direct precursor for Newfoundland. Did that mean the king himself disagreed with Cabot's claims of having reached Cathay? The portentous words may have been only clerical shorthand for phrases already employed in support of Cabot. The August 10–11, 1497, reward in Henry's household books went to "hym that found the new Isle." Cabot's 1498 patent had empowered him to press ships to sail to the "londe and Iles of late founde by the seid John."

Such mentions of *new* lands or islands would have upheld Cabot's entitlement to what he had discovered, regardless of whether they were actually the land of the Great Khan—or, according to Bristol mutterings, represented a rediscovery of Brasil. Even so, the language in English records was failing to embrace terms evoking the Indies, as Columbus's renewed capitulations and other legal documents did. From the beginning of the English experience of what proved to be the New World, there was a strong reservation about formally crediting Cabot with reaching anything like the Indies.

Whatever Cabot's 1498 voyage managed to achieve in fresh exploration, it did not find a market in Cathay for its English goods or return with riches of the Orient. The 1498 Cabot expedition indeed could have been almost immediately forgotten to history—and ignored by Spanish diplomacy—because it was so resounding a commercial failure. Henry may have experienced a wavering or an outright loss in confidence in Cabot's vision, not unlike the one that had come over Fernando and

Isabel in April 1495 when they marginalized Columbus's role in the Indies enterprise without tearing up his capitulations. Although Weston's voyage could have been undertaken with a sublicense of Cabot's rights and the Venetian's full approval, it also could have been an effort by Henry to independently verify what Cabot claimed to have found, in the face of disappointing results from the 1498 voyage, in which the king had invested personally. After all, whatever Cabot had found was within Henry's realm. The king was free to send anyone he wished there, provided they did not infringe on Cabot's patent rights through commercial activity.

"Henry has aged so much during the last two weeks that he seems to be twenty years older," Pedro de Ayala informed Fernando and Isabel on March 26, 1499, two weeks after the king ordered the stay of proceedings against Weston. Henry was becoming very devout, hearing a sermon every day during Lent and continuing his devotions for the rest of the day. But his love of money remained unchanged. His riches were increasing daily. "I think he has no equal in this respect," Ayala concluded. Once a gold coin entered one of his strongboxes, Ayala assured, it never came out again.

Henry had arranged to pay Cabot his annual pension out of customs revenues at Bristol "for the time being." If Cabot's discoveries had no real hope of increasing trade, then Cabot was going to be an unnecessary financial burden to the crown. In early 1499, the king appeared duly motivated to employ a fact-checking Weston.

Some Bristol merchants in 1498 had banked on Cabot being correct in that he had found a profitable route to Cathay. Others suspected Cabot had found only what men in Bristol had already discovered, a distant wooded shore they called Brasil. There was another, emerging option: The Isle of Brasil was in fact mainland, as Hugh Say conveyed to Columbus, but was *not* Cathay. In that case, Cabot had discovered—rather, had rediscovered—a massive impediment to reaching the Indies by sailing west. Some way around it would have to be found. Weston's 1499 voyage could have been the first to probe for a Northwest Passage. The Portuguese voyages of the doomed Corte-Reals also seem to have been an early effort to determine if this new landmass could be surmounted to the north.

If Henry had lost confidence in Cabot's claim to have found a quick and easy route to Cathay in northern waters, the reversal of fortune nearly coincided with Columbus's own renewed plunge in stature with Fernando and Isabel. On March 21, 1499, nine days after the English king ordered the stay of proceedings against Weston, the Spanish monarchs granted Francesco de Bobadilla, brother of Columbus's former lover, a commission with sweeping powers for investigating the rapidly deteriorating state of Española, where colonists were in revolt at Santo Domingo.

Columbus had sailed on to a rude welcome in Española after his discovery of the Caribbean coast of South America in the summer of 1498 and was still there when Bobadilla arrived. It had taken fourteen months for Bobadilla to depart for the Indies, his preparations possibly disrupted by Columbus loyalists in Spain.

Bobadilla already had earned a reputation for harshness as a commander of several Castilian towns that belonged to the military order of Calatrava and had been sued by residents of two of them for malfeasance. When he reached Santo Domingo on August 23, 1500, he immediately installed himself as governor, imprisoned Columbus, and then sent the explorer home in irons.

It would take Columbus until 1501 to regain limited standing with his monarchs and launch a fourth and final voyage, in 1502. When he arrived at Santo Domingo that June, the new viceroy and governor, Nicolás de Ovando, refused him permission to anchor. Columbus's nemesis, Bobadilla, was departing with a fleet carrying the entire year's haul of gold. A hurricane in the Mona Passage all but destroyed the fleet and drowned Bobadilla. The only ship to survive was the one carrying Columbus's personal share of the gold. His Genoese partners in Seville, Francisco de Riberol, Francisco Doria, Francisco Catanio, and Gaspar de Spinola, were financially devastated by the hurricane, but Columbus was finally able to call himself a wealthy man.

Departing Santo Domingo on his further explorations, Columbus reached the Yucatán peninsula of Central America, thus filling in a crucial portion of the La Cosa map concealed beneath the portrait of St. Christopher. The essential evidence for the Americas was now in hand. Columbus still argued he was in Asia.

NOTWITHSTANDING THE LA COSA MAP, we still have no certain idea of what Cabot's enigmatic 1498 flotilla saw or what Weston found that warranted his subsequent reward. But the geographic regimen of Ptolemy, of Pierre d'Ailly, of Marco Polo, and of Toscanelli that had inspired Portuguese adventurers and a German knight named Martin Behaim and that had fueled the ambitions of both Columbus and Cabot could not continue to dictate the nature of the world. There was no port of Quinsay, no empire of the Great Khan full of precious goods on the far shore of the Ocean Sea. Nor was that far shore an island called Brasil. Beyond the horizon these adventurers dared to chase, *another world,* a *new world,* a *new founde land* was rising.

AFTERWORD

ALWYN RUDDOCK continues to hold historians spellbound with the claims in her book outline for Exeter Press that survived the posthumous destruction of her papers. A number of her key assertions have already been substantiated by the Cabot Project, including the role of the Florentine House of Bardi in financing Cabot's English voyages. But her truly extraordinary statements remain unproven, perhaps even improvable. No one yet knows if there was a documentary basis to them or if Ruddock had stitched together a scenario based on highly educated guesses. I remain confident that much of what she asserted was based in fact, in no small part because of the faith of Jeffrey Reed, whose work in transcribing letters between Ruddock and David B. Quinn in Quinn's papers at the Library of Congress has been so important to furthering the hunt for Ruddock's sources. After reading her stillborn book's chapter outline in the 2008 *Historical Research* paper by Evan Jones, "Alwyn Ruddock: 'John Cabot and the Discovery of America,'" Reed told me, "I was struck by what she claimed. The obvious criticism of the paper was that Ruddock had never published much of her findings, which raised the possibility that her claims were those of a mad old woman. But it was clear to me that she was one of those people who, if she said she had found something, she had found it. Anyone who met Ruddock would quickly realize that she was a real old-fashioned archival scholar. I knew both Alwyn Ruddock and David Quinn, and he took seriously everything she said."

"I think we're now well past the stage of wondering whether Ruddock simply made her claims up—which I was asked a lot at the time my first article came out [as a preview online] in 2007," Jones has told me. "We've corroborated too many of her finds now to doubt her on that score. On the other hand, that doesn't mean that everything she said was correct."

Foremost among Ruddock's unproven assertions is the scope of the role of Giovanni Antonio de Carbonariis in the 1498 Cabot voyage. Ruddock believed Carbonariis and his fellow Augustinian friars had participated with their own ship, the *Dominus Nobiscum*. The Spanish ambassador Ayala had reported in July 1498 that a ship carrying Carbonariis ("another Friar Buil") was forced into port in Ireland by a storm on the outbound passage, but Ruddock asserted that Carbonariis and his ship made it to Newfoundland. There they established a settlement with a church on Conception Bay, in a location that was preserved through folk memory as Carbonear.

The idea that Carbonear might be linked to Carbonariis did not originate with Ruddock. David O. True, a Miami geographer, posited in 1954 that John and Sebastian Cabot were the discoverers of Florida; at the same time, True found Carbonear resonantly intriguing. As James A. Williamson wrote in 1962 in *The Cabot Voyages*: "Mr. David O. True very kindly notified me of a point that has attracted his attention, the existence of the old place-name Carbonear on the eastern shore of Newfoundland. Its similarity to the unique personal name de Carbonariis is suggestive. It might be supposed that Antonio de Carbonariis was in some way linked with this place in the voyage of 1498, or equally that he was there in the course of some subsequent expedition."

Ruddock assuredly was inspired by this observation and fleshed out a scenario involving an actual settlement. The friars overwintered at present-day Carbonear and the next summer made an exploratory voyage up the Labrador coast in the *Dominus Nobiscum*. Ruddock must have been aware of the record of such a ship; she claimed the account of the voyage was passed down through the decades in garbled memories, until the sixteenth-century English historiographer Richard Hakluyt mistakenly turned it into a 1527 Northwest Passage search with a ship he misspelled as *Dominicus Noviscum*, confusing the voyage's details with the actual expedition of the *Sampson* and the *Mary of Guildford* of that year. Ruddock also appeared to believe that Ilha de Frey Luis (Island of Brother Luis), which appeared on a Portuguese chart from around 1503, referred to a hermit retreat associated with Carbonariis and his friars. Carbonariis in Ruddock's scenario never returned to England, and we know he was replaced in his proctor's duties by Polydore Vergil.

There was more. Three of the other four ships in the 1498 Cabot flotilla engaged in fishing, while Cabot struck out on a solo passage to the south, sailing all the way to the Caribbean. Here Ruddock's thesis merged with the familiar scenario of a supposed encounter with Spaniards. It's not clear if she actually had fresh evidence in this regard; she may only have been elaborating on the known materials related to the La Cosa map and the expedition of Alonso de Hojeda and Amerigo Vespucci. Nevertheless, her outline for chapter XIII promised: "The arrival in the Caribbean. Columbus in Hispaniola and Hojeda and Vespucci exploring the South American coast. Evidence from Spanish archives and narratives. The encounter with Cabot's ship at Coquibaçoa and the homeward voyage. Repercussions in Spain."

Unless Ruddock had stumbled on fresh evidence in Spanish archives, Cabot's encounter with Hojeda and Vespucci at Coquibaçoa is the most speculative of her unpublished ideas. Her assertions about Carbonariis are more promising; her work sifting through unindexed materials in British archives apparently yielded a number of additional insights that researchers are chasing down. Among them are clues to previously unknown relationships within the Cabot enterprise.

Ruddock's outline for "Chapter XII (Preparations for the Voyage of 1498)" avowed that Henry VII loaned money to the "Esterfield family" and Thomas Bradley. She also asserted links between the Thirkill family of London and the Bristol community. Bradley we know had a ship pressed by Cabot for the 1498 voyage, as did Launcelot Thirkill. Ruddock appeared to be following the lead of C. Raymond Beasley, who in his 1898 volume on the Cabots qualified the king's payment of twenty pounds to Thirkill in the March 17–22 day books entries of 1498 not as a payment for a ship press, but as a "loan;" Beasley also called a subsequent payment to Thirkill and Bradley of thirty pounds in the April 1–3 entries a "loan." While Beasley was mistaken in not recognizing that ships were pressed from these men, Ruddock had revisited these archival records and concluded that Henry VII was indeed financing these men as voyage participants. The Cabot Project has discovered the initiation of legal proceedings against Launcelot Thirkill and Thomas Bradley in June 1500 for nonpayment of a loan the king had advanced them in 1498 for going to the "new isle."

As for Ruddock's assertion that Henry loaned money to the Esterfield family for the 1498 voyage: We know of John Esterfeld from the suit he filed against William Weston, for which Henry VII issued a stay of proceedings in March 1499 so Weston could make an exploration voyage on the king's behalf. If all of Ruddock's assertions with respect to these families and individuals and the 1498 Cabot voyage prove correct, they will significantly enhance—and complicate—our picture of the dynamics of the relationships among the king, Cabot, and the Bristol and London merchant communities.

Confirmation of John Esterfeld's involvement in Cabot's 1498 voyage would not come as a surprise, as he was one of Bristol's most prominent citizens and merchants. Esterfeld traded mainly with France's Gascony region and the Atlantic ports of Spain and Portugal. He dominated Bristol trade there in cloth, according to customs records in the late 1480s, but also dealt in woad, wine, sugar, cloth, hides, calfskins and oil. For the *Trinity* voyage of 1480–81 to Andalusia that called at Columbus's haunt of La Rábida, Esterfeld secured the ship's purser, John Balsall, as his agent in trading in cloth. No records connect him directly with the Bristol search for Brasil under way at the time, but Esterfeld certainly knew the men involved.

Like William Weston's late father-in-law, John Foster, Esterfeld held the usual public offices of a leading citizen: sheriff, bailiff, and mayor (in 1487 and 1494–95), and represented Bristol in Parliament in 1485–86 and 1487, immediately before Foster became the city's member of Parliament. He also invested in land with Weston in 1493. In 1495, Esterfeld was commissioned to execute the office of Admiral of England for the city and county of Bristol, a post that was renewed in 1498. Who knows what Esterfeld might have thought of Cabot being styled the "Great Admiral" on his return in 1497?

If any Bristol merchant had the means to invest in Cabot's 1498 voyage, it was Esterfeld, who was also well known and loyal to Henry VII. Why the king would have felt obligated to lend money to Esterfeld for the 1498 voyage is another issue. And how Esterfeld managed to become entangled in a bitter legal fight with Weston—with whom he had invested in real estate and who was an apparent associate of Cabot who had already been compensated by Henry in January 1498—is a true conundrum. Esterfeld may have had no choice as executor of the Foster will but to initiate the chancery petition against the Westons, but the ongoing action threatened to toss Foster's daughter and son-in-law out on the street and put Esterfeld at odds with the king's interests.

Foster had died in 1492, and a house he owned on Corn Street in Bristol was left to the use of his daughter Agnes during her lifetime, on condition that she honored a number of financial stipulations. It was a rather begrudging bequest, and apart from ensuring that he continued to have a roof over his head, Agnes's husband, William Weston, could not benefit from it. Esterfeld had launched the prosecution because William and Agnes Weston had not kept up with the quit-rent and had barred him from entering the property to ensure it was being maintained in accordance with the will, which Esterfeld said it was not. The Westons were on the verge of being evicted when the king stepped in so that William Weston could make the exploration voyage.

The recent emergence of Weston as an explorer in his own right raises many questions about Cabot's status with Henry around the time of the 1498 voyage and about the English perception of what had been found. The suit involving Esterfeld and Weston layers on additional intrigue. The history of Bristol's late fifteenth-century maritime community, and its role in the early exploration of North America, is suddenly alive with unanswered questions and fresh lines of inquiry.

WHERE JOHN CABOT'S STORY promises the recovery of a lost history, Martin Behaim's may be destined to remain an intriguing riddle. Between his strange letter of March 1494 to his cousin Michael and his impoverished death in Lisbon in 1506 lie twelve yawning years of documentary silence, at a most conspicuous time in exploration history. The nineteenth-century historian John G. Morris summed up well the enduring mystery, and the possible solution: "The years between 1494 and 1506 were rich in expeditions to the west and east, and we can only conjecture how Behaim was employed during that period. We do not certainly know whether he took part in any of them, but this is certain that he became poor, and for this we cannot account, for he brought a considerable sum with him from Nürnberg."

Something had consumed the time, energy, ambition—and money—of a man who, after being denied his opportunity to strike westward with Dulmo and Estreito in 1487, had devoted himself to creating the world's earliest extant terrestrial globe and had then unquestionably used that project as a springboard for crafting with Jerome Münzer the 1493 proposal to João II for a northern passage to Cathay that was pitched to the wrong monarch at the wrong time. Nothing of interest occurred in the life of his friend Münzer after his four dinners with João II and his remarkable series of encounters with leading figures in the Columbus enterprise. After Münzer concluded his eventful tour of Spain and Portugal in the spring of 1495, he evidently never again left Nürnberg and died there in 1508. But the parallel dozen-year silence of Behaim should not necessarily stand as a similar case of idle retirement, which in Behaim's case would have involved a distressing bleeding of an inherited fortune.

Morris could not help but suspect that Behaim went to sea with *someone*. "It may be that Behaim lost his fortune in some unsuccessful private expedition, for we can hardly suppose that such an adventurous, restless spirit as he would be content with the inactive life of a plain citizen. He may have joined one of those numerous expeditions of the day, and like many other bold adventurers before him and since, paid the price of his rashness by the loss of his fortune."

It is hoped that the reassessment of the historical record in this book encourages a fresh consideration of this long-discounted or marginalized figure. Behaim emerges as a bridge among the careers of Columbus, Cabot, and the Portuguese voyagers of little Terceira, including the celebrated Corte-Reals. His actual participation in the Cabot voyages is plausible yet ultimately circumstantial. Raimundo di Raimundis may have caught a glimpse of him at Henry VII's court in December 1497, the nameless Burgundian who could vouch for everything that Cabot, the Columbus doppelgänger, said and who expected to be made a count with an island to his own name on the next voyage. One can well imagine that the misadventure that broke the back of Behaim's fortune was the 1498 Cabot expedition, although a debilitating insistence on helping bankroll the fruitless Terceiran ventures, including those of the luckless Corte-Real brothers, cannot be discounted.

The circumstantial nature of Behaim's career and his ultimate fate is typical of early exploration history. Rare are the figures as copiously documented as Columbus, but for all the paperwork his career produced, there are enough holes in the record that people continue to bitterly debate something as basic as where he was born, which is fundamental to the issue of who Columbus was. We continue to find fresh questions to pose about his character, his motivations, and his world, which extended to the *orbe novo* he refused to believe he had discovered.

BIBLIOGRAPHY

Adams, William. *Adams's Chronicle of Bristol*. Bristol, UK: J. W. Arrowsmith, 1910. Originally published 1623.

Albardaner i Llorens, Francesc. "John Cabot and Christopher Columbus Revisited," *Northern Mariner/Le Marin du Nord* 10, no. 2 (July 2000): 91–102.

Arquivo dos Açores, Vols. 1–15. Arquivo Digital, Universidade dos Açores, http://arquivodigital.uac. pt/aa/index.html.

Asociación Cultural Cristóbal Colón. "En busca de la verdad: el verdader o origen de Cristobal Colon." Archived online at http://www.yoescribo.com/publica/especiales/buscaverdad.aspx?cod=1.

Attreed, Lorraine. "Henry VII and the 'New-Found Island': England's Atlantic Exploration, Mediterranean Diplomacy, and the Challenge of Frontier Sexuality," *Mediterranean Studies* 9 (2000): 65–78.

Autoridad Portuaria de Valencia. "Notas Históricas Sobre El Puerto De Valencia." Accessed at http://www .valenciaport.com/en-US/ValenciaportEntorno/Historia/Valencia/Paginas/HistoriaValencia .aspx.

Avalon Project, Yale Law School. "Treaty between Spain and Portugal Concluded at Tordesillas, June 7, 1494." Accessed at http://avalon.law.yale.edu/15th_century/mod001.asp.

Beasley, C. Raymond. *John and Sebastian Cabot: The Discovery of North America*. London: T. Fisher Unwin, 1898.

Bergenroth, G. A., ed. *Calendar of State Papers, Spain, Vol. 1*. London, UK: Public Record Office, 1862.

Berggren, J. Lennart, and Alexander Jones. *Ptolemy's Geography: An Annotated Translation of the Theoretical Chapters*. Princeton, NJ: Princeton University Press, 2001.

Bernáldez, Andrés. *Historia de los Reyes Católicos D. Fernando y Doña Isabel, Tomo I, II*. Seville: D. José María Geofrin, 1852.

Biblioteca Oliveriana de Pesaro. http://www.oliveriana.pu.it/.

Biggar. H. P. *The Precursors of Jacques Cartier 1497–1534*. Ottawa: Government of Canada, 1911.

Birden, Isabel, and Evan Jones. "John Cabot in Seville, 1494." Accessed at http://www.bristol.ac.uk/ history/research/cabot.html.

Breazeale, Kennon. "Editorial Introduction to Nicolò de' Conti's Account." *SOAS Bulletin of Burma Research* 2, no. 2 (Autumn 2004): 100–199.

Brown, Rawdon, ed. *Calendar of State Papers Relating to English Affairs in the Archives of Venice, Vol. 1, 1202–1509*. London, UK: Public Record Office, 1864.

Busch, Wilhelm. *England under the Tudors: King Henry VII (1485–1509)*. Translated by Alice M. Todd. London, UK: 1895. Reprint, New York: Burt Franklin, nd.

The Cabot Project. Accessed at http://www.bristol.ac.uk/history/research/cabot.html.

Caunedo del Potro, Betsabé. "Los 'Medianos': Mercaderes y Artesanos," *Medievalismo* 13–14 (2004): 157–179.

Chambers, David, and Brian Pullan, eds. *Venice: A Documentary History 1450–1630*. Toronto, Canada: University of Toronto Press, 2007. Reprint.

Columbus, Christopher. "Columbus Manuscript." Letter of November 20, 1493.World Digital Library. Accessed at http://www.wdl.org/en/item/2962.

———. "Letter from Columbus to Luis de Santángel." Doc. No. AJ-063. Wisconsin Historical Society Digital Library and Archives, www.wisconsinhistory.org/libraryarchives/collections/digital.asp.

"Covilham (Covilhão, Covilhã), Pero or Pedro de." *Encyclopaedia Britannica*, Vol. 7, 1911.

Diffie, Bailey W., and George D. Winius. *Foundations of the Portuguese Empire, 1415–1580*. Minneapolis: University of Minnesota Press, 1977.

Dursteler, Eric. "Reverberations of the Voyages of Discovery in Venice, ca. 1501: The Trevisan Manuscript in the Library of Congress." *Mediterranean Studies* 9 (2000): 43–64.

Fernández-Armesto, Felipe. "God Bless Amerigo," *Tufts Magazine* (Fall 2007). Accessed at http://www.tufts.edu/alumni/magazine/fall2007/features/amerigo.htmlv=.

Fernández-Armesto, F. F. R. "La financiación de la conquistade las islas Canarias en el tiempo de los Reyes Católicos," *Anuario de Estudios Atlanticos* 28 (1982): 343–378.

Fundación Casa Ducal de Medinaceli. Accessed at www.fundacionmedinaceli.org.

Gaio, Felgueiras. *Nobiliário de famílias de Portugal*.17 vols. Edited by Agostinho de Azevedo Meirelles and Domingos de Araújo Affonso. Braga, Portugal: Pax, 1938–41.

Gairdner, James, ed. *Letters and Papers Illustrative of the Reigns of Richard III and Henry VII*. Vols. 1–2. London, UK: Longman, Green, 1861.

Ghillany, F. W. *Geschichte des Seefahrers Ritter Martin Behaim*. Nürnberg, Germany: Bauer und Raspe, 1853.

Giuffrida, Edoardo. "New Documents on Giovanni Caboto." In *Attraversaregli Oceani: Da Giovanni Caboto al Canada multiculturale*, edited by Rosella Mamoli Zorzi (pp. 61–72).Venice, Italy: Marsilio Editori, 1999.

Görz, Günther. "Martin Behaim." In *The Biographical Encyclopedia of Astronomers*, edited by Thomas Hockey. Berlin, Germany: Springer, 2007.

Görz, Günther, and Norbert Holst. "The Digital Behaim Globe (1492)." Fourth International Conference on Hypermedia and Interactivity in Museums, 1997, Le Musée du Louvre, Paris.

Gould, Alicia B. *Nueva Lista Documentada de los Tripulantes de Colon en 1492*. Madrid, Spain: Real Academia de la Historia, 1984.

Hakluyt, Richard. *Divers Voyages Touching the Discovery of America and the Islands Adjacent* (1582), edited by John Winter Jones. London, UK: Hakluyt Society, 1850.

———. *Principal Navigations, Voyages, Traffiques and Discoveries of the English Nation* (1598–1600), edited by Edmund Goldsmid. Unpaginated transcription accessed at http://ebooks.adelaide.edu.au/h/hakluyt/voyages/.

Hardy, Sir Thomas Duffus. *Syllabus (in English) of the Documents Relating to England and Other Kingdoms Contained in the Collection Known as "Rymer's Foedera," Vol. 2, 1377–1654*. London, UK: Longman and Co., and Trübner and Co., 1873.

Harrisse, Henry. *Jean et Sébastien Cabot: Leur Origine et leurs Voyages*. Paris, France: Ernest Leroux, 1882.

———. *John Cabot, the Discoverer of North America, and Sebastian, His Son*. London, UK: Benjamin Franklin Stevens, 1896.

———. *Les Corte-Real et leurs Voyages au Nouveau-Monde*. Paris, France: Ernest Leroux, 1883.

Hinds, Allen B., ed. *Calendar of State Papers and Manuscripts in the Archives and Collections of Milan, 1385–1618*. London, UK: Public Record Office, 1912.

Hunter, Douglas. "Rewriting History: Alwyn Ruddock and John Cabot." Archived under "Readings" at www.douglashunter.ca.

Ife, B. W. "Diary: Christopher Columbus." Unpaginated translation at King's College London, "Early Modern Spain." Accessed at http://www.ems.kcl.ac.uk/content/etext/e020.html#d0e434.

Igual Luis, David, and Germán Navarro Espinach. "Los genoveses en Espana en el transito del siglo XV al XVI." *Historia, Instituciones, Documentos* 24 (1997): 261–332.

Jones, Evan. "Alwyn Ruddock: 'John Cabot and the Discovery of America,'" *Historical Research* 81, no. 212 (May 2008): 224–254.

———. "England's Icelandic Fishery in the Early Modern Period." In *England's Sea Fisheries: The Commercial Sea Fisheries of England and Wales Since 1300*, edited by David J. Starkey, Chris Reid, and Neil Ashcroft (pp. 105–110). London, UK: Chatham Publishing, 2000.

———. "Henry VII and the Bristol Expeditions to North America: The Condon Documents." *Historical Research* 83, no. 221 (August 2010): 444–454.

———. "The *Matthew* of Bristol and the Financiers of John Cabot's 1497 Voyage to North America." *English Historical Review* 121, no. 492 (June 2006): 778–795.

———. "The Quinn Papers: Transcripts of Correspondence Relating to the Bristol Discovery Voyages to North America in the Fifteenth Century." Accessed at http://www.bristol.ac.uk/history/research/cabot.html.

Jones, Evan, ed. "Will of John Foster, Merchant of Bristol, 6 August 1492," National Archives, PROB 11/9, fos. 65–66. University of Bristol, ROSE, 2008. Accessed at http://www.bristol.ac.uk/history/research/cabot.html.

Jones, Evan, and Harvey Sharrer. "Salazar's Account of Bristol's Discovery of the Island of Brasil (pre-1476)." Accessed at http://www.bristol.ac.uk/history/research/cabot.html.

Jones, John Winter, and George Percy Badger. *The Travels of Ludovico di Varthema.* London, UK: Hakluyt Society, 1863.

King's College, London. "Early Modern Spain." Accessed at http://www.ems.kcl.ac.uk/content/etext/.

Kostylo, J. "Commentary on the Venetian Statute on Industrial Brevets (1474)." In *Primary Sources on Copyright (1450–1900),* edited by L. Bently and M. Kretschmer. Accessed at www.copyrighthistory.org.

Leland, John, and Thomas Hearne. *Joannis Lelandi antiquarii De Rebus Britannicis Collectaneorum,* Vol. 4. London, UK: Benj. White, 1770.

Lemonnier, Henry. *Charles VIII, Louis XII, François Ier et les guerres d'Italie (1492–1547).* Paris, France: Éditions Tallandier, 1911.

León-Portilla, Miguel. "Men of Maize." In *America in 1492: The World of the Indian People before the Arrival of Columbus,* edited by Alvin M. Josephy, Jr. (pp. 147–176). New York, NY: Vintage Books, 1992.

Littlehales, Henry. *The Medieval Records of a London City Church—St Mary at Hill, 1420–1559.* London, UK: Early English Text Society, 1905.

Lyon, Eugune. "Search for Columbus." *National Geographic* 181, no. 1 (January 1992): 2–39.

Major, R. H., ed. *India in the Fifteenth Century.* London, UK: Hakluyt Society, 1857.

Marshall, Ingeborg. *The Beothuk.* St. John's, NL: Breakwater Books, 2009.

Martz, Linda. "*Toledanos* and the Kingdom of Grenada, 1492–1560s." In *Spain, Europe, and the Atlantic World: Essays in the Honour of John. H. Elliott,* edited by Richard L. Kagan and Geoffrey Parker (pp. 103–124). Cambridge, UK: Cambridge University Press, 1995.

McGregor, James Harvey. *Venice from the Ground Up.* Cambridge, MA: Belknap Press of Harvard University Press, 2006.

Morris, John G. *Martin Behaim, the German Astronomer and Cartographer of the Times of Columbus.* Baltimore, MD: John Murphy and Co. for the Maryland Historical Society, 1855.

Murr, Christoph Gottlieb von (Christophe Theophile de Murr). *Histoire Diplomatique de Martin Behaim,* 3rd ed. Translated by H. J. Jansen. Paris, France: Treuttel et Würtz, 1802.

Murray, G. W. "Felix Fabri's Pilgrimage from Gaza to Mount Sinai and Cairo, A.D. 1483." *Geographical Journal* 122, no. 3 (September 1956): 335–342.

Münzer, Jerome. *Jérôme Münzer: Voyage en Espagne et au Portugal.* Translated by Michel Tarayre. Paris, France: Les Belles Lettres, 2006.

Nader, Helen, ed. and trans., and Luciano Formisano, philologist. *Repertorium Columbianum Vol. II: The Book of Privileges Issued to Christopher Columbus by King Fernando and Queen Isabel 1492–1502.* Eugene, OR: Wipf and Stock, 1996.

Nowell, Charles E. "The Columbus Question." *American Historical Review* 44, no. 4 (July 1939): 802–822.

Otte, Enrique. *Sevilla y sus mercaderesa fines de la Edad.* Seville, Spain: Universidad de Sevilla, 1996.

Pané, Ramón. "The relación of Fray Ramón Pane." Translation accessed at http://faculty.smu.edu/bakewell/BAKEWELL/texts/panerelacion.html.

Peacock, Annabel. "The Men of Bristol and the Atlantic Discovery Voyages of the Fifteenth and Early Sixteenth Centuries." Master's thesis, University of Bristol, UK, 2007.

Pescador, Carmen. "Un Documento Curioso sobre el Descubrimiento de America (Nueva Interpretacion)," *Revista Chilena de Historia del Derecho* 2 (1961): 63–67.

Phillips, William D., ed. and trans. *Repertorium Columbianum, Vol. 8: Testimonies from the Columbian Lawsuits.* Turnhout, Belgium: Brepols, 2000.

Pilorgerie, J. de la. *Campagne et Bulletins de la Grande Armée d'Italie Commandés par Charles VIII, 1494–95.* Paris: Didier et Co., 1866.

Pollard, A. F. *The Reign of Henry VII from Contemporary Sources,* Vol. 1. London, UK: Longmans, Green and Co., 1913.

Polo, Marco. *The Book of Ser Marco Polo the Venetian Concerning the Kingdoms and Marvels of the East.* Translated and edited by Henry Yule; 3rd ed. revised by Henri Cordier. London, UK: John Murray, 1903.

Porro Gutiérrez, Jesús María. "Una antinomia protorrenacentista: secreto de estado y divulgación en los descubrimientos luso-castellanos. La cartografía (1418–1495)," *Anuario de Estudios Americanos* 60, no. 1 (2003): 13–40.

Portsteinsson, Björn. "Henry VIII and Iceland." *Saga-Book of the Viking Society* 15: 67–101.

———. Letters of May 15, 1967 and August 2, 1969, and manuscript, "The Voyages of Englishmen to Iceland in the 15th Century, and Their Discoveries." Box 80, David B. Quinn Papers, Library of Congress, Washington, DC.

Prescott, H. F. M. *Once to the Sinai: The Further Pilgrimage of Friar Felix Fabri.* London, UK: Macmillan, 1947.

David B. Quinn Papers. Library of Congress, Washington, DC.

Quinn, David B. "État présent des études sur la redécouverte de l'Amérique au XVe siècle." *Journal de la Société des Américanistes* 55, no. 2 (1966): 343–381.

Quintanilla Raso, María Concepción. "Los Grandes Nobles." *Medievalismo* 13–14 (2004): 127–142.

Reddaway, T. F., and A. A. Ruddock, eds. "The Accounts of John Balsall, Purser of the Trinity of Bristol, 1480–1," *Camden Miscellany* 23, Fourth Series, no. 7 (1969): 1–28.

Regiomontanus, Johannes. *Kalendarium* (1476). Digitized and composed by H. Petsch and A. Partl, University Library of the Vienna Institute of Astronomy. Accessed at http://www.univie.ac.at/hwastro/books/regioBWLow.pdf.

Ricart, Robert. *The Maire of Bristowe Is Calendar.* Edited by Lucy Toulmin Smith. London, UK: Westminster, for the Camden Society, 1872.

Roover, Raymond de. *Money, Banking, and Credit in Mediaeval Bruges.* Cambridge, MA: Mediaeval Academy of America, 1948.

Ruddock, Alwyn. "Columbus and Iceland: New Light on an Old Problem," *Geographical Journal* 136, no. 2 (June 1970): 177–189.

———. *Italian Merchants and Shipping in Southampton 1270–1600.* Southampton, UK: University College, 1951.

———. "John Day of Bristol and the English Voyages across the Atlantic before 1497," *Geographical Journal* 132, no. 2 (June 1966): 225–233.

Rumeu de Armas, Antonio. *Alonso de Lugo en la Corte de los Reyes Católicos 1496–1497.* Madrid, Spain: Consejo Superior de Investigaciones Científicas, 1954.

———. "Los amorios de doña Beatriz de Bobadilla." *Anuario de Estudios Atlanticos* 31 (1985): 413–456.

Ryan, A. N. "Bristol, the Atlantic and North America, 1480–1509." In *Maritime History, Vol. 1: The Age of Discovery,* edited by John B. Hattendorf (pp. 241–255). Malabar, FL: Krieger, 1996.

Sanuto (Sanudo), Marino. *Diarii di Marino Sanuto,* Vol. 4. Venice, Italy: F. Visentini, 1880.

Sharrer, Harvey L. "The Passing of King Arthur to the Island of Brasil in a Fifteenth-Century Spanish Version of the Post-Vulgate *Roman du Graal,*" *Romania* 92 (1971): 65–74.

Sneyd, Charlotte Augusta. *A Relation, or Rather a True Account, of the Island of England . . . about the Year 1500.* London, UK: John Bowyer Nichols and Son, for the Camden Society, 1847.

Stevenson, Edward Luther. *Marine World Chart of Nicolo de Canerio Januensis 1502 (Circa): A Critical Study with Facsimile.* New York, NY: American Geographical Society and the Hispanic Society of America, 1908.

Suárez Acosta, J. J., Félix Rodríguez Lorenzo, and Carmelo L. Quintero Padrón. *Conquista y Colonización.* Santa Cruz de Tenerife, Canary Islands: Centro de la Cultura Popular Canaria, 1988.

Symcox, Geoffrey, ed. *Repertorium Columbianum, Vol. 10: Italian Reports on America 1493–1522, Letters, Dispatches and Papal Bulls.* Turnhout, Belgium: Brepols, 2001.

———. *Repertorium Columbianum, Vol. 12: Italian Reports on America 1493–1522, Accounts by Contemporary Observers.* Turnhout, Belgium: Brepols, 2002.

Tafur, Pero. *Travels and Adventures (1435-1439).* Translated and edited with an introduction by Malcolm Letts. New York, NY, and London, UK: Harper & Brothers 1926.

Thacher, John Boyd. *Christopher Columbus: His Life, His Works, His Remains.* 2 vols. New York, NY: G. P. Putnam's Sons, 1903.

Thomas, William. *Travels to Tana and Persia by Josafa Barbaro and Ambrogio Contarini.* London, UK: Hakluyt Society, 1873.

Tiepolo, M. F. "Documenti Veneziani su Giovanni Caboto," *Studi Veneziani* 15 (1973): 585–597.

Vignaud, Henry. *Histoire Critique de la Grande Entreprise de Christophe Colomb.* 2 vols. Paris, France: 1911.

Vigneras, Louis-André. *The Discovery of South America and the Andalusian Voyages.* Chicago, IL: University of Chicago Press for the Newberry Library, 1976.

———. *État présent des études sur Jean Cabot.* Lisbon, Portugal: Congresso Internaçional de Historia dos Descobrimentos, 1961.

———. "New Light on the 1497 Cabot Voyage to America," *Hispanic American Historical Review* 36, no. 4 (November 1956): 503–506.

———. Unpublished papers, compiled and edited by Jeffrey Reed. Private collection.

Waters, D. W. *The Art of Navigation in England in Elizabethan and Early Stuart Times.* New Haven, CT: Yale University Press, 1958.

Williamson, James A., ed. *The Cabot Voyages and Bristol Discovery under Henry VII.* Cambridge, UK: Cambridge University Press, for the Hakluyt Society, 1962.

Wolf, Eric R. "Unforeseen Americas: The Making of New World Societies in Anthropological Perspective," *Proceedings of the National Academy of Sciences USA* 93 (March 1996): 2603–2607.

NOTES

on SELECTED SOURCES

and COMMENTARY

AS A COMPANION to the full bibliography, these notes provide guidance on selected sources and a few elaborating comments. I have focused here on primary sources related to the main exploration figures. The bulk of transcribed and translated documents and extracts from the standard early histories related to Columbus (including works by Barros, Herrera, Las Casas, Martire, and Oviedo, as well as extracts from the Fernando Columbus biography) can be found in Thacher's *Christopher Columbus* (Vols. 1–2) and in Vignaud's *Historie Critique*. See also Bernáldez's *Historia de los Reyes Católicos*. As I have identified these early historians in the text and the sources are well known to scholars, I have mainly reserved these notes for specific documentary evidence where Thacher and Vignaud are concerned. For general historical material, consult the bibliography. I have referred to documents in the volumes of *Repertorium Columbianum* and Williamson's *Cabot Voyages* by item number. Although I have listed the better-known and more recent Williamson volume as the source for documents, most were published earlier by Biggar in *The Precursors of Jacques Cartier*, and Biggar's effort was superior in including transcriptions as well as English translations. Harrisse's works can also be relied on for original transcriptions of documents.

In citing sources here, I have listed only the author's or editor's last name unless there is more than one work credited to that person in the bibliography, in which case I have also provided an abbreviated title. See the bibliography for full citations. The Nader volume of *Repertorium Columbianum* (*Vol. 2*) was particularly useful for its contextual essays on the Columbus enterprise.

The Las Casas abstract of the 1492–93 Columbus log or journal has been widely translated into English; I have relied on "Diary: Christopher Columbus" by B. W. Ife. For the succeeding Columbus voyages, I turned to the translation of the Navarrete version of the Las Casas abstracts in Thacher, *Christopher Columbus*, Vol. 2. Quotations from the journal of Jerome Münzer are translations by me from Münzer, *Jérôme Münzer*, the French translation by Tarayre of the original Latin manuscript.

CHAPTER 1

For Sanudo, see "Praise of the City of Venice, 1493," in Chambers and Pullan. For an analysis of dialects in Cabot's signatures and its implications for his origins and for a discussion of his citizenship, see Giuffrida. Ayala's letter is item 37 in Williamson. Martire categorized Columbus as a Ligurian in the *First Decade* of his *History of the New World* and more specifically as a Genoese in the seventh book of the *Second Decade*. See Thacher, *Christopher Columbus*, Vol. 1, Part I. The 1504 libretto of Trevisan is item 14 in Symcox, *RC Vol. 12*. Documentary evidence for Columbus's Genoese origins is well covered by Thacher, *Christopher Columbus*, Vol. 1, Part III, and is summarized by Lyon. The controversy over Columbus's origins, while neverending, was addressed well in 1939 by Nowell. Gallo's 1506 recollection is item 10 in Symcox, *RC Vol. 12*. The Tafur quote is from Tafur. For my discussion of the Assereto document and Columbus's relationship to the di Negros and Gaspar de Spinola, including the solution to the tale of Columbus and the 1476 attack on the Flanders Galleys, I am indebted to Louis-André Vigneras' unpublished papers edited by Jeffrey Reed, which are in his private possession. The Fernando Columbus account of the sea battle is translated by Thacher in *Christopher Columbus*, Vol. 1, 216–217.

CHAPTER 2

For a discussion of early Portuguese voyages in the Atlantic, see Gutiérrez, "Una antinomia protor-renacentista," and Diffie and Winius. For the Sanudo comment, see "Praise of the City of Venice, 1493," in Chambers and Pullan. Columbus's marriage into the Perestrello-Moniz family is explored by Thacher in *Christopher Columbus*, Vol. 1. See Gaio for genealogy. For details of Cabot's membership and acceptance in San Giovanni Evangelista and the character of this *Scuola Grande,* see Giuffrida as well as McGregor. For a discussion of the Flanders Galleys, see Sanudo's "Praise of the City of Venice, 1493," in Chambers and Pullan, and Ruddock, *Italian Merchants and Shipping in Southampton,* 22–27. Cabot's property records are item 11 in Williamson. For Cabot's identification as a *pellizer,* the possible range of his trading activities, his purchase and sale of a slave, and the community of mariners associated with San Giovanni Evangelista and Cabot's properties, see Giuffrida. The Tafur quote is from Tafur. Nicolò de' Conti is discussed by Breazeale. For Venetian patents, see Kostylo.

CHAPTER 3

For Pietro Martire's discussion of Sebastian Cabot in his third *Decades,* see Thacher, *Christopher Columbus,* Vol. 1, Part I. The testimony of Sebastian Cabot is item 25.4 in Phillips, *RC Vol. 8.* Toscanelli's letter is discussed in Thacher, *Christopher Columbus,* Vol. 1. For an explanation of India Sinus, India Magna, and India Parva-Ethyopis, see Nader, 19. Gallo's commentary is item 10 in Symcox, *RC Vol. 12*. For Ptolemy's geography, see Berggren and Jones. Note that Ptolemy didn't explicitly advocate degrees of latitude. Rather, he divided the Earth into horizontal zones called climates, which reflected the lengths of the day in daylight hours. However, degrees of latitude were naturally applied to cartography along the general Ptolemaic scheme and were described as an elevation above the equinoctial, or equator. The geographic distances of the Toscanelli scheme as interpreted by Columbus are discussed by Phillips, 6. The possibility that Febo Capella could have been the conduit through which Toscanelli's ideas reached Cabot's Venice is proposed by Giuffrida. Gallo's discussion of Bartolomé Columbus is item 10 in Symcox, *RC Vol. 12*. The evolution of navigation science is thoroughly explored by Waters.

CHAPTER 4

For a discussion of early Portuguese voyages in the Atlantic, see Porro Gutiérrez, and Diffie and Winius. Note that João de Barros is our sole source on the existence of the Portuguese sun-sight junta, as discussed by Vignaud (*Histoire Critique,* Vol. 2, 433, n25). Vignaud cautioned that it is uncertain whether the junta ever existed, with the members cited by Portuguese authors. Nevertheless, Vignaud felt it was certain that the king submitted to learned and competent cosmographers the questions bearing on voyages of discovery the Portuguese were then undertaking. Geraldini's recollections are item 17.5 in Symcox, *RC Vol. 12*. The testimony of the physician Fernández is item 19.5 in Phillips. The

Trevisan recollection is item 14 in Symcox, *RC Vol. 12.* Columbus's 1500 letter to Juana de La Torre is Chapter 94 in Thacher, *Christopher Columbus,* Vol. 2. The testimony of Rodríguez Cabezudo is item 7.2 in Phillips. Note that despite long-standing claims that Columbus was allied with Enrique de Guzmán, second duke of Medina-Sidonia (who died in 1492), Fundacíon Casa Medina-Sidonia notes there isn't a single document among millions preserved in its archive indicating a formal relationship. Regarding Columbus's initial contact with Isabel, in the 1492–93 voyage journal, Columbus on January 14, 1493, states how "I came to serve you, now seven years ago on 20 January this present month." January 20, 1486 could have been the date his formal voyage proposal was first made to Isabel. For Cabot's flight from Venetian creditors and their biographies, see Tiepolo as well as Giuffrida. Giuffrida notes the important role of Marin Mocenigo in Venetian trade with England. Fabri's description of Venetian prisons is in Chambers and Pullan, 97–98. Documentation of Cabot's sojourn in Valencia is item 12 in Williamson.

CHAPTER 5

Geraldini's recollections are item 17.5 in Symcox, *RC Vol. 12.* For the letters of Martire, see Part I ("Peter Martyr") of Thacher, *Christopher Columbus,* Vol. 1. See Phillips for the testimony of Vélez (22.3), Maldonado de Talavera (11.2), and González (7.3). Columbus's recollection of the fall of Granada is in Thacher, *Christopher Columbus,* Vol. 1, 435. Giuffrida speculates that the hide trade may have drawn Cabot to Valencia. For Genoese merchant activity in Valencia, see Igual Luis and Navarro Espinach. Documentation of Cabot's harbor project in Valencia is item 12 in Williamson.

CHAPTER 6

Columbus's initial connections to Berardi and Riveroli are mentioned by Nader, 215, n40. The presence of Berardi in Seville from 1486 to 1495 is noted by Otte, 191; see also Otte for a discussion of the Genoese merchant community in Seville, 184–89. For the financing and conquest of the Canary Islands, see Fernández Armesto, "La financiación de la conquista;" Rumeu de Armas, *Alonso de Lugo;* and Suárez Acosta et al. Cuneo's letter of 1495 is item 7 in Symcox, *RC Vol. 12.* For the life and loves of Beatriz de Bobadilla, see Rumeu de Armas, "Los amorios de doña Beatriz de Bobadilla." For the history of Valencia's harbor, including Antoni Joan's pier (and photographs of its foundations), see Autoridad Portuaria de Valencia. For Cabot's Venetian creditors, see Tiepolo. For the Spanish correspondence regarding Cabot's harbor proposal, see item 12 in Williamson and Albardaner i Llorens.

CHAPTER 7

For the letters of Martire, see Part I ("Peter Martyr") of Thacher, *Christopher Columbus,* Vol. 1. For the Arawakan people, see León-Portilla. Toscanelli's letter is discussed in Thacher, *Christopher Columbus,* Vol. 1. For Marco Polo's travels, see Polo. For the men of the Columbus flotilla, see Gould. Historic trade between the Arawaks and Maya is noted by León-Portilla. See Phillips for the testimonies of the mariner Fernández (18.1), Vélez (22.3), and the physician Fernández (19.5).

CHAPTER 8

See Phillips for the testimonies of Pérez Pinzón (19.12) and Medel (22.11). Comments about Charles VIII by the Florentine and Venetian envoys are in Lemonnier, 13. For the orders to Torres to begin the Valencia harbor construction, see Albardaner i Llorens. English translations of Columbus's letters to his monarchs and Santángel can be read online at King's College, London, "Early Modern Spain." See also Columbus, "Letter from Columbus to Luis de Santángel," as well as Part VI of Thacher, *Christopher Columbus,* Vol. 2. For Columbus's letter to João II on his return from the Caribbean, see the Las Casas abstract of his journal as translated by Ife. Columbus's 1500 letter to Juana de La Torre is Chapter 94 in Thacher, *Christopher Columbus,* Vol. 2. A copy of the March 9, 1493, letter by Annibale De Zennaro (Hanibal Ianuaris) made by Giacomo Trotti is item 1 in Symcox, *RC Vol. 10.* See Phillips for the testimonies of Pérez Mateos (23.1) and Arias (22.2).

CHAPTER 9

For the March 30, 1493, letter from Fernando and Isabel to Columbus, see Nader, *RC Vol. 2*, 70. For the denouement of Cabot's Valencia harbor project, see Albardaner i Llorens, and item 12 in Williamson. For the records of Cabot's employment on the Seville bridge project, see the translation of and commentary on Juan Gil's findings by Birden and Jones. The March 1496 letter by Fernando and Isabel to their ambassador Puebla is item 16 in Williamson but has been retranslated for me by Janet Ritch. See notes for Chapter 17 for details. Note that Harrisse in *Jean et Sébastien Cabot* gives his name as "Ruy Gonzáles de Puebla"; Williamson calls him "Gonsalez de Puebla." I have followed the example of Bergenroth. The letter by the Milanese ambassador Raimundo di Raimundis (*aka* Raimondo de Raimondi de Soncino, among other variants) is item 24 in Williamson. The Scillacio letter relating the experiences of Coma is item 6 in Symcox, *RC Vol. 12*.

CHAPTER 10

The papal bulls of 1493 are discussed and translated most authoritatively in Symcox, *RC Vol. 10*. See also Chapter 2.3 in Nader. Cuneo's account of the 1493 voyage is part of his 1495 letter, item 7 in Symcox, *RC Vol. 12*. For the relationship between the Arawaks and Caribs and the later discussion of Arawak culture and settlements, see León-Portilla. Nicolò de'Conti's experiences on his Indies travels, as reported by Poggio Bracciolini, are translated in Major. Dr. Chanca's account is Chapter 77 in Thacher, *Christopher Columbus*, Vol. 2. The Scillacio letter relating the experiences of Coma is item 6 in Symcox, *RC Vol. 12*. The testimony of Martín is item 22.10 in Phillips.

CHAPTER 11

An English translation of Columbus's letter to Santángel can be read online at King's College, London, "Early Modern Spain." See also Part VI in Thacher, *Christopher Columbus*, Vol. 2. Isabel's September 5, 1493, letter to Columbus is in Nader, 92. Fernando and Isabel's August 16, 1494, letter to Columbus is in Nader, *RC Vol. 2*, 99. For the Treaty of Tordesillas, see the translation at the Avalon Project. For the letters of Martire, see Part I ("Peter Martyr") of Thacher, *Christopher Columbus*, Vol. 1. For the statement of the notary Perez de Luna, see Thacher, *Christopher Columbus*, Vol. 2, 327–32. For Martire's writings in *Decades*, see Part I, Chapter 7 of Thacher, *Christopher Columbus*, Vol. 1. The Columbus letter of November 20, 1493, was authenticated in 1978. See Columbus, "Columbus Manuscript." For the mentions of Antilla in association with Columbus in contemporary documents, see Vigneras, *Discovery of South America*, 3–4. The Strozzi letter is item 13 in Symcox, *RC Vol. 10*. Its original Italian reads "*sono segnate ditte isole più de .XLIII. gradi .XXVI. in gradi .XXXI. sotto l'Equinotio; per aviso.*" The RC translation renders this as: "these islands extend more than forty-three degrees, [from] twenty-six degrees north to thirty-one degrees below the Equator, according to report." The editors observe: "This report clearly does not make sense. It represents deliberate misinformation to keep the actual location of the newly found islands secret." Yet the Strozzi letter does make some sense, if the translation is reconsidered. The key verb is *segnare*, which means to mark or place. The letter is concerned with where the islands have been located, cartographically speaking, not with where they "extend." The fact that 26 and 31 do not add up to 43 indicates that Strozzi was writing not about a north-south span in latitude but rather a westward measure of longitude. "More than 43 degrees" is as good as a perfect result for the span between São Vicente in the Cape Verdes and the eastern edge of Española. The Martire letter of December 29, 1494, which conveys similar figures in latitude and longitude, supports this interpretation of the Strozzi letter. Columbus's eclipse results in his *Book of Prophecies* are recorded by Thacher, *Christopher Columbus*, Vol. 2, 631, n2. Cuneo related the abbot's rejection of the idea Cuba was mainland in his letter of 1495, item 7 in Symcox, *RC Vol. 12*. Gallo's 1506 recollection is item 10 in Symcox, *RC Vol. 12*.

CHAPTER 12

For the *comitres* of Triana and the local community, see Vigneras, *Discovery of South America*, 33, 36, 41, 84, 86. For Seville's role in the mid-Atlantic trade, see Igual Luis and Navarro Espinach. Rodríguez de la Mesquita's maintenance contract for the Puente de Barca is reported by Vigneras, *Discovery of*

South America, 86. For the records of Cabot's employment on the Seville bridge project, see Birden and Jones. For the career of Martin Behaim and his plans with Münzer for a westward voyage, see Vignaud, *Histoire Critique,* Vol. 2, "Sixième Étude: Le projet de Behaim et celui de Mûntzer. Leurs rapports avec le grand dessein de Colomb"; Morris; von Murr; Ghillany; and Görz. For letters written by and pertaining to Behaim, the most complete transcriptions (in German) appear in Ghillany. For Huerter and the first few generations of his Portuguese descendants, see *Arquivo dos Açores,* Vol. 1, 152–156. Regarding the friendship between Behaim and Columbus, Herrera in his *Historia general de los hechos de los Castellanos en las islas i tierra firme del mar oceano* (Decad I, Book. I, Ch. II.) stated: "Martin de Bohemia . . . su amigo . . . gran cosmographo." Cited by Vignaud, *Histoire Critique,* Vol. 2, 436. The first Decad of *Historia general* was published in 1601. While Herrera had access to court documents as Felipe II's official chronicler of Castile and the Indies, as Vignaud notes, it's not clear how he formed his conviction that the two men were friends. The text suggests the information originated with Columbus.

CHAPTER 13

For a transcription of the Dulmo-Estreito patents in their original Portuguese, see *Arquivo dos Açores,* Vol. 4, 440–446; for the award of Terceira to Jacome de Bruges, see ibid., 207; for documentation with respect to the Corte-Reals on Terceira, see the overview in ibid. beginning on page 157. For the claims that Corte-Real and Martins had discovered Terra do Bacalhau, see Diffie and Winius. For the larger story and genealogy of the Corte-Real family, see Harrisse, *Les Corte-Real.* For the explorations of Barcelos and Fernandes and the Bristol patent that succeeded Cabot's, see source notes for Chapter 24. For the Toscanelli letter, see Thacher, *Christopher Columbus,* Vol. 1. For sources on Behaim and Münzer, including letters, see the publications listed for Chapter 12. For the Behaim Globe, see also Görz and Holst. Behaim's letter to João II survived as a partial draft in Latin in the papers of Hartmann Schedel and as a Portuguese transcription discovered in the library of Munich. The two versions were collated in a French translation by Vignaud in *Histoire Critique, Vol. 2,* from which I have made the English translation; see "Pièces Justicatives," No. 25. Regarding the curious "Grulanda" of Münzer's letter, there seems to be an almost mischievous coincidence: One of the five families whose crests appear on the Nürnberg globe as evidence of their support for the project was that of Nicolas Groland.

CHAPTER 14

Cuneo's account is part of his 1495 letter, item 7 in Symcox, *RC Vol. 12.* The travails of La Isabella are well summarized by Nader. The records of Cabot's employment in Seville are covered by Birden and Jones. Regarding the identity of "Luis Méndez Portocarrero," according to the database of the Fundacíon Casa Ducal de Medinaceli, Luis Méndez de Haro y Sotomayor married Pedro Portocarrero's daughter Beatriz at an unknown date. It would not have been unusual for him to append the name of his wife's noble family to his own. See also the Fundación's database for information on the other Spanish nobles mentioned. The decree appointing Alfonso Enríquez admiral of Castile is item 48 in Nader. For the Cisneros petition, see Pescador. Juan Gil proposed a petition date coincident with Cabot's time in Seville (see Birden and Jones), but it may have dated to 1497 when the monarchs were passing through Zamora. The letter of December 3, 1494, mentioning the return of Buyl is cited by Gould, 307. For the letters of Martire, see Part I ("Peter Martyr") of Thacher, *Christopher Columbus,* Vol. 1.

CHAPTER 15

Ayala's letter to his sovereigns is item 37 in Williamson. My appreciation to Conrad Heidenreich for securing a fresh translation of the March 11, 1494, Behaim letter (transcribed in Ghillany).It has been long proposed that the letter indicated Behaim was sent to Burgundy by João II to secure the support of other monarchs for his plan to have his illegitimate son (and sole offspring), Jorge de Lencastre, succeed him. But this is a serious misinterpretation, as the letter never mentions João II or Jorge. The oft-stated idea that the "king here in Flanders" employing Behaim was João II is impossible, not only because João II was in Portugal but also because his only male offspring, the illegitimate Jorge, could not be "the king's son" in the Burgundian Netherlands, as is also routinely stated. Jorge was only twelve years old and never left João II's court in Portugal. The "young King from England" has illogically been identified as Henry VII, who was neither young (he was thirty-seven) nor living with the King of the Romans, Maximilian I. Behaim clearly was referring to the pretender Perkin Warbeck, who was being sheltered by Maximilian I. The Raimundis letter to the Duke of Milan is item 24 in Williamson.

CHAPTER 16

For Columbus's April 1493 letter, see the sources in Chapter 8. For the friar Pané's account, see Pané. Cuneo's letter of 1495 is our main account of the roundup of slaves on Española and also provides his account of his female slave; see item 7 in Symcox, *RC Vol. 12*. News of the arrival of the Torres flotilla on April 12, 1495, is noted by Gould, 308, n1. The new permissions for the Indies of April 10, 1495 are item 12 in Nader. The status and nature of Spanish "subjects" and "citizens" are discussed by Nader, 201, n4, 5. For the surge of Italian merchants into Spanish citizenship, see Otte, 186. See also research by Juan Manuel Bello León compiled in *Extranjeros en Castilla (1474–1501)*, 1994, cited by Asociación Cultural Cristóbal Colón. Bear in mind that the Asociación champions the theories of Gabriel Verd Martorell, which dispute the Genoese origin of Columbus. The Berardi flotillas, including the Sosa flotilla, are discussed by Gould, 309–317. For the Canary Islands conquest, see the sources in Chapter 6. For the Genoese domination of Canary Islands sugar plantations, see Suárez Acosta et al., 62.

CHAPTER 17

The Flanders Galley disaster and the correspondence of the doge Barbarigo are found in Brown. The Milanese ambassador's remarks about Henry VII's attitude to France is in Hinds. Lemonnier makes the point (p. 30) that Henry VII seemed to go to war to extort money from his subjects and made peace to obtain it from his enemies. The many uses of saffron are noted by Brown in his introduction. The Venetian ambassador Marcantonio Contarini's senate report on Sebastian Cabot and the recollection by the "Mantuan Gentleman" in Ramusio are items 57 and 58 in Williamson.

Regarding the connections between Cabot and the men involved with the Bragadina and the Flanders Galleys crisis in general, one of them is found in the run-down property Cabot acquired in San Giacomo dell'Orio in 1482. Cabot purchased it from a guardian of "Donna Marieta, daughter of the late Messer Pasqual Bragadin." (Williamson, item 11.) So the property was from the Bragadin (Bragadino) family. In 1495, Piero Bragadin, captain of the *Bragadina*, was dining aboard ship in Southampton when the French pirates struck and carried him away. Cabot also had joined the Scuola Grande of San Giovanni Evangelista in the same year as the ship's carpenter Zuan de Zorzi, who may have been from the Zorzi de Zuan family of shipbuilders. The merchant ship that was with the *Bragadina* in Southampton Water was the *Zorza*, owned by the noble Hieronimo Zorzi and his brothers. Also, the *Pasqualiga*, the ship tasked by the Venetian senate in 1497 to provide haul-back service for Venetian merchants from England, belonged to the Pasqualigo family; Lorenzo Pasqualigo wrote home from London with news of Cabot's exploration success on August 23, 1497. Lorenzo Pasqualigo's uncle and father were members like Cabot of the Scuola Grande of San Giovanni Evangelista. Giuffrida turned up the connection between Cabot and the Pasqualigo family via their scuole membership but did not connect Lorenzo Pasqualigo with the vessel *Pasqualiga*.

Regarding the March 1496 letter of Fernando and Isabel to the ambassador Puebla, the standard translation by Biggar, first published in *The Precursors of Jacques Cartier* (1911) and reproduced in Williamson, is in error. Biggar rendered the critical sentence: "In regard to what you say of the arrival there of one like Colon for the purpose of inducing the king of England to enter upon another undertaking like that of the Indies, without prejudice to Spain or to Portugal, if he [the king] aids him as he has us, *the Indies will be well rid of the man*" (my italics). Biggar thus has the Indies becoming rid of Cabot, not the "one from the Indies" (*lo de las Yndias*) being at liberty. Janet Ritch undertook this fresh translation for me. She informed me that "there is no justification for assuming that that the Indies will be well rid of Cabot," as the Biggar translation put it. Her version is more in line with the effort by Beasley, whose abstract in *John and Sebastian Cabot* (1898) said the final words meant, "He is quite at liberty." But Beasley sidestepped the problem of *lo de las Yndias* altogether simply by using the pronoun "he." An abstract had previously been included by Bergenroth, but it also omitted the "one from the Indies." An alternate interpretation would be to read it as calling Cabot "the one of the Indies [scheme]," thus avoiding the issue of Cabot's physical presence in the Indies. But that requires injecting a word that is not there. It also leaves the problem of accounting for Cabot's whereabouts for some fourteen months that dovetail with the second Columbus voyage, and further denies us an explanation for why the correspondent of the Milanese ambassador in 1497 described Cabot as having experience in discovering new islands. Another option, of reading *lo* as a pronoun referring back to the Spanish affair or enterprise of the Indies, is problematic on two fronts. I cannot make sense of the resulting sentence, and the writer should have used the subject pronoun *el*, which he had in fact already done in his mention of "another affair like that of [or "the one of"] the Indies," *el de las Yndias*. I have also considered the possibility that there was either a flaw in the trancscription or a botch by Alvarez of his dictated instructions, as *lo de* in modern Spanish at least means "about," and *y lo de* "what about." The passage could have been intended to convey something radically different: "If King Henry aids Cabot, then like us, what aspect of the Indies will be free from interference?" But as this is a rather free interpretation, I have not chosen it as the ultimate solution. The character of Alvarez is discussed by Martz, 106.

CHAPTER 18

Evan Jones of Bristol University suggested to me that Cabot's Italian origins might have given him a cachet of Renaissance sophistication at the court of Henry VII. Regarding the Count of Penamacor and the links of his children to Columbus, the count's eldest son, Afonso Garcia de Albuquerque, married Leonor de Perestrelo, an in-law of Columbus. An adopted son, Diego Mendéz de Segura, would testify in the Columbus suits that he had been "in the royal camp and in the city of Grenada" when Columbus secured his 1492 capitulation and had also been at Barcelona in 1493 when Columbus returned from the first voyage, "and saw that he brought some Indians and great samples of gold" (Phillips, item 24.5). Mendéz would sail on the fourth Columbus voyage as secretary of the flotilla and write an account of it. He would also serve as *alguacil mayor* (assistant mayor) of Santo Domingo. The Latin original of the Cabot patent is transcribed in Biggar's *Precursors of Jacques Cartier* (appendix IV), along with an English translation. An English translation only is item 18 in Williamson. Puebla's character, the origins of his ambassadorship, his attempt to arrange a marriage between James IV and Fernando's illegitimate daughter, and his feud with Ayala, are covered by Bergenroth in his introduction. For Columbus's capitulations, see Nader. For the papal bulls, see Symcox, *RC Vol. 10*. For a transcription of the Dulmo-Estreito patents, see *Arquivo dos Açores*, Vol. 4, 440–446. Regarding possible licensing of Cabot's rights to silent partners or backers, Evan Jones made this crucial point in his 2006 paper, "The *Matthew* of Bristol." As a poor man, Cabot effectively would have "secured the support of his financiers by mortgaging his future. In Cabot's case, such a mortgage could have taken the form of a deed or charter in which he assigned a share of his rights to his financiers. By doing this, Cabot would not have been doing anything particularly novel, since rights granted through letters patent were often, not only assigned, but treated as negotiable assets." While Jones had no evidence of a specific license, he noted such licenses were assigned in the case of the 1501 and 1502 royal exploration patents to Bristol interests (ibid., 781–782).

CHAPTER 19

For an overview of contemporary banking practices, see de Roover. See also Ruddock, *Italian Merchants and Shipping*, for a portrait of Italian merchant and financial activity in London and Southampton. For Raimundis's observation of Henry VII's reliance on Florentine advisors, see Hinds. Alwyn Ruddock claimed in her Exeter Press chapter outline that she knew of an actual loan document and of a letter written by Cabot's Italian bankers relating his 1497 voyage results on August 10, 1497, which should be taken seriously. In a note to an editor at Exeter Press, she alluded to two managing partners in an Italian bank off Lombard Street. Ruddock never revealed the identity of these bankers in the outline or in the surviving notes. (See Jones, "Alwyn Ruddock.") But in September 2010, Evan Jones discovered in additional notes in Ruddock's former home evidence that she had linked Cabot through Giovanni Antonio de Carbonariis to the Florentine House of Bardi. In October 2010,

Francesco Guidi Bruscoli of the Cabot Project located the House of Bardi ledgers in Italy that contained a record of Cabot as a client. Jones shared the basic news of the discovery with me and has allowed me to identify the House of Bardi, prior to the Cabot Project publishing its complete findings. I am also indebted to Jones for encouraging me to consider whether "Bardi" and "Berardi" were one and the same family.

The spelling of Vespucci as *Bespuche* is noted by Gould, 316. Francesco Bardi's appearance in Seville records is noted by Otte, 191. For Berardi's dying rant against Columbus, see Fernández-Armesto, "God Bless Amerigo." Regarding Carbonariis, he was already known incidentally to Cabot scholars from his participation in the 1498 Cabot voyage, but Ruddock left behind a series of statements and clues that greatly expanded his role in the Cabot enterprise. Jones's paper "Alwyn Ruddock" summarizes what could be determined about Carbonariis following the discovery of Ruddock's book outline and notes at Exeter Press and provides far more detail. For my discussion of the nature of "Brasil," I am indebted to the unpublished papers of Louis-André Vigneras compiled by Jeffrey Reed. Vigneras in particular points out the equivalence of Terceira with Brasil. For the early English experience of Iceland and possible knowledge of the sagas, I have relied on the Bjorn Portsteinsson letters and manuscript in the Quinn papers at the Library of Congress (Box 80, "Iceland, 1967–1969") as well as Portsteinsson's "Henry VIII and Iceland." For the Salazar account of the island of Brasil, see Sharrer and see Jones and Sharrer. For the account of Henry VII's 1486 visit to Bristol, see Leland and Hearne, 199–202. For Bristol's condition in 1490, see Adams, 76–77. For the fishery treaties between England and Iceland, see Jones, "England's Icelandic Fishery," 106. Regarding the idea of a "secret fishery," David B. Quinn proposed Bristol mariners found "Brasil" between 1481 and 1491 but kept the news to themselves so they could exploit its cod without competition. Ruddock (and others) dismissed it. Ruddock supported what might be called the "lost-discovery" theory put forward by Vigneras, stating: "the land found had been lost again, and that there was no permanent contact between Bristol and whatever had been discovered across the Atlantic before 1497" (Ruddock, "John Day of Bristol," 231). In a 1988 letter to Quinn, Ruddock advised: "I take the line that the Bristol discovery was pre-1470 but lost again until Cabot made landfall in 1497." See Jones, "The Quinn Papers."

CHAPTER 20

The status of the Flanders Galleys service in 1496 is ambiguous in Brown. Ruddock in *Italian Merchants* is firm that the galley service was suspended for two years following the 1495 attack. A striking omission of her Cabot book outline for Exeter Press is any mention of the suspended Flanders Galleys service. Vigneras notes Columbus's presence at the wedding at Burgos in *Discovery of South America*, 3. Columbus's confirmation of his capitulations in 1497 is in Nader, Chapter 3.5. For Maurice Toby's account in the *Bristol Chronicle,* see Williamson, item 19. For the documentary finds regarding William Weston, see Jones, "Henry VII and the Bristol Expeditions." For Weston's background, see Peacock. For the Raimundis account of Cabot's 1497 voyage, see Williamson, item 24. Note that Toby's account in the *Bristol Chronicle* is the source of the local tradition that Cabot's landfall was June 24, 1497. The details of the "black king" of the Canaries are discussed at length by Rumeu de Armas in *Alonso de Lugo*.

CHAPTER 21

For the accounts of events in England from the Venetian and Milanese perspectives, see Brown and Hinds. The king's household books payment to Cabot of August 10–11, 1497, is item 26 in Williamson. For the rebuff of the Cornish rebels by Bristol, see Ricart, 48–49. The report by an unknown correspondent to the Duke of Milan on Cabot's voyage is item 23 in Williamson.

CHAPTER 22

For Andrea Trevisan's comments on England and the character of its people, as expressed in his *Relazione* of 1498, see Sneyd. Note that at the time of Sneyd's translation, its author was unknown. The Contarini establishment in London *wher nowe one peter Conteryn dwellith* was described in the parish record of St. Mary at Hill. See "An Isolated Inventory of the Furniture of a House in 1485," in Littlehales. The Pasqualigo letter describing Cabot's voyage is the standard Biggar translation that is item 22 in Williamson, which gives Cabot's name as "Talbot." But the translation is from the Sanudo diaries, where the name is "Calbot"; I have corrected it accordingly. The account of the Cornwall mob's butchering of the proctor of Penrynis from the Kingsford's "Chronicles," is item 123 in Pollard. The confession of Perkin Warbeck, also from the Kingsford's "Chronicles," is item 124 in Pollard. Nicolò de' Conti is discussed by Breazeale; the account of his travels is in Major. For the Raimundis account of his encounter with Cabot, see Williamson, item 24. Note that Raimundis's observation of the plentitude of fish has caused historians to overestimate the importance of Cabot's discovery to the English fishery. Despite the promised replacement of the Icelandic fishery, the English were slow to exploit the Grand Banks fishery, leaving it largely to the French, the Portuguese, and the Basques. Ludovico Sforza's letter to Agostino Spinola is in Hinds. For Varthema's clandestine visit to Mecca, see Jones and Badger. For Fabri's travels, see Murray and see Prescott. Columbus's 1500 letter to Juana de La Torre is Chapter 94 in Thacher, *Christopher Columbus*, Vol. 2. The journeys of Barbaro and Contarini appear in Thomas. Reliable information about Covilham is scant. The most thorough summary is the entry "Covilham (Covilhão, Covilhã), Pero or Pedro de" in Vol. 7 of *Encyclopaedia Britannica*, 1911. Santo Stefano's journey is recounted in Major.

CHAPTER 23

Vigneras published a brief account of his 1955 discovery of the "John Day" letter in 1956 ("New Light"). His further research on the mysterious Day turned up the 1499 suit at Sanlúcar de Barrameda. Vigneras never published this additional material; I was apprised of it through the Vigneras papers provided to me by Jeffrey Reed. Vigneras did not provide biographical material on the Spanish figures mentioned. For "Batista Negron" I have used Igual Luis and Navarro Espinach, the Fundación Casa Ducal de Medinaceli, and Vigneras's *Discovery of South America*. Pinelo and the Dorias and their connections to Columbus's financiers can be found in Nader as well as in Gould. For the English merchant community at Seville, see Otte. Vigneras's translation of the letter is item 25 in Williamson. Vigneras's Spanish transcription of the Day letter is in his 1961 paper "État présent des études sur Jean Cabot."

Alwyn Ruddock made the breakthrough find that "John Day" was an alias of Hugh Say, in 1966 ("John Day of Bristol"). Much of the Say biography presented here, including the quotation from his will, derives from that article. Ruddock performed more research on Say, which turned up his family's connections to the Warbeck insurrection, none of which was ever published. I have provisionally accepted some of her undocumented findings, as revealed in a February 9, 1992, letter to David B. Quinn (see Jones, "The Quinn Papers").

Regarding the disputed "cape" at which Cabot made his landfall, a world map from about 1544 printed in Antwerp places the landfall on Cape Breton and attributes it wrongly to 1494 and also to both John and Sebastian Cabot. Although a 1549 second edition of the map printed in London is explicitly accredited to Sebastian Cabot, it's not certain the map was Sebastian's work or that he thought the 1497 landfall was in Cape Breton. Sebastian was otherwise remiss in the extreme for failing to give his father any credit of discovery.

With respect to the unknown Indigenous peoples Cabot seems to have glimpsed but not met, and who created the artifacts he reportedly brought back, archaeologists identify the "Little Passage" people as coastal inhabitants of Newfoundland from around A.D. 850 to 1500; the Beothuk were their descendants. Marshall (Chapter 2) notes that the Labrador Innu and the Beothuk probably were not only culturally similar, but genetically related as well. Marshall discusses population figures in Chapter 3 and the timing of the annual salmon run in Chapter 4.

Regarding Columbus's latitude fix errors, on his 1498 voyage, according to Las Casas, Columbus placed Trinidad at 6° north, which is too low by 4 degrees. He also mentioned in the same voyage account that Espanola was at 24° north, when its north coast is actually at 20° north. The errors seem genuine, although it's possible that when the letter was printed for public consumption, deliberate mistakes were inserted to obscure Spanish discoveries.

The disputed origins of the name "Labrador" is beyond the scope of this work, but the basis for it being the result of Portuguese exploration relies on the 1506 deposition by Pero de Barcelos in which he asserts having explored for three years with his fellow Terceiran João Fernandes Lavrador. But "Lavrador" was probably a description of Fernandes's occupation—farmer or small landowner— as he is thought to be the Johan Fernandez named in the October 1499 letters patent from Manoel I. "Labrador" first appears in cartography on the world map at the Biblioteca Oliveriana de Pesaro, which is thought to date to 1508 to 1510. The "Mappamondo di Pesaro" contains the labels *Cavo Laboradore* and *Insula Laboradore*.

For the documents on the 1480–81 search for Brasil out of Bristol, see Williamson, items 6 and 7. See also Ryan. Vigneras addresses these voyages as well as the notions of Brasil in his unpublished papers, which may substantially reflect his work *La búsqueda del paraíso y las legendarias islas del Atlántico*, published by Casa-Museo de Colón, Seminario de Historia de América de la Universidad de Valladolid, 1976.

For the 1480–81 *Trinity* voyage to Andalusia, see Reddaway and Ruddock. Vigneras discusses the Andalusia voyage in his unpublished papers and makes the point that this *Trinity* could not have been the same *Trinity* that searched for Brasil in 1481. Note that the 1480–81 visit to La Rábida by the *Trinity* could explain how the Fernando Columbus biography managed to attribute to Christopher Columbus a voyage to Iceland and 100 leagues beyond it in 1477. It is a controversial aspect of a troubled book, and has been used by some historians to advocate secret Columbus knowledge of Norse passages to the New World. Ruddock demolished the notion that Columbus ever visited Iceland in "Columbus and Iceland," suggesting the *Trinity* visit to Andalusia of 1480–81 as a source of Bristol-based knowledge that found its way imperfectly into the Fernando Columbus biography.

CHAPTER 24

For the payment of Cabot's pension, see items 27 to 29 in Williamson. The award to William Weston was discovered by Evan Jones and Margaret Condon in 2009 and has not yet been published. For the renewal of Cabot's patent, see item 35 in Williamson. For the king's household payments to Thirkill, Bradley, and Cair, see item 26 in Williamson. Evan Jones has communicated to me the discovery of a document (which has not yet been published) indicating the initiation of legal proceedings against Launcelot Thirkill and Thomas Bradley in June 1500 for nonpayment of a loan the king had advanced them in 1498 for going to the "new isle." The *Great Chronicle of London* account of the 1498 voyage is item 31 in Williamson. For the Spanish diplomatic correspondence, see Bergenroth. The translation of *Esmeraldo de Situ Orbis* is from Vigneras's unpublished papers, as is the translation of the Barcelos evidence. For the documentation of these Portuguese voyage plans to the northwest, see "A Terra do Labrador," *Arquivo dos Açores*, Vol. 12, 353–368. See also Biggar for transcriptions and translations. Agostino Spinola's June 1498 letter to the Duke of Milan is item 36 in Williamson. Ayala's letter of July 1498 is item 37.

CHAPTER 25

Puebla's letter of July 25, 1498 (the year is missing, but it is unquestionably from 1498), is transcribed (in Spanish) by Harrisse as item XII in *Jean et Sébastien Cabot*. The letter was transcribed by Bergenroth in the course of preparing *Calendar of State Papers, Spain*, but was omitted from the print edition. Harrisse received a copy from an official at the Public Record Office. Beasley mentioned the letter in his volume on the Cabots, but it was overlooked by Biggar in compiling *The Precursors of Jacques Cartier* and consequently was also missed by Williamson, who relied particularly on Biggar for *The Cabot Voyages*. My thanks to Janet Ritch for undertaking the English translation. Ayala's letter of the same date is item 37 in Williamson. The *Great Chronicle of London* mention of Cabot's 1498 voyage is item 31 in Williamson. Vergil's account is item 33 in Williamson. Columbus's letter to Fernando and Isabel is in Thacher, *Christopher Columbus*, Vol. 2, 399.

CHAPTER 26

The accounts of the *per verba de præsenti* marriage of Catherine and Arthur and the correspondence involving the Spanish envoys, are in Bergenroth. Note that following Arthur's death in 1502, his widow Catherine became the first wife of his brother, the future Henry VIII. Pietro Pasqualigo's letter regarding the 1501 voyage of Gaspar Corte-Real is item 38 in Williamson. Note that João Fernandes, Francisco Fernandes, and João Gonsalves teamed up with three Bristol merchants, Richard Warde, Thomas Asshurst, and John Thomas, to secure a letters patent from Henry VII on March 19, 1501. See item 42 in Williamson. Transcriptions and translations of documents relating to Portuguese expeditions that followed Cabot's are in Biggar. Regarding the return of at least some of the ships from Cabot's 1498 flotilla, as well as Cabot himself, Evan Jones of the Cabot Project informed me in late 2009: "We've got a number of documents that support [Alwyn] Ruddock's claims about the return of Cabot's 1498 voyage. In particular, we have the initiation of legal proceedings against Launcelot Thirkill and Thomas Bradley in June 1500 for nonpayment of a loan the king had advanced them in 1498 for going to the 'new isle.' And we have documents that seem to put John Cabot, mentioned by name, back in London by May 1500." These findings have not yet been published. See Hunter, "Rewriting History." For Henry VII's stay of proceedings against William Weston, see Jones, "Henry VII and the Bristol Expeditions." Stevenson's monograph on the 1502 Caneiro map provides a good contextual overview of the La Cosa map and other early sixteenth-century maps. Harrisse covers well the sources of sixteenth-century historians on the Cabot voyages in the syllabus of *John Cabot, the Discoverer of North America, and Sebastian His Son.* Fernando and Isabel's orders to Hojeda are in Vigneras, *Discovery of South America.*

AFTERWORD

Alwyn Ruddock's unpublished theories on the 1498 Cabot voyage are covered by Jones in "Alwyn Ruddock." Williamson commented on True's interest in Carbonariis on page 93 (n5). For Beasley's discussion of "loans" to Thirkill and Bradley, see Beasley, 102–03 and 271–72. For fresh evidence of the king's loans to Thirkill and Bradley, see the sources for Chapters 24 and 26. For new research on Esterfeld and Foster, see Peacock. For the Esterfeld suit against Weston, see Jones, "Henry VII and the Bristol Expeditions." For Foster's will, see Jones, "Will of John Foster." Morris speculated about the final years of Behaim on 46–47.

INDEX

Monte Cristi, 67, 68, 88
Morris, John G., 250–51
Muliart, Miguel, 33
Münzer, Jerome, 7, 9, 31, 35, 51–2, 105–9, 125,
    128–30, 131–2, 146, 162, 166, 251
    and Behaim, 116–20, 128, 133, 137, 140, 147,
        156, 161, 166, 168–9, 172, 187, 215
    in Portugal, 31, 108, 128, 129, 156, 168, 251
Muslims, 11, 23, 27, 34, 36, 48, 99, 105, 141, 145,
    201, 202

Naples, 132, 151
    and Cabot's origins, 13
Napoli, Nicolo da, 149
navigation
    dead reckoning, 100, 103, 222
    instruments, 24, 29–30, 62, 110, 187
    pilotage, 29, 184
    polestar, 29–30, 61, 62, 187, 188
    solar observation, 29–30, 32, 110–11
    true and magnetic north, 187
Negro, Battista di (Batista Negron), 208
Negro, Giovanni Antonio di, 16
Negro, Paulo di, 15, 16
Newfoundland, 115, 174, 187, 210–12, 215,
    242–3, 244, 248
Norse exploration of, settlement in North
    America, 174, 210

Ovando, Nicolás de, 246
Oviedo y Valdéz, Gonzalo Fernández de, 26,
    40, 69

Paganus, Francesco, 173
Palos, 33, 41, 42, 43, 47, 63, 64–5, 75, 91, 107,
    125, 197, 214
Pané, Ramón, 142
papal bulls,
    Aeterni Regis (1481), 18, 32, 85, 137, 162
    Inter cetera (1493), 85–7, 95–6, 137, 143, 162,
        166, 219
    Dudum siquidem (1493), 86–7 95–6, 143,
        162, 166, 219
Pasqualigo, Lorenzo, 196–7, 210–11, 239
Pasqualigo, Pietro, 239–40
Payva, Alfonso de, 203s
Peraza, Hernán de, 49
Pereira, Duarte Pacheco, 221
Perestrello, Bartolomeu, 18, 34
Perestrello, Bartolomeu (son), 19
Perestrello, Filipa Moniz, 18–19, 33
Pérez, Juan, 34, 35, 43, 65
Perez de Luna, Fernand, 98
Pesaro, Fantin da, 186–7
Pinelo, Francisco, 50, 208, 223
Pinzón, Arias Pérez, 67

Pinzón, Martín Alonso, 41, 58–60, 62, 63–5,
    67–70, 73–5, 77, 89, 90, 91, 92
    and River of Martín Alonso (Río de Martín
        Alonso), 68, 69, 75, 90, 91, 147
Pinzón, Vicente Yáñez, 64–5, 69
piracy, 13, 39, 71, 136, 137, 149–50, 152, 174,
    181, 184
Pisani, Domenico, 129
Pizzigano, Zuanne, 27
Pliny, 26, 120
Poggio Bracciolini, Giovanni Francesco, 23, 87,
    99, 203
Polo, Marco, 11, 23, 32–3, 59, 61, 119, 201, 209,
    215, 246
Portocarrero family, 125
Portugal,
    and Atlantic exploration, 14, 17–18, 34, 74,
        86, 223
    and West Africa, 22, 29, 32, 57, 81, 110, 222,
        223
Pozzo, Taddeo da, 22
Prieto, Diego, 36
Priuli, Francesco, 37
Ptolemy, 28, 29, 235, 246
Puebla, Roderigo Gondesalvi de, 5, 6, 7, 79,
    80, 133, 156–9, 162–5, 173, 180, 219–21,
    223–7, 229–33, 237–9, 243
Puerto Rico, 68, 87, 98, 144, 235

Quinn, David B., 2, 3, 8, 247
Quintanella, Alonso de, 50
Quintero, Cristóbal, 48

Raimundis, Raimundo di, 138, 139, 140, 171,
    184, 185, 191, 192, 193, 198, 199, 200, 201,
    202, 203–5, 211, 213, 218, 225, 226, 229,
    231, 251
Ramusio, 153, 154
Reed, Jeffrey, 8–9, 247
Regiomontanus (Johann Müller), 101, 102, 103,
    110
Riberol, Francisco de (Sir Francesco di Riveroli),
    48, 49, 50, 59–60, 72, 145, 146, 148, 208, 246
Richard III (King of England), 134, 135, 177,
    190
Rizzardo, Paolo, 36, 37
Rodriguez Bermejo, Juan (Roderigo de Triana),
    106
Rodríguez Cabezudo, Juan, 35
Ruddock, Alwyn Amy
    Cabot research, 2–4, 7, 8, 9, 247–9
    death, 1–2
    and Exeter Press, 2–3, 247
Rull, Gaspar, 45, 51, 52, 54–5

Salazar, Lope García de, 175